**NATIONAL SECURITY AND
THE U.S. CONSTITUTION**

National Security and the U.S. Constitution

THE IMPACT OF THE POLITICAL SYSTEM

EDITED BY

George C. Edwards III AND Wallace Earl Walker

The Johns Hopkins University Press

Baltimore and London

To Carmella and Susan

Library
University of Texas
at San Antonio

The Johns Hopkins University Press, 701 West 40th Street, Baltimore, Maryland 21211
The Johns Hopkins Press Ltd., London

Library of Congress Cataloging-in-Publication Data

National security and the U.S. Constitution.

  Bibliography: p.
  Includes index.
  1. United States—National security. 2. Civil-military relations—United States. 3. United
States—Constitutional history. I. Edwards, George C. II. Walker, Wallace Earl, 1944–
III. Title: National security and the US Constitution.
UA23.N2483   1989   355'.033073   88-655
ISBN 0-8018-3684-0 (alk. paper)

Contents

Foreword   vii
WILLIAM W. KAUFMANN

Preface   xi

Introduction   1
GEORGE C. EDWARDS III AND WALLACE EARL WALKER

Part I. STATECRAFT

1. Mobilizing Political Support   13
   BERT A. ROCKMAN

2. Making National Strategy: The Practitioner's View   37
   STANSFIELD TURNER AND GEORGE EDWARD THIBAULT

3. Producing Foreign Intelligence   50
   HARRY HOWE RANSOM

Part II. NATIONAL DEFENSE

4. Raising the Armed Forces   73
   HOBART B. PILLSBURY, JR.

5. Organizing the Armed Forces   92
   DANIEL J. KAUFMAN

6. Equipping the Armed Forces   121
   HARVEY M. SAPOLSKY

7. Waging War: Structural versus Political Efficacy   136
   ASA A. CLARK IV AND RICHARD M. PIOUS

Part III. FOREIGN RELATIONS

  8. Protecting Citizens Abroad   161
     IRA SHARKANSKY

  9. Conducting Diplomacy   182
     ROBERT H. FERRELL

10. Negotiating International Agreements   202
     NORMAN A. GRAEBNER

Part IV. ECONOMIC POLICY

11. Budgeting for National Defense   237
     LEE DONNE OLVEY

12. Engaging in International Trade   258
     ROGER B. PORTER

13. Managing International Monetary Policy   282
     NORMAN C. THOMAS

Conclusion: The Constitutional System and National Security   305
GEORGE C. EDWARDS III AND WALLACE EARL WALKER

Contributors   329
Index   333

Foreword

WILLIAM W. KAUFMANN

The Constitution of the United States is a remarkably brief document. In its original form it contains only a prologue of objectives and six articles. To them, twenty-six amendments have been added since 1789, of which the first ten define the Bill of Rights, adopted in 1791, another fourteen modify, clarify, or amplify the first six articles, and one (the Twenty-First) repeals the Eighteenth (Prohibition). Only the Second and Third Amendments make reference to what might be called national security issues: "the right of the people to bear arms," and the proscription against quartering soldiers in peacetime in any house without the consent of the owner.

The original Constitution is not a great deal more specific on this score. At the outset it lists six great objectives. The third among them is to "provide for the common defense." Section 8 of Article 1 defines the powers of the Congress in pursuit of this objective: mainly to raise and support armies and a navy, to declare war, and to regulate the relationship with the state militias. Section 2 of Article 2 makes the president commander in chief of what have become the U.S. armed forces (including the National Guard and reserves when called to national service). From this slight edifice has grown one of the most powerful defense establishments in history.

Steeped as they were in history, political literature, and recent experience, the Founding Fathers saw no greater threat to the "blessings of liberty" than an executive (whatever his title) who could raise and maintain military forces independently of a representative body and use those forces to tyrannize the nation or engage in dubious and unauthorized foreign adventures. Hence the separation (or perhaps more accurately the sharing) of powers; hence the right of Congress to raise and maintain armies and a navy and declare war; hence the assumption of civilian control over the military in the form of the president as commander in chief.

Underlying the nature of the decentralized political system that has evolved in the past two centuries is the question that gives this book its focus: what are the consequences of the U.S. constitutional system for national security policy? It is toward the balanced appraisal of those consequences that this volume is directed.

Such an appraisal is no small task, for conditions have changed dramatically since 1787. The United States has become a great power; its interests are truly worldwide and extend into space. It remains, after forty years, the bulwark of the noncommunist world. The American active-duty defense establishment consists of more than 2.1 million men and women; still another 1.2 million serve in the "militia" and other forms of reserves; the Defense Department alone employs more than a million civilians to help administer and operate its vast organization. Congress, however, still controls the purse, declares war, and has enacted the War Powers Act to reduce the incidence and duration of undeclared wars.

Yet, national security concerns are not limited to traditional notions of the employment of military force. The international political and economic systems penetrate every aspect of American life. Arms control negotiations, balance of trade deficits, access to natural resources, and the indiscriminate violence of terrorism are but a few of the issues that affect the "national security" of the United States. Domestically, concerns about the appropriate allocation of resources for security and nonsecurity programs shape the political environment in which such decisions will be made and, at root, determine the level of effort that will be devoted to security matters.

In light of the increasingly complex international and domestic environments with which decision makers in the United States are confronted, the editors of this volume rightly define national security to include, not only defense, but also statecraft, foreign relations, and economic policy. The authors have written authoritatively and lucidly about the impact of the U.S. constitutional system on national security policy and policy making, broadly defined. The editors have added cogent introductory and concluding chapters that link the individual essays and place them in perspective. The essays combine insights from trained analysts and academicians, experienced practitioners, and authors who hold both sorts of credentials.

It is not the purpose of this volume to arrive at some consensus concerning the desirable or undesirable consequences of the constitutional system for national security. Rather, the purpose is to explore the nature of the political system that has emerged from two hundred years of development under the Constitution and assess the ability of that system to provide for the common defense in the face of an increasingly complex international environment. Several of the authors show an understandable impatience with the thickets of bureaucracy that have grown so lushly in and around the Department of Defense. Others complain about the dilatoriness of Congress and about the way that body has used the power of the purse to involve itself in matters seen as more properly the province of the executive branch. One author has even suggested that increased congressional involvement is the price that is paid when consensus breaks down; furthermore, that substitution of a parliamentary system (an oft-heard "solution" when frustrations with the present structure peak) would not improve matters much, and could make them worse.

The authors have concentrated on the impact of the constitutional system on national security policy and policy making. Readers will find little about the state of civil-military relations in the United States. Are civil-military relations still a problem worth discussing? There seems little ground for concern. No "man on horseback" has appeared. Still, changed conditions have brought forth a new set of problems in civil-military relations that could become as important as those envisaged two centuries ago. Recent events involving commissioned officers in the national security policy-making process and the continued application of U.S. military force in ambiguous situations exemplify the difficulties inherent in defining the appropriate role of the military in setting national priorities. Although for practical reasons these issues could not be explored at length in this book, they certainly remain the appropriate focus of another.

Preface

This book seeks to understand the impact of the U.S. Constitution on the making and implementation of national security policy. Although much has been written on the substance of national security policy and, separately, on the American political system, little attention has been devoted to the connection between the two. Our object is neither reform nor apology. Instead, it is our hope that this volume will contribute to a richer understanding of the Constitution and the political system it structures.

To examine the consequences of the Constitution for national security policy, we delineate thirteen national security functions in the areas of statecraft, national defense, foreign relations, and economic policy that all states must carry out in one way or another. We invited practitioners in national security affairs and a collection of leading political scientists, historians, and economists specializing in national security to write essays addressing the theme of the book. Both the editors and the authors found the task a challenging but rewarding one.

Our debts in this project are many. Among our colleagues in the Department of Social Sciences at West Point, Donne Olvey, Jim Golden, George Osborn, Ace Clark, Dan Kaufman, Dick Norton, Fred Black, and Hobie Pillsbury served as our "wise men," providing a wide range of advice and enthusiasm. Several also contributed chapters to the book. Brigadier General Roy Flint, dean of the U.S. Military Academy, provided unflagging support in tackling administrative obstacles. A number of others at West Point were uncommonly patient and helpful to us. Specifically, we wish to thank Dave Phillips, Don Rowe, Kevin O'Brien, Bob Strati, and Kim Flint. Diane Hughes and Susan Riley skillfully typed uncounted manuscripts and letters for this project. We also relied heavily on Barbara Thomas, whose unflagging good humor and administrative skill sustained us throughout.

We gratefully acknowledge the Ford Foundation for its underwriting this volume and a related panel at the 1987 American Political Science Association. Gary Sick, David Arnold, and Nancy Feller of the foundation were especially supportive. The Association of Graduates of the U.S. Military Academy provided much needed and appreciated support for administering this grant.

Six of the essays in this book appeared in slightly different form in the Fall 1987 volume of *Armed Forces and Society*. David Segal and Dorothy Totz, the editor and managing editor, respectively, of the journal, contributed substantially to the development of the project, and we are grateful for their professional advice and support. We are also appreciative of Seven Locks Press for permission to reprint the material that appeared in the journal.

Henry Tom, Social Sciences editor of the Johns Hopkins University Press was an early supporter of the volume, and he and his colleagues at the press have skillfully managed the production of this book. Sam Sarkesian, Tom McNaugher, Mike Freeney, and the late Robert Osgood reviewed several chapters each and made very worthwhile suggestions. George Quester read the entire manuscript and was most helpful. We are also grateful to Peter Dreyer for his excellent copy editing.

Our biggest debts, however, are to our wives, Carmella Edwards and Susan Walker. They continue to be sources of encouragement, counsel, and sustenance. The dedication of this book is but a small token in repayment of their love and friendship.

Although this book exists only because of these many sources of support, we must claim responsibility for what follows. The material contained herein does not necessarily represent the views of the U.S. Army or the U.S. Military Academy.

Introduction

GEORGE C. EDWARDS III and WALLACE EARL WALKER

Two centuries ago the framers of the U.S. Constitution established the basic outline and features of government for a distinctively new nation. Although much has changed in American society since the late eighteenth century, the essential features of the framers' constitutional design remain. Equally important, these characteristics of our political system continue to have a significant influence on both the process and substance of U.S. public policy.

This book focuses on one prominent area of public policy: national security. Whether one is a hawk or a dove, a liberal or a conservative, national security is a central component of public policy. Two-thirds of the employees of the national government and approximately 40 percent of the budget are devoted to national security policy. At this juncture in our history as the Constitution enters its third century, it is appropriate to appraise our constitutional system in terms of its impact on national security policy and policy making.

We center our attention on how both the Constitution and the political system it structures affect the national security system, composed as it is of organizations, processes, and policies. We view the U.S. political system as the institutionalization of the Constitution, which is in fact a vague document, laden with ambiguous provisions that have provided generations of lawmakers with leeway in the development of our political institutions. Nevertheless, the essential structure of the system is based upon and legitimated by the Constitution. Its parameters are broad, but they nonetheless place significant constraints on the rules of the game of politics and policy making, and such rules are never neutral.

The constitutional system, then, is our independent variable and the national security system is our dependent variable or, more simply, the subject of our investigation. The preservation of its national interests and freedom of action is a paramount concern of every state. To protect and advance those interests, all countries must establish a national security system that in some degree performs certain functions. This book considers the ability of our constitutionally based political system to perform each of the functions described below.

THE CONSTITUTIONAL SYSTEM

The word that best characterizes the American political system is *decentralization*. Both the fear of the concentration of power and concern for obtaining the support of the original thirteen states prompted the framers of the Constitution to diffuse political power throughout the political system.

Perhaps the most widely recognized aspect of decentralization at the national level is horizontal, more commonly called separation of powers. Our constitutional precept of separation of powers is really a system of shared powers. The president usually finds it difficult to act without the acquiescence of Congress. The president and the executive branch spend money, but Congress must first authorize and appropriate it. The president proposes laws, but Congress must approve them. The president nominates people to serve in official positions, but the Senate must confirm most of them. If the president vetoes a bill that has been passed by Congress, the latter may override the veto.

Even in national security policy, where the president has more leeway because he and his representatives constitute the sole organ of the U.S. government representing the nation abroad, he must rely on Congress to exercise his power effectively. Although the president is commander in chief of the armed forces, Congress decides if and when there will be a draft, how much military personnel will be paid, the rules governing the armed forces, and whether or not the United States will declare war. Out of such precepts has grown a constitutional system bounded by numerous laws. For example, the War Powers Resolution of 1974 buttresses Congress's power to limit the president as commander in chief by restricting his authority to engage in sustained combat without explicit congressional approval.

With presidential urging, Congress has seen fit to create a sprawling national security establishment to advance and implement policy. Since the creation of the State and War Departments in 1789, Congress has not only fashioned new departments and independent agencies, but has also added national security–related bureaus and offices to what originally were domestic departments. A list of only a few of the new organizations includes the Defense Department, the Navy Department, the Air Force Department, the National Security Council, the office of the U.S. Trade Representative, and the Agency for International Development. Organizations added to existing departments include the Foreign Agricultural Service (Agriculture Department), Coast Guard (Transportation Department), International Trade Administration (Commerce Department), and the International Affairs Office (Labor Department). In fact, virtually every cabinet department has a subsidiary bureau with an important role in national security affairs.

Constitutional precepts and developments in the political system ensure that the judiciary also shares power with the executive and legislature. Sometimes it constrains the other branches, even in matters related to national security, as it did President Truman in his attempt to run the steel mills during the Korean War. At other times the courts referee disputes between the executive and legislature, as in the case of Congress's use of the legislative veto.

The separation of powers also affects the role of extraconstitutional institutions such as political parties and interest groups. Because the president remains in office even after losing important votes in Congress, there are fewer costs for members of his party in opposing him and less incentive to support their party leader than in a parliamentary system. This in turn greatly complicates the process of coalition building.

The absence of centralizing power makes the national government especially permeable to a wide range of interests, including those of other countries. In addition to the decentralization of power within each branch of government, which is not mandated by the Constitution, the presence of several power centers provides alternatives to outside interests in their efforts to influence policy. If one branch is unsympathetic to their requests, another might be more responsive. Once again, the incentive to organize and press demands complicates national security policy making.

Vertical as well as horizontal decentralization characterizes the American constitutional system. Federalism has fundamental consequences for national security policy making. States define congressional constituencies. Senatorial districts consist of the states themselves, and state legislatures determine House districts, none of which ever cross state boundaries. States also determine the rules for obtaining a party's nomination, further weakening the potentially centralizing role of party leaders. Furthermore, the states organize, and in peacetime control, much of the U.S. reserve military force, the army and air force National Guards.

As a result of this decentralization, there is a natural tendency for U.S. legislators to be especially responsive to those interests that are predominant in their constituencies. Wide-ranging interests—from ethnic and minority groups to defense contractors and communities near military bases to companies threatened by foreign trade and truck farms reliant on alien workers—are concerned with national security matters. Taking advantage of their special access, they lobby members of Congress in an effort to influence policy decisions.

Underlying all of the above is the First Amendment. The world's freest press, most limited libel laws, and broadest freedom to assemble, petition, and disseminate information both encourage and facilitate broad-scale participation in national security policy making. The result is a very complex policy-making environment.

NATIONAL SECURITY FUNCTIONS

The functions that any national security system must perform fall into four categories: statecraft, national defense, foreign relations, and economic policy. Each function stresses constitutionally based democratic political systems in different ways.

In part 1 of this book, we are concerned with statecraft, the efforts of governments to mobilize support for and to develop an overall national strategy, or what some call grand strategy. We begin our analysis in chapter 1 with a focus on the mobilization of political support for national security policy. This is a task for national government and party leadership and requires that citizens be informed, legislatures mobilized, and elites persuaded. The support of elites and of mass publics is perhaps more crucial in this realm than in other policy arenas because national constituencies do not exist around the collective good of national security. Legislative action is also crucial to ensure that programs for implementing national security policy are authorized and that funds are appropriated to sustain policies and organizations.

A national strategy typically reflects the state's international standing, as well as the dictates of its international environment and its domestic culture and capabilities. Successful strategies supply an agenda for government attention that provides for a clear decision to guide action and for sensible choices about the allocation of resources. Policies growing out of a strategy address international responsibilities and regional concerns. Ideally, national strategy should be an integrated product of a state's disposition toward its allies, its potential adversaries, neutral states, and international organizations. Thus chapter 2 deals with the institutions and processes for making strategy and assesses the impact of our constitutional system on our ability to produce a consistent and flexible strategy that is responsive to political direction and accountable to the public.

The formulation of such a strategy relies upon foreign intelligence, the topic of chapter 3. Intelligence production usually relies upon a "cycle" that involves the planning of information gathering, the collection and processing of raw data, the assessment of its meaning, the production of estimates, and the dissemination of intelligence to various government agencies. Intelligence organizations are generally involved with the collection of human and technically generated data, the protection of state secrets, the coordination of intelligence gathering across a broad array of agencies, and the conduct of covert operations abroad. The cycle and techniques used in intelligence collection and analysis require secrecy to be effective, and yet democratic governments demand accountability. Thus, intelligence production is inherently a controversial subject and invariably involves not only the executive and the legislature but also the courts and the press.

Part 2 considers national defense. Here the U.S. Constitution is much more specific about allocating responsibilities to American political institutions. We have therefore broken up this facet of national security into four functional areas, each of which is of vital concern to any state. Each of these areas entails difficult choices among competing alternatives. A state's choice among these alternatives can have a profound impact on its civil-military politics and on its economy. National defense, as we conceptualize it here, fulfills three missions: to make available military force to back up diplomatic initiatives; to deter hostile states from the use of military force or from coercive measures against vital interests; and finally, when all else fails, to defend ths state or its allies from attack.

Chapter 4 examines the function of raising the armed forces. The choices here are enough to daunt even the most determined political leader. Should the force be composed of conscripts or volunteers? What demographic characteristics are preferred in terms of age, sex, and racial or ethnic background? What are the roles and sizes of the militia and of reserve forces to be? How is the military officer corps to be constituted and structured? These choices involve very difficult policy questions and invariably embroil political institutions and private interests in enduring conflict.

Choices about the organization of the defense establishment, discussed in chapter 5, are no less overwhelming. Among the issues involved in fulfilling this function are the structure of the defense ministry and the armed forces, the distribution of responsibilities for policy development and program administration, and the mechanisms for integrating the advice of senior military chiefs and commanders into the design of national strategy and policy. Also, the mission responsibilities of the various services must be allocated, and joint and service doctrine must be developed.

The function of equipping the armed forces is reviewed in chapter 6. Military equipment may be produced by private industry or by public arsenals and may be procured domestically or from foreign arms producers. Such equipment can be highly sophisticated and designed for intense conventional wars, as with the U.S. Army's TOW (a tube-launched, optically tracked, wireguided antitank missile), or more modest, as with the Soviet RPG-7 (a short-range antitank missile that is aimed by means of a simple sight). Furthermore, it can be researched and developed in university-affiliated laboratories staffed by academic scientists or in government research centers manned by federal employees. Finally, at issue in this function are the costs of modern equipment, the development and testing procedures, and the distribution of defense contracts. Such choices involve considerable technological and political uncertainty, with administrators vying with politicians to produce sophisticated weapons that also satisfy regional and local needs for defense contracts to sustain employment.

Chapter 7 considers the impact of the constitutional system on waging war. Forces may be deployed at home or abroad and assigned a variety of contingencies, from repelling attack on the homeland to interdiction against enemy forces intruding on a friendly nation to service in an allied force repelling a foreign attack. Forces may be used in a variety of operations, including low-intensity conflict (peacekeeping, blockades, anti-guerrilla warfare), mid-intensity conflict (limited conventional war), or high-intensity conflict (all-out conventional or nuclear war). In addition to choices about deployment and contingencies, states must have mechanisms to decide how willing they are to use force, what level of forces are to be used in a conflict, and when their reserves are to be mobilized.

The third part of this book examines foreign relations and looks at the protection of citizens abroad, the conduct of diplomacy, and the negotiation of international agreements. In seeking to protect citizens abroad, states must provide traditional consular services, which include the issuing of passports and overseas embassy services, but in an era of worldwide terrorism, they have had to go beyond these traditional roles. In fact, they have had to take active measures to safeguard, to negotiate for, and, if necessary, to rescue their citizens from piracy and terrorist acts of violence, kidnapping, and extortion. These more active measures are affected not only by each state's constitution, but also by the laws of foreign nations where hostages are held, the domestic political concerns of those nations, and the current international political issues among the states involved. Chapter 8 therefore discusses the protection of citizens abroad.

The topic of chapter 9 is the conduct of diplomacy, which involves a plethora of communications and coordination between governments. Diplomacy involves not only bilateral relations between states, but multilateral relations among allied states, as in the North Atlantic Treaty Organization, or among states meeting in unison at the United Nations. Diplomacy can be conducted at home by the president or the members of the legislature; it can also be conducted abroad by a team composed not only of an ambassador and his political and economic counselors, who represent the Department of State, but also of military, commercial, agricultural, and public affairs attachés. This team is responsible for ceremonial representation of the state abroad, the collection of information about foreign objectives and programs, the articulation of a state's policy positions, and propaganda initiatives. It also is called upon to make recommendations to the home state and to persuade the host nation as to the proper direction of relationships on broad policy matters and on specific programs.

Chapter 10 focuses on the negotiation of international treaties and executive agreements. Although negotiation is also a technique discussed in chapter 9 on diplomacy, here we are concerned with high-level negotiations, which almost always involve the president and other senior officials, and with legislative reactions that may involve congressional concurrence in the forms of Senate approval and congressional appropriations. Such negotiations address concerns about the protection and extension of national values and the advancement of vital national interests. Invariably, issues such as arms control, the reduction of military forces, and forging new alliances and commitments with friendly, neutral, and potentially hostile states evoke negotiations at the highest government levels. Geographic and economic issues may also be involved, such as the acquisition of new territory and access to mineral resources or fishing rights. All such negotiations may be conducted bilaterally, multilaterally, or within international organizations.

The fourth and final part of this book considers the requirement for each state to address the relationship between economic policy and national security affairs. This aspect of economic policy involves not only budgeting for defense, the topic of chapter 11, but also foreign economic policy, which includes international trade and international monetary policy.

Budgeting for defense occurs in the face of competing claims from other national priorities. A constitutional system may promote or discourage defense spending in the face of domestic demands for social services, income security, economic stabilization, and environmental protection. Not only do existing national values as institutionalized in the constitutional system affect the choice, but so do existing political arrangements. That is, whereas the system may yesterday have favored one political institution to resolve these disputes (such as the legislature), today and tomorrow it may favor another as the dominant partner in the allocation of resources (such as the executive or appointed federal officials). Clearly the character of the favored institution will affect not only what proportion of resources are allocated to which priority, but also the criteria used in deciding such allocation. The constitutional system must also resolve whether national security is one of many competing claims on national priorities or whether it has an absolute claim that transcends all others, including the private economy.

In chapter 12, we are concerned with foreign trade. Every state must promote foreign trade to some extent to ensure that sufficient foreign credits are available to purchase abroad the raw materials and finished goods it cannot efficiently produce at home. Yet a state must also decide which domestic industries to protect or promote so as to sustain its domestic economy and how to ensure the viability of its vital defense industries while satisfying powerful domestic constituencies for free trade. A range of options are available in the pursuit of satisfactory trade relations with foreign nations. They include tariffs on imported goods; export controls such as embargoes or restrictions on the flow of high-technology items; multilateral or bilateral trade agreements such as those provided by the General Agreement on Tariff and Trade (GATT) and U.S.–Canadian agreements on natural gas shipments; government-funded adjustment mechanisms to foreign-inspired trade shocks such as stockpiles of raw or refined materials; and techniques to promote sales overseas such as credits to foreign governments.

The final national concern in the area of economic policy is managing international monetary policy so that the influx or flight of capital does not damage national security. As all advanced industrial economies have become internationalized, capital flows among developed and less developed states have affected not only the relationships among states but also the political economy within each state. Among the many issues involved in chapter 13 are foreign purchase or sale of U.S. firms or subsidiaries; purchase of public or private debt instruments by foreign governments or individuals; investment abroad by U.S. multinational firms; and foreign loans by U.S. banks to both governments and foreign companies. The aggregate monetary outcome of these many choices and other decisions involving foreign trade in turn affects a state's balance of payments with foreign states. A sizable negative monetary balance can create domestic unemployment, while positive balances can promote inflation; either balance affects the state's international economic strength and reputation. Currency exchange arrangements also affect national security. The current area of floating, state-managed exchange rates requires nations to decide if and when to intervene in the international marketplace to stabilize their currencies.

The conclusion summarizes the points developed in the substantive chapters and addresses the ability of the U.S. political system, built as it is on an eighteenth-century constitution, to effectively ensure national security. Finally, we discuss the implications for the U.S. Constitution and political system as it carries the nation into its third century.

THE FOCUS

The primary concern of each author is the linkage between the U.S. constitutional system and national security policy making. Obviously, not every feature of the political system is relevant to each national security function. Thus each chapter describes the systemic features of policy making in each functional area, including the authority allocated to relevant policy makers, the level of participation of nongovernmental actors, and other system-based constraints and influences on policy makers. We are not therefore focusing here on issues within each function, but rather on the constitutional and the national security systems.

Because the impact of the constitutional system varies not only among national security functions but also between the stages of policy making, authors have sought to emphasize both policy creation and policy execution. In addition, the national security policy system is not static; it has evolved over time. Our discussion thus also seeks to account for its development into its current state.

In addition to establishing the essential features of policy making, our authors consider how the constitutional system affects the ability of the United States to carry out the functions essential to national security. We seek to answer such questions as: What difference does it make that the United States formulates the implements national security policy as it does? In other words, what are the consequences of the U.S. constitutional system for national security policy? How do policy makers cope with the constraints the system imposes upon them? Is the constitutional system adequate to meet the needs of a superpower? Can the United States correct problems within the constitutional system, or are more basic reforms in order?

As editors, then, we have asked the authors for a description of both constitutional and national security systems, an explanation of why the national security system handles particular functions as it does, and the implications and consequences of why policy making is handled as it is. Both we and the authors hope that this appraisal will contribute to a richer understanding of the U.S. Constitution as it enters its third century of structuring American politics and national security policy.

STATECRAFT

1

Mobilizing Political Support

BERT A. ROCKMAN

What exactly is the effect of the American constitutional system on the national security policy-making capabilities of the American government? I pose this question not because it is answerable in the way I have put it but because it provides a necessary perspective from which to assess the connection between institutions, consensus or the lack thereof, and normative theories about how national security policy should be made and by whom.

The constitutional system of divided powers has long been a source of dismay to those bent on achieving a state of policy, whatever the arena, that can be described as "coherent." Discontent with the hyperpluralized decision making characteristic of American government has a clear lineage dating back to the emergence of "the new nationalism" associated with Herbert Croly in the first decades of the twentieth century. The "new nationalism" envisaged a unitary conception of "the public good." Such a conception naturally requires a prescription for unitary institutional outlets—a condition that the Madisonian framework seems inevitably to stymie. Traditionally, the "unitary" institutional outlet has been the presidency.

In the realm of national security policy making, however, the issue became significant primarily after World War II. The United States was then the preeminent world power in virtually every respect and, among all the major parties to the upheavals of the two world wars, the country that in relative terms had suffered the least. The emergence of the United States as a global power and the simultaneous movement toward a bipolar world gave salience and visibility to a national security policy that hitherto had been only regional in focus and sporadic in effort.

The fear particularly of a Soviet challenge to Western interests and values precipitated an unusual level of international involvement for the United States, whose isolationist propensities followed from its advantageous defensive geopolitical position. The development of a bipartisan national security consensus, promulgated through an alliance of Senate Foreign Relations Committee Chairman Arthur Vandenberg and the Truman administration, provided critical support to a global political posture dedicated to (1) stopping the spread of communist governments and movements; (2) reining in the growth of Soviet military and political power; and (3) stabilizing a Western political and economic order and, ultimately, cementing a Western military alliance. This relatively rare circumstance has since been shrouded in legend as a norm from which the American policy-making process has deviated in recent times presumably moving from consensual premises and presidential leadership to conflicting premises and frequent policy disagreement.

The institutional supposition behind this conception dictated a virtually presidentialist outlook on American national security policy making—a realm of activity removed from the tugs and pulls and parochial pressures of domestic policy making. That conceptualization has diminished for many reasons, including the growing indistinctiveness of domestic and foreign policy as separable realms of activity. Nonetheless, the contemporary inheritors of the tradition of Croly's "new nationalism" have been partisans of presidential supremacy in national security policy, and often partisans of presidentialism in general. To create the means necessary to generate a coherent voice and mission for national security policy and to immunize it from day-to-day political pressures, as well as from conflicting views that may weaken resolve, executive supremacy (really meaning presidential supremacy) was accepted as an essential mechanism. It is this view that has come under attack, especially in the past two decades—peaking perhaps in the 1970s. The "repluralization" of national security policy making is, of course, related to the growth of fundamental disagreement about policy. But institutional availability provides opportunities for the opposition not readily found elsewhere.

As I have indicated, however, it is hard to demonstrate the precise effects of institutions on policy making—though I am convinced there are some, and I hope to suggest how these operate. More fundamental is this question: Can consensus or leadership override institutional obstacles? Equally fundamental is the converse: Do institutions influence the ability to forge consensus and to exercise leadership? Relatedly, how much does institutional structure influence process and behavior? How much of the policy-making equilibrium evolves through institutional norms? How much is shaped by political conditions?

Above all, what is the connection between institutions and conditions of fundamental agreement or disagreement about the aims and means of national security policy? Even more, what ought to be the relationship between institutions and policy making? Has the Madisonian system of competitive forces given way to a Hamiltonian conception of executive power in contemporary national security policy making? Or is the need for a Hamiltonian system of executive authority still hamstrung by the Madisonian precepts of fragmenting authority?

In the course of this chapter, which deals with the capacity to mobilize political support, I begin with an effort to define domains of national security policy. Subsequently, I probe into the nature of mass and attentive constituencies on national security policy—the pressures these create and the prospects for a broader educational effort from national security policy makers. I then, secondly, emphasize the fundamental importance of conflict and consensus on the ability to conduct national security policy, from the presidential vantage point. Thirdly, I focus on specific institutional effects as these influence the process of national security policy making. Finally, I want to touch briefly on the possibilities for presidential latitude provided not only by the Constitution but by the modern plebiscitary presidency. At the end, I try to draw together some observations that address, if indirectly, the very broad questions I have raised here about the impact of institutions on the ability to forge a unified *and* unifying national security policy.

DOMAINS OF NATIONAL SECURITY POLICY

As Hugh Heclo and Aaron Wildavsky put it, public policy is not like a cadaver on a slab to be dissected.[1] What is called policy is often pronouncement as much as it is action. In the form of pronouncement, "policy" is at its most coherent. As the product of choices made in the context of a continuous flow of events, constraints, and opportunities,[2] however, policy is often less coherent. It is this context to which Heclo and Wildavsky's picturesque simile applies. But even if policy does not lie still for dissection, we can draw some rough distinctions about the broad domains of decision making to which we give the label "national security policy."

There are many places from which we could start to draw these distinctions. One way of distinguishing the domains of national security policy is by the scope of the actors involved in decision making and the nature of their relationships to one another. Thus, Randall Ripley and Grace Franklin define three modes of national security policy: (1) structural, (2) strategic, and (3) crisis.[3] Structural policy involves implementing prior strategic decisions and includes such matters as deciding on specific weapons contractors, closing specific military installations, and making decisions about military personnel, including salary and benefits. Policy making on such matters has many attributes in common with domestic distributive policies, which, in fact, they closely resemble. The hypothesized relationship of influential actors here is that of subgovernmental dominance in which key agency interests, important members of authorizing and appropriating subcommittees, and relevant private contractors are often the dominant actors. The politics of key constituency interests is believed to be at work here, sometimes representing an obstacle to more effective procurement and logistic decisions. Since Robert McNamara's reign as defense secretary, however, none of his successors or the presidents they have worked for have been especially inclined to rub powerful interests, as represented in Congress, the wrong way—at least not without good political reason.

Srategic policies are composed of those setting large-scale (and presumably long-term) policy direction. These involve such matters as mixes of weapons systems, overall trade policies, foreign assistance, and, to some degree, basic adversarial or cooperative postures toward other states and international or multinational organizations. The principal actors involved in this genre of activities, according to Ripley and Franklin, are the president and central executive decision makers and Congress in plenary form. The point at which Congress gets involved and the intensity with which it does are likely to vary in accordance with the particular policy domain within this broader definition of strategic policy. Congress is, for example, likely to be relatively more active in regard to trade policies than in regard to either mixes of strategic weapons and forces or adversarial and cooperative postures by the United States toward other countries. This may help account for the greater success of presidents in getting defense-related legislation through Congress relative to most non-defense-related items of foreign policy.[4] Once it is taken into account that many of the non-defense items deal with trade issues, which are inherently domestic ones, and to requests for upgraded foreign assistance of various sorts, for which no congressional constituency exists, the disparity between defense and non-defense legislative success is understandable.

Ripley and Franklin's last national security policy category is crisis policy. By definition, this set of responses is to immediate problems of an unanticipated nature. Here, an almost exclusive role is played by the top executive leadership (the president and his inner advisory and cabinet circles). Usually, the top congressional leadership is taken into account, but more through consultation about decisions already arrived at than through advisory processes.

From the classification above, we can conclude that some elements of national security policy fall into fairly routine and disaggregated form, involving constituency benefits and pork barrel politics. Bureau routines, powerful lobbies, and constituency-tending members of Congress (usually on the key subcommittees) exert a powerfully fragmenting set of obstacles to any synoptic, rational planner. Since in regard to these issues presidents typically are at least as concerned with how they play in Peoria as with how they play at, say, the Kennedy School at Harvard, they are not likely to push hard to achieve some overarching concept of rational management behavior, at least for its own sake. Of course, they may have their own preferences as to who should get what benefits or bear what costs, but these preferences are more apt to be embedded in motives of political advantage (even if sometimes highly indirect) than in motives of managerial merit.

At the diametrically opposite end of things is the response to (or initiation of) crisis. Here, presidents have extraordinary powers stemming from their constitutional role as commander in chief and the implied presidential powers granted by the "take-care" clause of Article 2, Section 3 of the Constitution. These powers stem also from contemporary expectations shared by elites and mass publics that crisis decision making is, more or less, the exclusive province of the president and his inner national security circle.

These short-term, highly visible behaviors are thought also to provide presidents with rallying points in public opinion, almost regardless of their outcome. Some recent views, in fact, tend to emphasize the notion of a crisis-driven presidency whose incumbent is capable of finding popular solace in foreign policy crisis episodes.[5] Careful analysis, however, suggests that the so-called rally phenomenon built around presidential visibility in foreign affairs may be oversold. Such events apparently do not produce appreciably greater effects than other changes in the environment.[6] Whatever the facts of the case are, the prospect that elite actors believe that a president can rally opinion through visible international activity is often what is important. Because the power of initiative lies with the president, short-run and highly visible behavior negates congressional influence and public opinion as obstacles to executive action. In this regard, even prior statutory inhibitions imposed by Congress are readily circumvented when: (a) the event turns out well or action is thought necessary, (b) there is sufficient ambiguity (there is always sufficient ambiguity!) for alternative interpretations to be given to the situation to which a statutory inhibition applies; and (c) above all, the political coalitions and conditions that motivated the prior inhibitions are no longer strong.

Between the polarities of structural decision making and crisis decision making are those elements of national security policy making that require full legislative support. These are what Ripley and Franklin call "strategic policy." Here, a president typically is dependent upon Congress for Senate ratification of treaties, authorization and appropriations for weapons systems and military forces, military and economic assistance programs, trade legislation, and so on. These, in turn, are decomposable into specific packages. Typically, as noted, presidents have found it easier to get congressional support for defense-related matters than for others. It is especially in these other matters, but perhaps now in defense-related issues as well, that the so-called (and, as we shall see, short-lived) bipartisan consensus has dissipated.

The picture, in brief, is that the concept "national security policy" is merely a convenient cover for an assortment of diverse policy sectors with equally diverse political configurations surrounding them. National security policy appears most coherent when presidents utter words, less coherent when presidents must deal with the varied perspectives within their own executive departments and from their advisory circles, and probably least coherent when congressional support must be activated and solicited. The extent to which a president can gain coherence is, however, in no small part attributable to his own navigational system and the sorting out of his own priorities. Coherence, though, is not necessarily the same as analytic clarity. At least at the level of pronouncement, forceful ideological premises can provide the basis for coherence, if not clarity.

In regard to this point, the image of the bully pulpit is often invoked, along with a somewhat more sedate image of the president as the great educator in matters of foreign policy. Although it is frequently the case that "the great educator" is in need of a great deal of educating himself, the question of whether presidents can attain popular support for their objectives depends not only upon what these are but also upon what the capabilities of the citizenry are. Trigonometry is beyond the capability of third graders to absorb, but multiplication probably is not. The bully pulpit and the great educator both raise important issues of leadership, but one image has to do with simplicity, the other with complexity. Are these at all compatible? We need to know something about "the teacher," obviously, and the extent to which a president is capable of recognizing complex patterns and orchestrating sophisticated responses,[7] given that he is inevitably an amateur in international affairs. (Presidents do not, as a matter of course, float to the top of the political system from either the diplomatic service or the ranks of international politics theorists.) We need, however, to know something also about "the students"—the citizenry—and what their typical response patterns and capabilities are. That is what we turn to now.

MASS OPINION ON FOREIGN POLICY

Despite the enormity of its potential effects on their lives, national security policy is ordinarily perceived by most people as being removed from their daily existence. Although the images of presidential candidates as peacekeepers and international leaders have some significance to voters, the low salience of national security policy to ordinary citizens means that "opinion" about concrete issues is relatively unstable, created by the flow of events and the nature of elite cues. According to Gabriel Almond's major postwar study of mass foreign policy opinion, the limited knowledge of mass publics engenders great volatility in public opinion about international events.[8] Almond posited the existence of "moods" among the mass public that are susceptible to great swings. The swings themselves are a function of external events. During low visibility periods, there is little mass attention to foreign affairs, but when salient events arouse mass interest, a foreign policy mood is created. By definition, the characteristic of a mood is that it is unstable. Almond concluded that public opinion mood swings on foreign policy issues fail to provide the necessary stability and ballast from which elites can sustain direction and develop policy strategy.[9]

While Almond's concept of mood swings has been subject to critical analysis,[10] the view that there is a lack of political foundation in mass opinion for coherent or complex national security policy strategies is common (and probably correct). That also means that there is little support (except at the speech-making level) for policies that entail broadly dispersed sacrifices.

There is a good deal of evidence on the latter point. For example, among OECD countries, the United States devotes a relatively small percentage of its Gross National Product (GNP) to economic assistance abroad, although, of course, because of the gigantic size of the U.S. economy, that still involves a lot of money. Despite the growing internationalization of the American economy, moreover, the United States still exports a relatively smaller percentage of its products than most other advanced industrial nations.

On matters involving the protracted engagement of military force, impatience and the erosion of support become dominating features of public opinion whatever the initial level of support. Inherently, such an erosion is fully predictable if the decision to engage forces follows from motives of maximum expected utility, which assume that going to war is based on the expectation of winning and gaining.[11] John Mueller's study of the similarities in mass opinion during the three-year war in Korea and the even lengthier engagement of American military forces in Vietnam is instructive.[12] Although in retrospect it seems as though the American involvement in Vietnam was more controversial, the characteristics of mass opinion in these two cases are stunningly similar.

In spite of the fact that opposition to the war in Vietnam was more vocal and mobilized than to the war in Korea (which may have had to do with the growth of the attentive public and its polarization), support for continued involvement in Korea eroded even more quickly than in Vietnam. In each case, a major event that apparently changed the expected advantage to be gained from involvement brought the erosion of public support into sharp relief. In the case of the Korean War, it was the entrance of Chinese troops onto the side of the North Koreans in November 1950. In the case of the Vietnam War, it was the Tet offensive by the North Vietnamese regular army and its allied Viet Cong irregulars.

These patterns lead to a seemingly obvious conclusion—namely, that protracted engagement of military forces with mounting casualties in distant locales will bring growing disillusionment and political dissent at home. Pressures to end engagement clearly will be generated under such conditions. Yet despite the similarities in opinion structure among the American public across the Korean and Vietnam wars, one war produced overt protest not associated with the other. Moreover, there also is evidence, however fragmentary, to indicate that clarity about the goals being pursued by the United States in World War II was in question.[13] The moral virtues that some commentators have associated with the World War II effort (the "good war" as it has been dubbed by the journalist Studs Terkel) seemed less clear in the war's midst than at its end.

Mass impatience with long-term engagements is understandably great, and it may also be universal. There is no reason to think that the American public is unique in its dissatisfaction with costly engagements, nor is there any reason to believe that the Vietnam episode was unique, despite the remarkable length of the engagement. What does appear to be unique about Vietnam was the arousal of particularly activist centers of opposition emanating especially from those with the skills and means of communication—university intellectuals and journalists.[14] The weakest support for the war effort in Vietnam stemmed from isolationist sentiment, which was found disproportionately among the elderly, the least educated, blacks, and women.[15] These groups are among the hardest to mobilize. Though numerically only a very small portion of opposition to the war sprang from the nation's intelligentsia, it, in contrast, is an obviously mobilizable population, typically with a well-articulated view of foreign affairs. Equally important, the intellectuals disproportionately found their political home in the party of the president (Lyndon Johnson) who was principally responsible for enlarging the American involvement.

For the most part, it is not clear what the electoral consequences are, other things being equal, of mass dissatisfaction with war policy. Although Truman's popularity suffered directly from the Korean War, Johnson's own fall in public approval was not, according to Mueller, attributable to Vietnam in any significant degree.[16] The consequences of strong elite dissatisfaction, of course, are more powerfully exhibited. Undoubtedly, internal opposition is but one factor of many in calculating a settlement. But at some point, the costs of further military engagement are essentially unsupportable. In spite of the greater immediacy to the French of the Indochinese and Algerian colonial wars than of Korea or Vietnam to the United States, the French too had to pull out when they no longer cared to bear the costs of staying in.

Most fundamentally, however, Almond's concern was with the ability of the citizenry to comprehend the complexities of foreign affairs, and thus to provide a public base for a sustained and sophisticated national security strategy. By its very nature, of course, sophisticated strategic policy is not amenable to overt and unambiguous positions. Simple moral principles or highly dramatic positions are not likely to travel far as operational policies, no matter how appealing they may sound on the home front. Moreover, restraint, prudence, and caution are easily turned into political liabilities at home. Yet the underlying reasons why this is so have less to do with the relatively inert and uninformed sectors of the public than with the relatively more informed.[17] It is, therefore, to the relatively informed and elite sectors of foreign policy opinion that we now turn. In doing so, we shall also be better able to comprehend a setting in which national security policy is both relatively more salient and also more conflictual.

CONSENSUS AND CONFLICT IN FOREIGN POLICY MAKING

One of the key propositions frequently encountered about the recent history of U.S. national security policy making is that a bipartisan consensus and fundamental agreement has been displaced by a partisan outlook on foreign policy and sharpened disagreement since the growth of dissent on the Vietnam War. Greater conflict between Congress and the president presumably reflects this sharpened disagreement. To be addressed, this argument needs to be broken down in several ways.

First we need to focus on the nature of the population being discussed. Is it the mass public? Is it an elite population, if not necessarily a decision-making one? Alternatively, is it an elite decision-making group with palpable influence on decisions, such as members of Congress? Is there more disagreement within Congress? Is it especially the case that presidents are having a more difficult time with Congress on foreign policy than once was the case? It is difficult, of course, to define a threshhold appropriate to all of these levels at which one can comfortably talk about consensus or conflict. But there is an even more pressing problem: finding comparable data to draw appropriate comparisons over time. Mostly, we shall have to settle for very rough comparisons by most criteria. Unfortunately, that may not conclusively answer the questions being raised here.

Second, we need to define an appropriate time frame. At what point was consensus lost—if it was? Has it been regained? If so, when?

A third need is to define intensity and policy arena. How central has national security policy become? To whom? About what? Have some policy domains become differentially salient? Is interest group activity growing? If so, on what types of issues? Interest group activism is clearly one of the key indicators of the salience of an issue domain. The flowering of ethnic interest group activities in the 1970s was a reflection of both the growth of such groups and the relative intensity of the interest that particular foreign policy domains have held for certain sectors of American society.

As a general proposition, the more national security policy becomes salient, the more it becomes political, and the more it becomes political, the less presidents will find national security policy making exclusively within their jurisdiction. This increase in actors and widening of interests in the national security policy-making process certainly is one feature of the present era, but it is not clear that this is aberrational in the American experience.

Mass Publics

Strategic national security policy issues are largely abstractions to the general public. For the most part, they do not touch directly the lives of most people. Ironically, however, it is often just exactly these large strategic issues—concerns about war, threats of various sorts, nuclear weapons, and so on—that rise to the top of lists of most important issues that the public cites when asked to do so. Yet, aside from crisis situations, these are not the kinds of matters to which mass publics are particularly attentive or in respect to which, traditionally, there is any significant degree of attitude stability.[18]

In the environment of approximately the past twenty years, however, foreign policy issues have tended to become more salient politically, while at the same time they have fallen off to some extent in the most-important-problem sweepstakes.[19] Until 1964, for example, the relationship between votes and opinion on foreign policy issues (no doubt influenced by the internal instability of the latter) was weak. The relationship changed markedly at that point, however, despite some later oscillations in the magnitude of the correlations.[20] The rise of foreign policy issue voting is connected to a general rise in issue voting (obscured somewhat by the Carter candidacies), which, in turn, is connected to several other factors—the weakening of traditional party-based voting, the growth of more highly educated publics, a declining center within both Republican and Democratic parties at both mass and elite levels, and the disunifying nature of key foreign policy issues within this time frame. At the same time, national security policy issue attitudes among mass publics apparently became more linked to attitudes on domestic issues.[21] Although these findings are themselves controversial and possibly the consequence of variability in the measuring instrument, there is a clearer structuring of opinion even within the mass public, no doubt greatly influenced by contextual considerations, than had been the case in the pre–1964 period.

All of this must, of course, be seen in relative terms. Opinion structure at the mass level is at best more like a gelatin mold than a firm substance. If it is somewhat more defined than in the past, that is because the political context of national security policy issues may be somewhat more sharply defined than in the past. In order better to understand that context, we have to shift our focus to look at those who are especially attentive to national security policy—the elites who give definition and structure to national security policy debates.

Elites

One thing—but I believe *only* one thing—is clear about elite opinion on national security policy, and that is that it is more definitively structured than mass opinion. That is not particularly surprising because, in general, real opinion tends to be harder and more stable than responses based on little information.[22] Two leading analysts of U.S. national security policy making, Ole R. Holsti and James N. Rosenau, make an impressive case for the emergence among elites of a set of clear-cut and mostly conflicting world views about U.S. national security policy. Their argument is that the costly and protracted engagement of American forces in Vietnam stimulated a breakdown of foreign policy consensus into a more definitive and clashing set of perspectives. Yet their claim that there once was a clearer consensus on national security policy, and that Vietnam was the principal agent for its breakdown, is not so well sustained.

Holsti and Rosenau admit, to be sure, that their assumption that U.S. national security policy-making processes were more consensual in the period between the end of World War II and the Vietnam War is "tentative and impressionistic."[23] In fact, Holsti and Rosenau are very careful to indicate that a solid empirical base upon which to draw the inferences they do is lacking. For that, they need comparable data over time. They are also careful to point out that very sharp disagreement on national security policy concerning both substance and process occurred before the onset of World War II. They observe, for example, that even after the Nazi conquest of France in June 1940, there was no consensus to enter the war on the Allied side until the Pearl Harbor attack. Their presumption, a not uncommon one after all, is that a basic consensus was forged out of the World War II and Cold War experiences, which then broke down as a consequence of the dissent from the Vietnam War.

To reiterate, however, although every available elite survey indicates substantial division on firm ideological grounds among American elites over the course of American national security policy since the 1970s,[24] there simply is no precisely comparable evidence to suggest that equally sharp attitudinal divisions (however differently they may have been structured) did not exist in the period before the falling out over Vietnam. Relevant studies have existed only since this time period. Moreover, from a comparative perspective, evidence of strong division on matters of national security policy direction, particularly having to do with NATO, can be found among West German elites.[25] Nor is it necessarily the case that such disagreements are unhealthy. As with Holsti and Rosenau, my impression too is that post–World War II and pre-Vietnam foreign policy operated in the context of an establishment consensus, brokered by major East Coast diplomatic and financial figures active in the Council on Foreign Relations. That is not, however, to say that major differences of view did not exist. Congress, Samuel Huntington has argued, was often outside of that consensus (though on the whole compliant with it) because its members were (and still are) more attuned to Main Street than to Wall Street.[26] In short, my impression, like Holsti and Rosenau's, is just that— an impression, and one undoubtedly reinforced only by equally impressionistic, if forcefully argued, commentaries. Thus are legends created.

It is true, of course, that during a time of considerable challenge, a Republican Congress acted to support a number of very significant proposals made by the Truman administration to stave off the Stalinist threat in Europe. This gave rise to the idea of bipartisanship in national security policy and to the notion that national security policy making represented a water's edge of normal politics. This circumstance and some temporally limited empirical data on congressional treatment of presidential national security policy initiatives gave rise to the "two presidencies" notion—the idea of a more or less embattled domestic policy presidency and a congressionally deferential national security policy one.[27]

To what extent is there evidence here to support the notion of a bygone foreign policy consensus and a more recent environment of partisan strife? To examine that, we need to turn to the congressional arena.

The Congressional Arena

Aaron Wildavsky's notable hypothesis of "the two presidencies" has been amended from time to time by analysts suggesting that it may have been temporally limited,[28] or by those suggesting limitations connected to the measures Wildavsky employed.[29] The most thorough analysis accounting both for temporal and measurement considerations, however, is provided by George Edwards.[30] The two presidencies idea receives considerable debunking by Edwards as he analyzes the differential between presidential support in Congress on domestic and foreign policy issues over a thirty-year period. Between 1953 and 1983, for example, Edwards finds only a 3 percent differential in key congressional votes on domestic and foreign policy support for the president.

The differential between domestic and foreign policy was by far the greatest during the Eisenhower presidency. It lessened during the Kennedy and Johnson presidencies and further declined during the Nixon and Ford presidencies. Partisan differences especially help account for these findings. Although partisan differences were relatively small during the Eisenhower administration, they became greater (especially in the House) during the Kennedy/Johnson and Nixon/Ford administrations. Support from the opposition party as well as domestic and foreign policy support differentials reached new lows during the Carter administration. Yet, party differences on key foreign policy issues have been sharpest during the Reagan presidency, and the differential between domestic and foreign policy on the part of the opposition party is virtually nil.[31] There is a good bit of evidence to suggest that in many respects Reagan is the most polarizing president the country has known during the thirty-year time sequence.[32] For example, in 1984 he was "more disliked by opposition voters than any previous victorious candidate"—in fact, the most unpopular (among opposition voters) of any major candidate since 1952, *wining or losing*.[33] This is masked, of course, by the fact that he is also the most strongly supported by his supporters since Eisenhower.

In any event, Edwards' analysis is both compelling and yet inconclusive on at least one key issue. Although it casts strong doubt on the "two presidencies" as a norm, it nonetheless does suggest that there was greater consensus earlier, during the Eisenhower period. However, we lack comparable data for the frequently controversial Truman period. Except for the short spurt during the 80th Congress in which Senator Vandenberg abandoned his traditional midwestern Republican isolationist moorings and rallied support for Truman administration initiatives, this hardly appears to have been a period of great consensus. Edwards suggests that the Eisenhower case is anomalous, mostly the result of a Republican president with policies closer to the preferences of the opposition party and the eastern establishment wing of his own than to the main corps of Republicans in the Congress. To paraphrase Edwards, then, the key to the Eisenhower anomaly is not presidential deference but policy preference.

The issue as to when there was a change to a more conflictual relationship between president and congressional opposition is still not fully determined. We do not know for certain whether Truman's key proposals over the course of his presidency were as kindly treated as Eisenhower's, nor are the early years of the Kennedy and Johnson administrations separated from the publicly more contentious later period. The consequence is that we are uncertain as to whether Eisenhower represents an unusual blip in a normally conflictual pattern or whether that conflictual pattern fundamentally came into being coincident with the great controversy over Vietnam policy.

Intensities and Arenas

Gauging the intensity of national security policy issues and whether or not it has changed over time is no easy matter. As noted earlier, national security policy issues often top the list of most important issues when the public is surveyed. But that by itself does not necessarily register intensity. At the mass public level, as also noted, the correlation between national security policy issues and the presidential vote greatly increased (where it once was negligible) during the 1964–72 period. In fact, among issues, national security policy opinion correlated most closely with the presidential vote in both 1964 and 1972, suggesting that at least for some segments of the population these issues were salient ones, even if mostly at the level of symbols.

Another indication of intensity is political mobilization, including extrasystemic mobilization such as street demonstrations. This clearly was what distinguished opposition to the war in Vietnam from that in Korea. Although war weariness appears to have accounted for most of the verbalized opposition to each war, during the Vietnam conflict the opposition of the intelligentsia, especially centered on major university campuses, transformed disgruntlement into active and mobilized opposition. Although there is no indication that support for the American involvement was less in Vietnam than in Korea, it is clear that the intensity of opposition was greater, if only because it was clearly mobilized. Before drawing any unambiguous conclusions, however, it is well to remember the riots provoked in northern cities by instituting conscription during the Civil War.

Intensity, of course, may be especially passionate when national security policy deals with the ethnic loyalties of citizens. A number of commentaries have made note of the growth of lobbies for other states that tap the external loyalties of American ethnic groups. The growth of interest groups, the role of political action committees (PACs), the global reach and interests of the United States, and the constituency dependence of members of Congress all seem to have facilitated these influences on American national security policy.[34] The pro-Israeli and pro-Greek lobbies are most routinely cited because in recent times they especially have come into visible conflict with presidential decisions and proposals.

The tradition of the so-called "hyphen vote" is, however, a fairly longstanding one. Opposition to American entry into World War I on the side of the Allies was fairly strong among German-American groups; pressures for exotic pledges to "roll back" the communist regimes installed in Eastern European countries after World War II were also exerted by various Eastern European ethnic groups and organizations. Since the United States emerged as an ethnically diverse immigrant state, such pressures probably were inevitable once American involvement and prowess were exerted globally.

From a constitutional standpoint, the independence of Congress from the executive and the political dependence of its members lend themselves to a receptivity to passionate claims by ethnic organizations, especially those that have substantial political assets. Whatever the merits, or lack thereof, of this sort of well-focused pressure (putting aside, for the moment, the often strong proclivities for agreement between members' personal views and those the groups are pushing), it is hard to ascertain specific constitutional effects, because while a few other democratic nations have a good bit of ethnic diversity too, they do not have an equivalence of global reach. Canada comes to mind as an obvious example. It is probably fair to say, however, that the present active role of ethnic-related interest groups with specific national security policy agendas is not discontinuous with our past.

We have begun at last to ask what difference institutions make. To that intriguing question there is no unambiguous answer. But in the next section of this chapter, I shall explore some of the ways in which we might think about this very central issue. For a great many discussions about the need for coherence in national security policy begin with the supposition that, in some quite fundamental sense, Congress should play only a limited role.

Unfortunately, presidents and those purportedly acting on their behalf often mistake secrecy for coherence, as the recent Iranian arms deal suggests, and as the 1971 opening to China (with its accompanying disruptions in relations with Japan) also indicates. Moreover, yet quite understandably, presidents are also apt to mistake coherence in their policies with longer-run continuities in national security policy to which Congress has been a partner, as recent efforts to interpret the 1972 ABM treaty reveal.

THE ROLE OF INSTITUTIONS

It is important to appreciate that the U.S. Constitution does not really limit presidential powers, but rather, implicitly—and in some cases explicitly—through the separation of powers endows other institutions with powers as well. Despite the Madisonian checks, in certain respects presidents have extraordinary crisis powers that are constitutionally derived. Notwithstanding the congressional power of appropriations, the War Powers Act, and the congressional authority to declare war, for example, presidents have gone virtually unchallenged once they have acted to deploy military force.

The extent to which Congress is likely to act as a direct deterrent to presidential aspirations in national security policy depends significantly upon a president's legislative needs. Of course, Congress can jump into anything for which it has developed a collective concern and relatively clear preference. Formerly ordinary matters such as arms transfers are now subject to congressional approval. This also happens to be an arena in which American ethnic organizations have been particularly active.

Divided government, made possible by the separation of powers, is an especially sizeable obstacle to presidential plans, inasmuch as the norm is for members of the president's party to support him and those of the opposition party to not do so. The difference between the American system and party government systems is, of course, that the norm is not as rigidly held to in the United States. In the absence of a great deal of internal division within a president's party over the course of his national security policy, a president whose party is in command on Capitol Hill (the Senate is especially important) generally will fare well. It is not very surprising in this regard that in recent decades the existence of political division between the White House and the Congress has put some crimp into presidential plans.

Beyond this, however, and regardless of the party division, there is a tendency for Congress to try to micromanage aspects of national security policy. This phenomenon, though, is not an especially new one. The former chairman of the Senate Foreign Relations Committee, J. William Fulbright, took note of congressional intrusions in the mid 1960s (pre-Vietnam) and spoke of them disparagingly. Congress, he concluded, should set policy with a capital P, not with a lowercase one.[35] Huntington, on the other hand, concluded that Congress was likely to perform these oversight and supervisory functions better than it was able to define the broader parameters of policy.[36]

Political division between branches of government certainly brings to a head the ultimate logic of the American constitutional system: Do not proceed without agreement unless an immediate crisis impinges. Although we cannot directly compare systems with different institutions and practices that seem to be at variance with American traditions, it is very important to take basic levels of consensus and disagreement into account.

We might, then, begin to think about this comparison if we asked what the United States would look like with a parliamentary system of government. No one can answer that precisely, although there is no shortage of speculative opinion on the subject.[37] It may well be that a parliamentary government would not look appreciably different from the conditions that prevail in contemporary Washington. Thus, if the political process produced majority party government, that government, because of the political benefits needed to keep it together, would undoubtedly exhibit somewhat diverse political predispositions, as is already common within the American political parties.

These diversities might well be more commonly exhibited in the cabinet than in the legislative body. For a parliamentary cabinet, as such, is not equivalent to a president's. The American system of superordinate-subordinate presidential-cabinet relationships makes the cabinet, in theory, a presidential instrument. The cabinet is part of the president's team. A prime minister, however, is rather more like the coach of an athletic team. He or she inherits people; under normal circumstances, a president does not. Cabinet members are a president's subordinates, but they are, strictly speaking, a prime minister's peers. Of course, a prime minister with will can also find ways to dump cambinet members overboard. That is particularly true under majority government conditions. In general, however, a cabinet system requires collective decision making and responsibility, and usually, therefore, more attentiveness to diverse points of view and to coalescing them than is found in the American presidential system. Although the parliamentary body has less maneuverability to constrain initiatives once a government has committed itself to them, it is presumed that essential voices have been heard in the cabinet.

It is at least equally probable to imagine that, were the American constitutional system restructured to produce a parliamentary one, the result would look more like a multiparty coalition. (Naturally, that depends a lot upon the voting rules and the representational scheme employed.) Under these conditions, bargaining is undertaken before a government is arranged. Once bargains are sealed, they are to be kept. Understandably, that may limit considerably the range of options that a government can explore. Often such governments fall when an unanticipated crisis occurs for which no clear bargain had previously been arranged and about which one or more of the parties dissents from the government's response. Because foreign affairs is the realm of the unanticipated, crisis incidents often provoke the decomposition of multiparty cabinet governments. It is important in this regard to realize that if a president fails on a policy matter, he does not also fall.

Much has been made of the growing fragmentation of Congress and an increased tendency for Congress (from the executive perspective) to micromanage or (from the legislative perspective) supervise national security policy making.[38] This is not, as I have noted, entirely new. Monuments to this tendency, such as the Hickenlooper Amendment (which pegged foreign economic assistance to private enterprise) abounded prior to the "new congressional" era. It is possible that more of it is occurring as a consequence of (1) more opportunities to influence policy resulting from congressional dispersion of authority; (2) a greater desire to influence policy on the part of a different generation of members of Congress; and (3) a more salient view of national security policy making in both its substance and process, which makes the normal adversarial relationships more central.

It is clear, however, that neither a parliamentary system nor the American separation-of-powers system can remain unaccountable to political forces. But one is a more closed, privatized, and bureaucratized operation; the other more open, public, and accessible to a multitude of political forces. In a parliamentary system, bargains are struck at the level of party leadership, usually in the cabinet, and debated mostly for show in parliament. Agreements tend to come unstuck only when the unanticipated occurs. In the American system, by contrast, policy stances are put on public display prior to being bargained. That, of course, heightens the stakes for all involved because it commits the actors to public positions.

Since by the totality of a mix of powers it endows to each institution, the Constitution makes the roles of executive discretion and legislative supervision ambiguous, presidents have a natural tendency to claim a variety of powers implied in the exercise of their duties. On matters where the power of initiative is vital, that usually gives the president the upper hand; on matters on which congressional support is clearly required (usually legislative requests), the president is most often a supplicant.

It is exceedingly difficult to separate the role of institutions from the political and cultural norms that influence their operation. In the American polity, the national security policy-making process enjoys (or suffers from) a high degree of visibility, the influence of many hands and interests, and consequently, to some degree, an often unpredictable policy course. Deals forged at the executive level are not always able to be kept when they require congressional commitment to sustain them. From one perspective, that represents a dangerous intrusion on the capacity of the executive to conduct international diplomacy. Viewed differently, however, it is unlikely that the leadership in other systems would fail to enlist the support of "relevant others" in their systems before they make commitments for which there is uncertain political support. The difference across systems is, of course, that "the relevant others" in the American case are both more numerous and less tied to the executive leadership.

It is not likely that institutions alone can forge consensus where little exists. In the presence of strong disagreement, a parliamentary government may also be checkmated by the nature of its own internal coalition.

But the process is likely to be less public. More negotiation behind closed doors takes place than in the American system. That decreases the public stakes for the actors. Of course, in the United States, the public stakes are actually employed as bargaining leverage by presidents in their relations with Congress. Numerous phrases attest to this—ranging from Lyndon Johnson's plea that he was, after all, the "one and only president" the county had to the more recent and oft-heard plea that Congress not eliminate this or that presidential "bargaining chip." Presidents, in brief, have learned to use their purported vulnerability before Congress as a political resource.

Still, there is no doubt that Congress can make a president's failures visible. If his reputation is on a downward slide, that will add to his troubles. In the absence of agreement, the independence of Congress and the publicness of our political processes are likely to make agreement harder to come by. Yet the virtue of these processes may be to clarify policy debates.

It should not be particularly surprising that under these conditions modern presidents seek to create the relative privacy and centralization of cabinet government minus any of the constraints that typically encumber it.[39] The natural advantage that presidents have lies in initiation; if Congress is to react, it often must do so in the face of a fait accompli. Alternatively, to the extent that a president is legislatively dependent in national security policy, he works at a considerable disadvantage.

What difference do institutions make? A lot and a little are both correct answers, but in different senses. Institutions make a difference in political strategy—who has to be convinced, at what stage, and how publicly. These are important matters, and a president dependent on, and interested in, agreement would be wise to reach those agreements before he makes public commitments. A president not so interested in or dependent on agreement, of course, can create facts and place the burden of initiating resistance on Congress.

Evidence that institutions can overcome deep and fundamental disagreement on national security policy is, however, unconvincing. Parliamentary governments nevertheless act in the face of disagreement, and so also do presidents. Still, the question that must be raised is to what extent any government can embark upon a policy course that generated divisiveness? Since it is fair to assume that division rather than consensus is, in fact, the norm, the real issue is to what extent should governments resist exacerbating division in national security affairs? The nature of institutions here is important because the parliamentary system leads to risk aversion—deep conflict within the cabinet likely will inhibit less supportable courses of action. On the other hand, the publicly conflictual nature of policy making in the American system gives it a propensity for risk taking. Presidents can lead in the hope (often misplaced) that others will follow.

PRESIDENTIAL POPULARITY AND FOREIGN POLICY LATITUDE

To what extent, then, can a president effectively lead in national security policy? As with any other form of policy making, the answer to that question rests principally on the president's political standing in Congress and his popular standing in the country. Naturally, presidents want policy coherence. This they define operationally as congressional compliance. The amount of compliance they get, though, depends on the party distribution of seats and party cohesion. It depends also on how much a president asks of Congress, as distinct from engaging in unilateral high diplomatic or military initiatives. Except in this latter regard, the usual political party–based cleavages tend to hold, because national security policy is not fundamentally distinct from domestic policy. Indeed, in the Reagan administration, there is some hint that division on national security policy is even stronger than it is on domestic policy. Divided government between the White House and Capitol Hill over much recent history has, then, managed—for better or ill—to bring the underlying conflicts among attentive publics to a head.

Other things being equal, however, presidential popularity in the country does have influence. Although performance in national security affairs is not a primary determinant of popular presidential approval,[40] a president's popular standing has a good bit to do with his national security policy latitude. Military shows of force, for example, appear to be most decisively influenced by presidential popularity.[41] These actions are unilateral ones, of course, and though Congress may react to them, the power of initiative lies in the president's hands.

For such data, it is difficult to infer presidential motives and calculations. Inferences of this sort require more finely grained studies of presidential decision making. Yet the dramatic penetration of plebiscitary influences in widening or narrowing what presidents perceive to be their opportunities and discretion in foreign affairs is impressive, if chastening from a republican and constitutional standpoint.

CONCLUSION

Since the end of World War II, the United States has been a global power with great, if limited, international economic, military, and political capability. The nation having emerged from its isolationist cocoon to play a continuously active role in the world, it is not surprising that this role and the costs and burdens it requires should be a matter of significant controversy.

A Democratic president, Harry Truman, was able to persuade the Republican 80th Congress of 1947–48 to respond immediately and institutionally to a potential Soviet political threat to all of Europe. Truman's Republican successor, President Eisenhower, confronted mostly with Democratic Congresses, mainly continued the Truman foreign policy agenda, despite noises to the contrary from the secretary of state, John Foster Dulles. A coalition of internationalist Republicans (of whom Eisenhower was the leader) and Democrats provided a relatively high degree of foreign policy accord throughout that period.

As the international environment changed, as generations of leaders changed, and as the limits of American power became more noticeable, underlying conflicts grew and became more salient. This, to reiterate, was not a deviant phenomenon but rather a normal and understandable one. Whatever the underlying realities behind the first decade and a half of the Cold War, presidents more or less seem to have drawn the conclusion that national security policy was their domain. To variable degree, presidents sought to immunize national security policy making from normal political processes, enveloping it in the mythology of bipartisan consensus.

Of course, presidents have self-interest at stake in sustaining the myth of bipartisan consensus. They, after all, shape policies, to which Congress mostly responds when it is able and willing to do so. Adverse congressional response is thus deemed conflictual. And conflict between Congress and the president is presumed to make our national security policy appear to be in disarray.

Regrettably, therefore, we end where we began—a not uncommon feature of political analysis. We began by asking what difference the American constitutional system makes in shaping national security policy. Relatedly, we asked to what extent the operation of institutions reflects underlying consensus and disagreement, and to what extent institutions shape these. Although we cannot know the answers for sure, we can be certain that the American system not only makes public policy, but also makes policy making very public. The publicness is related to the fragmentation of political authority and provides some access to intense interests. Disagreement may be more visible in the American system, but it also is less likely to be conducted on the streets than in many European polities. The cost of limiting access may be paid in the currency of mobilized social discontent.

Nonetheless, one cannot hope to achieve much clarity or strategic direction in policy merely by equilibrating and mediating between contending ideas and national security policy directions. To lead, presidents must take acceptable risks. And we should value their willingness to do so. At the same time, it is difficult to criticize Congress for engaging in a role that constitutionally is fully its right. National security policy is not, cannot, and ought not be immune from the need to engage in political persuasion. Given the state of the art of present-day presidential politics, however, that need is likely to be expressed in the form of "going public."[42] Thus, in national security as well as in domestic policy making, the inclination of presidents is toward plebiscitary rather than republican forms—an ironic twist of fate for this very republican form of government. For a government built on a foundation of sober thoughts, this indeed is a most sobering one.

How sobering that thought is has been highlighted by the Reagan administration's recent misadventures in its national security activities and its possible violations of law and congressional intent. When presidents forego the arts of political persuasion to practice those of political subterfuge, they run the risk (as Reagan now appears to have done) of damaging their own policy prospects—an individually irrational behavior. Worse yet, by escalating mistrust between Congress and the presidency, and even within their own administrations, they increase the likelihood that succeeding presidents will feel further compelled toward unilateral or covert policy making—a collectively dysfunctional behavior. The final irony, then, is that "going public," in general, also can be a resource for "going secret" in particular.

NOTES

I am indebted to George C. Edwards III for his excellent advice and to Kerry Manning for his able assistance.

1. Hugh Heclo and Aaron Wildavsky, *The Private Government of Public Money* (Berkeley and Los Angeles: University of California Press, 1974), p. 373.
2. This is often conceptualized as the ubiquitous "garbage can" model of choice. For a policy-making illustration of this, see John W. Kingdon, *Agendas, Alternatives, and Public Policies* (Boston: Little, Brown, 1984).
3. Randall B. Ripley and Grace A. Franklin, *Congress, the Bureaucracy, and Public Policy,* 3d ed. (Homewood, Ill.: Dorsey, 1984), pp. 28–31, 237–46.
4. Steven A. Shull, *Presidential Policy Making: An Analysis* (Brunswick, Ohio: King's Court, 1979), esp. p. 96.
5. For example, see Theodore J. Lowi, *The Personal President: Power Invested, Promise Unfulfilled* (Ithaca, N.Y.: Cornell University Press, 1985), esp. pp. 15–20.
6. See George C. Edwards III, *The Public Presidency: The Pursuit of Popular Support* (New York: St. Martin's Press, 1983), pp. 239–47.
7. For a more fully developed conception of presidential knowledge and style in foreign policy making, see Richard W. Cottam and Bert A. Rockman, "In the Shadow of Substance: Presidents as Foreign Policy Makers," in David P. Forsythe, ed., *American Foreign Policy in an Uncertain World* (Lincoln: University of Nebraska Press, 1984), pp. 65–104.

8. Gabriel A. Almond, *The American People and Foreign Policy.* (1950; New York: Praeger, 1960).
9. Ibid.
10. See especially William R. Caspary, "The 'Mood Theory': A Study of Public Opinion and Foreign Policy," *American Political Science Review* 64 (1970): 536–47.
11. For an exposition of this theory, see Bruce Bueno de Mesquita, "An Expected Utility Theory of International Conflict," *American Political Science Review* 74 (1980): 917–31.
12. John E. Mueller, *War, Presidents, and Public Opinion* (New York: Wiley, 1973).
13. Ibid., pp. 172–75.
14. Ibid., pp. 157–66.
15. Ibid., pp. 122–36.
16. John E. Mueller, "Presidential Popularity from Truman to Johnson," *American Political Science Review* 64 (1970): 18–34.
17. Relatively attentive opinion almost invariably is more polarized than is the case among the least attentive. Inevitably, it also is more hawkish (and equally more genuinely dovish). See here William A. Gamson and Andre Modigliani, "Knowledge and Foreign Policy Opinions: Some Models for Consideration," *Public Opinion Quarterly* 30 (1966): 187–99; Philip E. Converse and Howard Schuman, " 'Silent Majorities' and the Vietnam War," *Scientific American* 224 (June 1970): 17–25.
18. See Philip E. Converse, "The Nature of Belief Systems in Mass Publics," in David Apter, ed., *Ideology and Discontent* (New York: Free Press, 1964), pp. 205–61.
19. See Norman H. Nie, Sidney Verba, and John R. Petrocik, *The Changing American Voter,* enlarged ed. (Cambridge, Mass.: Harvard University Press, 1979), pp. 99–103.
20. Ibid., 1976 ed., pp. 187–89.
21. Ibid., 1979 ed., pp. 123–55.
22. Philip E. Converse, "Attitudes and Nonattitudes: The Continuation of a Dialogue," in Edward R. Tufte, ed., *The Quantitative Analysis of Social Problems* (Reading, Mass.: Addison-Wesley, 1970), pp. 168–90.
23. Ole R. Holsti and James N. Rosenau, *American Leadership in World Affairs: Vietnam and the Breakdown of Consensus* (Boston: Allen & Unwin, 1984), p. 222.
24. Ibid., see also Allen H. Barton, "Consensus and Conflict among American Leaders," *Public Opinion Quarterly* 38 (1974–75): 507–30.
25. Ursula Hoffmann-Lange, Helga Neumann, and Baerbel Steinkemper, "Conflict and Consensus among Leadership Groups in the Federal Republic of Germany," in Bogdan Denitch, ed., *National Elites: What They Think, What They Do* (London: Sage, 1979).
26. Samuel P. Huntington, "Congressional Responses to the Twentieth Century," in David B. Truman, ed., *The Congress and America's Future* (Englewood-Cliffs, N.J.: Prentice-Hall, 1965), pp. 5–31.
27. Aaron Wildavsky, "The Two Presidencies," in Wildavsky, ed., *Perspectives on the Presidency* (Boston: Little, Brown, 1975), pp. 448–61.
28. Donald A. Peppers, "The 'Two Presidencies': Eight Years Later," in Wildavsky, ed., *Perspectives on the Presidency,* pp. 462–71.
29. Lee Sigelman, "A Reassessment of the Two Presidencies Thesis," *Journal of Politics* 41 (1979): 1195–1205.
30. George C. Edwards III, "The Two Presidencies: A Reevaluation," *American Politics Quarterly* 14 (1986): 247–63.
31. Ibid.
32. Ibid. Edwards' analysis records the sharpest partisan differences on foreign policy voting in Congress for the thirty-year time period during the Reagan administration. My update for 1984 and 1985 on key votes reveals partisan differences on foreign

policy in the House for these two years actually to be greater than domestic differences. For a more general evaluation of the polarizing aspects of Reagan's presidency, see Martin P. Wattenberg, "The Reagan Polarization Phenomenon and the Continuing Downward Slide in Presidential Popularity," *American Politics Quarterly* 14 (1986): 219–45, and from an elite and policy-making perspective, see Bert A. Rockman, "USA: Government Under President Reagan," in Thomas Ellwein, Joachim-Jens Hesse, Renate Mayntz, and Fritz Scharpf, eds., *Jahrbuch zur Staats- und Verwaltungswissenschaft* (Baden-Baden, West Germany: Nomos Verlagsgesellschaft, 1987).

33. Wattenberg, "Reagan Polarization Phenomenon," p. 227.
34. For example, see Stephen S. Rosenfeld, "Pluralism and Policy," *Foreign Affairs* 52 (1974): 263–72, and Robert H. Trice, "Congress and the Arab-Israeli Conflict: Support for Israel in the U.S. Senate, 1970–73," *Political Science Quarterly* 92 (1977): 443–63.
35. J. William Fulbright, *Old Myths and New Realities* (New York: Random House, 1964).
36. Huntington, "Congressional Responses."
37. Lloyd Cutler, "To Form a Government," *Foreign Affairs* 59 (1980): 126–43.
38. Charles W. Whalen, Jr., *The House and Foreign Policy: The Irony of Congressional Reform* (Chapel Hill: University of North Carolina Press, 1982).
39. See my discussion here of the rise in importance of the national security adviser to the president in Bert A. Rockman, "America's *Departments* of State: Irregular and Regular Syndromes of Policy Making," *American Political Science Review* 75 (1981): 911–27.
40. Edwards, *Public Presidency*, pp. 239–50. This generalization holds in spite of Reagan's significant decline in popular standing apparently stemming from the Iran arms deal and the funneling of extralegal funds to the Nicaraguan Contras.
41. Charles W. Ostrom, Jr., and Brian L. Job, "The President and the Political Use of Force," *American Political Science Review* 80 (1986): 541–66. They note that "Holding all else equal . . . a good deal of the impetus for the large swings in the propensity to use force can be traced to the presidential approval rating" (p. 557).
42. The phrase is borrowed from a recent book title that documents the incentives and tendency for presidents to "go public." See Samuel Kernell, *Going Public: New Strategies of Presidential Leadership* (Washington: CQ Press, 1985).

2

Making National Strategy:
The Practitioner's View

STANSFIELD TURNER and GEORGE EDWARD THIBAULT

> Can a system with divided authority, with two major foreign policy
> decision making institutions, meet the need for united national action
> on life-or-death matters . . . ?
> —I. M. Destler, "The Constitution and Foreign Affairs"

"United national action" is what national strategy is all about. Ideally, a
national strategy is a plan to unify the nation's efforts to "shape world
events in ways that respond to America's national interests."[1] It sounds
simple and straightforward, In principle it is. In reality, especially in a
democracy, it is not.

Most administrations are criticized at some point for not having a
strategy. Easy to make and difficult to refute, the charge is usually based
on the way foreign affairs are conducted rather than their substance. A
core national strategy exists, and it is surprisingly consistent from administration to administration. As Henry Kissinger has observed, "It is remarkable how little domestic change affects the basic patterns of foreign
policy of either superpower. In the United States a conservative administration that six years ago had passionately proclaimed a new approach
to East-West relations is today pursuing the traditional agenda of the past
two decades with only minor variations. In the Soviet Union a formidable
new leader seeks to reform the domestic economy, but in foreign affairs he
is following basic directions inherited from his predecessor, albeit with
much greater public relations skill."[2]

That is not to say national leaders do not make strategy. The world
does not stand still. National interests are dynamic, priorities and emphasis change, and unexpected events occur. National leaders need a strategic agenda lest other nations set it for them. Yet no national strategy is
one-sided, playing itself out in a vacuum. A national strategy is but one
nation's preferred outcomes in a much larger world system. The president

would like other nations to conform to the U.S. view of what is best, but has no way of ensuring that that will happen. Consequently, he must not only provide national policy direction, but must also try to anticipate events that will affect national interests and maneuver to influence those events in our favor. Nonetheless, even if the president has a clear plan, in a democracy national strategy cannot be implemented by fiat. American leadership divides naturally into numerous different interest groups. A consensus on the strategy must be built, and that can be painstaking, if not impossible.

Is there, for instance, an agreed national strategy for U.S. relations with South Africa? The Reagan administration, seeing American business as an effective force for change, through which positive initiatives can be launched, has encouraged companies to stay and continue to set an example of blacks and whites working together in peace, with equal opportunity. However, American businesses are leaving South Africa in response to more direct pressures. Their motives are condemned on American campuses, and their corporate names are in danger of being tarnished by what many see as an acceptance of apartheid. Americans threaten to boycott South African goods. The Congress, not immune to public pressure, seeks more rapid solutions, such as sanctions, to pressure South Africa. It has echoed the call for American business to pull out, and has voted to reduce financial support not only to South Africa, but to other parts of developing Africa. How is a consensus built when each group's interests seem so clear and they conflict so profoundly?

Sometimes to bridge the seemingly irreconcilable positions of interest groups, someone suggests a broad, ephemeral, Delphic pronouncement as the nation's strategy. But even when there is agreement on the thrust of such a declaration, the need to satisfy everyone leaves the government with a policy statement that provides too little focus and direction to be useful. Although such expressions can give a sense of direction, they cannot serve as a serious national strategy within the government.

Nonetheless, looking back over the two hundred years of experience in managing America's national security affairs, strategic patterns do emerge. During that time, the United States has responded relatively consistently in similar situations, steadfastly embraced certain ideals, and traditionally aspired to certain goals. That legacy, modified by current interests, commitments, and goals, comprises today's national strategy.

Parts of the national strategy are drawn from the objectives of each government department and agency that makes policy and commands resources. If departmental policy objectives are consistent with the nation's general aspirations and goals, if they are broadly enough supported by the public, if they are flexible enough to provide long-term direction, if they are specific enough to permit structuring concrete programs from them, and if, once implemented, there can be accountability for results, then they stand a good chance of becoming part of the nation's enduring strategy. This chapter looks at the role of the key political institutions in making sound national strategy, and the degree to which they are guided by the criteria of consistency, flexibility, direction, and accountability.

CONGRESS—COLLABORATOR IN NATIONAL STRATEGY

The authority to make laws and appropriate funds gives the Congress the strongest hand in the government for making national strategy. However, more often than not, it eschews the leadership role it has the potential to assume precisely because of the difficulty in reaching a consensus. Even if the Congress could agree on a single list of objectives for the nation, which it cannot, that would not be enough to make a strategy. There must also be agreement on the means the nation will commit to achieving those objectives and in what priority. There is always competition for finite national resources, be they dollars, people, or materials. But, especially during periods of national crisis, when different parts of the government often compete for the same resources, the national strategy must provide the guidance for apportioning those resources. By deciding who should have first call on which resources, we affirm which objectives are most important to the nation. When there is no consensus on priorities, those experienced in government recognize that the strategy in question lacks a firm government commitment, and they proceed with caution. In the Congress the sense of priorities is shaped not by a national logic entirely, but to a large extent by the needs and interests of the individual states. The states' different levels of dependence on federal programs and the different effect world events have on local economies determine how they weigh the importance of federal strategies and what priorities they assign to them.

The result is that the president usually sets priorities. This is done in part through formal pronouncements like the *Defense Guidance* that is provided to the services in the budget cycle and in part through the final budget he submits to Congress. There is often agreement on the broad thrust of the president's budget, but almost always infinite disagreement on the priorities he sets in it. In our system, where power is expressly shared and endless debate seems to be encouraged, there are no clear answers. It can be extremely difficult to forge agreement as to which national interests are more important. Moreover, it is here especially, where the Constitution provides meager help, that the Congress and the president make full use of their implied authorities to exercise their preferences aggressively and, at times, creatively.

The Constitution says nothing directly about a national strategy. Fearing the concentration of power in one branch, the framers created a system of controlled decentralization. As Richard Neustadt points out, powers are not separate, but are shared by the separate branches of the government.[3] However, by giving both the executive and legislative branches powers to shape priorities, and neither a clear mandate for sharing the responsibility, the Constitution creates a need to find a way to reach an agreed national strategy. Neither the Congress nor the administration can go very far on its own in initiating programs or actions that affect the nation. In practice, the extent to which the two branches choose to assert their power, particularly in relation to each other, depends on the issue in question and their interest in it, the degree to which they are distracted at the moment with other issues, and the balance of power between the branches at that time.

For example, each fall, during the national budget debate in the Congress, the size and nature of the defense budge focuses intense congressional interest not just on budgetary issues, but on very detailed questions of defense organization, force employment, weapons development, research, and production. The lines between appropriate congressional inquiry for the sake of the budget and inappropriate detailed management of the Department of Defense's work become very blurred. Depending on the strength of the president, as measured by his popularity and his influence over relevant parts of the Congress, this debate can become a power struggle of one branch against the other. When this happens, clear direction in implementing the national security strategy is lost, and the course of strategy may weave back and forth so much as to be no real strategy at all. Actions may be taken that are inconsistent with past decisions. The fragmenting of accountability may constitute no accountability.

Building a national strategy, then, is in many ways like constructing a mosaic. Many pieces are fitted together over time, each in a sense discrete, by successive administrations in collaboration with the Congress. Because it is a collaboration, its main currents remain relatively constant, change usually taking place slowly. But, because it is a mosaic, it is a piecemeal effort. Pieces dear to the heart of the president or the Congress may not fit, yet may be forced to fit. This is most likely to occur when the president takes a strong leadership role in foreign or military affairs in response to a specific world situation, or when the Congress reacts strongly to what it perceives as the government getting out of control or the executive branch exceeding its constitutional authority.

The Nixon Doctrine, which relied on friends of the United States, like the shah of Iran, to protect our interests overseas; the Carter Doctrine, which declared southwest Asia a vital interest; and President Reagan's Strategic Defense Initiative, which moved the United States forcefully toward a defensive nuclear strategy and away from one built exclusively on offensive power, represent fundamental changes in the national strategy. Each has had significant implications for the nation. Each had merit in the context in which it was instituted. However, when presidents act resolutely, and especially when they act precipitously, as in the Carter and Reagan examples, they must take care not to veer very far from established policies unless they can reasonably anticipate congressional and public support. In the three cases cited, adequate public support was not built. The Nixon Doctrine lasted only until the fall of the shah, when it became obvious that the United States could not leave the protection or management of American vital interests to others. The Carter premise, that southwest Asia is a vital interest of the United States' for which we would commit military forces, has not been widely accepted even in the government, as evidenced by the failure to commit adequate forces to support it. And, there is skepticism that SDI will survive the Reagan administration, at least in its present form.

One of the truly ingenious aspects of the American constitutional system is the freedom it gives the government to react and to accommodate change through either presidential or congressional action, while holding both branches equally and fully responsible for the health and security of the state. Neither branch can put the state in serious jeopardy for long without the correcting ability of the other taking hold. Major new adjustments or, in the minds of some, wrong turns such as these, provide the fodder for accusations that the government has no national strategy. Because the Constitution does not put the power to establish and carry out a national strategy in the hands of a single individual or even a single governmental body, inconsistencies in the collection of declarations, understandings, programs, and initiatives that comprise a strategy are inevitable.

Does that mean there is no strategy? Not necessarily. The Nixon Doctrine served a purpose for a time. The Carter Doctrine at least goaded the military into paying somewhat greater attention to southwest Asia. And SDI may prove to be useful in the arms control arena. In practical terms, a good strategy is alive and must change. Unless it accommodates evolving national aspirations and world events that have an impact on those aspirations, it cannot be a sound basis for apportioning national resources. And unless that is done, few goals will be reached.

Consequently, the executive and the Congress are constantly challenged to ensure that the pieces of the changing mosaic on which they are focused at any moment will blend when combined. This is especially relevant when the nation becomes so absorbed with any single activity that it skews the national agenda away from the mainstream. This can happen most easily when an international event dominates the domestic scene, as with a war or a highly publicized act of terrorism, like the 444-

day hostage crisis in Iran. From late 1979 until early 1981, all other policy initiatives were forced into second place. Whether or not that was in our long-term interests, the government lost much of its capability to deal with anything else. Fortunately, such over-concentration is a great deal less frequent under a constitutional system, where more than one branch can influence national priorities, than under nearly any other type of government.

By controlling the budget, the Congress effectively forces an accommodation of the president's vision with its pragmatic accountability to constituents' interests. Despite Congress alone holding the formidable powers to declare war, raise and support armies, provide and maintain a navy, make rules for the government and regulation of the land and naval forces, ratify treaties, confirm ambassadors, and regulate foreign commerce, these powers normally follow presidential initiative rather than driving it. This is partially by choice and partially a recognition of what is feasible. It would be exceedingly difficult for a body as large and diverse as the Congress to raise, support, and run the military of the United States without the help of the White House and the Department of Defense.

A significant weakness of this collaborative arrangement is its cost. Members of Congress are always torn between what may be best for their constituents and what may be best for the nation. The sum of all constituents' interests across the nation may be less efficient and more costly than a single carefully designed solution to a problem. In equipping the military, for example, it can be difficult, and is often impossible, even to modify large, on-going military programs that bring business to many states. While a collaborative approach to national defense tempers philosophical extremes, it also causes us to buy some things we don't need and to pay more than we should for others. Probably the most dangerous consequence of this collaboration is the confusion of purpose that can result when domestic political and international security interests are mixed. The nation would be far better served if all military force decisions, for example, were made exclusively on the basis of our world interests and the threat to those interests, tempered by our ability to raise and maintain the forces to meet that threat, rather than even partially on what would best support domestic economic and political needs.

Often the Congress prefers to act after the fact and negatively, rather than stepping out ahead and providing direction for the nation. By withholding funds, or not ratifying a treaty, or excessively pressuring the executive branch to explain and rationalize its choices, it assumes the role of a powerful and critical overseer. Acting more by omission, more after the fact than before, Congress has considerable flexibility in ensuring that executive branch initiatives are fully consistent with the Congress's "sense of the nation" and within the law. At the same time, this denies the

Congress a leadership role in developing and influencing strategy. If the executive branch chooses to abide by a treaty's provisions despite the refusal of the Senate to ratify it, there is little the Congress can do. The basic motivation of both the executive and the legislative branches is to reach a consensus, because without it a policy is usually doomed wherever it originates. A negative position buys the Congress little except freedom of responsibility for results. It is free to criticize the executive if public support is not expected, or to ensure that only the executive branch is blamed when the risk of failure seems high. The executive branch is then put out on a limb and invited to saw itself off. Although this political maneuvering room appeals to instincts of self-preservation, it can contribute dangerously to the perception that the country has no agreed strategy.

Finally, because of its sheer heterogeneity and size, the Congress cannot assume much of a leadership role in shaping strategy. The Congress is a pressure group with a score of constituencies for every congressman. Five hundred and thirty-five persons subject to such pressures cannot hope to design a single, coherent national strategy. Instead, Congress is likely to push the national strategy in five different ways at once. Because no committee in the Congress has a monopoly on the consideration of national security affairs, Richard Haass points out, two types of jurisdictional tangles can result: "Not only are foreign and defense policy issues considered by a large number of separate committees, but often the same matter is considered by two or more committees. The chief consequence of this structural disunity is to divide the congressional perspective, making the creation of integrated and coherent legislation and policy almost impossible. Compromise becomes the paramount concern."[4] Unless the president is persuasive in communicating his vision of where the country should be going, as well as translating it into an agenda for action, the national strategy will be lost in the crowd of pressure groups.

THE PRESIDENT—PRINCIPAL ARCHITECT OF THE NATIONAL STRATEGY

If the principal architect of national strategy cannot be a committee, especially one as large as the Congress, the president is the only person in the government who is in a position to take the broadest view of what is best for the nation. He is the constitutional leader of the nation. As such he is the only one who can provide the long-range national vision of the future and some sense of how that future can be reached. But the president's choices are constrained, too, not just by the Congress, but also by his own executive departments and political constituencies. The executive departments and agencies have their own programs and interests, which compete with one another for funds. "Most organizations have a mission to perform, either overseas or at home, and some organizations need to maintain expensive capabilities in order to perform their missions effectively. All organizations seek influence."[5] Consequently, even with good intentions, departments are biased toward their own programs when priorities are set. His departments and agencies support him by generating ideas, responding to his ideas, developing the mechanisms to carry out his plans, and managing the government as it moves along the president's prescribed course. They are, in the end, just the counsellors and implementors of the national strategy.

The sole honest broker, ultimately, is the president. He is the only one who can appreciate the entire mosaic of the national strategy. His interests alone cover the entire range of foreign, domestic, and defense policies. Because his constituency is the nation, he alone has no competing parochial departmental interests. Again, the national budget is the place to find the president's priorities: "The preparation of the executive budget for submission to Congress presents the president with perhaps his greatest opportunity to affect national priorities. It is also at this stage that he faces the most difficult choices in reconciling the many conflicts and competing interests."[6]

Furthermore, the president must select individuals to head executive departments and agencies who see the world as he does and can help him achieve his vision in his limited time in office. He must entrust to them the detailed planning and execution of the initiatives that will move the country toward the objectives of his national strategy. Inevitably, however, those individuals develop a loyalty to the department or agency they head if they expect to be its effective leader. Secretaries are expected by their departments to be not just the president's man in the department, but the department's man with the president. Soon the secretary finds himself the department's advocate, defending departmental initiatives, most of which were in train before the current administration came into power, and many of which may not be fully in harmony with the president's strategy. So, more and more, as an administration matures, even these hand-picked helpers of the president become less able to support every presidential idea unquestioningly.

Presidents may be more or less natural strategists by temperament. Natural strategists have a clear and coherent vision of where they want to go and what has to be done to get there. They take a broad view of their responsibilities and rise above immediate issues. Great presidents come into office with an accurate vision of what the country needs and a preliminary sense of priorities for getting there. That vision can be simple, even simplistic. Its importance is not in its complexity or whether it is comprehensive, but in how accurately it reflects what the country needs and what it can realistically achieve. What is so important is its philosophical consistency and clarity.

When Ronald Reagan came into office, his agenda was to build up the nation's defenses, encourage business, reduce the role of the federal government, reduce social programs, emphasize law and order, and take a hard line with the Soviet Union, all without raising taxes. But these were slogans, not strategies. His administration was able to explain them to the public, however, and to generate public—and consequently congressional—enthusiasm and translate them into programs. Other decisions in line with this philosophy gave a sense of clear direction and consistency to the president's strategy. Fundamental, as well, was the president's ability to persuade the bureaucrats that it was in their interest to support him and actually act on his ideas. Whether or not one agreed with Reagan's policies, and despite the serious "theological" conflicts within his administration at times, for at least the first four years of his presidency, there was the perception of philosophical consistency.

In addition to a corps of appointees heading government departments, the president needs a staff of his own to which he can turn for unbiased, undiluted, and totally supportive help to assemble and implement the national strategy mosaic. It has been a long time since the cabinet has been able to function in such a capacity. Presidents have turned to an inner group of a few advisors either in or outside the government, often personal friends in whom they have had confidence. Unfortunately, although such groups can be helpful in generating ideas, when it comes to implementing those ideas, they are powerless. As outsiders, they are extra-organizational and cannot translate ideas into government action. Thus, the National Security Council staff has come to be the prime source of direct support to the president on national strategy.

The role and influence of the National Security Council staff has varied widely. Much depends on the personality of the president. Is he naturally a strategic thinker? Does he enjoy the give-and-take of discussion? Is he open to ideas? Much also depends on the national security advisor to the president. How does he envision his job? How secure is he personally? How close is he to the president? How objective can he be? Is he well informed and perceptive? If he is not well informed, if he is not a true confidant of the president, if he is afraid to express views that diverge from the president's views, then he will not be effective.

The greatest weakness of the NSC system in developing strategic consensus comes from the frustration with seemingly endless debate and the difficulty even for the president in making things happen. This can result in elements of the NSC becoming proactive, as in the Iran-Contra scandal. The NSC staff can become so consumed with day-to-day decision making, and so desirous of seeing the president's policies carried out, that they lose sight of the overall mosaic. It is easy to become swamped with the quantity of issues that come to the White House every day and with the perceived criticality of every decision, big or small. The danger of losing perspective increases in direct proportion to the pressure for a decision and the seeming importance of every decision. The ability to separate the important decisions from those others can make, and to step back from an issue and see all facets objectively, can be easily lost. The temptation is to disregard the bureaucracy and take action directly.

If the goal is a consistent national strategy and programs that will endure beyond the administration, the president also needs advice with respect to the interplay between his domestic political constituencies and national strategy. All presidents are their party's leader. They must continue to care about their party's political position, especially by helping to ensure as friendly a Congress as possible. If they want to institutionalize their imprint on the strategy, presidents eligible for another term in office must tend their personal political fences to be able to be reelected. Decisions that are inextricably part of the national strategy, such as major new thursts in military spending, can have important domestic political implications and are inherently fragile. The Strategic Defense Initiative, which different defense experts estimate will cost anywhere from $200 billion to well over $700 billion when fully funded, will profoundly affect the domestic economy. A program this large could not long survive in its initial stages, when decisions are still being made on how the funding will be spent, without the full force of the presidency behind it.

Finding a chief of staff or other close advisor who can keep the national strategy in mind as he advises on domestic politics can be even more difficult than finding a good national security advisor. All too often, domestic politics and national security strategy are viewed as separate, if not antithetical areas of concern. The infusion of domestic political elements in the consideration of national security policy may seem to place a major and unnecessary impediment in the way of good strategy making. That certainly can be the case. However, keeping the president sensitive to domestic political concerns can also provide an important check on presidential power by ensuring that he remains aware of the will of the people and the degree to which the public supports what he is doing.

The president can also affect national strategy through his relationship with other world leaders, the treaties his administration negotiates, the trade agreements to which he becomes a party, and the quality of his selected representatives to other nations. Here, the opportunities are nearly continuous during an administration for the president to forge important elements of the national strategy on his own. He can open relations with a former enemy, as President Nixon did with China, or set a precise arms control course for the nation, as President Carder did with SALT II.

The Constitution designates the president as commander in chief of the army and navy. However, the War Powers Resolution, enacted in 1973 over President Nixon's veto, restricts the president's ability to wage prolonged, undeclared war and attempts to legislate the collaboration of the president with the Congress before a commitment is made to go to war. Nonetheless, the president has the freedom under this resolution to order military action without asking for the consent of the Congress. In the Gulf of Tonkin in 1964, in Lebanon and Grenada in 1983, and in Libya in 1986, the president independently committed military forces to combat. In placing the power to use the nation's military arm in the hands of one individual, the potential is created for radical or ill-conceived foreign involvement that could change the national strategy quickly and fundamentally, and could embark the nation on a very high-risk journey unsupported by either the Congress or the American people. A more aggressive American involvement in Libya in 1986, for example, could have changed U.S. objectives from retaliation for terrorist acts against Americans, as advertised at the time, to unseating Mu'ammar al-Qadhdhafi and his government. It is doubtful that the Congress or the American people, or our allies, on whom we depended for support, would have concurred in the latter.

That is not to argue that a state should not be able to act quickly when its national interests are threatened or that the Congress can always act quickly enough to ensure the nation's security. At Pearl Harbor, after an unambiguous act of war against the United States, our armed forces fought back for a full day before Congress declared war on Japan. Regrettably, most threats are in gray areas where there is inadequate intelligence to make an easy decision, yet intense pressure to do something quickly. The president, acting alone, as he did with Lebanon and Libya, wields tremendous power. Whether, in retrospect, the president should have been constrained is difficult to say. It is precisely at times when the situation is unclear, but the danger is real, that the president must be able to act. Otherwise, a manageable threat may quickly grow to overwhelm the ability to respond. In such situations the American constitutional system permits the national strategy to be implemented cleanly. The direction can be clear and concise because the problem early on is often one-dimensional. Flexibility is preserved because there is but a single actor responding quickly to changes in the situation. The single thrust of the emergency often ensures an enviable consistency in national action, and, again, because there is but one actor, accountability is unambiguous.

However, given the enormous increase in destructive power that is being built into smaller and smaller weapons today, it is not unreasonable to ask whether presidential power has not increased too much and the time has not come for it to be restrained. Today the president can step in and, in one brief nuclear act, turn the nation's strategy on its head without having to consult the Congress, or the American people, or wait for war powers to be debated. However, even if it is unlikely that any president would launch nuclear weapons unilaterally or that the USSR would launch a first nuclear strike against us requiring a retaliatory nuclear response, the president can launch, with relatively few airplanes, ships, and "smart" conventional munitions, intense "small" wars of the kind that have been the norm since the close of World War II. It might take no more than that to draw the United States into a confrontation with the Soviet Union.

The counter to this argument is that when the president acts, he knows that he will have to explain his decisions to the Congress and the American people after, if not before, the fact. At that time he must be able to make the case that the action was necessary to the national security, that it was neither irresponsible nor resulted from a misreading of the evidence. He must show that his action did not draw the United States more deeply into a situation than necessary, given agreed national interests. But, is that good enough in the nuclear age? Here the Constitution gives us no help and the constitutional system seems to provide no special protections.

CONCLUSION

As the United States has shifted from intervention in Vietnam, to post-Vietnam isolationism, to intervention again in Lebanon, critics have charged that American national strategy lacks consistency. The argument confuses ends with means. The national strategy—the ends—has recognized, since at least the turn of the century and the popularization of the idea by Alfred Thayer Mahan, that our continued growth and well-being depend on our links with the rest of the world. Whether the means of maintaining those links should be through diplomacy, economic pressure, or active military intervention is debatable and depends on the situation. Yet, through it all, America's fundamental strategy must be consistent with our long-term national goals. The constitutional system guarantees to the electorate that there will be an accounting for how well that is done.

However, the real measure of the existence of a sound and coherent national strategy is whether, as policy makers add or subtract objectives and alter priorities, they look at the direction of the whole strategy, not just the elements that relate to what they are changing. This conscious stepping back to look at the effect their changes will have on the whole fabric of the national strategy is the only guarantee of its long-term consistency. This is difficult to do. The loss of perspective that can accompany the pressures of dramatic world events, powerful constituencies, swings in public attitude, and perceived threats to the life of the nation all affect judgment. But, even at moments of less intense pressure, very few individuals in the government beyond the president—a few cabinet officers, the National Security Council staff, and some enlightened and far-sighted members of Congress—ever have the incentive or the ability, by virtue of position and how they think about issues, to try to keep the whole strategic mosaic in mind.

Under the constitutional system, therefore, the ability of the United States to develop and carry forward a consistent and far-sighted national strategy depends on the quality of the people in a few key positions. This is indeed a weakness of the system. At the same time, however, it is ameliorated by the system's transparency. An open, democratic system nurtures informed citizens by their access to information. This should result in people coming into the government who are reasonably well informed and, with some luck, have imagination and vision. At least the probability is greater in a constitutional than in a closed system where open and critical discussion is less valued and the personal risk in disagreeing is high. Closed systems are far more dependent on a single leader to have a sound vision of the nation's direction and that leader's individual ability to develop national strategy.

Is the American constitutional system flexible enough to respond to future demands as more countries acquire nuclear weapons; as new forms of warfare, such as terrorism, threaten our global interests; and as our alignment of friends and allies evolves? Over the two hundred years of the life of the U.S. Constitution, effective national strategy has been made and implemented in very different and very difficult times and with the changing personal chemistry of the executive and the legislative branches. It is probably this flexibility that has permitted it to adapt over the years and accommodate the severest of national crises with strength. There is no evidence that it cannot continue to meet that challenge.

NOTES

Chapter epigraph: I. M. Destler, "The Constitution and Foreign Affairs," *News for Teachers of Political Science,* Spring 1985, p. 1.
1. Address by Secretary of State George Schultz before the Overseas Writers Club, Washington, D.C., 14 May 1986.
2. Henry Kissinger, "No More Talk of Never-Never Land," *Washington Post,* 8 March 1987.
3. Richard E. Neustadt, *Presidential Power* (New York: Wiley, 1980).
4. Richard Haass, "Congressional Power: Implications for American Security Policy," in Dan Kaufman et al., eds., *U.S. National Security* (Lexington, Mass.: Lexington Books, 1985), p. 264.
5. Morton H. Halperin, "Organizational Interests," in ibid., p. 201.
6. Lance T. LeLoup, *Budgetary Politics* (Brunswick, Ohio: King's Court, 1980), p. 131.

3

Producing Foreign Intelligence

HARRY HOWE RANSOM

Producing foreign intelligence is an implied and necessary government power in the Constitution. The intelligence function is to keep the nation's leadership informed accurately and promptly about external realities. In providing for the common defense, intelligence is essential. Accordingly, a vast intelligence bureaucracy has evolved since 1947 to perform the vital intelligence function. One consequence is that a secrecy-accountability dilemma confronts American constitutional democracy.

Fitting an intelligence capability into the constitutional framework poses specific problems. Intelligence operations and reports require secrecy. American democratic government expects disclosure and public accountability. American political culture suspects government secrecy. Furthermore, secret information and a capability for covert foreign operations in the hands of the executive branch are powerful weapons in the struggle—invited by the Constitution—between the president and Congress for control over foreign policy. This executive-legislative struggle may be viewed as a permissive-restrictive pendulum that swings between president and Congress as each branch attempts to dominate intelligence policy and operations.

When a strong consensus undergirds foreign policy, including agreement in the executive and legislative sectors on policy ends and means, the American system is permissive of a high degree of intelligence secrecy. Restrictions are relaxed on presidential discretionary action and a wide variety of secret operations. But when consensus evaporates with regard to either ends or means, Congress reasserts its claims to be consulted and fully informed of the details of secret operations overseas. Absent consensus, then, the pendulum swings in a restrictive direction and the secrecy-accountability dilemma becomes more acute. This is because the Constitution endows Congress with ultimate authority, just as it promises free speech and a free press.

My purpose here is to explore how intelligence has been accommodated to the conflicting requirements of secrecy and democratic accountability. The following analysis is based upon certain assumptions: first, that intelligence is a requisite for national security; second, that the intelligence product will be of increasing importance to decision makers as a consequence of technology; third, that secret intelligence activity must be managed by the executive branch; and fourth, that the U.S. Constitution does not permit the president to monopolize any function, and even the responsibility for intelligence must be shared with Congress as the agent of public accountability.

How the president and Congress have defined and played their respective roles regarding the intelligence function in various periods since World War II is the subject of this chapter. The evolution of the conflicts and adjustments between the president and Congress over the secrecy-accountability dichotomy are analyzed, particularly since 1947, when the central intelligence framework was established.

The president and Congress have for the most part occupied center stage in the delicate compromising act of determining controls over secret intelligence policy and operations. Other principal intervening actors are the federal judiciary and the mass communications media, which share with Congress a role in enforcing public accountability for intelligence and sustaining constitutional values. The designers of the Constitution in Philadelphia in 1787 intended that president and Congress play adversarial roles, with the Supreme Court as standby referee. Very soon guarantees of free press and free speech were added to the Constitution as a protection against censorship and monopoly of information. The Founding Fathers feared concentrated power and arranged for power to be dispersed within a system of legislative, executive, and judicial checks and balances.

How separate institutions sharing power would work in the realm of foreign and military affairs was of little apparent concern to the founders. Nor could they have realized that the First Amendment would lead to the creation of a "fourth branch of government" in the shape of the media. Although the intelligence function may be as old as the institution of war, it was not a matter of major organizational concern in 1787. Indeed, a century and a half elapsed before the nation saw the need to create a professional central intelligence system as a permanent unit of the national government.

Establishment of the Central Intelligence Agency in 1947 was not perceived as affecting the executive-legislative balance of power. In the early years, Congress played a passive role regarding the intelligence function, which was quietly managed through the National Security Council. The NSC in turn delegated wide discretionary authority to the leadership of the new intelligence system. Keep in mind that the CIA was created as an informational staff arm of the presidency. Very soon the agency was assigned large-scale operational functions overseas, including secret political intervention and counterintelligence in foreign areas. Not until after 1975, however, did Congress assert a claim of equal partnership with the executive on intelligence policy, organization, and operations.

Meanwhile the government's intelligence apparatus had grown into a huge multifunctional confederation of separate intelligence agencies, civilian and military. Adaptation of these new elements to the constitutional framework has created much controversy and challenged government leadership. Capped by the CIA, the intelligence system has come to include the National Security Agency (for code making and breaking), the Defense Intelligence Agency, State Department intelligence, intelligence sections in the army, navy, air force, and marines, and numerous other offices for the collection of specialized intelligence, including space satellite reconnaissance and counterintelligence, the domestic domain of the Federal Bureau of Investigation.[1]

A constitutional dilemma derives from the fact that secret intelligence operations require tight executive command and control and absolute secrecy, while the American democratic idea demands public accountability for all government activity. All government functions are monitored by the triad of president, Congress, and federal judiciary—all overseen by a free press. For nearly two hundred years of the Republic, the purposeful ambiguities of the Constitution have been negotiated by the various government units within a pluralist political process.

Conflict in the system has usually engendered compromises between the president and Congress on foreign affairs issues. The Supreme Court has, with a few major exceptions, remained on the sidelines for such "political" questions, once having certified the presidency as the sole organ of government for the conduct of foreign policy. When the court has intervened in the political fray, it has been on those occasions when legislative-executive power conflict reached stalemate, or when First Amendment freedoms were seen to be challenged by government secrecy. More often than not, the courts have favored the executive branch on foreign affairs issues.

When the Constitution was under debate, John Jay, arguing for ratification, made a telling remark in reference to the requirement that the president must have senatorial consent in forming treaties. Jay wrote that although the president must seek Senate approval, nonetheless "he will be able to manage the business of intelligence in a manner that prudence may suggest." Jay had argued that in treaty negotiations "perfect *secrecy* and immediate *despatch* are sometimes requisite. There are cases where the most useful intelligence may be obtained, if the persons possessing it can be relieved from apprehension and discovery." Jay argued that suppliers of secret information would more likely rely on the president for secrecy "but would not confide in that of the Senate and still less in that of a large popular Assembly."[2]

Although Jay's argument was in the context of treaty making, his rationale for executive secrecy and the doubts he expressed about the ability of Congress to keep secrets suggest an awareness of the problem in the Republic's formative period. But Jay's remarks implying a presidential monopoly on sensitive intelligence had to reckon with the dominant Madisonian doctrine requiring plural power in government, allowing no one branch to monopolize information.

Since the Constitution does not directly mention intelligence, one can argue that the intelligence function and the secrecy it requires derive from the president's role as commander in chief and as maker of treaties and conductor of foreign relations. But equally reasonable is the claim that Congress has authority over intelligence activities in keeping with the constitutional command that it "provide for the common defense"; "declare war"; give consent on treaties; make "necessary and proper" laws; and draw no money "from the Treasury, but in consequence of appropriations made by law." Furthermore, the Constitution requires the publication of a statement of all government expenditures "from time to time." Arguably, the Constitution gives Congress the power to specify exception to the publication requirement, as in secret intelligence expenditures.

The fact is that the Founding Fathers created separate institutions, sharing power, not excepting sensitive foreign operations. Whether such a system can work effectively, particularly with regard to intelligence, the most secret of all government functions, has been a matter of enduring debate. Efforts to make the system work, either through executive-legislative compromise or through judicial "balancing" of freedom and secrecy, have continued to the present time.

PERIODS OF OVERSIGHT: EXECUTIVE-LEGISLATIVE RELATIONS AND INTELLIGENCE

When the Central Intelligence Agency was created by statute in 1947, it was designed as an organization for the coordination of the government's best information for the presidency. Little thought was given to the congressional role in monitoring this new governmental unit. No discussion was recorded regarding a potential conflict between the president and Congress about intelligence policy, organization, and accountability for operations. Executive initiative prompted Congress to establish the CIA in an ambiguous and permissive section of the National Security Act of

1947. The result was a new central intelligence structure monitored loosely by the presidency, with the congressional oversight role left undefined.[3]

In the beginning, the CIA existed in the anonymity permitted by the Cold War consensus that "world communism" must be contained by the United States all over the globe. Early in the CIA's history, a major role in communist containment came to be assigned to a rather anonymous group of "honorable men" in the agency. They were to be asked few questions about their work, particularly by Congress or the media. Even so, little congressional jealously was apparent in these early years, either about such secrecy or about executive branch dominance of secret operations abroad.

Presidential-congressional relations regarding oversight of intelligence policy and management can be divided into three separately identifiable periods between 1947 and the mid 1980s.[4]

The first period, running roughly from 1947 to 1974, is best described as one of the benign neglect by Congress in its oversight function. These years were characterized by the Cold War consensus. Events abroad were perceived by President Truman and his associates as "communism on the move." The two major political parties, influenced by the communist scare, competed with each other as to which could assume the more aggressive anticommunist stance. Although some rumblings were heard in the mid 1950s about the adequacy of congressional oversight, major reform proposals were defeated by a bipartisan consensus that the "honorable men" of the intelligence services should be left to their own devices. Any supervision would come from the presidency. Congress, it was assumed, would play at most a passive role.

Under pressure from high-powered study groups such as the Hoover Commission, informal methods of monitoring intelligence operations were made more formal in both Congress and the executive branch. In the mid 1950s, the House and Senate created intelligence subcommittees of the Armed Services and the Appropriations Committees. Meanwhile, the White House formed a board of prominent private citizens to advise the president on the performance of the intelligence agencies.

From the mid 1950s until the mid 1970s, nominal oversight of U.S. intelligence operations was exercised by subcommittees in both houses of Congress. These units may now be viewed as the Potemkin villages of congressional oversight. There was a kind of symbolic oversight by the most senior leadership in Congress, who rarely challenged the intelligence system or demanded specific details of intelligence policy, budgets, and, especially, covert operations.

A small handful of legislators served, in effect, as defenders of the intelligence community on Capitol Hill. The rank and file in Congress were aware that congressional leaders such as Senator Richard Russell and Representative Carl Vinson were entitled to intelligence secrets if they sought them. Most members found this reassuring, and adequate. Executive jurisdiction over the management of intelligence was widely accepted in Congress and in the media.

One must not, however, overlook the congressional "backdrop" function. The White House and intelligence leaders knew that ultimate authority on policy and budgets for operations lay in congressional hands. They were aware, also, that media attention or a shift in public opinion could cause Congress to be more restrictive about certain kinds of intelligence activity. Intelligence leaders knew that if something went terribly wrong, congressional passivity could be transformed into aggressive investigative behavior. Doubtless this was an inhibiting factor and served as the kind of restraint, or counterweight, that James Madison had in mind. Individual members of Congress could always mount their own crusades against the CIA. Full-scale congressional investigations were always a possibility in a society with ambivalent feelings about government-sponsored dirty tricks abroad. After the Bay of Pigs and the subsequent Cuban missile crisis, Congress conducted special studies of these failures and criticized the CIA's performance. Even so, Congress did not challenge the executive's intelligence monopoly.

Congress's benign neglect of intelligence ended abruptly in 1974 when the intelligence system entered its second identifiable period as the pendulum swung. In 1974 the intelligence legitimacy crisis began, accompanied by an era of reform. The two main events of this year were congressional passage of the Hughes-Ryan amendment to a foreign aid act, and the disclosure, very late in the year, that the CIA had violated its charter by spying on Americans in the United States. This, more than any other disclosure in the Watergate context, stimulated major investigations by Congress and a presidential commission revealing a wide variety of intelligence establishment misdeeds and abuses of secret power. By 1975 the CIA was in a major legitimacy crisis.[5]

Hughes-Ryan symbolized the evaporation of the Cold War consensus, and its purpose was to require that the CIA cease secret political intervention overseas. When an exception was required to this new rule restricting the CIA to intelligence gathering overseas, the president was to declare covert political intervention a vital security interest and inform relevant congressional committees, numbering eight. This act sharply restricted covert actions and symbolized congressional disenchantment with U.S. secret intervention abroad at presidential discretion. It was a move to restore congressional influence over such operations. The "imperial presidency" was under attack across a broad foreign affairs front. An internal revolution was also under way in Congress in which foreign affairs and government operations committees also forced abandonment of the monopoly on secret foreign operations held by the Armed Services and Appropriations Committees.

The third era of national policy for the intelligence function, from 1977 to the present, is best described as a period of compromise and continuing intragovernmental conflict. It has been a period of sustained controversy, but one in which significant institutional and statutory changes and judicial interpretations occurred. These were the consequences of the second era. They may be briefly summarized at this point as follows:

— Establishment of the permanent select oversight committees in the Senate (1976) and House (1977) fortified with a mandate for full access to all intelligence secrets and assigned the duty of approving intelligence budgets. These committees are amply staffed, and their membership is carefully chosen by the congressional leadership.

— Passage of the Intelligence Oversight Act of 1980 requiring that the CIA and other intelligence agencies keep the select committees fully and promptly informed of all secret intelligence activities, past, present, and anticipated, including sensitive covert political interventions.

— Reestablishment within the executive branch of two oversight mechanisms, the president's Board of Foreign Intelligence Advisors and the Intelligence Oversight Board, both of which report to the president on the performance of the intelligence community.

— Assignment of stronger mandates to the Offices of General Counsel as well as to the inspector general in the intelligence agencies.

— Provision by statute for judicial monitoring of intelligence-related electronic surveillance within the United States. That is, the attorney general must report to congressional intelligence committees twice a year on government surveillance actions. The committees were also required to issue reports on the implementation of the Foreign Intelligence Surveillance Act of 1978.

— Congressional pressures on the executive branch that circumscribed presidential executive orders governing the roles and functions of the intelligence agencies. These executive orders, under Presidents Ford, Carter, and Reagan, have been in lieu of a new congressional charter for the intelligence system and may be viewed as not carrying the full legitimacy of a congressional statute, but they do reflect congressional input.[6]

All of these developments reflect compromises between the conflicting claims of national security and the promises and expectations of the Bill of

Rights. They demonstrate the swing of the pendulum away from the independence of intelligence operations and toward careful executive and legislative monitoring. Even so, the intelligence system was able to gain some legislative concessions to its concerns. In 1982 Congress made it a crime for any person to publicize the names of secret agents. And the Freedom of Information Act was amended to ease some of the CIA's administrative burdens from requests to release highly sensitive information.

But the overwhelmingly important development of this entire period was the abovementioned Intelligence Oversight Act.[7] It was important for several reasons. Notably, Congress was made an equal partner with the executive in intelligence policy and operations. Specifically, the act (amending Hughes-Ryan) reduced to two the number of committees to which the president must report all covert operations and required that the president must consult the intelligence committees in advance regarding secret political interventions overseas except in extraordinary circumstances. The act also gave the first unambiguous legitimacy to covert actions. The original purpose of Hughes-Ryan was to eliminate covert action as a CIA function, which reflected the original intention of the 1947 act that the CIA be an information-gathering agency only. But in a backhanded way, Hughes-Ryan and authorized covert action by permitting its use in special situations. The 1980 act for the first time acknowledged the covert action function, although only in exceptional cases.

After 1980, then, intelligence officials were directed by act of Congress to meet the following requirements: first, to keep the intelligence committees in Congress fully and currently informed of all intelligence activities; second, to notify the committees of all covert activities; third, to "furnish any information" that the committees might determine to be necessary to carry out the oversight function; and fourth, to report to the oversight committees any and all failures and illegal activities, and to do so in a "timely fashion." These new rules were clearly a compromise between leaving the operations of the intelligence establishment essentially an executive function, unsupervised by Congress, and the more restrictive proposals contained in a variety of draft intelligence "charters" in the late 1970s. On the crucial requirement that the president report all significant covert actions to the intelligence committees, note that this imposed an *informational* obligation on the executive, but did *not* require that the president seek congressional consent.

From the above brief digest of the principal developments in the great intelligence debates and executive-legislative actions of the 1975–86 period, we can see evolving an enormously complex system of laws and practices, as America searched for new ways to confront the secrecy-accountability dilemmas invited by separation of powers. For the most part, these developments have resulted from the reassertion of a congressional claim of responsibility for intelligence policy, organization, and operations.

THE REFEREES: THE COURTS AND THE PRESS IN INTELLIGENCE OPERATIONS

The roles of the Supreme Court over the years with regard to the intelligence function can be characterized in several generalizations. First, most foreign policy issues between the president and Congress have been judged to be "political questions," to be solved in the political arena. Judicial restraint is the most common posture of the federal courts regarding intelligence activities. Second, the Supreme Court has long since established that the president as chief executive and commander in chief is the "sole organ" of the government for the *conduct* of international relations.[8]

More specifically, on the rare occasions when the court has adjudicated a foreign intelligence issue, it has usually deferred to the president. With a few important exceptions, such as President Truman's steel company seizure and the "Pentagon Papers" controversy, the presence of national security considerations usually influences the federal judiciary to tilt toward the presidency rather than towards the constitutional right of individuals and to allow the president exceptional secrecy. Former CIA officials, for example, who have written books without clearance by the agency have discovered that claimed First Amendment rights had to yield, in the judgments of federal courts, to executive claims of secrecy.

The impact of the federal judiciary generally has been to sustain claims of extraordinary secrecy when sensitive intelligency matters are concerned. But the Supreme Court has been careful not to intervene in the continuing battles between president and Congress over control of foreign policy.

The Constitution guarantees freedom of speech and press. Fulfillment of this promise has run head-on into the necessity of secrecy for most intelligence activities. Can an intelligence system operate effectively within a constitutional system that provides free press guarantees and within a political culture that suspects government secrecy?

The relationship between the intelligence system and the mass media is complex and subject to extreme fluctuations. In World War I and World War II, a system of voluntary censorship was effectively in force. The press abandoned its "right to know" and accepted the government's claim of military necessity to manage the news. In the first twenty years of the Cold War, which had broad public support and a consensus among foreign policy elites, the media more often than not cooperated with government demands for secrecy. For example, prior to 1960, segments of the press knew of the U-2 flights over the Soviet Union, but refrained from disclosure. Prior to the Bay of Pigs in 1961, some journalists were aware of the plan but withheld the information. Intelligence activities in general were considered off limits by the mass media, tacitly accepting an informal government censorship.

In the late 1960s the Cold War consensus began to evaporate, and a "sea change" occurred in the media, which abandoned the self-restraints of earlier years regarding intelligence operations. Since then, journalists have been more disposed to publish what they please, including any intelligence secrets they may discover. At the same time, they have claimed a right to keep their sources confidential.

What restraints, legal or otherwise, should limit the media's discretion in disclosing highly secret information? Some have suggested legislation resembling the British Official Secrets Act that would punish journalists or editors for disclosing information known to carry a national security classification. Others, particularly editors and journalists, insist upon absolute freedom to publish anything at their discretion, on the argument that the public needs to know and that the Constitution guarantees such a right.

Tension between the media and public officials is inherent in a structure in which information is potential power. All administrations in modern times have been concerned with maintaining proper state secrets. At issue frequently is the question of what, indeed, proper state secrets are. In the 1980s agencies have been given more discretion to classify information as secret. The Reagan administration proposed that large numbers of officials with access to secrets be given lie detector tests and has demanded that officials agree never to publish books or articles without prior submission for review to protect national secrets. In addition, the generally unsuccessful war against news "leaks" was intensified.

A more vigorous effort to prosecute individuals for disclosing secret material also was undertaken. In 1985 the Department of Justice prosecuted Samuel L. Morison, a Navy Department intelligence analyst, for selling satellite photographs of a Soviet shipyard to a British defense magazine. He was convicted of violating the Espionage Act of 1917, a rarely invoked law assumed to cover those aiding a foreign enemy. In this case Morison was convicted for a "leak" to a Western publication.

More recently, in 1986, CIA Director William Casey disclosed that the government had considered prosecuting three newspapers, the *New York Times*, the *Washington Post*, and the *Washington Times*, as well as *Time* and *Newsweek* magazines, for publishing stories revealing how the National Security Agency gathers intelligence. Charges were not filed, but some of the nation's leading news outlets were forced to consider a tough new government posture on secrecy.

To those responsible for protecting national security, the constitutional guarantees of a free press may seem to be a handicap, particularly in the delicate realm of secret intelligence. Others make the argument that the government does not always know best. Furthermore, secrecy is seen as a dangerous weapon that will be used to hide incompetence, strategic mistakes, and abuses of power. A dynamic tension will always exist between the right to know and the need to know in a democracy. Secrecy is incompatible with democratic accountability. Disclosure is not compatible with effective intelligence operations. A proper balance between these conflicting claims may be crucial in determining survival of the Republic with democratic values intact.

Although the media have cooperated from time to time with voluntary censorship of highly sensitive information, they may be seen as the natural enemies of the intelligence agencies. The intelligence doctrine of absolute secrecy often confronts the news media head-on. The media nurture the political culture's natural suspicion of government secrecy. A belief that bureaucrats often are simply trying to conceal their own blunders drives the media. The net effect of the media may be more positive than negative, for what the media find out often discloses chronic intelligence problems. Publicity often also signals what adversaries also know of government "secrets."

THE POLITICIZATION OF INTELLIGENCE

By the mid 1980s the passive-restrictive pendulum had stalled in the middle, requiring new adjustments both by Congress and the executive branch. In the absence of a foreign policy consensus, particularly about means or instruments, the intelligence establishment no longer could carry out its functions in the same degree of isolation from presidential surveillance and congressional oversight. Yet Congress remained beholden to the good faith of the intelligence leadership to keep the intelligence committees significantly informed. And the incorporation of intelligence policy and operations into the more normal checks and balances of the governmental process invited the politicization of intelligence. What was the impact of this change on the principal intelligence agency functions of information collection, analysis, and reporting, and on covert political intervention overseas and counterintelligence? How has the new executive-legislative balance affected performance of the intelligence function?

Over the years, criticism has been widespread that CIA collection efforts are dominated by an obsession with the Soviet Union, especially with regard to military power. Some argue that this has led to neglect of political, economic, and social issues, in both Russia and other regions of the world, that may be more relevant to the future security of the United States than Soviet military capabilities.

Most of the collection effort against the Soviet Union is based upon use of high technology instruments. In recent years, major programs in electronic, imagery, and communications intelligence have been severely damaged by foreign espionage. We learn this from publicized espionage scandals, indictments, and court trials involving American, British, and Israeli spies. Problems raised by these cases initially received little attention from the congressional intelligence committees. Congressional oversight appears to have made little difference in this ongoing debate over collection priorities, or on other important issues such as collection duplication, waste of resources, and effective counterespionage. Since 1985, however, congressional interest in counterespionage has been rising, evidenced by a major 156-page Senate Intelligence Committee report in 1986 that made ninety-five recommendations for reform.[9]

Beyond collection, a second important function is analysis and interpretation. How well has the intelligence system kept decision makers informed of the realities of the outside world and how has the new oversight affected the quality of this performance? Here again the outside evaluator has difficulty garnering hard evidence for a generalized judgment. The intelligence system has been criticized for devoting too many resources to collection, while depriving the analysts of adequate support. One stereotype of the intelligence system is that of intelligence analysts inundated by a mass of data, with inadequate resources for analysis and interpretation. Under the new executive-congressional partnership, the two intelligence committees in Congress now have full access to the intelligence product: the daily briefs, special intelligence studies, and National Intelligence Estimates. Intelligence producers are now fully aware that Congress looks over their shoulders as they make estimates of the foreign situation, and that the intelligence product is shared by the executive and legislative branches. This alters the balance of executive power in foreign policy making. But what impact has it had on the quality of the intelligence product? This is difficult to measure with regard to a highly secret product. Yet what is reported to Congress in secret often is leaked, not just from Capitol Hill but also as a consequence of the internecine policy struggles among the various executive branch foreign policy agencies.

Evidence for public evaluation of intelligence performance comes primarily from congressional reports and observations of foreign policy behavior. In 1979 the Senate committee issued a report on the intelligence capability to monitor the SALT II treaty. In 1982 the House committee made public a report on the intelligence performance in Central America. The committees have also studied the intelligence performance in the fall of the shah of Iran, Soviet oil production, the oil crisis of 1973–74, and other specific events. Such studies are as much a part of the partisan policy struggle as a manifestation of congressional interest in evaluating performance, but they do provide some insight to outside observers into the quality of the intelligence performance.

The existence of a greater number of players in the intelligence game tends to politicize intelligence. Even so, the intelligence analyst gains some new freedom to analyze events with greater objectivity. Having to justify analyses may indeed magnify the bureaucratic instinct to play it safe, but it may also provide academic freedom to intelligence analysts. A wider clientele offers some protection against the misuse of intelligence and increases understanding that on many important questions, intelligence analysts can only deal in probabilities in their forecasting and will sometimes be wrong.[10]

The performance of the intelligence system has been of some concern to Congress, but aside from major intelligence failures, it rarely has been a source of major conflict between the executive and legislative branches. President and Congress share an interest in obtaining the best possible information for national security decisions. During the first half of the 1980s, the national intelligence budget doubled. Congress was generous in appropriations, recognizing the fundamental importance of intelligence for national security decisions. Although more openness about intelligence may inhibit some foreign sources of secret information, it does not seem that the separation of powers has damaged intelligence performance. To the contrary, the checks and balances of the American political process may stimulate the intelligence system to perform with greater efficiency. No evidence exists that they have been denied the financial resources for the intelligence function, as distinct from covert political operations abroad. Further evaluation of intelligence performance is given in the concluding section.

COVERT ACTION AND THE SEPARATION OF POWERS

Covert action has been the source of the most bitter controversy between president and Congress in the 1980s. Covert action is defined as secret political intervention in foreign areas that conceals the role of the government in such action. It is a function performed primarily by the CIA, at presidential initiative. The utility of covert action is justified by the argument that it offers an option for achieving foreign policy objectives between diplomacy and the overt use of military force.[11] Until 1974 covert action was of dubious legitimacy, because in creating the agency in 1947, Congress did not specify secret political intervention as a function of the CIA. Covert action was established by presidential order, first under President Truman, and was derived from a loose interpretation of the ambiguous clauses of the National Security Act of 1947.

Over the years, Congress gave nominal legitimacy to covert action through a secret process of funding such operations. In 1974 Congress for the first time gave statutory authority for covert action, but circumscribed presidential discretion by requiring that committees of Congress be fully informed. In 1980, by legislation, Congress imposed strict requirements that the president keep it informed of all intelligence activities, including covert actions. In emergency situations the president need inform only the congressional leadership. The point is that the pendulum had swung again, shortening the arc of executive permissiveness. Congress was now claiming full partnership with the executive in all secret operations. This had the effect of inhibiting the president's freedom of action, particularly in the absence of a foreign policy consensus.

Yet congressional oversight reforms of the post-Watergate era could not eliminate the presidential claim of a constitutional right to use covert action as a foreign policy instrument. Excepting a few cases, such as the Clark amendment (1973) prohibiting covert action in Angola, and the Boland amendment (1982) limiting the CIA's role in Nicaragua—both later repealed under presidential persuasion—the president's claim for some de jure covert action discretion remained intact. This results from the ambiguities of the constitution. Nonetheless, the political context for covert action has radically changed. Congress now tries to prevent covert action being used as a substitute for a consensus foreign policy. Accordingly, Congress has mandated that its intelligence committees be fully informed. Thus Congress has assumed a position to give advice, but has not tried to require congressional consent.

For any major foreign operation, of course, Congress must authorize a budget and make appropriations. Furthermore, a dissident member of Congress can "leak" information on a particular operation, which might have the same effect as a legislative veto.

Formal consent or not, perhaps the most significant change in the executive-legislative balance is the new reality that Congress has gained influence with regard to sensitive foreign covert actions. The president de jure may remain free to order covert action at his discretion. The de facto reality is that Congress is a new and powerful player in the game. A president's options in covert action are now limited. Only if covert action proposals reflect a strong legislative-executive consensus can foreign policy planners expect secrecy. A president might use contingency funds to set in motion a covert operation, but major covert action programs that extend over long periods must have the support of the intelligence committees in Congress.

Legislative attempts to redress the balance between the president and Congress have not resolved the constitutional ambiguities. The presidency continues to claim certain inherent national security discretionary powers, while Congress strives to narrow the circle of presidential discretion in foreign affairs, particularly with regard to covert action.

Three recent cases illustrate the continuing conflict, which has centered not on the straightforward intelligence function but on covert activities. The first example is the situation in Nicaragua in the 1980s, where the Reagan administration decided to put counterrevolutionary pressure on the Sandinista government. This was done in the context of a Congress divided on the issue. Many saw diplomacy as a better choice than aiding Honduras-based counterrevolutionary groups that sought to destroy the government in Managua. Senate and House intelligence committees were involved in this policy in a major way. Not only had the House committee by law prohibited CIA efforts to overthrow the Managua government, in January 1985 it issued a stinging report on other aspects of CIA-directed operations in Central America. The committee singled out the CIA-sponsored document entitled "Psychological Operations in Guerrilla Warfare," labeled the "CIA Manual" by the media.

After investigating the circumstances of the manual's production, the Democratic committee majority issued a report concluding that the manual: (1) violated the Boland amendment by advocating overthrow of the Sandinistas; (2) violated presidential orders prohibiting assassinations; (3) created profound embarrassment for the United States; (4) demonstrated that the CIA did not have effective procedures for controlling its agents; and (5) violated congressional spending guidelines placing a cap on aid to the Contras. Symbolized in this report is the new congressional posture of involving Congress itself in CIA management issues.

A second example is the CIA's role in the mining of Nicaraguan harbors. On 10 April 1984 CIA Director William Casey was required to report to the full Senate on the harbor-mining project. Consequent to this briefing, the Senate voted 84 to 12 prohibiting future funds from being used for mining of the ports of territorial waters of Nicaragua. Here again Congress was involved in secret operational issues. Shortly thereafter, Casey met with the Senate Intelligence Committee and apologized to senators for not keeping them properly informed. On 6 June 1984, with the president's approval, Casey signed a written agreement with the Senate committee pledging to follow precise procedures for fully informing the committee in the future.

A third example is the storm of controversy raised in November 1986 by disclosure of arms shipments to Iran in 1985–86. This operation, which went forward under direct White House supervision and control, with the CIA participating, was completely unknown to Congress until publicized in November 1986. More than any other "intelligence" controversy since the founding of the CIA, the "arms-for-hostages" episode magnified the national security dilemmas of the Constitution.

In this case the president claimed the right to withhold information even from the congressional leadership in the interest of the security of the operation. Some leaders in Congress asserted that the president had violated legislative statutes designed to force the chief executive to consult in a timely manner with Congress—at least its leadership—on even the most sensitive of operations. The controversy produced a crisis for Reagan's presidency, unresolved at this writing. The incident symbolized clearly that the permissiveness pendulum had swung to the restrictive mode. Some saw this as threatening to produce a foreign policy stalemate between Congress and a president unwilling to give up independent discretionary power in every circumstance.

No solution may exist to the problem of efficiently managing covert actions in a separation-of-powers system of government. Covert action and democratic accountability are incompatible. Without a strong foreign policy consensus, covert action may not be a feasible foreign policy instrument. Foreign policy leaders must, then, resist the temptation to substitute covert action as a expedient alternative to building a consensus foreign policy. Efforts by various administrations in recent history to circumvent Congress by covert action expedients have more often than not ended in disaster.

Nationally televised hearings by a House-Senate congressional committee during July 1987 offered the public a dramatic example of presidential-congressional conflict over the control of foreign policy, particularly covert action. The absence of a foreign policy consensus both within the executive branch and between the president and Congress had prompted the president to resort to unorthodox processes. Specifically, the National Security Council staff was assigned an operational role in an abortive effort to free American hostages in the Middle East by selling arms to Iran, contradicting publicized national policy. Proceeds from these sales were secretly and illegally diverted to antigovernment forces in Nicaragua.

In the Iran-Contra case, the decision-making structure was bypassed in pursuit of extreme secrecy. This resulted in confusion, deception, and the privatization of American foreign policy. The accountability system was short-circuited. Presidential and congressional investigations of the Iran-Contra affair in 1987 were highly critical of the decisions and the way they were made. Many reforms of the structures and processes were recommended. The central purposes of reform were to focus accountability and to assure timely notification of Congress of all covert operations.

Questions of law violations in the Iran-Contra case remain unresolved at this writing. But the following evaluations seem to be supported by the available evidence:

— The Iran-Contra crisis was a consequence of the extreme secrecy employed by the president's men because of deep distrust of Congress and lack of an internal policy consensus. The result was invisible government and policy disaster.

— The scandal reveals how, in the absence of accountability, intelligence agencies can be misused in both their informational and operational roles. The Iran-Contra hearings uncovered a dangerously politicized Central Intelligence Agency.

— The Iran-Contra experience displayed the necessity of careful oversight of all covert actions by both the president and Congress. This may be possible only with a new legislatively crafted intelligence "charter" that carefully incorporates the Constitution's demand for a system of checks and balances.

CONCLUSION

The decade after 1975 created a new environment for intelligence. The balance of power shifted as the pendulum swung from a permissive presidential dominance of the intelligence function to a more politicized system in which Congress and the mass media became major actors and inhibiting factors. The federal judiciary for the most part remained on the sidelines, intervening when matters of legal substance were involved, but viewing the legislative-executive conflicts primarily as a "political question." The mass media have also become major actors in the political process.

Meanwhile a massive intelligence establishment has evolved, at an annual cost in the tens of billions of dollars, bringing the whole world under U.S. surveillance. An information-seeking machine of vast dimensions has been created. The advances of modern technology are utilized in pursuit of the best possible estimates to inform the hard strategic choices to be made by decision makers. In addition, major capabilities have been developed for specialized functions such as covert political intervention, counterintelligence, and a variety of cryptological activities.

No political leadership in the world has at its command such a capability for gathering the hard, "knowable" facts of the international scene as have American leaders. But "knowable" facts are but one category of information needed by decision makers. Predictions of future developments and estimates of future intentions and behavior are a more challenging task for the intelligence system, for they are often the "unknowable." The performance record in regard to accurate forecasts is decidedly mixed insofar as can be judged from public information.

On numerous occasions the U.S. intelligence system has failed badly in the predictive function. The North Korean attack across the 38th parallel in June 1950 came as a surprise to American leaders. Intervention of China in the Korean War was another surprise, accompanied by military disaster. The failed Bay of Pigs expedition in April 1961 was not only the result of bad judgment, but also the consequence of erroneous information. The Cuban missile crisis in October 1962 developed from the placement of Soviet missiles in Cuba, an action that the intelligence system had advised the president would not occur. The Soviet army's invasion of Czechoslovakia in 1968 was an intelligence surprise, as was the Arab-Israeli war in 1973. More recently the fall of the shah of Iran was not expected by the American intelligence system, and the Iran-Contra scandal was in part the result of failed intelligence.

Analysis of intelligence failures is beyond the purview of this essay. Suffice it to say that intelligence failures can be ascribed only indirectly to the constitutional arrangements that have been under analysis here. Intelligence failure is a very complex phenomenon. In most cases, the failures were in anticipating the behavior of external persons or institutions. Such behavior must be classified generally in the "unknowable" or inevitably speculative category.

Intelligence failures are often apparent or publicized. Intelligence successes, on the other hand, are often unheralded. The absence of crises or strategic surprise may sometimes be attributable to great intelligence success. Often it is impossible to demonstrate this, sometimes for security reasons, sometimes because of the impossibility of proving a negative. For example, a terrorist attack that did not occur may be the result of great intelligence success. But public credit can rarely be given.

Failures in intelligence are more likely to occur in the later stages of the intelligence process, after information has been collected, analyzed, interpreted, and communicated to decision makers. A failure may occur at any one of those steps. But often the decision maker's perception and ultimate use of the intelligence available is the crucial element in intelligence failure. Selective perception is a well-established behavioral trait. This may in turn feed back to the intelligence analyst, who, albeit unconsciously, may tend to report what it is thought the decision maker wants to hear. Bearers of bad news are not always received hospitably.

A constitutional system that encourages the politicization of intelligence invites a distortion of the intelligence product. If intelligence becomes a weapon in policy debates, as it will be in a politicized intelligence system, this invites intelligence failure. The involvement of the principal intelligence agency in the implementation of foreign policy—as in covert political intervention overseas—can lead to a dangerous distortion of the intelligence function. Concern with policy success endangers the clear-eyed perception of reality.

Thus the aggressive role of Congress over the 1975–85 period in claiming a partnership with the presidency regarding intelligence policy has politicized intelligence. The wide publicity accompanying various public controversies over intelligence has certainly changed the working environment for intelligence professionals. Widespread public airing of sensitive intelligence problems, including counterintelligence and covert operations, may indeed have seriously inhibited some foreign sources of information, who now fear disclosure and are less willing to cooperate. Meanwhile a variety of "covert" actions have become a subject of public debate, eliminating the necessary "cover."

How, then, has the intelligence function been accommodated to the American system of separation of powers? A system of separated institutions sharing power has had its costs as well as its benefits with regard to the government's intelligence capability, perhaps the governmental function most vital to national security.

The costs are clear: secrecy is often in jeopardy, allied foreign intelligence services are sometimes reluctant to cooperate with an intelligence system in America's open society, foreign informers are sometimes inhibited by potential disclosure, and the pluralism of the American political process has impeded rationalized intelligence organization. The most significant cost, however, is the tendency of the American constitutional system to politicize the intelligence function. This may be the inevitable consequence of the Constitution's invitation to struggle between the president and Congress over foreign policy.

The benefits of separation of powers may be less clear. Yet accountability may be said to stimulate ultimate efficiency in performance. Lack of accountability, at worst, can result in abuse of power. At best, no accountability fosters the dead hand of bureaucracy that inhibits innovation and creativity. In the intelligence era of 1975–85, the system was badly shaken up and to some extent damaged by a vigorously enforced public accountability. Mistakes and misdeeds of the system were widely publicized. These damages are repairable. Unveiled was an intelligence system in need of reform. Intelligence scandals have stimulated ongoing efforts to establish a better balance of secrecy with accountability.

Power struggles between the president and Congress have not, however, prevented the creation of the best intelligence collection system in the world. The evolution of major intelligence institutions—the National Security Agency, Defense Intelligence Agency, National Reconnaissance Office, and others—has occurred without major public controversy. In this sense, the constitutional system has worked to foster the intelligence function. No other government's leadership has access to such a wide range of information on world affairs, and it is gathered by methods and techniques of the greatest variety and scope. Certainly it is difficult for the outside observer to establish criteria for evaluating intelligence performance and, particularly, to apply them to the secret product. But the institutional search for knowledge for national security has prospered.

Failures in intelligence—and there have been many—may in fact have been caused by the politicization of intelligence engendered by the American political process. Yet these failures may derive more from organizational mistakes than from the constitutional structure. At the heart of the organizational mistake may have been the assignment of foreign policy implementation to an agency created for the purpose of informing rather than doing. Covert action rather than intelligence has been at the center of most of the politicized debates over the intelligence function. It may be that this is the lesson to be learned from the record of controversy over the intelligence function.

Tocqueville, in *Democracy in America*, suggested long ago that foreign policy might be the Achilles' heel of American democracy. He wondered whether sufficient secrecy would be possible for an effective, consistent foreign policy. The question remains open even today, as the secrecy-accountability dichotomy continues to be debated with regard to the vital intelligence function. The Iran-Contra controversy of 1987 was one more illustration of the dilemma of national security secrecy versus accountable democracy, and of the conflict between the president and Congress that the Founding Fathers intentionally embedded in the Constitution.

NOTES

1. For an overview of the intelligence system, see Jeffrey T. Richelson, *The U.S. Intelligence Community* (Cambridge, Mass.: Ballinger, 1985).
2. *The Federalist Papers*, ed. Roy P. Fairfield (Garden City, N.Y.: Anchor Books, 1961), no. 64, p. 189.
3. For background on the creation of the CIA, see John Ranelagh, *The Agency: The Rise and Decline of the CIA* (New York: Simon & Schuster, 1986); Harry Howe Ransom, *The Intelligence Establishment* (Cambridge, Mass.: Harvard University Press, 1970); and Thomas F. Troy, *Donovan and the CIA: A History of the Establishment of the Central Intelligence Agency* (Washington, D.C.: Central Intelligence Agency, 1981).
4. See Loch K. Johnson, *A Season of Inquiry: The Senate Intelligence Investigation* (Lexington: University Press of Kentucky, 1985), esp. pp. 252–62.
5. For details, see Morton H. Halperin et al., *The Lawless State: The Crimes of the U.S. Intelligence Agencies* (New York: Penguin Books, 1976); David Wise, *The American Police State: The Government Against the People* (New York: Vintage Books, 1976); Frank J. Donner, *The Age of Surveillance: The Aims and Methods of America's Political Intelligence System* (New York: Vintage Books, 1981); Commission on CIA activities

within the United States, *Report to the President* (Washington, D.C.: GPO, 1975); U.S. Congress, Senate, Select Committee to Study Governmental Operations with Respect to Intelligence Activities, *Final Report* (Foreign and Military Intelligence), S. Rept. 94-755, 94 Cong., 2d sess. (Washington, D.C.: GPO, 1976); and various hearings and reports of the U.S. House Select Committee on Intelligence, 1975–76.

6. For additional details, see American Bar Association, *Oversight and Accountability of the U.S. Intelligence Agencies* (Chicago, Ill.: Standing Committee on Law and National Security, 1985).

7. Public Law 96-450, 1980.

8. *United States v. Curtiss-Wright Export Corp.*, 299 U.S. 304 (1936).

9. U.S. Congress, Senate, "Meeting the Espionage Challenge," *Report,* Senate Select Committee on Intelligence, 99th Cong., 2d sess. (Washington, D.C.: GPO, 1986).

10. For a discussion of intelligence performance, see Walter Laqueur, *A World of Secrets: The Uses and Limits of Intelligence* (New York: Basic Books, 1985), chaps. 3-6 and passim.

11. For sophisticated discussions of covert action, see Harry Rositzke, *The CIA's Secret Operations: Espionage, Counterespionage, and Covert Action* (New York: Reader's Digest Press, 1977); Jay Peterzell, *Reagan's Secret Wars* (Washington, D.C.: Center for National Security Studies, 1984); and John Prados, *Presidents' Secret Wars: CIA and Pentagon Covert Operations since World War II* (New York: Morrow, 1986).

II

NATIONAL DEFENSE

4

Raising the Armed Forces

HOBART B. PILLSBURY, JR.

Who will serve in the armed forces when not all are required to serve? Who will decide? How will those to serve be chosen? These enduring political questions must eventually be addressed in every discussion of national security. The purpose of this chapter is to explore how the U.S. constitutional system has influenced the way our nation has answered them.

Not surprisingly, over the past two centuries those answers have often changed. We have normally relied upon the "invisible hand" of the market. Reliance upon volunteers is clearly consistent with the emphasis of our political heritage and the guarantees of freedom within our constitutional system. Yet periods of crisis have demanded extreme measures curtailing that freedom of choice, and the nation has resorted to conscription of its citizens in peacetime as well as in war.

Decision making about manpower policy has normally been the task of the executive branch, and Congress has allowed wide discretion over specific policies and administration. Legislative review has been nominal and judicial interpretation of executive action has been accommodating. On occasion, however, in response to public outcries or perceived usurpation of power, Congress has reasserted its right to direct the most minute details of how the armed forces will be raised. The federal courts, on the other hand, have tended to be accommodating to the other branches.

Nor has the evolution of truly integrated active and reserve forces—"One Army" comprised of active, reserve, and National Guard elements—eliminated the tension that has existed between the states and federal government since the Constitution was ratified. Although the Constitution specifies that the Congress shall be responsible for how the militia is organized, armed, and equipped for use in the federal service, and that the appointment of officers and training of the militia shall be reserved to the states, the arrangements to accomplish these tasks have historically created conflicts. The long-term shift from reliance upon a small armed force backed by sizable reserves to a large force in being has resulted in a different, but still critical, role for the National Guard.

One ostensible national goal has been armed forces representative of the nation's youth. Yet we typically have had higher participation rates from the lowest socioeconomic groups of our society. During wartime, that insured disproportionate casualties among those groups. On the other hand, when we have used manning policies for the armed forces consciously to promote integration and as a vehicle for upward mobility, it is quite possible that operational effectiveness has been reduced.

It would appear that anyone hoping to find consistency in the historical mosaic of the policies adopted to man the armed forces is likely to be disappointed. There seems to be no pattern—we have relied upon volunteers and conscrption, executive discretion and detailed legislative oversight, national control and state influence. We have used manpower policy to shield the privileged from danger and to promote the cause of the disadvantaged. At times, we have accepted policies that resulted in shortages and qualitatively inadequate forces, and at other times we have used the coercive power of the state to fully man the force structure with very high caliber people.

Yet the explanation of these developments is really not at all mysterious. It accurately reflects our American political culture and the constitutional framework of our political system. Here I shall briefly review how the United States has raised its armed forces and assess how it remains constrained in that task by focusing on three fundamental features of the American constitutional political system—the primacy of individual rights, separation of powers, and federalism.

THE HISTORICAL CONTEXT

An understanding of our military manpower policies is obviously facilitated by an appreciation of the historical context in which they have evolved.[1] The prevailing belief of adult Americans may be that the current policy of manning the armed forces in peacetime with volunteers deviates from "normal" practice. In fact the post–World War II peacetime draft was the policy aberration in the long-term context of our history, and contemporary debates over the wisdom of paying volunteers are hardly breaking new ground. The arguments on both sides actually are older than both the Constitution and the Republic itself.

In the liberal tradition of the citizen soldier, colonial America, understandably suspicious of standing armies, adopted the British militia system of relying upon a small regular army backed by sizable reserves of able-bodied men organized locally to be called upon to serve as the need arose. In practice, however, the ideal of a universal military obligation for all citizens was undermined by the proliferation of exemptions and deferments in the various state militias.[2] Such colonial precedents led to reduced training and widespread unwillingness to leave home. That posed little problem in the context of colonial defense requirements. Routine duties were confined to scheduled parades and home defense of the colony, with an occasional muster to suppress an insurrection or pursue outlaws as a posse comitatus.

These precedents of the state militias, unfortunately, made the task of General Washington during the Revolutionary War particularly difficult. His complaints to the Congress detailed a wide-ranging assessment of the deficiencies of his forces, but to little avail. Eventually all of the states resorted to conscription during that war, but the inequities of existing laws made the burden of service very uneven—the rich were permitted to hire substitutes or pay fines rather than serve. When the war ended, Congress disbanded the Continental Army, relying upon the explicit principle that "standing armies in time of peace are inconsistent with the principles of republican governments."[3] The volunteer army of 1789 had a total strength of 718 officers and enlisted men.[4]

Conscious of the hostility toward ratification of the proposed Constitution that any attempt to establish a standing federal army might generate, the framers of that document granted Congress the power to "raise and support armies," but made no attempt to specify any action toward that end during the Constitutional Convention. It is not difficult to understand why. The Articles of Confederation provided for the requisitioning of troops from the states to provide the army for the central government, a system that was widely condemned. On the other hand, having just freed themselves from a government perceived to be tyrannical, the colonists were reluctant to grant to their central government a means of enforcing a new tyranny. Providing for the common defense while preserving civilian control posed an apparently insoluble dilemma for the new nation.

Under the Articles of Confederation, Congress had only the power "to agree upon the number of land forces, and to make requisition from each State for its quota." The clauses of the Constitution that gave Congress authority to raise and support armies were not intended to provide the national government with greater power, but to designate the department of government that should exercise the power to raise the army. The precedent for the placing of such power in the legislative branch was the 1688 act of Parliament prohibiting standing armies in peacetime without the consent of Parliament, effectively restricting the power of the king, who had previously been able to raise armies in time of peace at his own pleasure.

Aside from the issue of the appropriate branch, the Constitution also specified controls to preclude unfettered power. Limiting appropriations to a maximum of two years and prohibiting of the quartering of troops in peacetime and during war unless prescribed by law effectively further limited the power of the executive branch.

RECURRING TENSIONS

Within the framework of this constitutional system, competing objectives and purposes have complicated the development and implementation of military manpower policies. Each choice has struck a balance between mutually exclusive alternatives—freedom or compulsory service; executive control, legislative oversight, or judicial interpretation; and states' rights or national interests. Typically, the effort to better serve one desired purpose or objective has limited accomplishment of the other.

Individual Rights and National Security

The conflict between individual rights and the need for national defense remains the most salient of these issues. Conscription obviously represents a severe infringement of individual liberty. Any policy requiring involuntary service of only some citizens, as we rediscovered most recently during the Vietnam War, must be perceived favorably as both equitable and necessary to have any prospect of public acceptance.

The arguments of advocates for and against conscription have appeared regularly in the debates over manpower policy. In considering the appeal for a draft after military reverses and manpower shortages in the War of 1812, Daniel Webster claimed that the Constitution was "foully libelled" by such proposals:

> The people of this country have not established for themselves such a fabric of despotism. They have not purchased at a vast expense of their own treasure and their own blood a Magna Carta to be slaves. Where is it written in the Constitution, in what article or section is it contained, that you may take children from their parents, and parents from their children, and compel them to fight the battles of any war, in which the folly or the wickedness of government may engage it?[5]

As it turned out, conscription was not necessary in that conflict, and military manpower concerns were no longer salient when the war ended. In the 1820s army strength dropped to approximately 6,000; on the eve of the Civil War, it had risen to only 16,000—all volunteers. That conflict, first of the modern wars in which the impact of technology and mass production played important roles, forced both sides to rely heavily upon conscription. The enormous needs for manpower to supply and support as well as fight this war quickly outstripped the numbers of volunteers available. Both sides enacted conscription laws during 1862 that permitted substitutes and favored the rich: the North with a $300 commutation fee for draft exemption (which was eventually repealed) and the South with an exemption for owners or overseers of twenty or more slaves.

In practice, the payment of bounties to volunteers and to veterans willing to reenlist in the Union forces made it necessary to draft only between 2 and 3 percent of the force, with another 6 percent drafted as substitutes. Only a relatively small part of the two million men who fought for the North were actually drafted. Conscription was far more important to the South, with one-third of its force made up of draftees.

At the war's end, consistent with the Anglo-American tradition, the army was again disbanded; by 1869 only 25,000 men were serving in the Indian Wars. Although the Spanish-American War required a temporary increase to 300,000 men, the need was easily met with volunteers, and conscription was never considered.

Prior to U.S. entry into World War I, Congress approved an increase in the regular army to 175,000 and authorized a 450,000-man reserve force in 1916. When the United States entered the war, however, only 380,000 were in uniform and only 36,000 more were willing to enlist during the following two weeks. President Wilson's view that enough volunteers would come forward soon proved overly optimistic, and in April 1917 the administration was forced to propose a draft. When the war in the trenches ended, the armed forces were again largely disbanded. Army strength dropped from 2.3 million at war's end to just over 200,000 by 1920.

The National Defense Act of 1920 again relied upon volunteers to man the small force maintained during the interwar period. Although an authorized strength ceiling of 280,000 men was approved by Congress, funds were not appropriated at a level that would support even that force. Army strength was 140,000 in 1930 and, when Germany began its invasion of Poland in 1939, stood at 190,000—seventeenth in size in the world.

The first American peacetime draft legislation was not passed until September 1940 when the likelihood of U.S. involvement in World War II increased. A Gallup poll taken at the time showed the public evenly divided on the issue of compulsory service.[6] Opposition to the law was spearheaded by U.S. Senator Burton Wheeler of Montana, who viewed it as placing a disproportionate burden on the unemployed and poor. The Congress of Industrial Organizations (CIO) also opposed the measure, as did religious organizations and groups of pacifists, socialists, and Republican isolationists. Socialist Norman Thomas viewed conscription as "the first essential to the totalitarian state," while Senator Robert Taft of

Ohio, the most prominent Republican isolationist, labeled it "absolutely opposed to the principles of individual liberty."[7]

In 1940, after rejecting Taft's proposal to double entry-level pay, the Senate instead voted 58 to 31 and the House 263 to 149 to pass the first peacetime draft. The law imposed a conscript enrollment ceiling of 900,000; limited service to one year; and restricted service to the United States, its possessions, and the Western Hemisphere. By a single vote margin, the House voted in the fall of 1941 to extend the terms of draftees beyond one year. After Pearl Harbor, geographical restrictions were lifted and the term of enlistment was extended for the duration. The following year voluntary enlistments were no longer permitted.

By the end of the war nearly fifty million men had registered and over ten million had been inducted; two-thirds of the manpower needed for the war was provided through the selective service system established by the law. During the war, public opinion in support of compulsory military service grew substantially.

As the war in Europe was ending, Congress was faced with the decision of whether to renew the draft law, due to expire 15 May 1945. Despite support of the draft during the war, public pressure for demobilization understandably rose as victory over Japan appeared likely. Based on the much smaller forces believed necessary after the war, the services anticipated being able to return to a volunteer system. Ultimately, however, uncertainty over possible manpower shortages that might occur without the pressure of the draft, coupled with the anxiety generated by the Soviet invasion of Iran, led Congress to extend the draft until 31 March 1947.

Despite the fact that Congress twice acquiesced in extending the draft for one-year periods after the war, the political pressure for returning to a volunteer force was strong. Various proposals were made during this period for increasing pay to make the services more attractive, to permit recruitment of aliens, and to lower entrance standards.

Reliance on the market to raise armed forces indisputably eliminates the tension inherent in conscription. Volunteers presumably must be those willing to serve at the pay rates and under the contractual arrangements offered to them. As long as enough volunteers are available to satisfy manpower goals, the loss of individual freedom appears to be a moot point.

There remain, of course, some legitimate concerns with this approach. Manpower goals are not static, and occasional crises may require increases in manning levels. That can be accomplished by calling upon the reserves, as President Kennedy did for the Berlin crisis of his administration, or it may be necessary to increase the active force. The period of greatest need, unfortunately, is likely to be a time when volunteers, faced with the prospect of imminent danger, are least inclined to step forward.

Indeed, regardless of the effectiveness of economic and other incentives, the conflict between individual rights and national security persists, because a draft, even if on some sort of "standby" basis, continues to be perceived as necessary in order to respond to threats that cannot be precisely anticipated.

During the Vietnam War, there were thousands of demonstrations, often violent, protesting not only American involvement but the draft that provided the manpower to continue the war. Over that period, 2,000 to 4,000 draft violators were prosecuted each year. Although opinion polls taken early in the war suggested strong majorities willing to "follow the flag" and support government action in Vietnam, prolonged fighting and increased casualties eventually led to intense opposition. One of the most obvious targets of public opposition was the draft itself, widely perceived as inequitable and unfair.

As the United States began its withdrawal from the war, the debate over elimination of the draft led the Nixon administration first to a lottery system, which effectively neutralized some of the criticism of the features perceived as most inequitable, and, ultimately, to proposals to rely completely upon volunteers. Despite strong reservations of many key players in the executive and legislative branches, the early years of the "all-volunteer force" showed encouraging results. Raising pay and improving some conditions of service life seemed to provide adequate incentives to keep the ranks filled. By the late 1970s, however, after several pay "caps" that prevented military pay scales from keeping pace with inflation, the services experienced serious problems in recruiting and retention. A major "catch-up" pay increase in 1980, subsequent pay hikes that nearly matched inflation, and better management of recruiting activities have permitted the services to meet their manpower objectives since then.

Acceptance of the all-volunteer force, coupled with standby registration for the draft, seems for the present to have eliminated the conflict between individual freedom and the services' needs for manpower. By Christmas 1986 the Pentagon announced that all of the services had met their recruiting objectives for the fiscal year that ended 30 September, the seventh consecutive year in which they had done so. Assistant Defense Secretary Chapman B. Cox took the opportunity to note that the administration would continue to resist suggestions for reinstatement of a draft.

Similarly, although it has been argued that the current registration requirement is an infringement of personal freedom, public acceptance of the policy is reflected in widespread voluntary compliance. By 1 January 1987, the first registrants under the standby system had passed through the "window of eligibility." The 2.1 million men who reached eighteen in 1980 have now turned twenty-six and would not be drafted now even if a draft call-up were ordered upon the outbreak of war. This era has witnessed nothing comparable to the widespread, often violent, opposition to draft laws of recent times.

The answer to the question of "who will serve?" when not all are required to serve has other aspects that are troubling to many even when the market model seems to achieve a satisfactory level of volunteerism. Today, no less than during the nineteenth century, reliance upon direct incentives has the potential to fill the ranks of the armed services disproportionately from the least privileged categories of our society. Although the effect of this in peacetime may be to provide real opportunities for the disadvantaged, the inescapable consequence during hostilities will be for casualties to fall disproportionately upon the minority and lower economic status groups that fill the ranks.

The inherent underlying tension between competing objectives remains, of course, notwithstanding that the conflict between freedom and manpower requirements may appear resolved for the moment. Two possible developments might quickly restore the salience of these issues: a serious foreign challenge might require an increase in manning requirements, or the cumulative impact of demographic influences might reduce the flow of recruits. Either of these would quickly force policy makers to refocus their attention on the underlying dilemma: manning the armed forces must be accomplished through some form of compulsory service whenever numbers of volunteers are inadequate to meet the need.

In the first case, return to some form of draft seems quite likely. After the national experience in Vietnam, it is difficult to imagine scenarios in which volunteers would be adequate for significant manpower increases in response to anything less than a major, direct threat to U.S. interests. In the second, as the traditional pool from which recruits have been drawn levels off, while service skill requirements increase, there are more options—and complications. Greater reliance upon civilian employees,[8] greater reliance upon women,[9] and greater reliance upon minorities[10] in manning the armed forces at the very least arouse concerns about deployability in wartime, equity in assignments, and unrepresentative forces respectively.

Even if all of these issues could be resolved to everyone's satisfaction, there remain other grounds for conflict over policies for raising the armed forces created by the structures of our constitutional system. Despite the satisfaction with the all-volunteer military expressed by Pentagon officials from former Defense Secretary Caspar W. Weinberger on down, at least some key Democratic congressional leaders have continued to discuss reimposition of the draft or the imposition of some other form of national service requirement. Their proposals reflect the second set of tensions inherent in the development and implementation of military manpower policy—the potential differences arising from a structure based upon checks and balances and the separation of powers.

Checks and Balances

The tug-of-war between executive and legislative direction and control of military manpower policy has, as we have seen, been a consistent feature of our national history. What has changed, of course, are the stakes in peacetime that our status as a world power has created. Although the Congress was amenable to executive initiatives over manning small forces in the aftermath of major wars and in the absence of major threats, a standing force of roughly three million service members and budgetary issues measured in hundreds of billions of dollars have generated an unsurprising level of congressional interest in almost every aspect of military manpower policy in the post-Vietnam era.

That interest has followed the familiar pattern of congressional involvement whenever defense issues led the national agenda. Reasserting control of military manpower policy on the eve of World War I, for example, Congress passed draft legislation, and by 5 June 1917, nine and a half million men registered. During the war almost two-thirds of the armed forces of four and a half million men were conscripts. In 1918 voluntary enlistments were no longer permitted—the draft was much more efficient and became the only means of manpower procurement. Not surprisingly, events of the interwar period aroused little concern over military manpower issues. Public indifference to the matter of manning the armed forces was reflected in congressional deference to executive initiative and control.

Reinstatement of the draft for World War II was widely accepted by the public, and there was no disagreement between the federal executive and the legislature over the necessity for such action. Differences resurfaced, however, once the war was over.

In 1945 President Truman lifted the ban on voluntary enlistments, and by 1 January 1946, the army recruiting force contained almost 10,000 men. By January 1947 the army was meeting its goals with volunteers and anticipated early release of some draftees. Draft calls ended that month and induction authority was allowed to lapse. Meanwhile, the process of demobilization reduced active strength substantially. Army manpower actually dropped from 8.2 million in 1945 to 1.9 million the following year.

The combination of lower manning requirements and intensified recruiting shifted the focus of military manpower policy to administration and War Department proposals for universal military training (UMT) as a means of insuring adequate reserve forces to back up the regular army.

The services, however, were not in complete agreement on the issue. Navy and army air corps recruiting successes during the war led their service leaders to favor larger forces in being; army leaders, with an appreciation for the greater difficulty they were likely to experience in manning a larger active force, tended to favor mobilizable reserves.[11]

In the political battle that followed, the administration was supported by the American Legion, other veteran's groups, and the Chamber of Commerce, while UMT opponents included the NAACP, most of organized labor, and a variety of leftist groups.[12] UMT advocates argued that the demands of modern war, unlike those of previous conflicts, required prior training and forces that could be quickly mobilized; in their view, there would simply be less reaction time for industrial and manpower buildups than the United States had during the two world wars. Opponents countered that rapid changes in technology would make prior training obsolete and "push-button war" would not require large forces.

For the next year, the services relied on volunteers, but problems developed as the pace of demobilization, the decline in military pay relative to civilian wages, and an increase in army test standards for volunteers resulted in twice as many men leaving the army each month as were recruited.[13] Related to the question of quality as a key variable affecting the size of the eligible population for military service was the issue of enlisting greater numbers of women. In 1948, anticipating serious recruiting shortfalls during the first AVF experiment, Congress passed the Women's Armed Services Integration Act and seriously considered the possibility of drafting women. Many of the arguments on both sides over that proposal would be revisited in the 1970s when the country turned again to an all-volunteer force. Again, the lines were drawn—the executive favoring higher standards and, consequently, a relatively narrow pool of eligible service members, the legislature preferring lower threshholds and greater reliance upon women to fill the ranks.

After the communists gained control in Czechoslovakia, and with relations with the Soviet Union continuing to deteriorate, the Truman administration proposed restoration of the draft and, once again, legislation for UMT. This time the debate over military strategy focused on the conflicting proposals of advocates of air power and proponents of a "balanced force" of air and ground elements.[14] UMT opponents, joined now by air power advocates, again persuaded Congress to reject the administration proposal.

In March 1948, as the Soviet blockade of Berlin was taking shape, and with active U.S. military strength at 1,384,500, Truman asked Congress temporarily to restore the selective service system. By this time, key administration figures were convinced that demobilization had been too rapid, and both the Joint Chiefs of Staff and Secretary of Defense Forrestal supported a two-million-man force. By default, resumption of the draft as a temporary measure now became the cornerstone of the nation's military manpower policy. In June Congress passed the Selective Service Act of 1948, authorizing an active strength of just over two million and restoring induction authority for a period of two years. Although neither the Truman administration nor the Congress ever intended to continue conscription in peacetime, this "temporary" measure was destined to remain in force for the next quarter century.

Although a few thousand men were inducted over the next few months, enlistment rates began to rise in 1948, and the draft authority was not required at all during the year and a half prior to expiration of the law in June 1950. Only thirty thousand men were inducted during the final quarter of calendar year 1948, and draft calls were ended in January 1949. Since adequate numbers of volunteers were available, those drafted were released after twelve months of service. The intent of the 1948 law was to provide a means to make up the gap between manpower requirements and voluntary enlistments, which it was hoped would be a small one. With no inductions at all in 1949 and 1950, it was a reasonable expectation when Congress extended the law to 9 July 1950 that it would not be needed after then.

Although an administration request for a three-year extension initially appeared unlikely to gain congressional approval, the North Korean invasion of South Korea on 23 June caused the matter to be reconsidered. With Truman's commitment of U.S. forces to the war, Congress rapidly passed his requested extension of draft authority. In the midst of the Korean War, it was extended again until 1955, the induction age was lowered to eighteen and the term of active service was lengthened. Once again Congress supported the executive lead on manpower policy during a period of national crisis.

Ironically, despite the "New Look," "more bang for the buck," and reduced military manpower requirements, the influence of the Eisenhower administration led to continued reliance upon the draft during the 1950s. As active force strength fell from 3.5 to 2.5 million between 1953 and 1961, the shift to more technical jobs and the relative increase in air force and navy personnel created a greater demand for skilled individuals. The selective service authorities and Department of Defense argued that the draft remained essential, and after perfunctory review, Congress endorsed executive initiatives by extending conscription authority for four years in 1955, 1959, and 1963.[15]

U.S. involvement in Vietnam required continuation of a compulsory draft during the 1960s, of course, but the widespread public opposition to the draft, as well as to the war itself, eventually forced Congress to press for change. Initiatives by the Nixon administration to shift first to a lottery system and then to an all-volunteer force were an understandable reaction to popular pressure and the resulting congressional insistence that the system be revised.

Although the preceding decade found the legislature willing to defer to executive initiatives, the Vietnam War resulted in a reassertion of congressional control over the armed forces. The War Powers Act was the most obvious evidence of this shift, but control of military manpower policy specifically by the legislature was also strengthened in less visible but equally effective ways of limiting executive power. A cursory comparison of the authorization and appropriations hearings on manpower issues for the 1970s with those of the earlier postwar period reveals a clear trend towar detailed and growing involvement by the Congress in every aspect of military manpower policy. The recruiting and advertising slices of the service operation and maintenance (OMA) appropriations, for example, became "special interest" items that were closely scrutinized during the budget cycle. Growing congressional interest covered a host of other issues relating to military personnel, ranging from specific pay rates, bonuses, and enlistment standards to retention incentives and quality-of-life issues.

U.S. military forces experienced a gradual quality decline during the 1970s, and Congress "capped" military pay despite accelerating inflation. By mid decade, as the purchasing power of military pay lagged behind inflation and cost-cutting by Congress fueled the perception of "eroding benefits" across the board, there were serious discussions of military unionization. Readiness was hampered by an alarming exodus of skilled noncommissioned officers. When the services failed to meet quantitative recruiting goals in 1979 despite lower standards, Congress reversed the trend toward declining pay in real terms and renewed emphasis upon improving service life. Subsequent improvements in pay, starting with the "catch-up" raise of 1980, coupled with support of service initiatives in several other areas, then reversed the disturbing trends of the 1970s.

Today, higher quality, defined in terms of the relative percentages of high school graduates and based upon standardized test scores, has reached and remained at reassuring levels. Retention has improved in critical skill areas, and indicators of disciplinary problems have improved significantly since the late 1970s. The prospects for raising the armed forces through voluntary mechanisms—forces that by historical measures still remain very large for peacetime—remain encouraging for the near term. As advocates of the volunteer force insisted from the beginning, the "market model" appears adequate to the task.

These developments have, however, occurred with policies that have typically evolved only after negotiation and compromise between the executive and legislative branches. On the one hand, key players in the executive branch remain critical of "micromanagement" of manpower policies by the Congress, which they perceive as infringing on the president's role as commander in chief; on the Hill, key players respond that specific controls and directions imposed in the authorizations and appropriations bills are the proper exercise of their constitutional responsibility to raise the armed forces.

Although these two branches have often disagreed upon the appropriate policies for raising the armed forces in the exercise of their respective powers, judicial review of their action has generated little conflict. The courts have consistently supported legislative and executive action designed to raise the armed forces, whether through contractual arrangements or conscription.

The authority of Congress to determine how armies shall be raised was explicitly acknowledged by the judiciary a century ago: "All citizens capable of bearing arms constitute the reserved military force or reserved militia of the United States as well as of the States" and are subject to such military service as Congress may require.[16] The rights of conscientious objectors, the courts have further stated, thus exist only at the discretion of the legislature—the "conscientious objector is relieved from the obligation to bear arms in obedience to no constitutional provision, express or implied; but because, and only because, it has accorded with the policy of Congress thus to relieve him."[17]

Enlistment is a voluntary contract for military service for a certain term entered into by a civil person with the United States. The contract is unusual in the sense that it is a contract made with the government, under the specific authority of the Constitution, and thus governed by those principles or considerations of expediency and economy expressed in the term "public policy." Thus the soldier alone may be held to the contract, while the government may put an end to it any time and discharge the soldier without his consent, or otherwise modify it, such as by reducing pay and allowances. Thus this contract is entered into with the understanding that it may be modified in any of its terms, or wholly rescinded, at the discretion of the government.[18]

The other approach to raising the armed forces, of course, has been to rely upon conscription. Although not used by the federal government until the Civil War, many of the states had exercised the power of exacting compulsory military service from their citizens prior to that time—indeed, nine of the original state constitutions contained explicit provisions permitting conscription.[19] As noted earlier, during the Civil War more than a quarter million men were drafted. The constitutionality of that measure was only raised once during the war, and then only in a state court, where the draft was upheld.[20]

The Supreme Court settled the issue of constitutional power to compel military service at the federal level in a 1918 decision upholding the validity of the Selective Draft Law of World War I. In that instance defendants failed to register under the Draft Act and were prosecuted for failing to obey the law. Their defense was based on the claim that there was no power conferred upon Congress by the Constitution to compel military service, and that if such power had been given to Congress, the terms of the Draft Act caused it to go beyond such power so as to be repugnant to the Constitution. They were convicted of violating the Draft Law and appealed to the Supreme Court.

Indicative of more recent times, the registration law of 1980 was attacked not only by traditional antiwar groups and others making the case for individual freedoms, but by women's rights groups on equity grounds because of sex discrimination. Unsurprisingly, once the law had passed, it was promptly challenged on the grounds that it discriminated against men.

A three-judge panel in a Pennsylvania federal district court declared the new draft law unconstitutional on 18 July 1980 and enjoined the selective service system from proceeding with registration. Once again deferring to the other branches, Supreme Court Justice William Brennan stayed the district court order, thereby allowing registration to begin as planned. The Supreme Court held the following July that an all-male draft did not violate the Constitution, since women, ineligible for combat duty, were not "similary situated" for draft eligibility. This most recent decision dealing with how we raise the armed forces once more supported the action of the other branches, following the consistent pattern of previous judicial rulings.

The separation of powers and checks and balances of our constitutional system have, then, resulted in two patterns in recent times that are likely to persist in the future. On the one hand, there has been consistent tension between the executive and legislative branches over the design and implementation of manpower policies; on the other, there has been an equally consistent pattern of judicial endorsement for the compromises eventually hammered out.

The ultimate impact of legislatuve involvement in the specific design of peacetime manpower policies is obviously indeterminate. Although the immediate effect of detailed review of specific executive initiatives has undoubtedly made the task of developing and defending budget proposals more difficult for the executive branch, it is equally plausible that such review will result in better expenditure of defense dollars in the long run. Acquiescence by the judicial branch, of course, has rendered this "check" largely irrelevant.

This leaves a final arena in which the design of the Constitution has important implications for raising the armed forces—the federal structure of the government itself and the continuing division of forces into active and "militia" components.

Federalism: States' Rights and the National Interest

The existence of federal and state governments with explicitly defined roles for raising the armed forces establishes still another area in which our constitutional system creates conflict over competing policy objectives. The need for armed forces in being at levels far above those historically deemed appropriate has obviously imposed enormous costs upon our government. The manpower costs of those forces today typically consume roughly half of every defense dollar. To the extent that Army and Air National Guard units can meet national defense needs, there are likely to be significant savings here. Also the fact that National Guard forces remain under state control in peacetime, a position upheld by the judiciary in *Johnson v. Sayre*,[21] has always influenced congressional willingness to underwrite their expenses.

Public laws passed between 1903 and 1920 established the basic framework for the manning and use of the reserve forces that exists today. The highlights of these laws were to task wholly federal reserve forces primarily with support, technical, and specialist missions, while assigning ground combat roles to the National Guard. Federal control and funding of National Guard training, organization, and equipment increased, along with greater liability for federal service and without any decrease in militia responsibilities.

As a powerful pressure group in its own right, the National Guard has had notable successes in pursuing its objectives on those occasions when its political allies and a congressional predisposition toward defense combined to support its cause. On other occasions, however, congressional control of the purse has clearly led to increased federal control over every aspect of guard activities. Although Congress has retained its special attachment to the guard as the military component closest to the home state, that special relationshiop has also clearly changed over time. Where hostility toward federal military power dominated the Congress at the time our Constitution was written, now there is a clear recognition that the United States must be prepared to respond to the international demands inevitably placed upon a world power in the latter part of the twentieth century. Moreover, since the resource requirements to meet that challenge are far greater than those that existed when that document was written, the decisions that affect manpower allocation between active, reserve, and National Guard forces have become extremely important even in peacetime.

Calling the National Guard into federal service, as President Kennedy did during the Berlin Crisis of 1961, provides dramatic evidence that the "militia" retains an important role in the defense manpower picture. Although only 65,000 Army and Air National Guard service members were part of the 300,000-person expansion in the armed forces of that time, their participation suggested a national determination to stand firm that may well have been more important than any military contribution they could have made.

During the 1970s, the pool of individual reservists left over from the Vietnam War draft era declined substantially, of course. Without the reserve obligation following a period of active duty to keep the reserve ranks filled, and without the incentive of the draft to at least partially encourage participation in the guard, the reserve components began to experience serious problems in meeting authorized strength levels. Since that time, the evolution of the "One Army" concept of active, reserve, and guard forces has resulted in increases in the support provided to the reserve components and substantial improvements in the manning picture. Nonetheless, the debate over the proper distribution of resources by component remains a perennial feature of the budgetary process.

Today the problems experienced from reliance upon the militia during the early history of the nation are unlikely to be repeated, but reservations about the nationalization and commitment of the National Guard for any federal purpose remain.[22] From the federal perspective, those reservations center on the capability of some guard units to perform their intended missions within the time frame likely to be necessary. From the state perspective, any requirement for rapid, widespread activation and deployment of guard forces would result in serious disruption of the lives and economic affairs of the families and areas from which units were drawn. The National Guard as a state militia also meets the continuing requirement for dealing with domestic disturbances, such as the race riots of the 1960s, and for providing aid after natural disasters or state-declared emergencies. As a result of these multiple missions, the possibility of conflict between the states and federal government over the use of the National Guard persists to this day.

This conflict, though muted, is highlighted each year in the annual appropriation process as the Congress wrestles with administration requests and local and state political pressures before reaching decisions about manpower policies for the various components of the armed forces. On balance, dollars spent on the guard buy more force structure than those spent upon the active forces. The trade-offs obviously come in some combination of immediate readiness, deployability, and military effectiveness—all difficult to measure, but equally legitimate concerns.

The potential impact of state control of National Guard units upon federal policy objectives was most recently dramatized by the refusal of several states early in 1986 to allow their units to conduct their annual training in Central America. Although Congress thereupon passed legislation limiting the power of governors to stop their units from deploying to Central America for training, the incident once again, as the chief of the National Guard Bureau, Lieutenant General Herbert R. Temple, Jr., noted, "raised the question of the reliability of the National Guard in its federal responsibilities."[23]

The trade-off for raising the armed forces that results from maintaining the National Guard is difficult to isolate precisely. To the extent that young men otherwise eligible for military service join the guard, obviously, whatever recruiting success the guard achieves may come at the expense of the active and reserve forces. On the other hand, since the guard is best prepared to perform some activities in the service of the states, the regular forces that might otherwise be required for such tasks as disaster relief may remain available on call to perform direct military missions.

CONCLUSIONS

In terms of the tensions suggested earlier, the American experience in manning the armed forces has reflected some clear patterns that are likely to persist. First, although individual freedom has occasionally been held subordinate to national security interests, the preference throughout our history has been to rely upon volunteer forces. When we have turned to coercion, public acceptance has been proportional to the imminent danger to the state. During peacetime, the issue of who serves typically has lacked salience for most Americans. Given volunteer forces as the norm, the consensus in recent times has been that those who serve choose to do so. There has also been little public resistance to specific related policies such as the need for a standby draft; nor has there been widespread support for fundamental alternatives such as compulsory national service.

The second pattern likely to persist is continuing tension between executive control and legislative oversight in shaping manpower policies. Although some observers perceive less interest in military issues on the part of congressmen as the number of senators and representatives with any firsthand military experience has declined, the importance of national defense and the fact that manpower costs remain a substantial part of every defense budget assures continuing attention to this issue.

At the same time, although the separation of powers and checks and balances of our constitutional system have fostered continuous tension between the two branches with explicit responsibilities for raising and commanding the armed forces, little conflict has arisen through review of their activities by the judiciary. There is no reason to expect any substantial shift in the manner in which the courts have interpreted federal power in manning the armed forces. Unlike other substantive areas, such as criminal law, in which judicial activism has occasionally dominated policy, this is likely to remain one arena in which executive initiative tempered by legislative oversight is left largely unchallenged by the courts.

Finally, national control should continue to dominate state initiatives in the military manpower arena as far as the manning and use of the militia are concerned. Whatever the initial intent of the Constitution's framers may have been, the contemporary reality is that congressional control of the authorization and appropriation strings all but guarantees strong national influence on how the National Guard is manned and operated.

Throughout U.S. history, the adequacy of our armed forces' manpower has been evaluated in the context of several distinct, but interrelated, policy issues, including the volunteer basis of military service; the level of appropriate compensation for such service; the social representativeness of our armed forces; and the likely effectiveness of those forces in combat. The shared power of the legislative and executive branches and the accommodating interpretations of the judicial branch have allowed a precarious journey through policies that have at times preempted liberties in the name of common defense, and at other times possibly jeopardized our security in the interest of personal freedom. That the nation has been preserved while guaranteeing individual freedom to the extent that it has is reassuring evidence of maintaining a reasonably proper balance of those often mutually exclusive objectives.

NOTES

1. The history of military manpower policy has been extensively covered in several excellent secondary sources. Detailed historical accounts and a wide range of original documents, extracts from congressional debates, and summaries of various other primary sources upon which this section is based include John Whiteclay Chambers, ed., *Draftees or Volunteers: A Documentary History of the Debate over Military Conscription in the United States, 1787–1973* (New York: Carland, 1975); James M. Gerhardt, *The Draft and Public Policy: Issues in Military Manpower Procurement, 1945–1970* (Columbus: Ohio State University Press, 1971); James L. Lacy, "Military Manpower: The American Experience and the Enduring Debate," in Andrew J. Goodpaster, Lloyd H. Elliott, and J. Alan Hovey, Jr., eds., *Toward a Consensus on Military Service: Report of the Atlantic Council of the United States* (New York: Pergamon Press, 1982), pp. 20–51; John Franklin Leach, *Conscription in the United States: Historical Background* (Rutland, Vt.: Charles E. Tuttle, 1952); Gus C. Lee and Geoffrey Y. Parker, *Ending the Draft—the Story of the All Volunteer Force* (Alexandria, Va.: Human Resources Research Organization, 1977); John O'Sullivan and Allan M. Meckler, eds., *The Draft*

and Its Enemies: A Documentary History (Urbana: University of Illinois Press, 1974); and Lillian Schlissel, ed., *Conscience in America: A Documentary History of Conscientious Objection in America, 1757–1967* (New York: Dutton 1963).

2. O'Sullivan and Meckler, eds., *The Draft and Its Enemies,* pp. 4–5, provides several examples. The Massachusetts Militia Act of 1647, for example, exempted members of the General Court, officers, fellows, and students of Harvard College, elders and deacons, schoolmasters, physicians and surgeons, masters of vessels over twenty tons, fishermen employed in all seasons, and all other individuals with physical problems or other causes excused by a General Court or the Court of Assistants.

3. Walter Millis, *Arms and Men* (New York: Putnam, 1956), p. 46.

4. Lacy, "Military Manpower," p. 21.

5. Ibid., p. 21.

6. *The Gallup Poll,* vol. 1 (New York: Random House, 1940), p. 226.

7. Lacy, "Military Manpower," p. 31.

8. See Martin Binkin, *Shaping the Defense Civilian Work Force* (Washington, D.C.: Brookings Institution, 1978), for an excellent discussion of the fiscal and military effectiveness implications of this course of action.

9. William J. Gregor, "Women, Combat and the Draft: Placing Details in Context," in William J. Taylor et al., eds., *Defense Manpower Planning* (New York: Pergamon Press, 1981), pp. 34–60, reviews the issues involved with this option. See also Martin Binkin and Shirley J. Bach, *Women and the Military* (Washington, D.C.: Brookings Institution, 1977).

10. See Martin Binkin and Mark T. Eitelberg, with Alvin J. Schexnider and Martin M. Smith, *Blacks and the Military* (Washington D.C.: Brookings Institution, 1982).

11. Ibid.

12. James M. Gerhardt, *The Draft and Public Policy* (Columbus: Ohio University Press, 1971), pp. 12–15.

13. Lee and Parker, *Ending the Draft,* p. 16.

14. The positions of the two groups are documented in the Finletter and Haslip Reports respectively. See President's Air Policy Commission, *Survival in the Air Age* (Washington, D.C.: GPO, 1948), p. 4 (Finletter Report), and War Department Policies and Programs Review Board, *Final Report* (Washington, D.C.: GPO, 1947), pp. 111, 46–47, 110–11 (Haslip Report).

15. Lee and Parker, *Ending the Draft,* pp. 21–23.

16. *Presser v. Illinois,* 116 U.S. 262, 265 (1886).

17. *United States v. Macintosh,* 283 U.S. 605, 623 (1931).

18. William Woolsey Winthrop, *Military Law and Precedents* 538 2d ed. (Washington, D.C.: GPO, 1920).

19. *Selective Draft Law Cases,* 245 U.S. 366, 380 (1917).

20. *Kneedler v. Lane,* Pa. St. 238 (1863).

21. *Johnson v. Sayre,* 158 U.S. 109 (1895).

22. See "Part II: Reserve Forces," in Taylor et al., *Defense Manpower Planning.*

23. "Guard Units Ready for More, Chief Says," *Army Times,* 15 December 1986, p. 52.

5

Organizing the Armed Forces

DANIEL J. KAUFMAN

Organizing the U.S. defense establishment has become much more difficult, and much more important, since the nation assumed the responsibilities of a world power in the years following World War II. When the
United States had few responsibilities outside its own borders, questions
of defense organization were of little consequence; today such is no longer the case. The structure of the Defense Department and the armed
forces, the distribution of responsibilities for policy development and
program administration, the mechanism for integrating the advice of
senior military officials into the design of national strategy and policy are
all critical considerations that bear on this country's responsibilities as
the leader of the Western alliance.

How does the U.S. constitutional system affect the ability of the United
States to organize its armed forces for its own protection and for the
protection of important national interests around the world? In order to
address this fundamental question, I begin with a description of the
constitutional basis of the structure of the national security system and
consideration of other, nonconstitutional, constraints and influences that
affect the nation's approach to defense organization. Following this discussion is a brief examination of the evolution of the national security
system as it pertains to the organization of the armed forces. The historical discussion provides the basis for an examination of the consequences
of the constitutional system and the implications for the ability of the
United States to organize its armed forces effectively and efficiently.

THE STRUCTURE OF THE SYSTEM

The decentralization that characterizes the U.S. constitutional system is
especially evident in the functions relevant to organizing the defense
establishment. The constitutional allocation of authority between the

executive and legislative branches in dealing with issues of national security created, in Richard Neustadt's phrase, "a government of separated institutions sharing power."[1]

Executive Authority

The president's constitutional authority as chief executive and commander in chief of the armed forces vests in him the authority and responsibility for the structure of the armed forces. The president's constitutional authority and institutional position as chief executive make him responsible for the articulation of a coherent national strategy and the design of a national security system that will translate that strategy into an effective national security policy.[2] The defense establishment should, therefore, be organized in such a way as to facilitate the implementation of that security policy.

The Department of Defense is not the only executive agency concerned with the issue of organizing for national defense. The Central Intelligence Agency (CIA) is not only responsible for the collection and dissemination of intelligence information, but also has become directly involved in armed conflicts through its sponsorship of paramilitary organizations during the Vietnam War and, more recently, in Central America. Other involved agencies include the Department of Energy, which directs the development and production of nuclear warheads, and the Office of Management and Budget (OMB), which supervises the preparation and execution of the president's budget. Additionally, the assistant to the president for national security affairs and the National Security Council staff, acting either as the president's personal staff or to facilitate interagency coordination, can be sources of influence in the organization and use of the nation's armed forces.

The various organizations of the executive branch bring different, and often competing, perspectives to bear on specific issues of national policy. As chief executive, the president is responsible for the resolution of bureaucratic conflict and for the effective development and implementation of policy. The manner in which these competing views are redressed depends in large measure on the president's management style. Some presidents, such as Eisenhower and Nixon, have preferred formal systems characterized by clearly drawn lines of authority, well-defined procedures, and an orderly flow of information up through the various organizational levels to the president. Other presidents, such as Kennedy, Johnson, and Carter, have preferred more informal systems, with interagency debate encouraged, where the president is more likely to communicate with subordinates in various departments or seek outside advice or information. Whatever the president's management style, the fragmented institutional structure of the executive branch contributes to the decentralization that characterizes the American decision-making system.

The Department of Defense (DoD) is the executive agency directly responsible for the organization and supervision of the armed forces. The secretary of defense is the principal assistant to the president in all matters relating to the Department of Defense. The statutory authority of the secretary of defense for "direction, authority, and control"[3] over the Department of Defense is clear. However, competing bureaucratic interests can combine to reduce that power considerably. Indeed, one should be careful not to consider the Defense Department as a monolith. It is comprised of a number of institutional actors, all of whom bring different perspectives to bear on the problem of organizing for national defense. The secretary of defense, other senior officials within the Office of the Secretary of Defense, the Joint Chiefs of Staff (JCS), and the individual military services are all influential actors that have, to varying degrees, statutory authority to pursue their own interests.[4] For example, the secretary of each military service has the right, by statute, to submit matters directly to Congress, regardless of the position, preferences, or decisions of the secretary of defense or the president. Decentralization, then, affects not only executive-legislative and executive branch relations, but also relationships within the Department of Defense as well.

Congressional Authority

The authority for congressional oversight of the organization and procedures of the defense establishment derives from specific constitutional powers. Article 1, Section 8 of the Constitution provides inter alia that Congress shall have power:

> To make Rules for the Government and Regulation of the land and naval forces . . . To make all Laws which shall be necessary and proper for carrying into Execution the foregoing Powers, and all other Powers vested by this Constitution in the Government of the United States, or in any Department or Officer thereof.

The constitutionally mandated separation of powers with regard to the organization of the armed forces ensures that Congress will be an active participant in deliberations concerning this issue. Indeed, since the establishment of the War Department in 1789, Congress has maintained a keen interest in the nature, size, and structure of the nation's armed forces. Therefore despite the president's position as chief executive and commander in chief, the constitutional system deliberately and specifically allocates authority to both the president and the Congress on the issue of organizing for national defense.

Historically, Congress has been ambivalent in its attitude toward increased centralization in defense organization. Although the constitution assures Congress a role in overseeing the structure of the nation's defense establishment, Congress faces a dilemma on the issue of centralized control: decentralization, with its attendant shortcomings, enhances congressional control. Centralization, with its promise of improved performance, reduces effective congressional influence. Historically, the services always have cultivated relations with specific members or committees in Congress. By so doing, the services ensure a degree of institutional autonomy from the centralized management of the Department of Defense. In return, Congress has been able to exercise influence on issues about which the individual members are most likely to be concerned, such as procurement and basing.

The manner in which Congress has chosen to carry out its constitutional responsibility for regulating the armed forces has changed dramatically in recent years. Although a complete discussion of the causes of increased congressional involvement in the details of defense management is beyond the scope of this chapter, it is clear that the degree of congressional participation in matters of defense policy, programs, and organization has grown significantly.[5] For example, the organizational structure to support congressional involvement has expanded considerably. In 1947 the staffs of the Senate and House Armed Services Committees numbered ten each. Today the figures are forty-one and fifty-six respectively.[6]

Furthermore, Congress has reduced its reliance on the executive branch for information and improved its ability to conduct independent analysis. The Congressional Budget Office (CBO), the General Accounting Office (GAO), the Office of Technology Assessment (OTA), and the Congressional Research Service (CRS) can and do provide Congress with systematic analysis of timely issues.

Congressional involvement in the details of defense budgeting has also increased. During the past twenty-five years Congress has gradually but consistently expanded the requirement that portions of the defense budget be authorized for appropriation. Prior to 1959 the Armed Services Committee would authorize a program or activity once, then let the Appropriations Committee fund it annually. Since that time, however, practically every element of the defense budget has been brought under the requirement for annual authorization. Consequently, defense officials spend a considerable portion of their time preparing and presenting testimony to the numerous subcommittees of the Armed Services and Appropriations Committees of both houses of Congress. As discussed in more detail below, concentration on the annual budget cycle tends to focus both executive and legislative attention on the details of defense procurement rather than on the larger issues of national security and military policy.

Finally, Congress has become involved to a considerable extent in the day-to-day functions of the Defense Department. In 1970 Congress requested 31 reports or studies from DoD. By 1985 that number had grown to 458. General provisions in laws prescribing how the Defense Department should carry out certain of its functions increased from 64 in 1970 to 213 in 1985. During the same period, annual congressionally mandated actions requiring specific DoD compliance increased from 18 to 202.[7]

In sum, it is clear that Congress seems intent on retaining its increasingly activist role in defense policy and management. Indeed, the JCS reform legislation passed in late 1986, discussed in detail at the end of this chapter, was initiated in the face of intense opposition from DoD. The fact that the most sweeping reform in defense organization since 1958 was the result of congressional initiative is indicative of the desire and willingness of Congress to exercise its constitutional prerogatives concerning the organization of the nation's armed forces in a most forceful way.

American Political Culture

The decentralization of responsibility for defense organization that is inherent in the constitutional system has its roots in American political culture. Critical public attitudes about the desirability and necessity of maintaining large standing forces represent nonstatutory, but nonetheless very real, constraints on the organization of the armed forces. The public's desire for firm civilian control is manifested in a defense organization that maintains a fragmented military structure that until 1986 had not vested the responsibility for military advice in a single military officer and that resists the development of a general staff for the integration of service efforts.

American preoccupation with domestic matters has made it difficult for the nation to prepare for war prudently or to retain significant military forces on active duty once hostilities have been concluded. The absence of compulsory military service for most of the nation's history has had a direct impact on the organization of the U.S. armed forces, putting a relatively fixed cap on the size of the active force that can be maintained, requiring increased reliance on reserve and National Guard forces, and leading policy makers to search for technological innovations whereby qualitative superiority will offset quantitative inferiority.

The federal system also influences the organization of the nation's armed forces, practically ensuring the continued importance of the National Guard. The individual states are responsible for the peacetime administration of their National Guard units, a responsibility that is an important source of political leverage for state officials. Therefore, the individual states have been, and continue to be, powerful proponents of the National Guard system. The states are opposed to proposals, such as those made by Secretary of Defense Robert McNamara in the early 1960s, to unify the National Guard and reserve structure and reduce state influence over the administration of guard units. Consequently, a significant portion of the nation's armed forces continues to be located in the National Guard.

Traditional public attitudes about the nation's role in world affairs were directly confronted by the challenges facing the United States in the post–World War II era. Two generations after the United States assumed its role as the leader of the Western nations, public preoccupation with domestic issues limits the level of effort that the nation devotes to national security matters. Even after the significant increases in defense spending in the first Reagan administration, defense spending consumes less than 28 percent of the federal budget and measures only 6 percent of gross national product (GNP).[8] The point here is not to judge the desirability of these attitudes, but only to indicate the effect that they have on questions of defense organization.

The influence of nongovernmental actors on the organization of the armed forces is indirect. The intense media coverage accorded operational failures such as the Iranian hostage rescue attempt in 1980 and the destruction of the marine barracks in Beirut, Lebanon, in 1983 focuses public attention on the ability of the services to carry out their functions and raises questions concerning the command arrangements for deployed operational forces. Public concern over waste, fraud, and mismanagement, exemplified by the highly publicized accounts of $600 hammers purchased by the Defense Department, also can affect defense organization, particularly with regard to the public's willingness to support annual increases in defense spending.

The indirect influence of public opinion can be substantial. The current interest in reforming the structure and responsibilities of the Joint Chiefs of Staff and various elements within the Office of the Secretary of Defense stems, at least in part, from public concerns about operational command and control arrangements following the episodes at Desert One, in Beirut, and in the invasion of Grenada in 1983.

Decentralization is a fundamental aspect of the American political system, and constitutional authority vested in the president and the Congress specifically ensures that the principle of decentralization applies to defense organization. Deeply held public attitudes about the armed forces reinforce the constitutionally mandated separation of powers. Given the distribution of authority and the public influence described here, it is not surprising that the defense organization of the United States has evolved into its current state over the past two centuries.

THE EVOLUTION OF DEFENSE ORGANIZATION

> The benefits derived from it, I flatter myself will be considerable tho' the plan upon which it is first formed may not be perfect. This like other great works in its first edition, may not be entirely free from error. Time will discover its defects and experience will suggest the remedy, and such further improvements as may be necessary; but it was right to give it a beginning.
> —George Washington at the Creation of the War Office in 1776.

The national security system that has developed since Washington made this observation reflects the constitutional imperatives and public attitudes outlined in the preceding section. A brief examination of the evolution of the nation's defense establishment will illustrate the extent of these influences and provide the basis for the measured consideration of their consequences for defense organization and the implications for U.S. national security.

The Legacy of Decentralization

Decentralization has been a hallmark of the U.S. national security system since the founding of the Republic. The War Department (established in 1789) and the Navy Department (created in 1798) operated as independent agencies from their inception until the creation of the Department of Defense in 1947. For over 150 years, the president was the sole coordinator of the two departments and the only official empowered to resolve disputes between them.

Decentralization was also the primary organizational characteristic within each service. Prior to the twentieth century, there was no chief of staff or general staff to coordinate the activities of the various branches of the service. For example, from the end of the War of 1812 until 1903, the chiefs of the army's technical services (e.g., Quartermaster, Engineers, Ordnance, Signal, Medical, and Finance) reported directly to the secretary of war.[9] As administratively independent agencies, the technical services controlled their own organizations, procedures, personnel, training, supply, and planning functions. They also had control of their own budgets (which usually accounted for over half of the appropriations for the entire army). The technical services dealt directly with the Congress on appropriations matters, an arrangement that ensured the bureaus' administrative independence from centralized supervision and accommodated congressional desires for both administrative and budgetary control.

During the nineteenth century, the small size of the army and navy and the relatively clear division of military missions made presidential supervision of the departments workable. However, as the United States began to emerge as a world power at the turn of the twentieth century, the need for a more effective national security organization became clear. The Spanish-American War, particularly the Cuban campaign, demonstrated serious deficiencies in the performance of the army and navy in both operational and administrative matters. (The deployment of army troops to combat in Cuba dressed in wool uniforms is perhaps the best-known example of administrative deficiencies.) However, despite operational shortcomings, the War and Navy Departments remained autonomous and independent of meaningful central direction. A general staff was established for the army in 1903, removing the secretary of war from the direct supervision of the services' subordinate agencies and bureaus.

The first proposal to create a single executive department for the nation's defense establishment was published in 1921 by Frank Willoughby of the Institute of Government Research (later renamed the Brookings Institution).[10] Willoughby's proposal received considerable attention and became the basis for unification proposals considered by the Congress from 1921 until 1945. Not surprisingly, both the War and Navy Departments opposed the proposals and argued against unification throughout the interwar period. Between 1921 and 1945, Congress considered fifty bills to reorganize the armed forces. Given the opposition of the armed services, only one of these bills reached the floor of the House of Representatives, where it was defeated in 1932 by a vote of 153 to 135.

Movement toward Unification

American entry into World War II demonstrated the need for centralized control of the armed forces. Modern warfare required combined operations by land, sea, and air forces, operations that in turn required not only unity of operational command, but also a coordinated approach for developing the most effective force structure. Shortly after the United States entered the war, President Roosevelt created the Joint Chiefs of Staff. Established initially for the purpose of coordinating with the British Chiefs of Staff, the JCS soon assumed an important role in the planning and direction of U.S. military operations.

The experiences of World War II provided the major impetus for establishing centralized control of the U.S. military establishment. Although the successes of the wartime command arrangement virtually ruled out a return to the prewar independence of the services, they certainly did not suppress the divergent pressures that emanated from traditional attitudes within the services toward organizational independence and from the constitutional balance between the executive branch and Congress.

The National Security Act of 1947 created, in addition to the National Security Council, the nation's first "unified" military establishment. The position of secretary of defense was created to provide the president with a principal staff assistant "in all matters relating to the national security." However, the powers granted to the secretary of defense reflected congressional reluctance to bestow upon the executive branch any additional powers that might weaken the role of Congress in oversight of the military departments. Rather than presiding over a single executive department, the secretary of defense was to preside over a national military establishment composed of three executive departments—army, navy, and air force—each headed by a cabinet-level secretary who retained all of the powers and duties of the office prior to "unification." The resulting organization was characterized some years later by President Eisenhower as "little more than a weak confederation of sovereign military units."[11]

The 1947 act also established the Joint Chiefs of Staff as a permanent body. The membership of the JCS was restricted to four officers: the chiefs of staff of the army and air force (which became a separate and independent service after World War II), the chief of naval operations, and the chief of staff to the commander in chief, "if there be one." The last position was never filled. The law specified that the Joint Chiefs of Staff (as a corporate body) would act as the principal military advisors to the president and the secretary of defense. Other duties of the Joint Chiefs included preparing strategic plans and providing for the strategic direction of the armed forces; establishing unified commands in strategic areas; formulating policies for joint training; preparing joint logistic plans; and reviewing major matériel and personnel requirements of the nation's military forces.

The defense organization created by the National Security Act of 1947 reflected the conflicting pressures inherent in the constitutional system: the recognized need for centralized management and control of the nation's armed forces, balanced against a strong tradition of decentralization and institutional independence, fear of a too-powerful centralized military establishment, and reluctance on the part of the Congress to enhance executive authority at the expense of its own. Not surprisingly, the organization that resulted soon displayed significant shortcomings that needed to be redressed if unification was to be effective.

The 1949 Amendments

In 1949 Congress amended the National Security Act. The resulting changes once again reflected a compromise between the conflicting concepts of unification and decentralization, but they generally represented a step toward unification. The Department of Defense became an executive department, with the secretary of defense responsible for its supervision and general direction. The executive departments of the army, navy, and air force became military departments, although each was to be administered separately. In the Joint Chiefs of Staff, the position of chief of staff to the commander in chief was abolished and replaced by the position of chairman of the Joint Chiefs of Staff. Although the chairman would serve as the presiding officer of the JCS, he was to have no formal vote in its deliberations. The corporate body, not the chairman, retained the statutory position as principal military advisor to the president and secretary of defense.

The 1958 Amendments

Despite the provisions of the 1949 amendment, dissatisfaction with the organizational scheme continued. Interservice rivalry and the national reaction that followed the successful launching of the Sputnik satellite by the Soviet Union in October 1957 led President Eisenhower to request substantial changes in the organization of the military establishment in 1958. The basic authority of the secretary of defense was redefined as "direction, authority, and control over the department of Defense," providing the secretary, for the first time, with the statutory authority to enforce the concept of unification. The office of the secretary of defense was enlarged to give the secretary the staff assistance he needed to carry out his new responsibilities.

The position of the chairman of the JCS also was strengthened. The chairman became a voting member of the body and assumed additional responsibilities in managing the Joint Staff. Later that same year, the operational chain of command was amended to run "from the President to the Secretary of Defense and through the Joint Chiefs of Staff to the commanders of unified and specified commands." In practice, the word "through" means that the JCS are transmitters, not originators, of command orders to deployed operational forces. The institutional adjustments made in 1958 were the last major statutory changes in defense organization prior to the 1986 reforms.

The Key West Agreement of 1948

The combined military operations conducted during World War II and the ensuing debate over unification prompted reconsideration of the roles and missions of the various military services. For example, should the Marine Corps continue to belong to the navy; or should it and its mission be subsumed by the army? What role was there for naval aviation? Shouldn't the newly created air force be responsible for all tactical aviation? Not surprisingly, the Joint Chiefs of Staff were unable to reach agreement on the detailed assignment of service roles and missions. As a result, Secretary of Defense James Forrestal met with the service chiefs at the Key West Naval Base in March 1948. At this conference (and a subsequent meeting in Washington), agreement was negotiated on the assignment of service roles and missions.

The fundamental issue addressed by the participants at the Key West conference concerned the most basic rationale for organizing the nation's armed forces: should each service be given the right to acquire all of the forces it needs to carry out its missions independently, or should the services endeavor to cooperate and prevent unnecessary duplication of forces and equipment? The navy favored the first view; the army and air force the second.

The navy got much of what it wanted. It retained its naval aviation to carry out air operations in support of sea battles; the right to provide its own air transport; and control of antisubmarine warfare. Further, the navy retained control of the Marine Corps and the close air support needed for Marine operations.

The navy insisted on self-sufficiency and largely prevailed. The army and air force decided to rely on navy assets and on each other rather than seek similar levels of independence. Therefore, while the army retained responsibility for land operations and sustained ground combat, it agreed to forgo development of organic close air support and strategic and tactical lift capabilities. For sealift, the army would rely on the navy; for close air support, strategic airlift, and tactical airlift, it would rely on the air force. For its part, the air force maintained primary responsibility for air operations and strategic air warfare.[12]

TABLE 5.1. Primary Service Functions (Key West Agreement, 1948)

Army
sustained combat operations on land
army antiaircraft artillery
primary interest in the development of airborne doctrine, procedures, and equipment

Navy and Marine Corps
sustained combat operations at sea, including operations of sea-based aircraft and their land-based naval air components
naval forces, including naval close air support forces, for the conduct of joint amphibious operations
seizure or defense of advanced naval bases and the conduct of such land campaigns as may be essential to the prosecution of a naval campaign

Air Force
sustained combat operations in the air
strategic air warfare
close combat and logistical air support for the army
air transport for the armed forces

Essentially, the services agreed to operate "by medium;" that is, the army was to conduct combat operations on land, the air force would fight in the air, and the navy would fight at sea. The primary service functions assigned by the Key West agreement are noted in table 5.1. Approved by President Truman on 21 April 1948, the "Key West Agreement" became the basis for the division of labor among the services.

The Key West agreement was, of course, a compromise that created as many problems as it resolved. However, despite a number of clarifications since it was established, there have been no major changes to the portion of the agreement dealing with service roles and missions. The general statements of service roles and missions contained in the agreement have enabled the services to define their legitimate areas of interest very broadly and to determine the relative priority to be accorded the different missions. Once again, the tradition of institutional independence frustrated attempts to construct a truly integrated defense organization.

Unified and Specified Commands

The final organizational development to result from the nation's experience in World War II was the creation of the unified and specified commands that control the deployed operational forces of the various services. As noted above, before World War II, the War Department and Navy Department operated as independent organizations; army and navy units rarely operated together. Interservice disputes during the Spanish-American War were so great that in 1903 the Joint Army and Navy Board was created to address "all matters calling for the cooperation of the two services." The board continued to deal with interservice matters until the Joint Chiefs of Staff were created in 1942.

The operational experiences of World War II, marked by numerous threats, multiservice operations, and increasingly sophisticated weapons systems, demonstrated that mutual cooperation between the services was no longer adequate. As General George Marshall, chief of staff of the army, remarked: "I am convinced that there must be one man in command of the entire theater—air, ground, and ships. We cannot manage by cooperation."[13]

The National Security Act of 1947 provided for the establishment of unified commands and assigned the JCS the responsibility for establishing "unified commands in strategic areas when such unified commands are in the interest of national security." In execution, however, the military department that raised and supported the forces also retained operational control of deployed forces.

The 1958 amendment to the national security act fundamentally changed the operational command arrangements. President Eisenhower, in proposing the revisions, stated:

Separate ground, sea, and air warfare is gone forever. If ever again we should be involved in war, we will fight it in all elements, with all services, as one single concentrated effort. Peacetime preparatory and organizational activity must conform to this fact. Strategic and tactical planning must be completely unified, combat forces organized into unified commands, each equipped with the most efficient weapons systems that science can develop, singly led and prepared to fight as one, regardless of service.[14]

Accordingly, the 1958 Reorganization Act established that the operational commanders would report directly to the secretary of defense. The military departments and service chiefs were eliminated from the chain of command. The command arrangements established by the 1958 act remain the basis for the current operational command structure. The commanders of the unified and specified commands report directly to the secretary of defense. The military services are responsible for the administrative and logistical support of the forces assigned to the various operational commands.

Today, there are eight unified commands and three specified commands in the operational command structure. The unified commands are mostly geographically based, whereas the specified commands are responsible for the execution of particular functions.[15] Currently, there are eight unified commands (European, Pacific, Atlantic, Southern, Central, Special Operations, Space and Transportation) and three specified commands (Strategic Air, Aerospace, and Military Airlift). The names of the commands designate their primary geographic or functional area of responsibility. (Central Command, created in 1983, has responsibility for the Persian Gulf region.)

Although the unified command structure establishes the concept of unification in theory, in practice the individual services retain a great deal of influence for two basic reasons. First, the subordinate commands of the unified commands are essentially single service commands. Further, the unified commander exercises operational command through the service component commanders. For example, the European Command is composed of the U.S. Army Europe, U.S. Air Force Europe, and U.S. Navy Europe, all single service component commands. The commander of the European Command exercises control through the commanders of these component commands.

The second reason for service influence is that the component commanders depend on their respective services for resources. The tanks assigned to the U.S. Army Europe are designed, developed, procured, and supported by the army, just as planes and ships are bought by the air force and navy. The unified commander has little direct control over the structure of the forces or the nature of the equipment assigned to him. Therefore, service perspectives on organization, doctrine, equipment, and mission priorities continue to be the dominant determinents of the structure of the nation's military forces.

Consequences for the Institutional System

The national security system that has evolved during the nation's history reflects both the constitutional division of authority and deeply held public attitudes concerning the desirability of maintaining standing armed forces. The assumption of great power responsibilities by the United States in the years after World War II led, perhaps inevitably, to conflict between constitutional imperatives, public attitudes, and the need for a defense establishment that reflects the nation's position in international political and military affairs. The acquisition of worldwide interests and commitments notwithstanding, the constitutional system and the public that supports it have had a significant impact on the organization of the nation's defense establishment. These influences have resulted in two significant consequences: incomplete centralization and the dominance of service interests.

Incomplete Centralization

As the discussion of the evolution of defense organization makes clear, decentralization has both constitutional and attitudinal roots. Only in the past half century has the United States made a serious effort to bring the disparate elements of its armed forces under centralized control and management. Although the desire to erect an organizational structure that facilitated the integration of the efforts of the separate services was the foundation of the reform acts of 1947 and 1958, the process has been completed only imperfectly. Although the statutory authority of the secretary of defense provides a legal basis for control, in reality the secretary's political authority is insufficient to enable him to manage the Department of Defense effectively. As John Ries notes, "Regardless of what the folklore of organization prescribes, leadership and control have a political rather than a statutory base.[16]

Powerful organizations such as the services vigorously pursuing their own agendas effectively reduce the authority of the secretary of defense. This decentralization is mandated in part by the constitution. The congressional role in the development and implementation of defense policy ensures that centralization will never be complete.

However, Congress is not the only source of institutional decentralization. Other executive agencies can also act in ways that limit the secretary's influence and control. The Joint Chiefs of Staff, the individual military services, even subordinate officials with independent political bases within the Office of the Secretary of Defense can pursue interests that do not coincide with those of the secretary.

Competition among public service organizations is not without benefit. William Niskanen has observed that competition among bureaus promotes efficiency by reducing the cost of a specific service. Furthermore, redundancy can ensure against the possibility of the catastrophic failure of one or more programs. In Niskanen's view, the Key West agreement was a cartel agreement among the military services to divide the major military missions among bureau lines.[17]

While there certainly are advantages to be gained by competitive approaches to the accomplishment of specific missions, there are important limits on the extent to which competition can contribute to the basic structure of U.S. military forces. In a budget-constrained environment, where the accomplishment of specific military missions is essential for the effective coordination and employment of military force, competition among the services in various mission areas would divert both effort and resources. Since success in modern warfare depends on the ability to carry out every necessary task, the requirement to ensure that such capabilities exist outweighs the marginal improvements in efficiency that might result from extensive interservice competition. Given the multitude of important tasks, the always limited resources available, and service predilections concerning mission priorities, the centralization of management authority is necessary to ensure the coherent development and maintenance of the forces and equipment required to carry out critical military tasks.

The impetus for the centralization of management authority in DoD and the vesting of statutory authority and responsibility over DoD activities in the secretary of defense was the recognition that the nature of modern warfare requires the integration of land, air, and sea capabilities. Opposing the acknowledged need for greater central authority are the constitutional division of responsibilities, long-standing public doubts about the accumulation of too much power by any one official, and powerful bureaucratic forces. Taken together, these influences seem to ensure that the centralization of decision-making authority in the Department of Defense will be achieved imperfectly, if at all.

The secretary of defense is not the only official who suffers from the effects of incomplete centralization. The institutional structure and statutory authority of the Joint Chiefs of Staff also reflect the reluctance of the American public to vest too much authority in a central military organization. The advisory and planning responsibilities of the JCS reside not in the chairman but in the JCS as a corporate body. Unity of command—that is, vesting decision-making authority and responsibility in a single official at every echelon—is gospel in military organizations. Ironically, at the very highest level of the nation's military establishment that principle has been purposively violated.

Not only has the central direction of the JCS been circumscribed by law, the very nature of the organization militates against integration. Every member of the JCS, save the chairman, is also the chief of staff of his respective service. This "dual hat" responsibility makes it extremely unlikely that the members of the JCS will subordinate their own natural predilections for their service's perspectives when addressing joint issues that have direct impact on their service.

The final manifestation of incomplete centralization is the absence of a general staff consisting of specialists trained to integrate the activities of the separate services. Normally, general staff officers become "purple suiters" who are no longer tied to a specific service. Public concern about a "Prussian style" general staff is evident in the reluctance of the nation to develop a true general staff. The services, with their tradition of institutional independence, also do not support the creation of such a staff. Rather than becoming members of a separate general staff corps, members of the Joint Staff retain their service affiliation. They are paid and promoted by their parent organization, and they must return to that organization upon completion of their tour on the Joint Staff. Not surprisingly, many Joint Staff officers tend to be spokesmen for their services rather than impartial evaluators of which policies and programs would best serve the interests of the nation. The lack of an effective general staff makes coordination and integration of the activities of the various services essentially impossible.

Service Dominance

The intent of the National Security Act of 1947 was to establish an organizational structure that provided for the integration of the armed forces "into an efficient team of land, naval, and air forces." However, the efforts at centralization have been, at least to a certain degree, unsuccessful. The effect of incomplete centralization is that the services have been able to maintain their organizational independence and influence.

Service dominance is manifested in two fundamental ways. First, the individual services determine what forces, weapons, and capabilities will be available to carry out national military strategy. Although the secretary of defense and the Joint Chiefs of Staff do have some influence on these issues, the services generally have been able to develop their organizational structure in accordance with their own institutional priorities. The services achieve this influence through their statutory responsibility for recruiting and training their forces, as well as for the administration and logistical support of deployed forces. Furthermore, each service is responsible for its own force planning and weapons acquisition (subject to supervision by the secretary of defense). Since military services train, organize, equip, and support the deployed operational forces assigned to the commanders of the unified and specified commands, it is hardly surprising that these forces reflect service interests, priorities, and decisions.

The second source of service dominance is through the policy-making apparatus. As Archie Barrett has noted, the services have coopted the joint decision-making structure through the dual roles of the service chiefs, overwhelming influence in the joint staff, involvement in the selection of unified and specified commanders, and predominant influence over the component commands of the unified and specified commands. As Barrett concludes, "the military input into decisionmaking, whether through the service secretaries, the JCS, the Joint Staff, CINCs, or components, is predominantly service-oriented."[18]

IMPLICATIONS FOR NATIONAL SECURITY POLICY

What are the implications of the institutional system described here for national security policy? What effect do the systemic characteristics of incomplete centralization and service dominance have on the mechanisms for integrating the advice of senior military officials into the design of national strategy and policy and in the structure and capabilities of the armed forces? In order to assess the implications of these characteristics, one must consider their impact on four critical functions of defense policy: (1) strategic planning and advice; (2) resource allocation; (3) force structuring; and (4) joint operations. An assessment of the ability of the United States to carry out these important functions will provide the basis for conclusions about the impact of the constitutional system on the development of an effective national security system.

Strategic Planning and Advice

Strategic planning is the process of linking ends (national objectives established by political authorities) and means (the military forces, weapons, and capabilities developed by the military services). Inherent in the process of strategic planning is the assessment of threats to national interests and of needs to meet those threats. Since resources inevitably will be constrained, strategic planning requires the determination of priorities among interests (e.g., Europe, Northeast Asia, the Persian Gulf) and among capabilities (e.g., nuclear versus conventional forces, forward deployments versus strategic mobility, active forces versus reserves, modernization versus sustainability). Strategic planning must address and resolve critical questions about how forces are to be employed: offensively or defensively, in a long war or a short war, simultaneously in many regions or sequentially across regions. Resolution of these conceptual issues leads to more specific considerations concerning the types of forces (ground divisions, carrier battle groups, tactical air forces) and weapons needed to implement the strategic plans.

Effective strategic planning, therefore, requires consideration of these issues from a national, rather than service, perspective. By law, the Joint Chiefs of Staff are responsible for the preparation of strategic plans. However, as the preceding discussion has indicated, the JCS system is not structured to provide the national, cross-service perspectives essential to the effective determination of priorities. Because the JCS system is service-dominated at the expense of any joint or national perspective, bureaucratic politics and service interests have a greater influence on JCS planning than systemic strategic thinking.[19] Instead of developing a system for coherent strategic planning, the members of the JCS continue to give priority to their role as spokesmen for their services, and Joint Staff officers continue to bargain among themselves, each trying to get the most for his or her service.

The inherent conflict of interest in the structure of the JCS system and its staff has three important consequences for strategic planning. First, strategic planning tends to be neglected. Attention is focused instead on issues affecting service interests, especially resource allocation. The JCS rarely, if ever, has taken the lead in developing new strategic concepts or approaches, with the attendant establishment of priorities among and across the services' roles and missions.[20] As Lawrence Korb concludes in his study of the JCS: "The JCS has become so bogged down in the cumbersome process which is so concerned with protecting each chief's own service interests that it has become addicted to the status quo and has never been a source of innovation in the national security policy-making apparatus."[21]

Second, to the extent that the JCS does develop strategic plans, they tend not to be constrained by realistic fiscal limits. This approach reduces the necessity to make tough trade-off decisions between service priorities and programs, thereby reducing interservice conflict and facilitating agreement on the plans by the individual chiefs. This approach also allows each service to develop the capabilities it wants. Furthermore, this unintegrated strategic approach allows the services to plan to fight different types of wars, resulting in a force structure that is not optimally designed to conduct joint operations.[22]

The third consequence of the inability of the JCS to conduct effective strategic planning is that the function has been assumed by civilian agencies. Subordinate bureaus within the Office of the Secretary of Defense, particularly that of the under secretary of defense for policy and the Office of Program Analysis and Evaluation, have become important actors in the shaping of national military strategy. Although the development of strategy by civilian agencies is not inherently undesirable, two points are pertinent to the problem. First, strategic planning is a primary function of the nation's military leadership; knowledgeable, experienced military officers ought to be intimately involved in the process, making recommendations to civilian leaders on cross-service priorities and the trade-offs necessary to construct a coherent defense program. Second, strategic plans have to be implemented by military officers. If these plans are to be realistic, pertinent, and appropriate, the senior military officials should provide the benefit of their expertise and experience in their development.

In addition to their responsibility for strategic planning, the Joint Chiefs of Staff are, by statute, the "principal military advisors to the President, the National Security Council, and the Secretary of Defense." Professional military advice is an essential ingredient for the effective management and direction of the defense establishment. Important issues on which the senior military leadership should advise civilian leaders include the formulation of national strategy, the allocation of service roles and missions, and the allocation of scarce resources among competing defense needs. However, just as with the task of strategic planning, the structure of the JCS system makes it difficult for the chiefs to provide effective, cross-service advice on issues that affect important service interests or programs.

The inadequacies of JCS advice have been observed for more than three decades. Blue ribbon panels investigating defense organization in 1949, 1960, 1970, 1978, 1982, and 1986 were unanimous in their verdict that the JCS system is generally seen by civilian leaders as unable to provide useful advice on many issues. Joint staff work is perceived as superficial, predictable, and of little help in resolving issues.[23]

The cause of the difficulty is, of course, the structure of the joint military system. As the senior military planning and advisory body, the Joint Chiefs are responsible for providing advice that transcends individual service interests. However, each chief also serves as the military leader of his service, making it difficult, if not impossible, for him not to defend his service's position in the joint forum. Further, the procedures of the JCS for drafting and coordinating documents ensure that each service must pass on every issue at every level. Therefore, when joint advice is proffered, it all too often will have been diluted by its passage through the cumbersome staff procedures that are designed to accommodate the interests of all four services.[24] Former Secretary of Defense James Schlesinger characterized the problem as follows:

The central weakness of the existing system lies in the structure of the Joint Chiefs of Staff. . . . The existing structure, if it does not preclude the best military advice, provides a substantial, though not insurmountable, barrier to such advice. Suffice it to say that the recommendations and the plans of the chiefs must pass through a screen designed to protect the institutional interests of each of the separate services. The general rule is that no service ox may be gored.[25]

The result of this process is advice that is not well received by those officials for whom it is intended. As David Jones, a former chairman of the Joint Chiefs of Staff, acknowledges, the corporate advice provided by the Joint Chiefs of Staff is not very useful or very influential. Consequently, "the resulting lack of credibility has caused the national leadership to look elsewhere for recommendations that properly should come from the JCS."[26]

Although civilian leaders consistently praise the advice they receive from the individual chiefs of the services, they also almost uniformly criticize the institutional products of the JCS as ponderous in presentation, predictably wedded to the status quo, and reactive rather than innovative.[27] The result, as James Schlesinger described bluntly, is that the "proffered advice is generally irrelevant, normally unread, and almost always ignored."[28]

The result of the inability of the JCS to provide useful advice is that the gap has again been filled by civilian advisors, serving as the major source of advice to the secretary of defense or the president on matters for which insightful military inputs would have been more desirable. Military advice from a national perspective is thus unavailable to civilian decision makers, who are therefore forced to provide this perspective themselves, whether or not they are qualified to do so.[29] The development of force structures and weapons within feasible budgets and the resolution of contentious joint military issues are the very decisions most difficult for the secretary of defense, the president, and the Congress to make. Thus, the views of senior military officials do not carry the weight they could in the decision-making process, especially in those areas where it could be most useful and influential. The ultimate result, as Schlesinger concluded, "is that decisions regarding the level of expenditures and the design of forces are made by civilians outside of the military structure."[30]

Resource Allocation

In no other area is the impact of the constitutional system on the national security system greater than with regard to the function of resource allocation. The constitutional allocation of budget authority to the Congress, coupled with increased congressional willingness to become involved in the details of the operation and structure of the defense establishment, ensures the active participation of the legislature in debates over resource allocation. Within the executive branch, the same organizational characteristics that inhibit strategic planning and advice also make rational, cross-service resource planning and allocation difficult, if not impossible.

The inherent conflict of interest between the joint and service responsibilities of the members of the Joint Chiefs of Staff prevents the use of the joint forum for effective resource planning and allocation. A service chief's responsibility to lead and manage his service virtually precludes his agreement to joint force planning recommendations that are inconsistent with the programs supported by his service. A chief of service cannot be expected to argue for additional programs for his service when preparing his service's budget request and then become a critic of that proposal in the joint forum or agree that another service's programs are more deserving of support. As a result, the Joint Chiefs of Staff are generally unable to establish cross-service priorities and make the necessary trade-off decisions required to construct a defense budget within realistic fiscal constraints. Instead, JCS recommendations generally endorse the full program proposed by each service.

Such recommendations are of limited value to the secretary of defense in the actual allocation of defense resources, since they make no judgments as to program priorities or trade-offs. The secretary of defense must therefore make force structure decisions without the benefit of fiscally constrained, cross-service military advice. Just as with strategic planning, he must rely on his civilian staff. Since budget requests are prepared by the individual services, budgetary priorities tend to be established in separate dialogues between the Office of the Secretary of Defense and the individual services, with minimal joint military participation.[31]

The result is that service interests rather than strategic needs play the dominant role in shaping program and resource allocation decisions. Instead of a rational choice of programs and weapons most needed to serve national purposes, the choices are determined largely by service needs and service interests. Service views on mission priorities determine which programs will be funded, which weapons will be developed and procured, and which roles will be neglected because of "budget constraints."

The predominance of service goals in the resource allocation process stems from the lack of strategic planning. Each service is essentially free to pursue its own vision of what the next war will be like and, hence, what forces it will need to fight that war. In the absence of strategic guidance, service goals tend to be expressed in terms of force structure: a 600-ship navy, an 18-division army, an air force with 40 air wings. The problem, of course, is that force structure is properly the instrument of strategy, not its goal. In the absence of realistic strategic planning, however, service goals tend to supplant strategic goals.[32]

The dominance of programs over strategy is exacerbated by the demands of the annual budget cycle. As Samuel Huntington points out, the annual authorization and appropriation processes divert the attention of senior military officials from planning to fight next year's possible war to planning to fight next year's inevitable budget battles. The military services may, understandably, be more concerned with the latter than the former.[33] The budget review processes of both houses of Congress reinforce the emphasis on programs rather than policies. When Congress reviews the annual budget requests, it tends to examine the details of the request as accounting inputs for functional activities rather than as defense mission outputs. Thus, the defense budget is considered by "line items" (tanks, planes, ships) rather than in terms of mission outputs (strategic deterrence, regional stability). This pattern of reviewing programs within categories of resource inputs makes it difficult for Congress to obtain a comprehensive picture of current defense capabilities. Further, Congress tends to review the services' programs in relative isolation. Funding trade-offs rarely cross service appropriation lines.

Finally, the budget review procedures of Congress force the senior civilian and military officials to follow suit. Congressional concern with specific programs makes the secretary of defense and the chiefs of the military services concentrate on justifications for individual programs rather than on service or department activities that, when taken together, provide a coherent and balanced defense effort.

The constitutional division of budget authority has led to the development of close ties between the defense-related committees and subcommittees of Congress and the individual military services. These ties can make the management and control of the defense establishment by the secretary of defense even more difficult, since Congress can be (and often is) used as a "court of appeal" to overturn an unfavorable budget ruling by the secretary on a favored service program. This noteworthy aspect of the constitutional system tends to perpetuate the independence of the military services. Congress historically has favored decentralization in the Department of Defense, since decentralization permits Congress to establish direct relationships with and control over those organizations within the services that are responsible for directing the allocation of resources, thereby maximizing congressional leverage over the distribution of those resources. In sum, the structure and decentralized procedures of Congress amplify the fragmentation of the defense establishment, which in turn inhibits the development of a coherent, integrated defense program.

Force Structuring

The implications of incomplete centralization and service dominance are pronounced in the function of force structuring. The tradition of organizational independence combines with the public and congressional presumption of professional expertise by officers of the separate services to make centralized control in the structuring and equipping of the services extremely difficult.

A service's structure tends to reflect what Morton Halperin has called "organizational essence," that is, the view held by the dominant group within the organization of what its missions and capabilities should be.[34] An organization will press hardest for those capabilities that it views as necessary to the essence of the institution. For the armed services, essence is reflected through the force structure (military units such as army divisions, air force wings, or navy fleets) and weapons systems (equipment such as tanks, planes, and ships) that give it the capability to carry out what it believes to be its primary functions. Furthermore, service views on organizational essence were sanctified by the Key West agreement of 1948. Since that time, the services have been free to develop force structures that they believe contribute to the accomplishment of the service's essential roles and missions. Consequently, service perspectives on mission priorities have been influential in determining the shape of both forces and programs.

The codification of roles and missions since the Key West agreement has had two important consequences for the structuring of the U.S. armed forces. First, service interests and priorities have led to imbalances in military capabilities. Although every service is responsible for a number of essential functions, fiscal constraints require the establishment of priorities among missions. Therefore, although high priority missions such as air superiority in the air force or power projection in the navy receive attention and funding, functions that are not central to a service's own conception of its essence tend to be neglected. As a result, when the capabilities required for effective joint military operations fail to coincide with the mission priorities of the individual services involved, significant deficiencies can develop.

For example, the Key West agreement gave the air force and navy responsibility for providing the army with crucial strategic (across a geographic theater) and tactical (within a geographic theater) lift support. However, providing airlift capabilities for army forces diverts resources from the essential air force missions of strategic bombing and air superiority, just as providing sealift is secondary to the navy's missions of sea control and power projection. Therefore, airlift and sealift have not been high priority programs for the air force and navy. As a result, the army lacks strategic and tactical lift capacity to deploy and sustain significant ground combat forces in accordance with existing U.S. security goals and contingency plans. The creation of the army's controversial light infantry divisions was, in large part, a reaction to the lack of adequate strategic airlift for more robust forces. Close air support of ground combat operations is another function that has not been accorded high priority by the air force. Since close air support is critical for the conduct of ground operations, the army, prevented by the Key West agreement from developing its own tactical air force, has been forced to develop expensive attack helicopters to accomplish that mission.

The second consequence of the division of responsibility established by the Key West agreement is that it has placed artificial constraints on the development of force capabilities to meet the changing needs of warfare. The services have been unable to adjust traditional missions and develop cooperative approaches to keep pace with the evolution of modern warfare.[35] New missions that could detract from more traditional ones are opposed. For example, the navy, interested primarily in sea control and power projection, not strategic bombardment, initially opposed assuming responsibility for the development of ballistic-missile-carrying submarines, but the air force was precluded from doing so by the rules of the Key West agreement. That agreement also precludes innovative solutions to problems. The ongoing development of the MX missile (now labeled Peacekeeper) program was expanded to address the problems of the perceived vulnerability of land-based intercontinental missiles. However, a militarily effective and politically acceptable basing scheme for the missiles on land has been elusive. Although many analysts believe that basing the missile on small submarines is an attractive solution to the problem, the option was never considered seriously. MX is an air force program; submarines belong to the navy.[36]

Modern warfare requires the accomplishment of missions that do not coincide with the accepted division of responsibility between the military services. Electronic warfare and command, control, and communications are functions that cannot be accomplished effectively by each service individually. Integration and coordination are essential if the nation's armed forces are to be able to operate on the modern battlefield. Furthermore, modern technology has provided capabilities that should be exploited, but that may not coincide with traditional approaches to mission accomplishment or to the accepted division of mission responsibility. Relatively inexpensive remotely piloted vehicles (pilotless drones), for example, can be used for electronic warfare, surveillance, target acquisition, even weapons employment. However, such systems do not conform to traditional air force notions about using piloted aircraft to accomplish these functions. The army, constrained by the Key West agreement, is limited to developing such vehicles for use by the field artillery as observation platforms. Consequently, the development of remotely piloted vehicles lags, making a significant (and demonstrable, as evidenced by Israeli use of such platforms) capability unavailable for use by the nation's armed forces.

Joint Operations

The final critical function for consideration is perhaps the most crucial. Can the nation's armed forces perform their most basic task—that is, can they conduct joint military operations, bringing land, sea and air power to bear in an effective, integrated fashion? Just as with the three functions already examined, incomplete centralization and service dominance have affected the ability of the armed forces to accomplish this aspect of organizational responsibility. These characteristics have resulted in two significant shortcomings: an unintegrated forces structure and inadequate command arrangements for the direction of deployed forces.

Effective joint operations require the development of, and adherence to, joint doctrine (that is, agreed-upon principles about how the services will carry out military functions, such as the use of tactical air power [air force, navy, or marine] by army or marine ground forces), the continuous conduct of joint training, and the practice of joint planning. However, the force structure of the nation's armed forces has been created by the institutionally independent services, acting in accordance with their own priorities and perceptions, without effective centralized control or direction. The result is an unintegrated force structure and an operational environment that does not promote emphasis on joint capabilities. Little attention has been paid to the development of joint doctrine, and the military educational system, as well as the services' career development practices, do little to encourage specialists in joint military planning and operations. Furthermore, the services have been reluctant to cooperate on the development of joint requirements for equipment; consequently, each service develops its own weapons and equipment independently, with little regard for the advantages of commonality or, at the very least, compatability and interoperability. This approach ensures an unintegrated force structure, as vividly illustrated by the well-publicized incident during operations in Grenada in 1983 when army soldiers on the ground were unable to communicate with navy pilots flying over them.

The tradition of service independence can also affect the command and control arrangements for the direction of employed operational forces. In Vietnam, for example, the commander of the Military Assistance Command, Vietnam, did not command the carrier task forces operating off the coast or the B-52 bombers flying from Guam. Instead of integrating their efforts, each service, as General David Jones has observed, "considered

Vietnam its own war and sought to carve out a large mission for itself. . . . Lack of integration persisted right through the 1975 evacuation of Saigon."[37] The desire for service participation and service autonomy was also evident in operations in Grenada. Although the island is a relatively small one, operational areas and command over the employed ground forces were divided between the army and the marines.

The effects of incomplete centralization and service dominance also limit the control that the unified and specified commanders exercise over the component commands. Since the services are responsible for the administrative and logistical support of their forces, the component commander is responsible to the unified commander on operational matters and his service for everything else. Furthermore, the unified commander has no direct control over the resources allocated to his command. Budget requests are submitted by the services, not by operational commanders. Although the unified commander can make his priorities for resources known through the component commanders, the services may or may not heed his recommendations. The chairman of the JCS is the spokesman for the operational commanders, but until the 1986 reorganization act, he had no substantive role in the budget process. As a group, the JCS is unwilling to make recommendations on cross-service or cross-theater priorities. Consequently, the services are the major influence on the structure of the forces assigned to the unified commanders. The training, equipping, and structuring of forces is not carried out by the individuals responsible for their employment in combat. In sum, an unintegrated force structure and service dominance over the component commands detract from the ability of the unified commanders to create and maintain forces capable of conducting effective joint operations.

CONCLUSIONS

What conclusions can be drawn from this examination of the effect of the constitutional system on the organization of the armed forces? What characteristics are the result of the influence of the constitutional system on the national security system rather than simply manifestations of organizational behavior common to all bureaucratic systems?

The fundamental impact of the constitutional system seems to be the inability of the United States to create a security apparatus that has a truly national perspective on the issues associated with organizing the armed services. The result of this fragmented national security system has been an organizational structure and decision-making process that reflect the incomplete centralization of authority over the armed forces. Incomplete centralization, in turn, allows the perspectives of the individual services to dominate the institutional environment and control to a considerable degree the functions and structure of the armed forces. The implications of incomplete centralization and service dominance for the nation's ability to carry out the functions of strategic planning and advice, resource allocation, force structuring, and joint operations suggest that the constitutional system has had a significant impact on the ability of the United States to create and maintain a defense establishment that emphasizes a unified, integrated, national approach to the problem of organizing its armed forces. Without such an approach, the United States is neither as effective as it could be in international politics nor as reliable as it should be as the leader of the Western nations.

The validity of this conclusion is buttressed by the passage of a defense reorganization act in September 1986, the first significant attempt at organizational reform since 1958. Public and congressional concern over the ability of the defense establishment effectively to carry out the functions described in this chapter resulted in legislation that fundamentally altered the statutory responsibilities of the Joint Chiefs of Staff and sought to enhance the authority of the unified commanders over their subordinate commands. The chairman of the Joint Chiefs of Staff has been given statutory authority as the principal military advisor to the president, the National Security Council, and the secretary of defense. The chairman also has been given supervisory control of the Joint Staff and a larger role in setting priorities and drafting military strategies. Finally, the chairman will play a much larger role in the budget process by providing realistic, fiscally constrained budget priorities to the secretary of defense and budget guidance to the services.

Although no one can predict whether the new organizational structure will alleviate the problems outlined here, it is clear that reform of the system was necessary and overdue. The new system is aimed at reducing the problems that result from incomplete centralization, especially that of service dominance. A vigorous chairman of the JCS and more influential unified commanders could make the institutional structure much more capable of carrying out its responsibilities effectively and efficiently. One should not expect change to come easily or quickly. Nonetheless, the legislative reforms of 1947, 1958, and now 1986 do represent attempts to reconcile the structural decentralization of the constitutional system with the requirements of modern military organization and planning. These efforts have made some progress. However, separation of powers in a federal structure is an inherent characteristic of the constitutional system, and it seems safe to assume that the national security system of the United States will continue to reflect the influence of its constitutionally inspired heritage.

NOTES

1. Richard E. Neustadt, *Presidential Power* (New York: Wiley, 1960), p. 33.
2. Daniel J. Kaufman, Jeffrey S. McKitrick, and Thomas J. Leney, eds., *U.S. National Security* (Lexington, Mass.: Lexington Books, 1985), p. 162.
3. Sec. 133(b), Title 10, U.S. Code.
4. For a complete discussion of the nature of organizational interests within the Department of Defense, see Morton H. Halperin, *Bureaucratic Politics and Foreign Policy* (Washington, D.C.: Brookings Institution, 1974).
5. For a more complete discussion of the causes of increased congressional involvement in national security affairs, see Richard Haass, *Congressional Power: Implications for American Security Policy,* Adelphi Paper no. 153 (London: International Institute for Strategic Studies, 1979), and Wallace E. Walker, "Domesticating Foreign Policy: Congress and the Vietnam War," in George K. Osborn, Asa A. Clark, Daniel J. Kaufman, and Douglas E. Lute, eds., *Democracy, Strategy, and Vietnam* (Lexington Mass.: Lexington Books, 1987), chap. 5.
6. Norman J. Ornstein et al., *Vital Statistics on Congress* (Washington, D.C.: American Enterprise Institute, 1984), pp. 125–26.
7. U.S. Congress, Senate, Committee on Armed Services, *Defense Organization: The Need for Change,* 99th Cong., 1st sess. (Washington, D.C.: GPO 1985), p. 592. Hereafter referred to as *SASC Staff Report.*
8. Caspar W. Weinberger, *Annual Report to the Congress, Fiscal Year 1987* (Washington, D.C.: GPO, 1986), p. 315.
9. James E. Hewes, Jr., *From Root to McNamara: Army Organization and Administration, 1900–1963* (Washington, D.C.: U.S. Army Center of Military History, 1975), p. 98.
10. *SASC Staff Report,* p. 49.
11. *SASC Staff Report,* p. 51.
12. Barry M. Blechman and William J. Lynn, eds., *Toward a More Effective Defense* (Cambridge, Mass.: Ballinger, 1985), p. 114.
13. Robert E. Sherwood, *Roosevelt and Hopkins: An Intimate History* (New York: Harper, 1948), p. 455.
14. President Dwight D. Eisenhower, message to the Congress, 3 April 1958, contained in *The Department of Defense: Documents on Establishment and Organization, 1944–1978* (Washington, D.C.: GPO, 1978), p. 149.
15. A unified command has a broad, continuing mission (usually geographically based) and is composed of significant forces from two or more services. A specified command has a functional mission and is composed primarily of forces from one service.
16. John C. Ries, *The Management of Defense* (Baltimore: Johns Hopkins University Press, 1964), p. 200.
17. William A. Niskanen, Jr., *Bureaucracy and Representative Government* (Chicago: Aldine-Atherton, 1971), pp. 161, 200. See chap. 15 for a discussion of bureaucratic behavior in a competitive environment.
18. Archie D. Barrett, *Reappraising Defense Organization* (Washington, D.C.: National Defense University, 1983), pp. 79–80.
19. For a more complete discussion of the role of the JCS in making strategy, see Robert W. Komer, "Strategymaking in the Pentagon," in Robert J. Art, Vincent Davis, and Samuel P. Huntington, eds., *Reorganizing America's Defense* (Washington, D.C.: Pergamon Press, 1985), pp. 212–15.
20. Samuel P. Huntington, "Organization and Strategy," in ibid., p. 236.

21. Lawrence J. Korb, *The Joint Chiefs of Staff: The First Twenty-Five Years* (Bloomington: Indiana University Press, 1976), p. 24.
22. Huntington, "Organization and Strategy," p. 237.
23. The panels were: 1949, Eberstadt Committee; 1960, Symington Report; 1970, Blue Ribbon Defense Panel; 1978, Steadman Report; 1982, Chairman's Special Study Group; 1986, Packard Commission. For a detailed history of the various panels that have investigated defense organization, see Edgar F. Raines, Jr., and David R. Campbell, *The Army and the Joint Chiefs of Staff: Evolution of Army Ideas on the Command, Control, and Coordination of the U.S. Armed Forces, 1942–1985* (Washington, D.C.: U.S. Army Center of Military History, 1986).
24. Blechman and Lynn, *More Effective Defense*, pp. 48–49.
25. U.S. Congress, Senate, Committee on Armed Services, Hearings, *Organization, Structure and Decisionmaking Procedures of the Department of Defense*, 98 Cong., 1st sess. (Washington, D.C.: GPO, 1984), part 5, p. 187. Hereafter cited as *Senate Hearings on Organization of DoD.*
26. U.S. Congress, House, Committee on Armed Services, Hearings, *Reorganization Proposals for the Joint Chiefs of Staff*, 97th Cong., 2d sess. (Washington D.C.: GPO, 1982), p. 54.
27. Blechman and Lynn, *More Effective Defense*, p. 48.
28. *Senate Hearings on Organization of DoD*, p. 187.
29. Barrett, *Reappraising Defense Organization*, p. 80.
30. *Senate Hearings in Organization of DoD*, p. 187.
31. Blechman and Lynn, *More Effective Defense*, p. 10.
32. Huntington, "Organization and Strategy," p. 241.
33. Ibid., p. 236.
34. Morton H. Halperin, *Bureaucratic Politics and Foreign Policy* (Washington, D.C.: Brookings Institution, 1974), p. 28.
35. *SASC Staff Report*, p. 633.
36. Blechman and Lynn, *More Effective Defense*, p. 115.
37. David C. Jones, "What's Wrong with Our Defense Establishment?" *New York Times Magazine*, 7 November 1982, p. 70.

6

Equipping the Armed Forces

HARVEY M. SAPOLSKY

Although the drafters of the Constitution would be awestruck by the sight of an Apache helicopter firing its missiles or of a Tomcat interceptor being launched from the deck of an aircraft carrier, they would find the issues that underlie the acquisition of these weapons much less unfamiliar. Today, just as they did in 1787, we seek to make representative government both responsive and effective. We wonder, as they did, whether or not a government sufficiently strong to meet external challenges is too powerful to allow liberty to flourish domestically. We struggle, again, as they once did, to find the right balance between regional and national interests, between individual freedom and collective security, and between administrative convenience and political accountability.

To be sure, our world is quite different from the one in which the representatives of the several states met to reformulate the government of the American union. No longer does the ocean provide the assured protection it once did. No longer can we depend on the mobilization of citizen soldiers alone to provide for our security. The past fifty years in particular have seen both America's status among nations and the weapons of warfare change drastically. Our national security interests have grown, while the time to prepare to defend them has shortened to the point of disappearing.

But the way we approach this twentieth-century world is shaped very much by the men who participated in the eighteenth-century constitutional convention. The decisions that they made then to constrain the exercise of political power through various structural checks and balances gave us the institutions and processes that must now cope with our current responsibilities. That we find the governmental framework that they devised at times exceedingly awkward for dealing with a changed world is not surprising. The fact that the framework survives unaltered stands as evidence of the enduring truths that they discovered. Apparently we fear more becoming like our enemies than we do our ability to match their strength within the limits of our constitutional system.

There is, however, reason for concern. The once-mundane task of equipping the military in peacetime has become a severe test of our form of government. More than ever before, the weapons at hand are the weapons that defend the nation. It is not an exaggeration to say that peace, and potentially even our freedom as well, depends upon our capacity to maintain technological advantage in the tools of war. And yet the political system gives little recognition to the danger, preferring instead to treat each weapon purchase, each new project, as another opportunity to bargain for personal, organizational, or regional gain. If they are to survive, it would seem, institutions and processes that have been so adept in absorbing domestic conflict through compromise among factions must now be able to choose among factions to find the appropriate support required for the military.

FROM ARSENALS TO THE ARSENAL OF DEMOCRACY

Memorable victories notwithstanding, our history is hardly a martial one. Our wars have been infrequent and, to be correct, ineptly waged more often than not. To paraphrase General David Jones, who served as chairman of the Joint Chiefs of Staff, we have not outfought our enemies so much as we have outproduced them.[1] Until recently, we did not maintain significant standing forces. The first battles of a conflict were usually disasters. In response we would mobilize our citizen forces and our industrial capacity to meet the challenge. Eventually our ability to replenish losses overwhelmed the exhausted enemy.

For most of our history, the military procurement function was essentially ministerial. Without large standing forces, the equipment needs of the military were modest. The important management problem was to be working on new designs between wars and to have the production capacity available to support expanded forces when they were mobilized. Little effective planning for the use of reserve production was required. Fighting was invariably slow to develop and when it did occur, civilian facilities were readily at hand and relatively easy to convert to war uses. The ocean barrier or a vast continent protected us from our enemies until we were ready to meet them.

Long periods of peace between mobilizations inhibited the development of a large arms industry. The army and the navy of necessity had to acquire their own weapons design and production facilities in order to sustain themselves in garrison. Some of these arsenals and naval installations date back to the founding of the nation. Others were established because of particular local pressures or wartime events. A small network of suppliers supplemented, and at times competed with, the government facilities, but was of no great consequence.

Officers assigned to the arsenals busied themselves exploring militarily relevant technologies. Progress was slow, in keeping with the slow pace of military activity, although important advances were occasionally achieved, especially in production techniques such as standardization of parts and metalworking.[2] Much of the benefit of these advances was absorbed by the civilian economy, which was expanding and in need of cost-saving innovations. Historians debate the extent of the contribution, but there is no doubt that the arsenal system played a role in the nation's industrialization, if only because it provided continuing support for manufacturing experiments.[3]

Scandal often accompanied mobilization as the inadequacies of preparation for war were revealed in reports from the field of troops without proper supplies and of weapons that were obsolete. The organizational response was to create specialized agencies in the military—the technical services in the army and matériel bureaus in the navy—to be responsible for procurement of supplies and weapons. The autonomy of these agencies within the military, enhanced by their ties with overseeing congressional committees and their control of budget allocations, encouraged bureaucratic rigidity, which in turn caused delay in the adoption of innovations and limited coordination among the agencies themselves and with the operating forces. After the Spanish-American War, the army managed to assert some centralized control over its technical services,[4] but the navy's matériel bureaus retained their organizational independence into the mid twentieth century.[5]

In both World Wars I and II, various civilian agencies were established to set priorities for critical materials, research, and industrial production.[6] The armed services resisted these efforts, the navy more than the army, seeking instead to continue with familiar routines and standard contract procedures.[7] After accommodation was forced, however, the full production capacity of the United States was mobilized for military needs. American participation in World War I was too short in duration for this capacity to be decisive, and our troops had to fight using much French and British equipment.[8] But in World War II it was American factories that carried the burden for the Allied cause.

Even before our forces were committed to combat in World War II, President Roosevelt pledged to make the United States the "great arsenal of democracy." Seemingly impossible production goals were established, including the promised output of 10,000 ships, 50,000 aircraft, and 100,000 armored vehicles, all of which were vastly exceeded.[9] A military force of over 12,000,000 was eventually raised. American scientists and engineers contributed by developing or improving such important new instruments of warfare as the proximity fuse, radar, napalm, and, of course, the atomic bomb. Because of the global nature of the conflict, an ability to land and supply forces great distances from our shores had to be perfected, a logistic skill that has since become an American trademark.[10] In the end, however, it was the capacity of American industry to sustain the armies of our allies until ours was ready that assured victory.

THE WATERSHED

World War II marked a major change in American foreign policy. With the war America abandoned its traditional isolationism and became a major military power. The commonly held lesson of the war among the nation's military and political leaders was that aggression had to be confronted early in order to avoid costly wars, that there would be no peace for America unless those who cherished freedom could convince potential aggressors that they were prepared to fight the erosion of freedom throughout the world. As the war approached its end, each of the armed services laid formal plans for expanded postwar force levels.[11] Disagreement with the Soviet Union over the pursuit of the war and its settlement, especially over the fate of Europe, gave cause for concern. The armed services were determined that America would not be caught unprepared again to defend freedom as it was when Germany and Japan began their march.

At the war's end an attempt was made through unification to increase interservice coordination and to assert continuing civilian direction over preparedness efforts. Although the Department of Defense was created, the autonomy of the armed services was preserved.[12] The enabling legislation that established the Department of Defense also established an independent air force and gained passage only on the assurance that the navy's full command prerogatives would be protected and that a viable and, for all essential purposes, independent Marine Corps would be maintained.[13] Subsequent amendments to the National Security Act, while increasing the standing of civilian-controlled central defense agencies, did not significantly alter the ability of the services, now four in number, to chart their own futures.

To varying degrees, the services saw their futures as intertwined with the advance of technology. All had an interest in aviation, with the air force seeking to make strategic bombing both its monopoly and the keystone of the nation's defense.[14] The three larger services claimed major roles in the deployment of nuclear weapons and, later, as technology evolved, in the management of ballistic missiles and spacecraft.[15] Once noted for their resistance to technological change,[16] the services now embraced innovation and willingly devoted substantial shares of their budgets to research and development activities in the hope of acquiring unique capabilities and new missions.

Rather than retreat to their own laboratories and arsenals, as was the usual pattern after a war, the services expanded beyond them. Ties to contractors were increased, as were those to the universities, the source of the nation's technical talent and much of its scientific progress. New organizations, nonprofit in structure, were created to provide specialized technical analysis and advice. The arrangements were flexible and intended to fulfill unique needs forced upon the military by the requirements of advanced technology. For example, RAND was established as an independent nonprofit corporation in part to advise the air force on strategic trends; Lincoln Laboratory was created at the Massachusetts Institute of Technology to help design radar for the air force's DEW line strategic warning system; MITRE Corporation was formed out of a division of Lincoln to provide technical assistance when the warning system became operational; and Aerospace Corporation was established to help the air force manage the development of ballistic missiles. The services came to rely upon major contractors to propose weapons innovations and for the construction and management of important defense facilities. Sensing an expanding market, researchers at universities and the major contractors formed hundreds of new businesses to specialize in advanced technologies and to seek their own contracts from the services. With mobilization growing permanent, an arms industry of unprecedented scale and scope developed.[17]

Weapons grew in sophistication, but rarely found a combat test. Instead they became obsolete, often quite rapidly, in statistical comparisons with their Soviet equivalents. The prevailing design philosophy pressed the limits of technical performance and involved the development of all related system components, including training, supply, and maintenance. Of necessity, each major system development required the assemblage of a multitiered network of contractors to work with the acquiring agency within the military and was accompanied by the risk of cancellation because of performance failure, cost escalation, or the appearance of counter systems.

Don K. Price has described the resulting procurement relationship as an unusual blending of the public and the private in the American economy.[18] What was traditionally public became private, and what was traditionally private became public. Through the military, the government assumed the role of the capitalist and entrepreneur, financing entire projects and absorbing all the risk of failure, while the contractors assumed the governmental tasks of project administration and weapon expertise. Contractors were protected from most of the hazards of government procurement with contracts that provided for full cost reimbursement and a fixed profit fee. The government acquired not only weapons, but project managers who made important design decisions and who provided technical support for the military. It was capitalism in a new guise.

For others, including some of those who presided over its creation, the procurement relationship was more troubling.[19] The armed services grew dependent upon the system contractors, unable to build weapons without them or even to shift to alternative suppliers once embarked on a particular design. The contractors in turn were dependent upon the services for much of their capital and, in many cases, most of their revenues. There was no price discipline because of the use of cost-plus-fixed-fee contracts, and there were often slippages in promised delivery schedules and system performance. Each major weapon project involved the employment of thousands, generating demands for its continuation because of local economic effects. The services found it difficult to distinguish their own survival from that of particular contractors and sought to maintain production capability with follow-on projects and, when necessary, loans or price adjustments.[20]

There were many attempts at procurement reform, but little improvement resulted.[21] During the 1960s the use of incentive contracts was emphasized. In the 1970s the theme was prototyping and design-to-cost. More recently there has been a requirement for increased contractor competition. To astute observers, the reforms seem merely repetitive, reminiscent of those tried without success during the services' early encounters with the development of aviation-related technologies as far back as the 1920s.[22] Yet, the search for solutions goes on, with each new administration proclaiming its determination to provide a more efficient way to procure weapons and ending up passing on a familiar litany of problems to its successors.

One other aspect of the postwar rearmament effort deserves mention. Like the commerce clause of the Constitution, which was used during the New Deal as a device to expand the regulatory power of the federal government, increased reliance on contracting for weapons procurement and the increased scale of defense purchases gave opportunity for further federal intervention in the economy. Procurement itself became a form of regulation, permitting the channeling of private sector behavior toward politically desired social objectives. Thus, the standard weapons contract came to include clauses requiring awardees to pay union scale wages, to hire minorities and the handicapped, to avoid pollution, and to seek subcontractors among small businesses and in areas in high unemployment. The most severe penalty, fines notwithstanding, is the threat of ineligibility for future awards, for it is a punishment few contracting organizations could survive. We buy not only weapons but also social reform with weapon contracts. It is not always obvious which purpose holds the higher priority.[23]

TWO KINDS OF UNCERTAINTY

Procurement problems persist because the weapons acquisition process is beset by two kinds of uncertainty, one inherent in the quest for advanced weapons and the other the product of our political system. The existence of these uncertainties both generates many of the procurement follies that are continually heralded in the media and frustrates the many efforts to achieve fundamental improvements in procurement outcomes.

Technological uncertainty results from the attempt to press the limits of technological knowledge. Matched as we are against a scientifically sophisticated opponent, we must seek to provide our forces with a vast array of weapons capable of performing under extraordinary tactical and environmental conditions. Consider the weapon requirements that follow from the need to defend an aircraft carrier from a missile attack that can be launched by surface combatants, submarines, or aircraft located hundreds of miles away, day or night, in any type of weather. What can be conceived as a defense then must be designed, developed, tested, produced, and deployed at a reasonable cost and before the threat itself changes.

Political uncertainty stems from the decentralized nature of our political system. A decision to move forward with a particular weapon project requires the concurrence of many independently situated participants and must be continually renewed. Although the navy, or at least parts of it, may favor the development of a new defense for carriers, to use the example cited above, various review authorities within the Department of Defense may not. And if agreement can be obtained within the Department of Defense, opposition may arise elsewhere within the executive branch or within the Congress. Literally dozens of agencies and committees hold a potential veto over projects. The kind of constitutional system that John Calhoun preferred, where the consent of protected minorities as well as of the majority must be obtained before authoritative decisions can be reached, seems to be in place.

Opposition may be based on different views of strategy or on disputes over budget and administration. Some may believe that aircraft carriers cannot be defended. Others may believe that the resources such a defense might require are best invested elsewhere in projects deserving greater priority. Still others may believe that the assignment should be given to their constituents. But always there is opportunity for opposition, bargaining, delay, and stalemate.

The chief characteristic of the system is its fragmentation. Action by the House of Representatives requires agreement by the Senate. The authorization process is separated from the appropriation process. The president proposes, but does not dispose. The secretary of defense holds formal control over the armed services, but must negotiate with them. The services themselves are structured into elaborate hierarchies, but in reality are fragile coalitions of interests, some centered around technologies and some not. The navy, for example, is composed of the surface navy, the aviators, the submariners, the amphibious navy, and the shore establishment, to identify only its major constituencies.

Much of the fragmentation is constitutionally mandated, intentionally crafted into the structure of government to constrain the exercise of political power in order to protect cherished liberties. In recent years, however, certain compensatory mechanisms that permitted the effective functioning of government have shattered. The Vietnam War and the Watergate crisis weakened trust in public authorities.[24] Party discipline in the Congress, never especially strong, fell before the political ambition of members who have to face an increasingly educated and independent electorate. And, most relevant for defense issues, the postwar consensus on foreign policy began to disintegrate, Vietnam and time having taken their toll among the supporters of the consensus.

With only slight overstatement, it is possible to argue that the current political paralysis approaches that of the unhappiest days of the Articles of Confederation. The impact of the fragmentation on procurement activities is considerable. Project managers need to be at least as skilled in political maneuvering as in the intricacies of their technologies.[25] Senior officials are constantly searching for a stable coalition. Much time is absorbed in preparing justifications and revising plans. Project goals are continually altered, causing schedule delays and adding to their costs. Budgets are forever in flux, denying the possibility of efficient management. The ICBM modernization program, in which we seemingly change missiles, basing modes, and numbers on a semi-annual basis, is but the most visible example of the procurement disarray that exists.[26]

It appears unlikely that either technological or political uncertainties will be reduced significantly in the foreseeable future. Technological uncertainty is the more malleable of the two. A commonly offered proposal is to seek less ambitious, more incremental advances in weapons—the acquisition strategy supposedly pursued by the USSR—in order to reduce the risks of cost increases and development failures.[27] The contrast between the American and Soviet strategies, however, may be overdrawn. The Soviet Union, after all, remains an effective competitor in most of the rapidly advancing weapon fields and even sets the pace in some (e.g., submarines and air defense missiles). Moreover, because we are unwilling to increase military manpower levels or match the Soviet Union in equipment totals, technology has to be our special edge and its uncertainties our special burden.

To the extent that it is their strategy, the Soviet leadership's practice of setting relatively modest goals for their weapons advances is surely in large part due to their ability to restrict political debate over weapons policies. Without the constant disruption in budgets and schedules that accompany political fragmentation, it is possible to plan for orderly progress in weapons programs. Our tendency to seek the major advance may reflect the need to exaggerate expected results so as to gather sufficient political support to initiate and sustain projects.[28]

Our allies supposedly also suffer fewer weapons development disappointments than we do. Their comparative success is attributed both to their conservative acquisition strategies and to their policy of using civilian rather than military procurement agencies.[29] But part of the difference in experiences may be due to the fact that our allies rely on us to provide, directly or indirectly, the protection afforded by the most exotic weapons. Moreover, it may matter less that these nations use civilian agencies to manage weapons procurement activities than that they have parliamentary forms of government that greatly restrict political interference once weapons plans are established by the party holding a majority.[30]

Clearly the decentralization characteristic of our political system does have costs, at least in terms of our ability to perform essential governmental tasks like acquiring weapons for our armed forces efficiently. The risk in attempting to curtail these costs is, however, that we may curtail the substantial advantages our political system provides even for the problem-plagued activity of acquiring weapons. One such hazard is the attempt to centralize procurement authority within the Department of Defense. Another is the increased secrecy about many major projects.

The recent reorganization of the Department of Defense moderately enhances the authority of the chairman of the Joint Chiefs of Staff and other defense officials, and in itself may not be of great moment. But as another step toward centralization, ever more the favored theme of congressionally devised solutions to defense policy problems, it is more worrisome. Competition among the services for roles and missions and in the development of weapons may be less an inducement to waste than an inducement to innovation.[31] Uncertain jurisdiction, the partner of interservice competition, keeps the services exploring alternatives, alert to new opportunities in technology and strategies. Reinforced hierarchy, in contrast, increases the possibility of doctrinaire judgments that court disaster.[32] Duplication by the armed services complicates not only our lives, but also those of our potential adversaries, who never know, for example, which of our several air forces they will encounter.

The practice of classifying entire projects—painting projects "black," as it is called—is intended to prevent the dissemination of information on advanced weapons by reducing the number of officials, including congressmen, aware of their existence. Coincidentally these projects avoid review by many of the agencies normally involved in acquisition decisions, no doubt an attribute that enhances the attractiveness of the practice for senior officials frustrated by the delays and changes imposed upon projects subject to standard procedures.[33] Tempting as it may be as a device for improving the efficiency of the acquisition process, this use of classification threatens representative government. What no one knowns, no one can criticize. It is the ability of citizens to criticize government that we seek to protect in the acquisition of weapons.

THE MILITARY INDUSTRIAL COMPLEX IN PERSPECTIVE

"Black" projects or not, the procurement process is much criticized, and for more than its inefficiency. The scale of the enterprise itself is enough to cause concern. No other activity has absorbed more federal resources since World War II than buying weapons. Literally trillions of dollars have been invested in equipment for the armed forces during this period. The taxes required to support weapons are given grudgingly. Some would prefer to devote the money to private consumption, others to address domestic social problems, such as health care for the poor or housing for the elderly.

A long-expressed criticism is that arms procurements are self-perpetuating, that the economic dependencies created in the quest for modern weapons are causing the continuation of the quest. This perspective on the acquisition of weapons easily, though not necessarily, drifts toward the formation of conspiracy theories. It is, some say, the armed services, or the contractors, or the weapons designers, or all in combination—the military-industrial complex—that drive up expenditures.[34] The fact that some high-ranking military officers find lucrative employment with defense contractors on their retirement and that senior officials are frequently recruited from the ranks of the same contractors feeds these beliefs. For the persuaded, Soviet weapons then are the product of equivalent machinations or are imagined threats conjured up to justify the flow of public funds to the conspirators.

However, one does not need to accept a conspiratorial explanation for weapons purchases to be concerned about their consequences. Much of the unease is directed toward a national strategy that relies heavily on the stockpiling and threatened use of nuclear weapons, with their ever-present potential for mass destruction. The fear of a nuclear holocaust is enough for some to decide the issue, to conclude that everything involving weapons is evil. But there is also concern that the economic opportunities created by the purchases distort the political process, converting debate over vital strategic issues into an effort to expand or gain access to the defense pork barrel. The available empirical evidence does not confirm such a view. For example, studies of congressional action on major weapons systems show that voting is largely independent of the distribution of contracts.[35] Nevertheless, suspicion persists that contract awards can be influenced by well-placed connections and are used to reward or garner political support, including that needed for the perpetuation of an overly large defense budget.

Recently the economic effects of the procurement process have become a focus of attention. Although Marxist and neo-Marxist claims that military expenditures are a necessary stimulant to the American economy are dismissed, the general belief has been that they hold advantage as a countercyclical measure, and especially as a spur to technological innovation. America, it is argued, gained significant economic benefit from military research and development investments in such fields as aerospace, electronics, computers, and telecommunications. But now, as our international trade competitiveness has deteriorated, these very investments are cited as an important retarding factor. Instead of supporting work on commercial products, we concentrate on creating exotic weapons. Too much of our scientific and engineering talent is diverted to military needs. The weapons procurement process itself generates inefficiencies that spill over into the civilian economy in the form of slovenly management practices and "goldplating" of equipment. Our trading partners who invest less in weapons and more in civilian technologies than do we, particularly the Japanese, gain markets at our expense.[36]

No doubt, there are economic costs associated with devoting over $120 billion a year to acquiring weapons. Although the advanced technologies cultivated for the weapons do have commercial application, we restrict their use for fear that they will be transferred to our adversaries. Our foreign arms sales are large, but they too must be restricted to protect their technical content and are often made on a subsidized basis.[37] As the dominant power in an alliance of many members, we are somewhat exploited by allies who prefer not to pay a fair share of the common defense. Research on weapons is now so specialized and conducted in such a unique cost environment that transfers to the civilian economy are limited. What benefits do spin off from weapons research could surely be obtained for less by more direct means. All of this, however, does not condemn the activity. We invest in weapons not to enhance the performance of the national economy, but rather to increase national security: $120 billion a year and some economic disadvantage is the price we pay. The real issue is always the security value of the investment.

Such an assessment is necessarily influenced by our attitudes to the interests directly affected by the allocations. Some elements of the armed forces are strongly attached to particular weapons technologies and want them advanced. Some weapons contractors know no other trade. Some communities could not survive the closing of an aircraft plant or a shipyard. Our political system, appropriately or not, is accommodating to these interests, considering organizational and geographic claims on public resources as deserving.[38]

The assessment must further take into account the political system's inherent fragmentation. So many have a role in making policy that accountability is often lost, and with it the need to act responsibly. The system's tendency is toward compromise, the splitting of differences rather than the rendering of clear-cut decisions and the formulation of coherent policies. No weapons project proceeds as planned or has an outcome that satisfies all who have supported it.

Ultimately, however, the judgment depends on acceptance of the underlying national strategies. Each security obligation the nation undertakes brings with it a series of weapons demands that is fulfilled, if imperfectly. The heavy tanks we acquire are for the defense of NATO's central front, the strategic missiles for deterrence, and the attack submarines for the battle of the North Atlantic. The armed services and the contractors attempt to control the specific weapons provided, but do not determine their need. Rather it is the choice of who and what to defend that is crucial.

Structure does affect policy, the determining form being constitutional arrangements that purposefully divide political authority. Lacking a final arbitrator, our government often pursues contradictory strategic objectives or mires in indecision. Muddled strategy lay behind the frustrations of the Korean and Vietnam wars. It makes our policy in Latin America and the Middle East chaotic. And it is the cause, much more than the obstinateness of the armed forces, for the persistent failure to purchase large amounts of airlift and sealift capacity that exercises so many defense critics.

Crisis can galvanize the political system. Witness the reaction to Sputnik and the Iranian hostage incident. To date though, direct military threats to our national survival have been rare, obvious, and sufficiently slow in developing to permit effective response. The existence of ballistic missiles makes life much more precarious, however, placing the burden of reaction to the threat of an attack entirely on existing forces. But we treat preparation for this awful possibility as hardly different from the kaleidoscope of normal politics. Two hundred years of good fortune discourages attempts to alter the constitutional structure so that it may conform to new realities. It also tempts the gods.

NOTES

The author wishes to acknowledge the very helpful comments received on an early draft from George Edwards, W. Earl Walker, Thomas L. McNaugher, Robert Osgood, and James Maxwell, none of whom share responsibility for the ultimate product.

1. David C. Jones, "What's Wrong with the Defense Establishment?" in Asa A. Clark IV et al., eds., *The Defense Reform Debate* (Baltimore: Johns Hopkins University Press, 1984), pp. 272–86.
2. Merritt Roe Smith, "Army Ordnance and the 'American System' of Manufacturing, 1815–1861," in M. R. Smith, ed., *Military Enterprise and Technological Change* (Cambridge, Mass.: MIT Press, 1985).
3. Alex Roland, "Science and War," *Osiris*, 2d Ser. 1 (1985): 247–72.
4. John C. Reis, *The Management of Defense* (Baltimore: Johns Hopkins University Press, 1964). See also William R. Roberts, "Reform and Revitalization, 1890–1903," in K. J. Hagan and William R. Roberts, eds., *Against All Enemies: Interpretations of American Military History* (New York: Greenwood Press, 1986), pp. 197–218.
5. Vincent Davis, *The Politics of Innovation: Patterns in Navy Cases,* Social Science Foundation and Graduate School of International Studies, University of Denver, monograph series, vol. 4, no. 3 (1966–67).
6. Robert D. Cuff, *The War Industries Board: Business-Government Relations during World War I* (Baltimore: Johns Hopkins University Press, 1973).
7. John K. Ohl, "The Navy, the Industries Board, and the Industrial Mobilization for War, 1917–1918," *Military Affairs* 40 (February 1976): 17–22.
8. R. F. Weigley, *History of the United States Army* (Bloomington: Indiana University Press, 1984).
9. Roderick L. Vawter, *Industrial Mobilization: The Relevant History* (Washington, D.C.: National Defense University, 1983); Irving B. Holley, Jr., *Buying Aircraft: Matériel Procurement for the Army Air Forces* (Washington, D.C.: Department of the Army, 1964).
10. See, for example, J. M. Heiser, Jr., *Logistic Support* (Washington, D.C.: Department of the Army, 1974).
11. Vincent Davis, *The Admiral's Lobby* (Chapel Hill: University of North Carolina Press, 1967); P. M. Smith, *The Air Force Plans for Peace, 1943–1945* (Baltimore: Johns Hopkins University Press, 1970); H. S. Wolk, *Planning and Organizing the Postwar Air Force, 1943–1947* (Washington, D.C.: U.S. Air Force, 1984).
12. Paul Y. Hammond, *Organizing for Defense* (Princeton, N.J.: Princeton University Press, 1961), and D. Caraley, *The Politics of Military Unification* (New York: Columbia University Press, 1966).
13. A. R. Millett, *Semper Fidelis: The History of the U.S. Marine Corps* (New York: Macmillan, 1980).
14. Thomas H. Coffey, *Iron Eagle: The Turbulent Life of General Curtis LeMay* (New York: Crown, 1986).
15. Harvey M. Sapolsky, *The Polaris System Development: Bureaucratic and Programmatic Success in Government* (Cambridge, Mass.: Harvard University Press, 1972).
16. For vivid examples of the military's former reluctance to innovate, see Edward L. Katzenbach, "The Horse Cavalry in the Twentieth Century: A Study in Policy Response," in Morton Halperin and Arnold Kanter, eds., *Readings in American Foreign Policy* (Boston: Little, Brown, 1973), pp. 172–90; and Elting E. Morison, *Admiral Sims and the Modern American Navy* (Boston: Houghton Mifflin, 1942).
17. See A. M. Agapos, *Government, Industry and Defense: Economics and Administration*

(Tuscaloosa: University of Alabama Press, 1975); and Adam Yarmolinsky and G. D. Foster, *Paradoxes of Power* (Bloomington: Indiana University Press, 1983).

18. Don K. Price, *The Scientific Estate* (Cambridge, Mass.: Harvard University Press, 1965). See also Gerald D. Nash, "The Managerial State: Government and Business Since 1940," in Robert Weibler, Oliver Ford, and Paul Marion, eds., *Essays from the Lowell Conference on Industrial History, 1980 and 1981* (Lowell, Mass,: Lowell Conference, 1981).

19. Dwight D. Eisenhower, "Liberty Is at Stake," Farewell Address of the President to the Nation, Washington, D.C., 17 January 1961. Reprinted in Jacob K. Javitz, Charles J. Kitch, and Arthur F. Burns, *The Defense Sector and the American Economy,* Moskowitz Lectures, no. 8 (New York: New York University Press, 1968), pp. 91–100.

20. James R. Kurth, "A Widening Gyre: The Logic of American Weapons Production," *Public Policy* 19 (Summer 1971): 373–404.

21. J. R. Fox, *Arming America* (Cambridge, Mass.: Harvard University Press, 1974); Robert Perry, "The American Style of Military R&D," in F. Long and J. Reppy, eds., *The Genesis of New Weapons* (Elmsford, N.Y.: Pergamon Press, 1980), pp. 89–112; William W. Crocker III, "Underestimating the Costs of Major Weapon Systems: Are Reforms on the Way?" *GAO Review,* Spring 1986, pp. 14–17.

22. See Holley, *Buying Aircraft;* and Kenneth P. Werrell, *The Evolution of the Cruise Missile* (Washington, D.C.: GPO, 1985).

23. Murray L. Weidenbaum, *Business, Government and the Public,* 2d ed. (Englewood Cliffs, N.J.: Prentice-Hall, 1981), pp. 169–83.

24. Seymour Martin Lipset and William Schneider, *The Confidence Gap: Business, Labor, and Government in the Public Mind* (New York: Free Press, 1983).

25. Thomas L. McNaugher, "Buying Weapons: Bleak Prospects for Real Reform," *Brookings Review,* Summer 1986, pp. 11–16.

26. See Lauren H. Holland and Robert A. Hoover, *The MX Decision: A New Direction in U.S. Weapons Procurement Policy?* (Boulder, Colo.: Westview Press, 1985); U.S. General Accounting Office, *ICBM Modernization: Status, Survivable Basing Issues, and Need to Reestablish a National Consensus* (Washington, D.C.: GAO, 1986); and Richard Halloran, "Soon, the Return of the MX Debate," *New York Times,* 16 December 1986, p. 10.

27. Perry, "American Style"; Arthur J. Alexander, *Soviet Science and Weapons Acquisition,* R-2942-NAS (Santa Monica, Calif.: RAND Corporation, 1972); Arthur J. Alexander, *Armor Development in the Soviet Union and the United States,* R-1860-NA (Santa Monica, Calif.: RAND Corporation, 1976).

28. Albert O. Hirschman, *Development Projects Observed* (Washington, D.C.: Brookings Institution, 1967); Paul R. Schulman, "Nonincremental Policy Making: Notes toward an Alternative Paradigm," *American Political Science Review* 69 (December 1975): 1354–70.

29. U.S. General Accounting Office, *Weapons Acquisition: Processes of Selected Foreign Governments* (Washington, D.C.: GAO, 1986); "A Job Too Important for Servicemen," *Economist,* 8 March 1986, pp. 31, 32.

30. There is surely no administrative magic to be found in civilian management of technology, as can be verified in a review of such projects as the Concorde, nuclear power, the Washington subway system, and any public construction project in Massachusetts.

31. Edward N. Luttwak, "Why We Need More 'Waste, Fraud and Mismanagement,'" *Commentary,* February 1982, pp. 17–30; and Martin Landau, "Redundancy, Rationality, and the Problem of Duplication and Overlap," *Public Administration Review* 29 (July–August 1969): 346–58.

32. Jonathan B. Bendar, *Parallel Systems: Redundancy in Government* (Berkeley and Los Angeles: University of California Press, 1985).

33. See David C. Morrison, "Pentagon's Top Secret 'Black' Budget Has Skyrocketed during Reagan Years," *National Journal* 18 (1 March 1986): 492–98.

34. See S. C. Sarkesian, ed., *The Military Industrial Complex* (Beverly Hills, Calif.: Sage, 1972); and Mary Kaldor, *Baroque Arsenal* (New York: Hill & Wang, 1981).

35. Lewis Dexter, "Congressmen and the Making of Military Power," in Raymond Wolfinger, ed., *Readings on Congress* (Englewood Cliffs, N.J.: Prentice-Hall, 1971); R. Douglas Arnold, *Congress and the Bureaucracy* (New Haven: Yale University Press, 1979).

36. Mary Kaldor, Margaret Sharp, and William Walker make this general argument for Britain with reference to the United States. See their "Industrial Competitiveness and Britain's Defence," *Lloyd's Bank Review*, no. 162 (October 1986): 31–49. See also Paul Lewis, "Military Spending Questioned," *New York Times*, 11 November 1986, p. D1.

37. David C. Morrison,. "Have Weapons, Will Trade," *National Journal* 18 (29 March 1986): 763–67.

38. Although personal gain is not considered legitimate, there is even some of that in the weapons acquisition process. See Patrick Tyler, *Running Critical: The Silent War, Rickover and General Dynamics* (New York: Harper & Row, 1986).

7

Waging War: Structural versus Political Efficacy

ASA A. CLARK IV and RICHARD M. PIOUS

> The circumstances that endanger the safety of nations are infinite,
> and for this reason no constitutional shackles can wisely be imposed
> on the power to which the care of it is committed.
> —Alexander Hamilton, *The Federalist*, no. 23

How does America's constitutional system affect U.S. warmaking—the ultimate task of any sovereign state? How have twenty decades of political evolution affected the issue of *who* decides *when* and *how* the United States will use force? How does the *structure* of the American political system affect the *process* and the quality of U.S. war making?[1]

The impacts of the constitutional system on U.S. war making are fundamentally important. The question of who should decide when and how the United States will use force in war was one of the most contentious issues debated during the constitutional convention. As the quotation from Alexander Hamilton illustrates, some argued for a powerful executive in whom singular war-making authority should be vested. Others were fearful of executive tyranny and insisted on shackling executive war-making powers to the legislature.

The Constitution is explicit on legislative powers concerning war making: Article 1, Section 8 of the Constitution grants Congress the power "to declare war." On the other hand, the Constitution is ambiguous on the war-making powers of the presidency. Some argue that the president's role as commander in chief grants him unique authority to engage the United States in war. For example, Sydney Hyman observes that the "decisions of any president have held this same potential since 1790: the cause lies in the functions the Constitution allocates to the presidency."[2] However, the Constitution is ambiguous about the intended meaning of the powers of the commander in chief. For example, the New Jersey Plan, featuring a plural executive, gave the president authority "to direct all military operstions," but also prohibited any executive from taking "command of any troops, so as personally to conduct any enterprise as General or in any capacity."[3] The fears of the Founding Fathers are well expressed in the remarks of this anti-federalist: "Who can deny but the president general will be a king to all intents and purposes, and one of the most dangerous kind too—a king elected to command a standing army. Thus our laws are to be administered by this tyrant."[4]

Although fears of an American tyranny have long since faded, the ambiguity and asymmetry in the U.S. Constitution continue to provoke disparate interpretations of executive and legislative war-making powers. These interpretations have sparked continuous debate over the structure of war-making authority, and in judgments about the efficacy of U.S. war making for two hundred years. Examples of this contentiousness are evident in the American Civil War, U.S. entry into World War I, the 1973 War Powers Resolution, and the furor over arms sales to Iran and covert operations in support of the Contras in Nicaragua in 1986.

This continuing controversy reflects the fundamental tension between two important parameters of America's use of force: *effectiveness* and *legitimacy.* Many factors influence the effectiveness of the use of force. Flexibility, the ability to rapidly shift commitments and resources, is inversely related to the number of constituents (decision makers, politically relevant constituents, allies, enemies) to whom policy is accountable. Thus secrecy is at a premium. Robert Kennedy's account of the secret deliberations of the president's entourage of personal advisors during the Cuban missile crisis illustrates the value of secrecy for maintaining a free hand in decisions regarding America's use of force against Soviet missile deployments in Cuba.[5] On the other hand, domestic public support adds greatly to the effectiveness of the use of force. Public political support depends, however, on disclosure of information. President Kennedy was adroit in disclosing information about Soviet missile deployments in order to catalyze domestic and allied political support for U.S. action against the missiles in Cuba. Legitimacy reflects the degree to which the public perceives that the policy effectively serves the public interest. Is the policy seen as accountable to the public interest? The legitimacy of the outcome of a war depends on its results; did the war effectively promote U.S. interests? The legitimacy of the conduct of the war requires disclosure of ongoing policies. Hence, these two important parameters of the use of force—effectiveness and legitimacy—confront policy makers with a tough dilemma.

This dilemma is clearly manifest in the debate over the respective war-making powers of the Congress and the president. Those who worry chiefly about the effectiveness of America's use of force advocate presidential preeminence; conversely, those concerned more about the legitimacy of the use of force espouse a major, if not primary, war-making role for the Congress.

One caution is in order: the pervasiveness of political change, conflict, and violence in the world confronting the United States today suggests that war making is an overly narrow focus for examining America's use of force. Traditional distinctions between war and peace have been overwhelmed by the dynamism, complexity, and diversity of today's world. It is unlikely that the United States will again enjoy total peace, interrupted, perhaps, by the necessity of engaging in a total war of national purpose for clear-cut objectives against a discrete enemy. Rather, today America is in a state of "semi-war" in the "modern age of conflict."[6] For example, U.S. strategic forces are constantly poised for instant use in the event of breakdown in nuclear deterrence, and U.S. military advisors continually participate in training and security assistance activities in many Third World countries. These examples represent ongoing instances in which U.S. military forces are used or are poised for use at virtually all levels of the spectrum of conflict. None of these examples, however, is likely to trigger the constitutional war-making process in which the Congress formally declares war.

Therefore, *war waging,* a broader term than *war making* and hence a more inclusive focus, is appropriate. War waging includes both the process of deciding to go the war and the process of conducting war. In traditional military terms, war waging subsumes declaratory policy (policy statements and doctrine about U.S. contingency actions under particular circumstances), deployment policy (decisions as to where forces will be stationed or based), and employment policy (decisions as to how forces will actually be used). In the context of the state of "semi-war" characterizing America's security environment today, war waging may also include the use of a variety of intelligence, security assistance, and developmental capabilities. Illustrative of these supplemental (but critical) dimensions of war waging are U.S. measures to construct airfields in Honduras, to provide training assistance, intelligence, and logistical support for the contras fighting in Nicaragua, to conduct U.S. military maneuvers in the Central American region, and to provide economic and developmental assistance to El Salvador. In this example of U.S. involvement in a semi-war in Central America, military measures play only a secondary role. Traditional distinctions between prewar planning and preparations versus conduct of wartime operations have become blurred. Although U.S. policy in Central America falls far short of any form of declared war, America's use of force is continuous, broad-based, low-key, and diffuse. A focus on war waging (rather than war making) also avoids freezing the assessment in sterile legal and constitutional debates that remain appart from political realities.

How can we evaluate the effects of the structure of America's constitutional system on U.S. war waging? Judgments about policy results for short- and long-run national objectives or for the public interest are peculiar to each instance. We can assess the quality and effectiveness of America's constitutional system by examining how its structure influences the *process* of war waging. Specifically, how well does U.S. war waging reconcile the dilemma between effectiveness and legitimacy? In order to assess the quality and appropriateness of these processes, a number of questions are examined. How does international change affect the nature, incidence, and severity of war waging in which the United States must engage? What is the nature of war-waging processes (both formulation and conduct) for different levels of conflict inherent in America's ongoing state of "semi-war"? What sort of policy processes are most compatible with the nature of war waging in this challenging environment of "semi-war"? How should the U.S. national security system be structured in order to promote the most appropriate war-waging process for each level of conflict? In order to assess America's constitutional system, three alternative models of presidential-congressional relations are evaluated here in terms of their relative appropriateness for U.S. war waging today.

Examination of these questions suggests conclusions about the fundamental quality, appropriateness, and vitality of America's constitutional system in today's world. Analysis of the degree to which U.S. war waging is capable of reconciling the tension between effectiveness and legitimacy leads to conclusions about the structure of the American constitutional system itself. Affirmative conclusions vindicate the constitutional system; conclusions that the national security system falls short on these criteria suggest consideration of revisions in America's national security system, or in the constitutional system itself.

U.S. WAR WAGING IN THE "AGE OF CONFLICT"

Before we can examine how America's constitutional system affects U.S. war waging, it is necessary to characterize the nature of the international environment with which U.S. security interests must contend.

The Pervasiveness of International Change

It is a truism to observe that change is a fundamental theme in America's political history. Consider aggregate change in the world during the two centuries of the U.S. Constitution. In the world of the constitutional convention, the international system consisted of fewer than 30 countries; the world of America's bicentennial features over 170 countries. During these two centuries, world population has quintupled (from roughly 980 million to more than 5 billion). World population has doubled since 1950 alone. Global manufacturing output has increased 1,730 times over the level of the late 1700s. This increase represents an average growth rate of 2.84 percent per annum (for the world)! Global trade has increased 460 times (an average growth rate of 2.47 percent per annum) over this same period.[7]

Similar trends are evident for the United States. America's share of world industrial production grew from only 4 percent in the late 1700s to 14 percent by 1860, 30 percent by 1910, and 42 percent by 1929. The U.S. share hovers around 30 percent in the 1980s. Although America's share of world exports was only 2 percent in 1780, it grew to 10 percent by 1890, 14 percent by 1929, and 20 percent by 1945. Currently the U.S. share of world trade stands at about 15 percent.[8]

More significant than these aggregate statistics are the effects of powerful political forces that have swept over the United States and the world during this period. Industrialization, urbanization, income redistribution, social mobilization, and the rise of nationalism have assaulted the political stability of governments around the world.

In particular, military power has been transformed from a personal, small-scale, intermittent activity to an efficient, utilitarian instrument of national purpose. Over the course of the past two hundred years, military power has been rationalized, popularized, centralized, and professionalized.[9] As modernizing states developed centralized administrative and political capabilities, the raising, training, and deployment of standing armies grew widespread. Development of professional officer corps, dedicated to the management of force and development of strategic thought, helped adapt the integration of modern weaponry produced by the industrial revolution into heavily armed, standing armed forces.

These effects were not limited to quantitative expansion of the military; the synergism of these changes qualitatively reshaped the role of military force. For example, the battleship and strategic airpower created military capabilities for rapidly projecting political influence far from home. Warfare and the use of force no longer affect only the military. Just as whole nations today are threatened by the prospect of nuclear war, the credibility of a nation's nuclear deterrent policy depends on strong domestic political support. Other nuclear states can be deterred only when they perceive one has sufficient political will to *perhaps* use nuclear weapons in retaliation for aggression.

Paradoxically, several features of these transformations of military power have undermined the integral subordination of this power to national foreign policy processes. Military managers tend to focus on internal military efficiency more than on strategic purposes. As the eighteenth-century French field marshal Maurice de Saxe observed: "In the military, very few men occupy themselves with the higher problems of war. They pass their lives drilling troops and believe that this is the only branch of the military art."[10] New military capabilities reflect the autonomous dynamics of technological development more than strategic designs of statecraft. The same long-range capabilities that permit extended political influence in peacetime make wartime control difficult. Finally, the advent of the nuclear age has shifted military power from an almost exclusive concern with fighting and victory to a greater stress on deterrence. On balance, the capabilities and roles of military power around the world have been enormously expanded during this period of change. More important, military power has been transformed into a far more potent and significantly more politically autonomous force in international relations.

International Conflict and Threats

Major international changes bearing on America's national security system since 1945 alone include America's emergence as a global superpower, the evolution of bipolar politics during the Cold War, the development of powerful nuclear arsenals by the superpowers and others, decolonization and the explosion of new and diverse states as an outgrowth of local nationalism, the tightening and subsequent erosion of alliance bonds in response to changing perceptions of military threats, global economic revitalization (although on very uneven terms), the emergence of Third World solidarity under the banner of the New International Economic Order, the explosion of economic and technological interdependence, the diffusion of more lethal conventional arms throughout the world, the spread of anti-Western Islamic fundamentalism and anti-Soviet nationalism, the growth of global financial interdependence, and the pall cast by international terrorism. During this maelstrom of change, the United States shed its historical mantle of isolationism and emerged as a superpower and world leader.

Threats facing the United States have never been more complex, constant, lethal, and insoluble; never in its history has America been confronted by a tougher world. At the upper end of the spectrum of conflict, war waging hinges on nuclear deterrence. As Leon Wieseltier comments: "A time in which there are 50,000 nuclear weapons in the arsenals of two great powers caught in political and philosophical competition is not a time to reform man. It is a time to manage him; that is, to deter him."[11] In this nuclear environment, U.S. war-waging policy must contend with the incompatibility between Western notions of assured destruction and the Soviet dictum of assured survival. The difficulty of this task is compounded by two paradoxes:

It is a paradox of deterrence that the longer it succeeds, the less necessary it appears.

We are confronted by the paradox of peace—that to preserve it, the peace-maker must be prepared to use force and use it successfully.[12]

Although these are terribly difficult and uncertain issues, the nature of war waging at the high intensity conflict end of the spectrum remains traditional in the sense that protagonists are known, military force has clear political value (for deterring the use of military force), and the units of war waging (ICBMs and SLBMs, warheads, targeting strategies, arms control limits) are highly discrete and identifiable. Much the same can be argued about the characteristics of conventional wars (so-called mid-intensity wars, such as the Iran-Iraq war or a potential conventional war in Europe). Such wars are horrifying to contemplate, especially given the potential for escalation to nuclear war. Nonetheless, mid-intensity war waging, too, involves what General John Galvin calls a "comfortable vision of war": "a theater with battlefields as we know, conflict that fits our understanding of strategy and tactics, a combat environment that is consistent and predictable, fightable with the resources we have, one that fits our plans, our assumptions, our hopes, and our preconceived ideas."[13]

International politics confront the United States with tougher challenges today because of more lethal threats at the higher end of the spectrum of conflict. However, it is the *variety, complexity,* and fundamental *intractability* of "small wars" that account for the qualitatively new challenges confronting American interests, and with which U.S. war waging must cope. Surrogate wars, terrorism, covert aid to insurgencies, small wars, subversion, civil war, and other forms of low-intensity conflict are increasingly the norm in international conflict. One analyst estimates that 90 percent of the international conflicts since 1945 have reflected some variant of low-intensity conflict and occurred in developing countries.[14] U.S. policymakers must anticipate that much of this political violence will focus on America. Not only is the United States the preeminent super-power, but its presence is most visible because of the great variety of America's global roles and the fact that America represents capitalism and Westernization—symbols that are rejected by a significant share of the world.

Small wars, commonly characterized as low-intensity conflicts, are "uncomfortable" for Americans for many reasons. First, they are hard to understand. Protagonists and combatants are difficult to identify. Distinctions between combatants and noncombatants are are not only difficult to make in civil wars, they are irrelevant. Second, societal factors such as ethnicity, perceived social and economic inequities, erosion of traditional authority structures, and social mobility are critical. Third, even if one understands a particular conflict, it is difficult to generalize to another. The peculiar circumstances of a small war are not just relevant; they are determinant. It is therefore difficult to assess the import of a small war outside of its particular context.

Finally, it is difficult for an external state, especially for the United States, to act constructively and appropriately in any given small war. Not only are Americans generally culturally insensitive to the local nuances so critical to small wars, but often the United States is perceived by those in the conflict to be *the* enemy. Thus constructive U.S. efforts are all but impossible. More fundamentally, many small wars are sparked by nationalism and hinge on internal perceptions of the state's political legitimacy. Well-meaning U.S. programs are often simply inappropriate for the nation-building challenges of developing countries. For example, although U.S. aid programs can assist in nation building, perceptions that a country's development program is being Americanized often generate significant political backlash against the host country's regime.

THE POLITICS OF U.S. WAR WAGING

America is in a state of semi-war. U.S. national security policy must simultaneously provide for war waging in terms of a credible and robust nuclear deterrent posture, a sufficiently lethal and flexible conventional force posture capable of responding to Soviet threats in Europe or a variety of regions, and a mix of intelligence, military, and development capabilities for engaging in small wars or military deployments aimed at regional powers (such as Iran). This state of semi-war confronts the United States with prospects for war of unprecedented likelihood and potential devastation.

What national security policy-making processes are associated with U.S. war waging today? How is war waging affected by the nature of these policy processes? Answers to these questions vary across the the spectrum of conflict. First, we must characterize the nature of policy-making processes. Policy making is usefully characterized in terms of the unity or fragmentation of the process.[15] A policy generates a unitary or unified policy process when there is significant consensus or likemindedness among policy makers. This situation normally reflects circumstances in which policy makers perceive similar distributive effects of a policy, or a crisis situation threatens to put national values at risk and, therefore, an immediate policy response is imperative. In either case, policy makers perceive that net policy benefits are evenly distributed across their constituencies or affect the nation as a whole. U.S. participation in World War II illustrates a unitary policy issue and an associated unified policy process.

Americans almost uniformly perceived the same high stakes at risk and agreed on the necessity of a total national commitment to end the war on terms favorable to U.S. interests.

Consensus in unified policy processes can serve useful roles: in promoting policy focus and coherence, in providing a framework within which actions can be handled by the bureaucracy, in facilitating implementation of policies in accordance with directives agreed upon in the policy formulation stage, in moderating debate and reinforcing policy continuity, and in articulating policy goals and objectives that serve U.S. national interests. However, as Ian Smart cautions, "consensus is not some sort of absolute good. Consensus is essentially a means to good or . . . evil ends."[16] There are many qualifiers that must be weighed in considering the value of policy consensus: on what scope of policy? on ends or means? among whom? by what means? for what motives? at what political price? These are critical questions for, as Smart reminds us, "there is no free consensus."[17]

On the other hand, perceptions among policy makers that a policy issue results in uneven distributions of net policy benefits will trigger controversy, debate, and political infighting. Unlike the consensus that characterizes unified policy making, fragmented policy processes reflect political tactics such as coalition building, expansion of the policy arena, leaks to the public, and log-rolling deals.

How do these different processes affect the content of policy? Unified policy making tends to involve fewer actors. Few may be affected by (and therefore care about) the policy; conversely, many may be affected, but all may agree on a course of action. In either case, relatively few decision makers participate in the policy process. As a result, it is less necessary to cut political deals in order to achieve support for a particular policy, and flexibility and substantive coherence are retained. On the other hand, fragmented policy making tends to be more politicized. Because disagreement is extensive, more deals must be cut in order to build political support. Flexibility and substantive coherence are circumscribed by the necessity of tethering the policy process to tactical deals with parochial political interests in order to build support.

The nature of the policy process—unified or fragmented—directly influences the quality of policy formulation and execution. Unified policy processes afford prospects for greater coherence, comprehensibility, flexibility, consistency, and executability. In a word, unified policy making is often viewed as more effective. These advantages are accompanied by disadvantages, however: the danger of groupthink, insufficient access to countervailing policy views, and a strain toward consensus over a comprehensive "world view." The price of policy coherence and flexibility may be policy dogma and insensitivity to local nuances and cultural limits on policy. Unified policy making runs the risk of holding to "bad" policy or of being denied legitimacy by an American public that perceives that it has been kept in the dark or, worse, has been deceived by policy makers. In addition, there is no assurance that unified policy making can attract and sustain the legitimacy conferred by broad-based public political support.

Fragmented policy processes offer prospects for more open debate and greater political accountability. However, these advantages are purchased only at the price of potential policy paralysis (caused by the difficulty of a large number of policy makers attempting to stay ahead of the press of world events), the tethering of security policy to parochial constituent interests, and the likely inability to conduct secret diplomacy or covert intelligence operations.

Implications for U.S. War Waging

The inherent character of war waging varies across the spectrum of conflict. For example, the nature of the threat, the identity of the protagonists, root causes, and the role of military force are different for small wars and mutual deterrence between the superpowers. Variance in such factors affects American perceptions of the stakes and consequences of U.S. use of force, and thereby shapes the nature of war-waging processes.

Three factors, in particular, help discriminate the unitary or divisive character of policy making for U.S. war waging. Time plays a powerful role in war waging. Ongoing and recurrent policy issues such as contingency planning, force structure design, and budgeting play out over extended time schedules. As a result, many actors participate, certain that positions lost in one round can be recouped in the next. Policy making tends to be fragmented and intensely politicized. On the other hand, crisis policy making (as to whether to employ force) outraces the ability of many actors to gain influence. Unified policy making is much more often the rule.

As discussed above, perceptions of the distributive consequences of a policy shape the nature of the policy process. Unified policy processes occur when many people perceive that the net benefits of a policy are evenly distributed (or when only marginal net benefits are at stake). For example, prospects for a secure America and the threat of nuclear war illustrate issues that generate more unified policy making processes. Conversely, fragmented policy making is the norm when people perceive uneven distributions of net policy benefits. Wartime conscription illustrates the divisive nature of such zero-sum game issues.

Finally, General Galvin's notion of the degree of "comfort" perceived with each level of war waging shapes policy making. "Comfort" reflects the relative ease of understanding—not any sense of moral acceptance—

of the various levels of conflict. Although nuclear war may be the most devastating form of conflict, its character is understandable in that it is consistent with traditional wars in terms of discrete protagonists and national commitments of military force for political goals. Terrorism, on the other hand, is much more difficult to understand—let alone designing a war-waging policy to oppose it that is either effective or legitimate.

Time available for war-waging policy, perceptions of the distributive consequences of this policy, and perceptions of the "comfort" factor associated with this form of war shape the politics of war-waging *processes*. By examining these factors for representative levels of the spectrum of conflict, we can characterize the degree to which the associated war-waging processes are more unified or more fragmented.

The threat of instantaneous nuclear war hangs equally over all Americans, and over humanity in general. Although its potential for enormous and almost instant destruction is awful to contemplate, the threat of nuclear war is profoundly understandable. Whether Americans ignore this threat (as being too remote) or fear its imminence, most agree that substantial war-waging measures are imperative in order to assure effective deterrence. Although political differences swirl around procurement and budgetary issues associated with nuclear forces, most Americans agree on the need for confronting the USSR with credible prospects of swift and measured U.S. nuclear retaliation in the event deterrence fails. Only then can Soviet military aggression be deterred.

The inherent nature of high-intensity conflict gives impetus to a broad policy consensus. Therefore, unified policy making is most appropriate for this form of war waging. War-waging processes associated with U.S. measures for assuring stable nuclear deterrence depend fundamentally on high levels of policy consensus. To the degree war-waging policy at this level is confounded by domestic and allied political disagreement, American and allied political cohesiveness are eroded. Accordingly, the credibility of U.S. nuclear deterrence is undermined. In the event of the failure of deterrence, prompt war-waging decisions must be made about the timing and character of retaliatory responses and negotiating efforts. War waging in this environment of immense uncertainties regarding communications, damage assessment, and motives behind any form of surprise attack must be both swift and considered. In this dimension of the spectrum of conflict, unitary policy making is at a premium in order to strengthen perceptions of both American political will and the flexibility of U.S. responses. No amount of enlightened public debate can clarify the root uncertainties of deterrence. Therefore, there is no premium on a policy process that assures intensive and continuous political debate in hopes that wiser policy can be developed. Like it or not, effective war waging in high-intensity conflict is possible only if authority is vested in the presidency.

On the other hand, small wars, reflecting diffuse and slow-brewing social, economic, and political factors, are "uncomfortable" for Americans. Small wars pose a mixed bag of implications for Americans: for example, tarnished U.S. credibility, prospects of danger for Americans traveling abroad, potential for Soviet exploitation, diminished security of overseas investments, perceptions of U.S. neo-imperialism, and potential for drawn-out and inconclusive military commitments (with risks of possible escalation). Moreover, such wars often do not admit constructive and effective policy measures from outside powers. Americans disagree on the import of small wars and the need for appropriate war-waging capabilities. The inherent nature of small wars triggers divisiveness in American politics. Only during the Cold War was a consensus over the necessity to confront threats of small wars sustained. This period was anomalous in American history. Fragmented policy-making processes are the norm for the politics of American war waging, particularly for small wars.

Unified policy making oriented on a grand strategy for dealing with small wars may lead to "bad" war-waging decisions because free-wheeling debate is stifled. The challenge is to avoid blunt application of "one-minded" doctrinal frameworks such as the Nixon and Truman Doctrines. Reliance on grand strategies or overarching foreign policy concepts runs risks of bad policy caused by hidden assumptions, unexamined prescriptions, camouflaged normative biases, and false comprehensiveness. Policy consensus often assumes too much and strains to prescribe too much. Unified policy processes risk imputing homogeneity to a world that is diverse and increasingly volatile.

This danger is especially keen for the United States because of the undercurrents of legalism, moralism, exceptionalism, and chauvinism that characterize American foreign policy attitudes. The price of unity in U.S. war-waging policy processes involving small wars may be increasing incongruence with the world and undesired backlash effects. Highly unified security policy has led the United States into dead-end situations: examples are American policy toward the PRC during the Cold War, the domino theory rationale of containment and U.S. war waging in Southeast Asia, and the illegal covert arms transfers to Iran and Nicaragua in 1985–86. As Irving Kristol has remarked, "consensus is what sustains an ideological foreign policy, and no great power—not the United States, not Russia, not China—can have a foreign policy that fits neatly into an ideological *Weltanschauung*."[18]

Moreover, the strains of prosecuting a small war, especially in an environment in which America is at semi-war, are too great and may overwhelm a policy consensus. As illustrated in the case of Grenada, Americans will support a small war that is quick and "clean." Such wars are the exception, however. Both Korea and Vietnam proved to be long-drawn-out and inconclusive wars, in which American support eroded rapidly as prospects for quick success faded.

Fragmented policy making is not only compatible with the nature of small wars, it offers a political environment more conducive to effective and legitimate war waging in that context. Time, reflection, and thoughtful debate are at a premium in small wars in order to assure wise war-waging policy. Fragmented policy making, based on vigorous public debate, is valuable for testing the validity of first-order assumptions and sharpening the quality of policy resolution. Rarely are low-intensity conflicts fast-breaking; in fact, the root causes of a small war have normally been at work for some time. Therefore, no crisis imperative normally operates that might obviate debate and politicized decision making over appropriate U.S. measures. Strong congressional war-waging roles are valuable for triggering vigorous policy debate. At the same time, potent presidential war-waging powers are necessary if the United States is to be able to carry out secret diplomatic and intelligence overtures over time.

Thus, at the end of the decade, while the United States celebrated the bicentennial of its Constitution, it found itself in a state of semi-war. U.S. national security policy must be capable of dealing with threats ranging from massive failure of nuclear deterrence to terrorist strikes against individual Americans. Given perceptions that scarce and highly valued resources will be unevenly distributed in defense budgetary, manpower, acquisition, and deployment policies, fragmented policy processes will continue to be the norm in the defense sector. War-waging processes, involving intelligence and military employment policies, vary at different levels of conflict. War waging at the high-intensity end of the conflict spectrum tends to be unitary. Unified war-waging processes are more than desirable; given the instantaneousness of potential threats, they are imperative. On the other hand, war waging in small wars tends to be more fragmented. In such cases, the full force of pluralistic politics better serves U.S. war waging.

Thus U.S. war waging better balances effectiveness and legitimacy through more unified policy making at upper conflict levels and through more fragmented policy making at lower conflict levels. How should America's national security system be structured in order to shape such a mix of war-waging policy processes? How well does America's constitutional system shape the national security system in order to achieve such a hybrid of policy-making processes?

THE STRUCTURE OF THE U.S. CONSTITUTIONAL SYSTEM
AND WAR WAGING

No stable structure of presidential-congressional relations for war waging has emerged over the course of American history. The Constitution remains an "invitation to struggle" over presidential and congressional war-waging prerogatives. U.S. war waging has evolved through custom, practice, ad implementing legislation. In order to evaluate the existing national security system (characterized here as the checks-and-balances system), three alternative structures are examined. How do these alternatives shape war waging in terms of unitary and fragmented policy making processes? How well do they balance effectiveness and legitimacy? Analysis of these alternatives for structuring the *process* of war waging in today's world serves as a baseline for assessing America's existing national security system.

America's Checks-and-Balances System

The framers of the Constitution feared the accumulation of power by either branch. The frictions and inefficiencies of a system of checks and balances were therefore explicitly employed in the Constitution in order to ensure that federal policy, including war waging, served the public interest. How are war-waging prerogatives distributed in America's existing national security system?

Article 1 of the Constitution assigns Congress the power to declare war, to raise, fund, and regulate the armed forces, to grant letters of marque and reprisal, and to punish piracy and other offenses against the laws of nations. The Senate must also consent to presidential commissioning of military officers. The "necessary and proper" clause provides a basis for broad legislative powers of waging war. In the aggregate, however, these legislative powers do not constitute plenary authority to make war. Nor do these powers conclusively determine how the executive should wage war. Proponents of executive authority argue that each power granted to Congress can be treated as an exception to the general power of war waging confided by the Constitution to the president. Alternatively, these powers can be considered a concurrent war-waging power to be exercised by a sovereign Congress over a compliant president. Finally, they can be considered a set of checks that the president must surmount, and a form of political constraint that requires him to seek support in Congress in order to gain a national consensus that allows him to pursue his war aims.[19]

The Constitution gives Congress discrete powers that are to be exercised intermittently while the nation is at war. Declaration of war officially commences hostilities. Appropriations are to be passed for no more than a two-year period. No general supervisory power to conduct hostilities is confided to Congress. Nor does Congress delegate war powers to the executive. Historically, congressional war-waging actions have had a "stop-go" quality to them: either the legislature acquiesced in a war or it did not; either legislative and budgetary authority was granted to continue hostilities or it was not; either Congress insisted that hostilities be terminated according to law or Congress did not. These congressional powers provide for intermittent influence over war waging. They do not add up to a *process* of war waging; no timetables or action-forcing deadlines are established. No requirements are stipulated for consultation, for reporting on executive initiatives, or for other collaborative procedures between the two branches.

The war-waging powers confided to the president by the Constitution include the prerogatives of the commander in chief of the armed forces (and state militias when called into national service), the executive power of the United States, and the responsibility to see that the laws are faithfully executed (including international commitments entered into by the United States or by the executive branch). Checks and balances established by the partial separation of powers assure presidential participation in aspects of the legislative process. The president recommends expedient measures to Congress and can veto legislation. These powers neither grant the president plenary authority to make war nor require Congress to subordinate its own authority to that of the executive.

What is most interesting about presidential war-waging powers is their character: because they are general terms and are not qualified by explicit enumeration, they can be interpreted in an open-ended way. Presidential war powers are easily expanded through doctrines of inherent presidential authority to exercise sovereign war-waging powers for the nation.[20] They provide scope for the president to claim implied war-waging powers that "fill in the blanks" or expand upon ambiguous aspects of his powers. For example, the Constitution makes no mention of aggressive war, acquisition of territory, interventions and interpositions, police actions, truces, armistices, disengagement, proclamations of neutrality, convoying in sea-lanes, undeclared naval wars, or covert wars and covert actions. Nonetheless, all these are considered acts of sovereign states under international law, and as such are part of executive war waging. They enable the president to fuse powers (the commander-in-chief clause and the executive power) and to combine obligations (the oath and duty to faithfully execute the laws). Interpreted expansively, these "resulting powers" can be applied to create a process of political supervision and control over the conduct of military operations, thus giving practical effect to abstract doctrine.

Whereas congressional war powers are exercised in a discrete "stop-go" manner, presidential war powers represent a continuum—ranging from the use of force for "signaling" to total war. The president can thus calibrate means and ends and take operational responsibility in war waging for the duration of hostilities, hoping that Congress will confine itself to specific acts in support of his actions rather than making specific checks against them.

A number of problems associated with war-waging plague America's constitutional system. The Constitution is woefully incomplete when it comes to war waging. First, consider the question of committing American forces to hostilities. The original understanding was that if the United States were invaded, the president could repel the attack on his own authority.[21] But if the president repels the attack, must Congress then declare war as soon as it is able? May Congress declare war for the purpose of acquiring territory or wage an aggressive war? The Supreme Court has, in fact, held the contrary in at least one case.[22] Must the president obtain the advice of Congress, or is the declaration simply a form of consent? Is the declaration a legislative act that goes to the president for potential veto (or even pocket veto)? Or is it one of those nonlegislative acts that is not presented to the president? Does it delegate power to the president, and, if so, may it present him with conditions or restrictions?

Second, consider how the United States disengages from hostilities. The Constitution mentions only the treaty power as a mechanism for ending war. No mention is made of other ways, such as a truce or an armistice. The president may enter into such agreements as commander in chief, but does Congress have a concurrent power, through law or resolution, to order military commanders to end hostilities? If Congress has declared war, may it later "undeclare"war? If so, can the president veto that act to keep the war going? Or is it his duty faithfully to execute the laws when it comes to the declaration? The literal text of the Constitution does not provide the answers, though the customs and usages of the "living Constitution" give us precedents to apply.

The War Powers Resolution has resolved neither these constitutional issues nor the failure to institutionalize war-waging processes. The language that purports to define the prerogatives of the president as commander in chief to deploy the armed forces in hostilities is contained in a "purpose and policy" section of the resolution that is not part of the operative law.[23] The consultation section is poorly drafted: it does not specify with whom the president must consult in Congress, nor the timing of such consultation, and it provides an escape clause if consultation is not deemed practicable by the president. Reporting requirements are loosely drawn. Various "clocks" are to be set when the president uses force, but the president is supposed to trigger them through his reporting.

If he delays months (as President Reagan did when sending troops to Beirut for "peacekeeping"), then the mechanisms of the resolution may be backed up until Congress decides to start the clocks itself. Should the clocks be set retroactively? At least one federal court has provided dicta indicating that various timetables must begin at the point at which Congress decides to act—and not before.[24]

The law provides for subsequent restraints on the use of force, but these, too, are poorly drafted. Whenever the president uses the armed forces in hostilities without a declaration of war or specific authorization (barring an extension granted by Congress), the legislature may direct by concurrent resolution that he withdraw these forces. In the aftermath of the *Chadha* decision, which declared a legislative veto unconstitutional, that has been interpreted to mean a joint resolution of Congress.[25] Even so, it is not clear that such a mechanism would be upheld by the federal courts. If the president chose to disregard it as an infringement upon his powers as commander in chief, the courts could sidestep the issue through declaring it a political question outside their purview or uphold the president's position. If the president has at any point received a declaration of war or other authorization, the courts might decide that the subsequent restraint was thereafter inoperative. Only at the beginning of hostilities, prior to any show of support, could such a check be deployed.[26]

Finally, it may be argued that the president has independent sources of war-waging prerogative. Although Congress may legislate, it may neither condition nor restrict what it does not possess or delegate. Indeed, the Supreme Court might interpret the existence of the resolution as an implied invitation to the executive to exercise his own war powers to further a war "acquiesced in" by Congress, following Justice Rehnquist's reasoning in upholding the 1981 Executive Agreement with Iran.[27]

The enduring constitutional patterns of war waging follow the contours of the American political culture: suspicion of executive prerogatives, insistence on checks and balances, and tentative, somewhat insincere, gestures by the president and the Congress toward collaboration. Presidents feel compelled to rely on prerogative and faits accomplis rather than collaboration, on briefings rather than consultation, and even on evasion. An example of minimal, rather than full, compliance with the terms of the War Powers Resolution is the case of the 1983 Beirut resolution in which President Reagan made compliance into a public relations initiative (complete with White House signing ceremony) while simultaneously releasing a statement that he was not bound by its terms.[28]

A collaborative war-waging mechanism such as the War Powers Resolution operates more as a symbol than as a process. Just as neither the president nor the Congress is willing to use the War Powers Resolution to force war-waging policies, neither is willing to renege on the resolution.

By the same token, both branches prefer to continue to conduct U.S. war waging by "pulling and hauling" rather than by trying to seek clarification of war-waging prerogatives or by overhauling the constitutional system itself.

Thus we see that the diffusion of war powers in America's constitutional system is *structurally suboptimal*. No mandate exists for war-waging authority exclusively in the hands of a single branch of the federal government. As a result, war-waging decisions—involving the highest stakes for U.S. national interests—remain fully entangled in American politics. Rather than optimally serving U.S. national interests, war waging decisions are "contaminated" by parochial political forces acting to serve disparate institutional, organizational, commercial, local, or personal interests. A degree of structural ambiguity and inefficiency is viewed as the price of retaining political accountability. As always, political realities rather than legal parchment or constitutional constraints shape the effectiveness and legitimacy of American war waging.

Alternative Models of Presidential and Congressional War Waging

In a *presidential supremacy* model, the president would fully exploit his war-waging prerogatives as commander in chief, as chief executive, and in accordance with his responsibility to ensure that the laws are faithfully executed. Such a concentration of political authority and focused control over war-waging capabilities would provide for responsive and consistent national security policy making. War waging would be effective because the president would be free to employ force appropriately and flexibly along the conflict spectrum, and to build national political support for his policies.

Nothing in the Constitution prevents adoption of a *parliamentary* model. Although it is without precedent, the president could establish a "war cabinet" and put his executive powers into commission (as presidents in the early 1800s did). The president could invite members of Congress to serve as "ministers without portfolio." Such a model does not comport with the American checks-and-balances system, and it is doubtful whether legislators would accept an invitation to participate in executive war-waging deliberations. Yet a president might decide to create informal consultative mechanisms with congressional leaders in order to formulate war-waging policies collectively and accountably. This was done by Eisenhower in 1954 in deciding not to intervene on behalf of the French at Dien Bien Phu.[29] In return, Congress might put its constitutional prerogatives at the president's disposal for the limited duration of a particular war situation. This is known as the constitutional doctrine of subordination. Institutionally it would be expressed through informal meetings and briefings with congressional leaders; politically it might be manifested in a bipartisan foreign policy in which political carping stops at the water's edge.

The Whig doctrine of *congressional supremacy* represents a third model—one with at least some historical precedent (congressional influence was dominant in the undeclared naval war with France, 1798–1800, and in the War of 1812). In this model, Congress represents the sovereignty of the nation; the president serves as its agent. Congress makes war-waging policy by declaring war or through legislation delegating war-waging powers. Congressional committees provide policy-making continuity through oversight. Although no one seriously advocates full-scale Whig theories today, Whiggish tendencies do appear in congressional attempts to constrain U.S. war-waging policies.

Analysis

Which of these structures of presidential-congressional war-waging prerogatives offers a mix of policy-making processes appropriate for each level of conflict? Which structure best shapes policy-making forms liable to achieve effective and legitimate war waging? Analysis of these alternative war-waging models provides insights into the relative appropriateness of America's existing constitutional system.

The *presidential supremacy* model obviously represents a structure conducive to highly unified policy making. Such a structure offers advantages such as greater policy coherence, comprehensibility, flexibility, and consistency. However, this policy-making structure runs the risk of vulnerability to groupthink and a tendency to rely on doctrinaire approaches to tough national security problems. Although a structure in which the president is dominant properly shapes policy making for high-intensity forms of war waging, the associated dangers of policy dogma and "true believership" can be lethal for the difficult and long-drawn-out nature of small wars.

Chief among the organizing principles of the *parliamentary* model is the notion of ministerial (or collective cabinet) responsibility. This feature offers many advantages: unified political support of the party leadership, policy coherence, flexibility, and discretion. On the other hand, cabinet-level groupthink too often plagues parliamentary policy making. This structure is also attractive because of the legislative accountability it gains. Again, the offsetting disadvantages are many: accountability is limited by the strength of party discipline (which in the case of war-waging policies is often strong), there are no midterm elections for registering public sentiment, and there are few legislative restraints.

A parliamentary structure fosters more unified policy making. Accordingly, parliamentary policy making is appropriate for waging war at the higher levels of the spectrum of conflict. However, parliamentary politics tend toward policy "one-mindedness," thus creating risks of wrong or inappropriately applied war-waging policy, especially in the case of small wars.

Congressional supremacy offers the advantage of legitimacy based on political accountability and the prospect that policy, based on rich and intense public debate, will tend to be "wiser." However, congressional war waging would reflect all the weaknesses of legislative politics: "too many chiefs," paralysis, parochialism, and inability to sustain secret diplomacy or covert intelligence operations. This structure is inappropriate for waging war at all levels of conflict.

Each of these alternative structures offers prospects for policy-making processes appropriate for achieving either relatively effective or relatively legitimate war waging. None promises to achieve both. America's existing checks-and-balances system, on the other hand, preserves presidential initiative, yet also retains legislative restraints on policy making. In spite of—indeed, because of—all the political friction and turmoil injected into policy making by the checks and balances, the constraining effects of America's constitutional system are politically optimal. In this constitutional structure, the national security system shapes policy-making processes that are compatible with the inherent character of war waging at the different levels of conflict. This system best matches policy-making processes and the character of war waging for all levels of conflict. America's existing constitutional system best shapes policy-making processes appropriate for both effective and legitimate war waging in today's world.

CONCLUSIONS

This chapter has assessed the effects of political structure on political processes in order to draw conclusions about the implications of presidential and congressional prerogatives for the quality of American war waging. One important caution is necessary: although political structure certainly influences political processes (and the ultimate quality of actual policy), many other factors are at work as well. Although the wonderfully constant, yet adaptable, U.S. constitutional system is the bedrock of American politics, factors such as the idiosyncratic character of the president and congressional leaders, the media, the tug of bureaucratic inertia, interest groups, allies, and shifts in the American public's mood also directly affect the effectiveness and legitimacy of policy making, including war waging.

The existing American constitutional system is structurally flawed. The tensions and frictions inherent in the constitutional system afflict U.S. national security policy with all sorts of inefficiencies, political turmoil, bad decisions, and waste. Examples of the poor policy that can result from this structural suboptimality include the U.S. refusal to recognize the PRC for over two decades, the Vietnam imbroglio, American security policy toward Iran in the 1970s, and the dysfunctions of the NSC system pinpointed by the Tower Commission in the aftermath of covert arms sales to Iran in the 1980s.

On the other hand, the structure of presidential-congressional war-waging prerogatives in the existing constitutional system is better politically than its alternatives in terms of shaping policy making likely to achieve both effective and legitimate war waging. The structure of war-waging powers shapes the most appropriate policy-making process for each level of conflict. It is interesting to note that this tension between policy effectiveness and legitimacy is sensitive to the ambient level of political consensus. Higher levels of political agreement mitigate this tension; lower levels of agreement exacerbate it. Thus this tension is assuaged in the case of the unified nature of war waging in high-intensity conflict. Political agreement promotes effectiveness of deterrence, which in turn confers political legitimacy on the associated war-waging policies.

By the same token, this tension is exacerbated by the inherently divisive character of war waging in the case of small wars. Fragmentation and political divisiveness assault and constrain policies for engaging in small wars. Except in the case of so-called "quick and clean" small wars, political pluralism forces fundamental debate over the stakes and policies relating to American involvement in such wars. This effect of the tension between effectiveness and legitimacy is a bonus: the separation of powers gives impetus to a creative tension that obstructs the policy strain toward unified, grand conceptions of national security affairs. This tension sustains fragmented policy making and triggers constructive impulses in American war waging: among others, a sense of "otherliness," cautiousness, and moderation. Considering the nature of the state of semi-war in which America finds itself, these merits are all the more important.

The remarkable stability of America's constitutional system is another reason to characterize it as politically optimal. The three keystones of American national security policy—the containment doctrine as the centerpiece of U.S. foreign policy, American strategic culture, and the structure of the American political system—have endured and are likely to continue to do so. Short of some major crisis that calls into question the political legitimacy of the constitutional system, the structural inertia of American politics will continue to endure.

In the long run, therefore, effectiveness and legitimacy are best balanced in U.S. security policy and war waging through the clumsy, erratic, often ponderous, and always politicized, structure of shared powers and collective, contentious collaboration between the presidency and the Congress. The strength of U.S. war-waging and national security policy is held to lie in the bedrock of America's durable, yet adaptable, political system. These conclusions add up to a mitigation of George Kennan's lament for the efficacy of U.S. security policy, given America's constitutional system. Kennan wondered "whether a government so constituted should deceive itself into believing that it is capable of conducting a mature, consistent, and discriminating foreign policy."[30] The answer, especially in the challenging international environment facing the United States today, is a resounding "No!" To paraphrase Tocqueville, however, this inefficacious political system is better than the alternatives its critics have proposed.

NOTES

1. Structure refers to the system of policy-making institutions and the distribution of policy-making prerogatives among these institutions.
2. Sydney Hyman, *The American Presidency* (New York: Harper & Brothers, 1954), p. 10.
3. Quoted in Raymond Tatalovich and Byron W. Daynes, *Presidential Power in the United States* (Monterey, Calif.: Brooks/Cole, 1984), p. 320.
4. *The Anti-Federalist Papers,* ed. Morten Borden (East Lansing: Michigan State University, 1965), no. 74, p. 212.
5. Robert F. Kennedy, *Thirteen Days* (New York: Norton, 1969).
6. These ideas were expressed by John Chancellor of NBC News in a speech at the U.S. Military Academy, West Point, New York, 2 December 1986.
7. W. W. Rostow, *The World Economy: History and Prospect* (Austin: University of Texas Press, 1978), parts 1 and 2.
8. Ibid.
9. For a full discussion of the transformation of military power, see Robert Osgood and Robert Tucker, *Force, Order, and Justice* (Baltimore: Johns Hopkins University Press, 1967), esp. pp. 41–70.
10. Quoted in Bernard Brodie, *War and Politics* (New York: Macmillan, 1973), pp. 433–34.
11. Leon Wieseltier, "When Deterrence Fails," *Foreign Affairs* 63 (Spring 1985): 828.
12. Caspar W. Weinberger, *Annual Report to the Congress, Fiscal Year 1985* (Washington, D.C.: GPO, 1984).
13. General John R. Galvin, "Uncomfortable Wars: Toward a New Paradigm," *Parameters* 16, no. 4 (Winter 1986): 2.
14. Caesar D. Sereseres, "Lessons from Central America's Revolutionary Wars, 1972–1984," in Robert E. Harkavy and Stephanie G. Neuman, eds., *The Lessons of Recent Wars in the Third World* (Lexington, Mass.: Lexington Books, 1985), p. 161.
15. This discussion reflects the rationale of the issue-area politics literature, which argues that the politics of policy making vary according to the character of the policy issue area. For representative examples of this literature, see William Zimmerman, "Issue Area and Foreign Policy Process: A Research Note in Search of a General Theory," *American Political Science Review* 77 (December 1973): 1204–12; and Theodore J. Lowi, "American Business, Public Policy, Case Studies and Political Theory," *World Politics* 16 (July 1964): 677–715.
16. Ian Smart, "Banquet Address to the Student Conference on United States Affairs," U.S. Military Academy, West Point, 18 November 1985.

17. Ibid.

18. Paraphrased from *Time,* 31 March 1986, pp. 14–15.

19. On expansive versus narrow interpretation of presidential and congressional pre-rogatives, see Alexander Hamilton, writing as Pacificus, Letter no. 1, June 1793, and James Madison, as Helvidius, Letter no. 1, August 1793, reprinted in Christopher Pyle and Richard Pious, *The President, Congress, and the Constitution* (New York: Free Press, 1984), pp. 54, 60.

20. The sovereign powers theory is developed by Justice Sutherland in *United States v. Curtiss-Wright Export Corp.,* 299 U.S. 304 (1936), and reaffirmed in *Perez v. Brownell,* 356 U.S. 44 at 57 (1958). On the other hand, consider Justice Black's statement in *Reid v. Covert,* 354 U.S. 1 at 56 that "The United States is entirely a creature of the Constitution. Its power and authority have no other source. It can only act in accordance with all the limitations imposed by the Constitution." For critical analysis, see Charles A. Lofgren, "United States v. Curtiss Wright Export Corporation: An Historical Reassessment," *Yale Law Journal* 83, no. 1 (1973).

21. For the intent of the framers, see Abraham Sofaer, *War, Foreign Affairs and Constitutional Power: The Origins* (Cambridge, Mass.: Ballinger Publishing Co., 1976).

22. *Fleming v. Page,* 50 U.S. 603 (1850), where the court stated that "the genius and character of our institutions are peaceful, and the power to declare war was not conferred upon Congress for the purposes of aggression or aggrandizement."

23. Chalmers Roberts, "The Day We Didn't Go to War" in Marvin Gittleman, ed., *Vietnam: History, Documents and Opinions in a World Crisis* (New York: Fawcett, 1965), pp. 96, 104.

24. For discussion of governmental collaboration (interbranch policy codetermination), see Thomas Franck and Edward Weisband, *Foreign Policymaking by Congress* (New York: Oxford University Press, 1979).

25. *Immigration and Naturalization Service v. Chadha,* 46 U.S. 919. On the weight courts attach to presumed consent and consistent direction of the branches, see *In Re Debs,* 158 U.S. 564 (1895), commending the executive for acting on behalf of the federal courts; *United States v. Midwest Oil Co.,* 236 U.S. 459 (1915), reading congressional acquiescence as an invitation for the executive to act; *Hirabayashi v. United States,* 320 U.S. 81 (1943), upholding a curfew on citizens of Japanese descent after an act of Congress ratified and confirmed a prior executive order; *Korematsu v. U.S..,* 323 U.S. 214 (1944), upholding exclusion of citizens based on ancestry from areas of the West Coast; and *Dames and Moore v. Regan,* 452 U.S. 654 (1981), upholding the validity of a presidential executive agreement and subsequent Treasury directives based on the intent of congressional statutes rather than their specific provisions.

26. War Powers Resolution, P.L. 93–148; 87 Stat. 555; 50 U.S.C., sec. 1541 48.

27. *Crockett v. Reagan,* 558 F. Supp. 893 (D.D.C. 1982).

28. *Chadha v. Immigration and Naturalization Service,* 77 L. Ed. 2nd 317 (1983).

29. See the discussion of subsequent restraints in Richard M. Pious, *The American Presidency* (New York: Basic Books, 1979), pp. 406–7.

30. George F. Kennan, *Memoirs* (New York: Bantam Books, 1969), vol. 1, p. 295.

III

FOREIGN RELATIONS

8

Protecting Citizens Abroad

IRA SHARKANSKY

The protection of American citizens abroad offers numerous problems for people concerned with national security. Politics is more prominent in these than military force. The kidnapping or killing of Americans overseas obviously does not threaten the nation in the same way as a conventional or nuclear attack by armed forces. Yet the concern of citizens and officials for the protection of individuals abroad has been of the highest intensity.

The recent scandal involving arms deliveries to Iran engulfed the White House, Congress, and the mass media. Several aspects of this scandal are parallel to issues to be considered here, and highlight their political sensitivity. Part of the scandal involved the administration's effort to secure the release of American hostages taken by Lebananese groups thought to be allied with the Shi'ite regime of Iran. This seemed to depart from the policy not to negotiate with or make concessions to hostage takers. Another aspect of the scandal was the use of funds generated by the arms deliveries to aid rebels fighting against the Sandinista regime in Nicaragua. Some critics take a cynical view of American policy against terrorism, and refer to those rebels as the White House's terrorists. Critics also charged that the administration violated the controls on arms deals and the support of the Nicaraguan rebels that had been defined by Congress.

"International terrorism" is the issue typically associated with the protection of citizens abroad. The State Department reports that American citizens, business firms, and government agencies have been targets of about a third of the attacks undertaken in the names of political causes and organizations in recent years.[1] American officials have staked out a posture against terrorism that is relatively aggressive by international standards. They have led efforts to legislate against terrorism in the United Nations and other international bodies, and have employed military force against foreign bases said to be sources of terrorist attacks against Americans.

The exposure of Americans to international terrorism is partly a function of the size of the U.S. population, the wealth of its economy, and a penchant to wander. Millions of Americans travel or work abroad, and there are substantial American investments overseas, plus extensive foreign representation of U.S. military, diplomatic, and other governmental agencies. The United States is viewed as the leader of an international camp of capitalist, Western, and developed nations. All this adds up to substantial American exposure to terrorist organizations based in foreign countries.

One can read the Constitution and conclude that it says nothing about the protection of citizens abroad. As in other fields of national security, however, several features of the Constitution do bear on the issue. Moreover, American politics and procedures for making and implementing policy that are structured by the Constitution affect the issue.

The elements of the Constitution that bear most directly on the protection of citizens abroad are the clauses granting authority to the president and Congress in the fields of defense and foreign relations. It is these provisions that stand behind the efforts of U.S. officials to reach agreements with foreign governments about the defense of American citizens or installations on their territory and attacks made by American forces against terrorists' bases. The provision in Article 1 that empowers Congress to "define and punish piracies and felonies committed on the high seas" seems to have lain dormant since the early days of the Republic,[2] but it may gain new importance with terror attacks against ships carrying American passengers or cargo.

As in other fields of security policy, the president's constitutional role as commander in chief of the armed forces and his priority in the making of treaties and other international agreements gives the executive branch the leading role in the protection of citizens abroad.[3] The roles of Congress derive from its power to "make rules . . . for the land and naval forces," its participation in defining the budget, the Senate's power to approve treaties, and Congress's general power to review the executive's activities. The judiciary enters the picture when it hears challenges to the activities of the legislature or the executive.

Constitutional provisions of civil liberties affect the way the executive and legislature can use their powers with respect to attacks on citizens abroad. The First, Second, Fourth, and Fifth Amendments provide freedoms of speech, press, assembly, and rights of petition; the right to bear arms; prohibitions against unreasonable searches and seizures; and due process in criminal cases. These provisions of the Constitution limit the means officials can use in gathering intelligence and apprehending suspected terrorists, and encourage some groups to organize in support of terror, while other groups press for severe antiterrorist action.

SPECIAL PROBLEMS OF DEALING WITH TERRORISM

The protection of citizens abroad has its own set of special requirements that distinguish it from other fields of national security. It is appropriate to examine these peculiarities before looking closely at the influence of the Constitution on policy making and implementation.

The simple label "terrorism" applied to attacks on citizens abroad is problematic in itself, and hints at some of the issues that complicate policy making and implementation. The epigram "one observer's 'terrorist' is another's 'freedom fighter'" summarizes much of the debate. It also highlights competing political perspectives that get in the way of precise definition and policy formulation.

Defining and Measuring the Problem

Several intellectuals have sought to sharpen the concept of terrorism. However enlightening their work, it does not simplify the tasks of policy making. Definitions feature ambiguous and contentious elements. Conor Cruise O'Brien defines terrorism in terms of the political context: as unjustified violence against a democratic state that permits affective and peaceful forms of opposition. Harold Lasswell defines terrorists as "participants in the political process who strive for political results by arousing acute anxieties." Martha Crenshaw would define terrorism by the morality of ends and means. She justifies Jewish terrorism against Nazis who sought to liquidate the Jewish people, but not the terrorism of the French Resistance, which caused worse horrors than those it sought to eliminate: Nazi reprisals that destroyed entire villages and slaughtered all their inhabitants.[4] Richard Schultz, Jr., and Stephen Sloan offer the component of "extranormal forms of political violence" to the definition of terrorism.[5]

William L. Waugh, Jr., has developed a multidimensional scheme to classify terrorism. The *ideological goals* of a group may be revolutionary or subrevolutionary. The *strategic goals* might be organizational enhancement, publicity, punishment of adversaries, provocation of authorities, or disruption. The *tactical goals* in a specific incident might include defined concessions (safe passage, ransom, release of prisoners) or the destruction of persons or property. Waugh writes that it may be unreasonable to pursue a hardline "no concessions, no negotiations" policy when facing subrevolutionaries seeking safe passage or money who have not yet killed their hostages. In contrast, a hard line might be appropriate when dealing with revolutionaries who have killed and who demand the release of incarcerated colleagues.[6]

Variations and ambiguities in definition lead to problems in defining the incidence of terrorism as well as the most likely targets. Data from the RAND Corporation and the CIA show striking differences in the incidents recorded. For the period 1968–77, RAND reported only 33 percent the number of international terrorist incidents and only 61 percent the number of deaths resulting from those incidents than did the CIA.[7]

It is common to report an increasing trend in terrorist incidents since the 1960s. The CIA's data show an increase from an annual average of 249 incidents worldwide during 1968–71 to an average of 756 during 1978–80. However, one prominent writer on the subject of terrorism—Walter Lequeur—is skeptical of the sophisticated quantitative research that has been reported. As of 1977, he was not convinced that terrorism was growing in incidence or was a fundamental threat to nations.[8]

A striking fact to emerge from the U.S. government's records of terrorist incidents is their tendency to occur outside the United States. As will become evident below, this has profound implications for those who make and implement policy against terrorists. CIA data limited to actions involving nationals of more than one country (what it labels "international terrorism") show the regions that recorded the most incidents during the 1968–80 period were Western Europe (2,206), Latin America (1,446) and the Middle East–North Africa (1,382). North America was a distant fourth (674).[9]

Why Isn't There More Terrorism within the United States?

This chapter focuses on the protection of citizens *abroad*. However, in order to put that problem in its larger perspective of providing security to citizens against terrorist attacks generally, it is worth raising the question of why so many attacks against American institutions and personnel perpetrated by foreign groups occur *outside* the United States. This hardly seems due to features of American institutions or policy that discourage domestic violence. A number of America's prominent traits—some of them derived from the Constitution and to be treated below as influences on the activities that can be pursued to protect citizens abroad—also seem to make the United States especially vulnerable to attacks on its own soil by the same groups that have perpetrated attacks overseas. These include:

— A multiplicity of largely uncoordinated police forces that vary considerably in their professional training and resources, weakening the security that can be mounted against domestic terror.

— The constitutional guarantees of civil liberties that restrict the activities of security forces, especially within the United States.

— The ease of obtaining weapons, ammunition, and explosives.

— The lack of mandatory population registration, with a requirement to carry official identification papers, that limits security forces in locating suspected criminals.

— A broadly defined "right to travel" that makes it difficult for the State Department to refuse passports to American citizens and allows the overseas travel of domestic dissidents to places where they might acquire training and logistic support for terrorist activities at home.

— ·Weak controls over the entry and continued presence of illegal immigrants that facilitates the presence of foreign-based terrorists within the United States.

— The diverse polity of the United States, with many ethnic groups, diverse perspectives, and a substantial incidence of individuals who are anomic or alienated politically, who can provide support to terrorist groups.[10]

The low incidence of terrorist attacks within the United States by foreign-based groups may reflect the problematic definitions and measures employed in the study of terrorism. In other words, there may be more attacks within the United States that could be labeled "terrorism" than revealed in the CIA reports cited above. The low incidence of terror within the United States may reflect the even greater ease of terrorist groups working in places like Beirut, Karachi, Athens, Rome, Vienna, plus other cities of Western Europe and Latin America. There they may take advantage of security forces even weaker than those of the United States. There are also sources of intelligence, logistic, and other support in the large ethnic communities that are friendly to their causes. In some of these cities there is support from foreign embassies that have close ties with the host government.

The low incidence of terror occurring within the United States may be a passing phase. The location of attacks may shift toward the United States if foreign-based terrorist groups retain their dedicated focus on American targets and learn to exploit the political fissures and administrative weaknesses in American society.

The Elusive Character of Terrorists

Several traits of terrorist groups make them difficult to locate and apprehend even in countries that do not provide their residents with the range of explicit freedoms enjoyed by Americans and where the authorities charged with internal security are professional and coordinated in a national hierarchy. Terrorist groups tend to be small and fluid, intensely concerned to maintain secrecy, and capable of severe discipline against members who violate their rules. Often they enjoy the financial or logistic support of foreign embassies, whose members can enter and leave a country freely, provide passports to their collaborators, and transmit "diplomatic pouches" without inspection.

These traits of terrorist groups make them poor targets for conventional security forces. Successful antiterrorist activities may depend on the use of agents who are intimately familiar with the language and culture of the terrorists and the infiltration of terrorist groups in order to gain access to their plans. In the case of attacks against Americans that occur in other countries, jurisdiction, effective defense against terrorism depends heavily on the cooperation of the host governments.

U.S. GOVERNMENT, POLITICS, AND ANTITERRORIST POLICY MAKING

Prominent features of American government and politics influence the way antiterrorist policy is made and implemented. The separation of powers and the numerous administrative agencies with a role in foreign relations and defense assure a variety of perspectives and problems of coordination. This variety is enhanced by the number of domestic groups with an interest in terrorism. Also, protections of civil liberties that appear in the Constitution and in legislation restrict the gathering of intelligence with respect to terrorists plans and operations, as well as the apprehension and conviction of suspected terrorists.

This section deals first with features of the U.S. Constitution and American politics as they affect the protection of citizens abroad. Then it is necessary to consider the foreign setting of terrorist incidents involving American citizens abroad, which requires international cooperation and assures that the laws and politics of other countries will bear heavily on what the United States can accomplish. In protecting citizens abroad, foreign conditions may outweigh U.S. constitutional provisions and American politics in determining the outcome of American policy efforts.

The Primary Actors: Who Is Responsible for What?

The constitutionally derived separation of powers and the extensive spread of administrative responsibilities within the American government complicate efforts to prepare for and react to terrorism. It is no small accomplishment to decide who is responsible for what and to hold each authority to preassigned activities.[11]

The primary actors in the protection of citizens abroad are the same as those who take a major role in other issues of national security. The president and the Congress derive their roles from constitutional powers dealing with defense, the making of treaties, and funding. Within the administration, the Departments of State and Defense and the CIA are prominent. Insofar as other bodies have a role in domestic security or the foreign interests of Americans—for example, the FBI, the Federal Aviation Administration, and the Department of Commerce—they also have an interest in the protection of citizens abroad. There is a parallel allocation of responsibilities among congressional committees and subcommittees with interests in national security and international relations.

The federal structure of American government that derives from the Constitution also has its implications for the protection of citizens abroad. Federalism—along with the tradition of local autonomy in most of the states—produces distinct state and local police forces, which guard their own turf against one another and against federal law enforcement and security bodies. Cooperation is something that must be pursued with diligence, and is by no means assured. The multiplicity of federal, state, and local security forces limits the single-minded pursuit and coordination of intelligence activities against the American partners of international terrorists. Also, the many security forces complicate efforts to maintain the secrecy of antiterrorist operations. State, local, and federal law enforcement bodies offer multiple sources of leaks to aggressive news media, who assert their own constitutional right to publish what they can learn about antiterrorist activities. According to one pessimistic assessment: "To control terrorism it is necessary for municipal police departments to cooperate with every federal investigative agency. . . . The federal agencies, however, find it most difficult to effect cooperation among themselves, and they are consequently unable to develop any lasting and mutually beneficial liaison with local police departments."[12]

Several bodies have been created to improve coordination among the different agencies with a role in antiterrorist activities. A cabinet committee on terrorism created during the 1970s was chaired by the secretary of state, and included representatives of twenty-three federal agencies.[13] In 1985 Secretary of State George Shultz announced the creation of the Overseas Security Advisory Council, composed of personnel from the State Department, American businesses operating abroad, U.S. law enforcement agencies, and other foreign policy agencies.[14]

Formal divisions of responsibility can become quite technical. Procedures in cases of airplane hijackings hold that the FBI is in charge within the United States if an incident occurs before an aircraft is in flying condition (doors closed); after that point the Federal Aviation Administration would be in charge of an incident.[15] The assignment of dominant roles for overseas incidents has turned on which agency has access to the most effective communications with the aircraft, authorities in the host government, the on-site U.S. ambassador, and various authorities in Washington and the airline. An analysis of Richard Starr's kidnapping in Colombia found that the government's response was delayed partly because of an unclear division of responsibility between the Peace Corps, in which he was a volunteer, and the State Department. This case, like others, also ran afoul of the American administration's policy of "no concessions, no negotiations." Starr was released eventually in response to activities of his mother, her representative in Congress, and newspaper columnist Jack Anderson, who acted as go-between with representatives of the kidnappers.[16] In another case suggesting fouled coordination, President Richard Nixon's dramatic but off-the-cuff assertion of "no concessions, no negotiations" may have resulted in the death of hostages in the Saudi Arabian Embassy seizure in Khartoum during 1973, just as intermediaries seemed likely to arrange their release.[17]

Thus, the plurality of actors in the protection of citizens abroad seems to assure competing perspectives. Politics does not stop at the water's edge. The response to the September 1984 bombing of the U.S. Embassy annex in Beirut produced a series of accusations and investigations that was not unusual. It was the third bombing of an American installation in Lebanon during a period of eighteen months. The first, at the old U.S. Embassy, killed more than 50. The second killed 241 U.S. military personnel at marine headquarters. The third killed 2 Americans and at least 12 other persons. Four congressional committees as well as the State Department and the CIA mounted their separate inquiries into the latest event.

Democrats in Congress charged the president and the State Department with not seeing that planned improvements in security were properly implemented. One response of the president was cast in his typical folksy style: "Anyone that's ever had their kitchen done over knows that it never gets done as soon as you wish it would." Three days later he was sounding more like a politician on the defensive: "We're feeling the effects today of the near destruction of our intelligence capability in recent years before we came [into office]."[18]

There was another division of responses after the American military strike against Libya in April 1986. Members of the president's own party, such as Senators Mark O. Hatfield and Lowell Weicker, spoke against the attack on account of the civilian casualties that it caused. Democratic Senators Robert C. Byrd and Sam Nunn asserted that the White House had only "notified" members of Congress about the military action and had not "consulted" as they felt was required by the War Powers Resolution of 1973. Yet Senate Foreign Relations Committee Chairman Richard G. Lugar and House Speaker Thomas P. O'Neill indicated that they were satisfied with the degree of consultation that had occurred.[19]

The definition of an appropriate stance toward terror has divided the administration at its highest levels. President Reagan and Secretary of State Shultz have proclaimed campaigns against international terror as being of the highest national priority, and they have spoken of the need to take preemptive strikes even at the risk of civilian casualties.[20] Vice President Bush and Secretary of Defense Weinberger have sought to limit military action to only the most narrowly defined targets, selected on the basis of firm information about the perpetrators of terror.[21]

The plurality of participants in the formulation and implementation of policy to protect citizens abroad includes administrative officials who disagree with the policies they are charged with enforcing. State Department employees—who are more than likely to be engaged in hostage episodes as captives or negotiators—have expressed opposition to the "no concessions, no negotiations" policy taken by their department. Beverly Carter, the U.S. ambassador to Tanzania, was reprimanded and denied an expected appointment for acting as an intermediary in a hostage situation in violation of that policy.[22]

Civil Liberties

The multiplicity of actors and differences in perspective can be thought of as one form of constraint that affects the American response to terrorism. Another constraint comes from the constitutional and statutory assurances of free expression, assembly, petition, privacy, due process, and the right to bear arms.

Freedoms of speech, prohibitions against unreasonable searches and seizures, and the assurance of due process in criminal cases limit the intelligence activities that can be mounted, especially within the United States, and restrict law enforcement officers in the apprehension and prosecution of suspected terrorists. Political dissidents have considerable freedom of speech and organization within the United States and are protected from casual searches and arrest by law enforcement authorities. A generalized "right to privacy" has been derived from those sections of the Constitution that deal specifically with freedoms of expression and association, freedom from unreasonable searches, and freedom from self-incrimination.[23] This provides additional support to those who oppose aggressive security forces or a national requirement to register one's address and carry an official identity card. The Second Amendment's "right of the people to keep and bear arms," reinforced by the failure to develop effective programs of weapons licensing and regulation, means that political dissidents have no trouble obtaining firearms.

The freedom of petition is the constitutional source that allows interest groups based upon ethnicity, ideology, or economic activities to bring their weight to bear in favor or against various policies. The prominence of Jewish groups among those that take a strong stand against terror reflects their identification with the victims of terrorist attacks against Israel and against synagogues and other Jewish institutions. The role of certain Irish-American groups as supporters of the Irish Republican Army (IRA) has served to complicate relations with the United Kingdom and to produce a situation in which the United States is accused of being soft on certain terrorists and their supporters. The prominence of American business personnel and facilities among the targets of terrorist attacks produces support for antiterrorist measures among the business lobby. However, the commercial motives of business firms may actually invite a higher incidence of hostage takings, insofar as businesses may be unconstrained by ideological inhibitions against paying ransom.[24] A number of the administration's strongest statements of antiterrorist policy have been made before Jewish groups or associations of multinational business firms.[25]

International political disputes linked to attacks on citizens abroad find expression in the postures taken by domestic American groups. Although Jewish-American organizations are likely to support a strong stand against the Palestine Liberation Organization, Arab-American organizations criticize the administration for "one-sided" support of Israel in the Middle East and cite the PLO as an appropriate representative of the Palestinian national movement.

The freedom of an aggressive press stands in the way of one recommendation offered by Walter Laqueur. He feels that the best way to combat terrorists is to deny them publicity and to remove from them the glorified image of desperate freedom fighters.[26] However, Laqueur offers no solution to the constitutional barriers against government control of the mass media.

The number of news media and the variety of their political perspectives have hampered any attempt to maintain what may have been at one time an informal agreement not to reveal sensitive issues related to national defense. Planning for the mission to rescue the Teheran hostages was flawed by a concern to keep the activity hidden from media likely to disclose the government's secret. Because of this concern, there was a lack of practice under simulated conditions. Some personnel met one another for the first time only when the mission was already under way and encountering unexpected difficulties.[27]

The freedoms of press and petition also provide the basis for the concerted attention given to an unfolding hostage crisis. Families of the hostages, individual politicians, and media personalities produce a national preoccupation with events and demands for immediate action. The Teheran hostage crisis was the longest-running drama. It preoccupied the country and President Carter throughout the 1980 election campaign, and may have contributed to Carter's defeat at the polls.[28] Each event also adds to the pressure on officials to do something in general terms about terror.

Both Republicans and Democrats in Congress have criticized legislative proposals by President Reagan designed to combat terrorists as being so broadly drawn as to threaten civil rights.[29] The American Civil Liberties Union said that certain of the president's proposals were largely symbolic and would not achieve anything not already provided by existing legislation.[30] The *New York Times* has taken a cautious stand in its editorials, urging the president not to overstep the bounds of law in his campaign against terror.[31]

Problems have been found in two administrative enactments designed to facilitate American intelligence activities with respect to terrorists: Presidential Executive Order Number 11905 of February 1976 extending the U.S. government's intelligence capacity to American residents thought to be operating in behalf of a foreign power; and the Privacy Act of 1974 facilitating the sharing of information about terrorism with foreign governments. These are said to be flawed by a lack of specificity as to the actions that are permitted and prohibited or by procedural errors in the manner of their proclamation.[32]

There is some dispute as whether U.S. actions against terror are limited more by formal restrictions or by the will of policy makers. Walter Berns argues that there has been a fundamental failure of political will to use the powers latent in the Constitution. He contrasts the divided and inconclusive postures expressed about terrorism with the forcefulness shown by President Abraham Lincoln, who found powers in the Constitution to use in defending the Union against the southern rebellion. Lincoln set himself up as the supreme law maker, entitled to exceed the limits set for him by Congress and the Supreme Court. The president ordered the incarceration of suspected secessionists contrary to Supreme Court orders upholding writs of habeas corpus.[33]

Bern's analysis is interesting for its historical analogy. However, Lincoln's success owed a great deal to the sense of emergency engendered by the Civil War. The contemporary issue of terrorism has hardly found a parallel position in political priorities.

The Foreign Setting and the Political Components

Several constraints with respect to American action flow from the foreign occurrence of terrorist attacks against U.S. targets. First, it is likely to be some other country's constitution, laws, politics, and administrative competence that define the defensive or retaliatory activities that can be mounted. Second, issues of international relations affect the legislation that can be enacted against terrorists in the United Nations and other multinational forums. Third, problems of coordinated planning and operations are made even more difficult by cross-national problems of communications, authority, and political sensitivities.

In order to clarify the dependence on foreign actors that appears in this area of national security, it will be useful to consider the frustrations faced by American officials who have tried to enact international legislation against terrorism.

Both the initial difficulty in enacting international laws or reaching agreements on bilateral arrangements and the subsequent problems of actually implementing laws or conventions that have been enacted derive from the sovereignty of individual nations. Behind many of these difficulties is the ingredient of political disputes embedded in terrorism. There are sharp disagreements in the international community as to what terrorism is and whether individuals labeled terrorists should be the subjects of sanctions or reward!

The United States has not been successful in persuading other nations that terrorism ought to be defined as a humanitarian rather than a political issue.[34] A common scenario is for an American legislative initiative against terrorism in an international forum to be smothered under antagonists' efforts to protect and praise those who use violence for purposes of national liberation or against colonialism, imperialism, racism, and other alleged oppressions. Some governments are proud to offer funds, technical assistance, or sanctuary to groups labeled "terrorist" by American officials.

"Political crimes exceptions" included in many existing treaties of extradition make them useless if a government holding a fugitive accepts the claim that the charge involved is a political one, such as violence perpetrated in the name of a political goal.[35] Disputes about the politics of terror occur within the Western camp of nations, as well as between the West and the East or the Third World. The United States is not only the accuser of states like the Soviet Union, Libya, and Syria for aiding terrorists.[36] The United States has also been accused by Great Britain of not doing enough to shut off the sources of funds and arms within the United States for Irish terrorists. The U.S. Senate only recently approved a treaty limiting the use of the "political crimes" exception in the case of extraditions between the United States and Great Britain. Under the treaty, murder, hijacking, kidnapping, and the planting of explosives will be exempted from the claim of having been political crimes.[37] For its part, the U.S. government protested when the British declined to adopt economic sanctions against Iran after the seizure of American diplomatic personnel in Teheran.[38]

One tactic that has been used to recruit support against terrorism in international forums is to limit the offenses to be outlawed. The following formulation of an illegal act was meant to avoid intrusion into the domestic disputes between governments and their residents, as well as to include enough ambiguities to appeal to those concerned with Palestinian interests:

> an act taking place or having effects outside the territory of the state in which the offender was a national; whose victims are citizens of a state other than that where the attack took place; where the attack is committed neither by nor against a member of the armed forces in the course of military hostilities; and where the attack is intended to damage the interests or obtain concessions from a state or international organization.

Despite the gaps purposely left in this formulation, its introduction in the United Nations led a Third World and socialist bloc to replace it with their own resolution condemning racist and colonial regimes as terrorist, and creating an ad hoc committee to consider the problem of international terrorism.[39]

It is in response to such frustrations that some activists have turned their attention to drafting international enactments that avoid the label of terrorism and are directed against specific activities that are widely condemned. There has been some success in legislating against aircraft hijacking and the kidnapping of persons who enjoy diplomatic protection[40] In their implementation, however, even these modest enactments are likely to run afoul of states' unwillingness to extradite those charged with "political crimes." Of the seventy-eight cases that produced requests for extradition of aircraft hijackers during the 1960–76 period, extradition was granted in only five instances.[41] An often-cited case of bowing to pressures of the moment is that of France's release of the suspected terrorist Abu Daoud in 1977, despite extradition requests being pressed by the United States and Great Britain.[42] Enactments against hijacking and kidnapping do not solve the problem of states that serve as sanctuaries for those who have committed certain crimes or crimes against certain countries.[43] Where there have been bilateral agreements to limit the application of the "political crimes exception" in extradition treaties, they have not yet proved their capacity to withstand the pressures mounted in difficult cases where perpetrators are members of well-known organizations.[44]

Some of the United States' problems in international forums may be attributed to the many Third World governments that identify the United States as a source of justifiable complaints that cause terrorism. Yugoslavia's credentials in the Third World and "uncommitted" blocs may have allowed it to succeed with a resolution that it introduced in the United Nations against the seizure of "protected persons" (i.e., diplomats).[45] Or Yugoslavia's success may have been due to the greater specificity of the resolution (directed against a specific action and avoiding the label "terrorism"), or to its focus on protecting the kinds of persons (i.e., diplomats) who draft and enact UN resolutions.

HOW THE UNITED STATES HAS COPED WITH THE CONSTRAINTS

There may be no solution for the security problem of protecting citizens abroad. The complexities of international politics that are intertwined with the issue of terrorism and the need for international cooperation in dealing with the issue limits what any one country can accomplish. The limits are especially severe for a global power like the United States. American personnel and installations are found in many countries whose governments are hostile to the United States or less friendly to the United States than to other governments or political movements that are hostile to the United States.

Although "solution" may have no place in this discussion, the United States has had some success in "coping" with the problem of protecting citizens abroad. It has won some victories in international forums and has taken military action against sources of terrorist attacks. Such actions may limit the damage that will be done by terrorists, even if they do not end the problem of terrorism.

The United States has achieved bilateral agreements between itself and countries with which it shares specific interests. An agreement with Cuba to return hijackers served to stop a rash of plane snatchings, and agreements with Canada, Argentina, Spain, and Great Britain limit the use of the political defense in existing extradition treaties.[46]

An ongoing hostage situation provokes several questions. Their consideration will show that constitutional provisions are of secondary importance in this area of protecting citizens abroad. More important are the foreign setting of the incidents and pressures coming from domestic and international politics.

Some questions have to be answered under the immediate pressures from captors, hostages, the families of hostages, the mass media, and involved politicians from the United States and the host government:

— Should there be negotiations?
— Should there be concessions?
— Should there be a rescue attempt?

Other questions are no less vexatious, but they can wait until the immediate crisis is past:

— Should there be reprisals against those who perpetrate or provide aid to the terrorists?

— Should there be preemptive strikes against the bases of suspected terrorists?

The United States has proclaimed a policy of "no concessions, no negotiations" with respect to hostage situations. For several years, this has been criticized and sometimes violated, even by State Department personnel charged with implementing it. Critics charge that the policy is too simple and too harsh. Although some demands of some terrorists might properly be resisted at all costs, other demands might be discussed or negotiated, especially if hostages' lives might be saved.

Israel's experience with terrorism and its efforts to maintain a "no concessions, no negotiations" posture helps to illuminate the American problem. Despite their reputation for toughness in dealing with terrorists, Israeli officials have negotiated in hostage situations. They ordered the storming of a school building in the town of Maalot only after it was decided that negotiations would not result in the release of hostages. During 1985 the Israeli government exchanged more than 1,000 prisoners, including some of the most notorious of its convicted terrorists (e.g., the Japanese Kozo Okamoto who participated in killing more than thirty incoming passengers at Lod Airport during 1972) for three Israeli soldiers held by organizations identified by the Israelis as terrorist. At the time, the defense minister said that this was a special case meant to convince Israeli soldiers that the government would do everything possible to gain their release from capture. However, the subtlety of the departure from a "no concessions, no negotiations" policy was lost on much of the Israeli public.

The crisis about American arms transfers to Iran that reached the mass media in November 1986 indicated that the White House may have abandoned this policy of "no concessions, no negotiations" with respect to American hostages held by Shi'ite groups in Lebanon, but without clarifying the change for leaders of the State Department or Congress.

It is not only that a "no concessions, no negotiations" policy suffers from a lack of workability under intense pressures to save certain individuals from the hands of terrorists. It is also not clear that a "no concessions, no negotiations" policy succeeds in dissuading terrorists from acting in the future. The limited evidence suggests the opposite. A comparison of the hardline U.S. policy with the willingness to negotiate of West German and Japanese governments during the 1970–75 period found that the United States continued to be subject to a higher incidence of attacks than those countries.[47]

In practical terms, the U.S. preference for a "no concessions, no negotiations" posture may take second place to the preferences of the government where hostages are held. Determining factors include national pride, the loyalties of the host country's politicians to the causes espoused by terrorists, the great distance from key American decision makers and the military forces that the United States has prepared for a rescue contingency, and local officials' desire to avoid the overt involvement of American officials or military units. Concessions have been pressed upon negotiators by local officials. Terrorists have been sent to safe havens in third countries. There have been ill-conceived rescue attempts by local forces that have paid a heavy cost in the lives of hostages.

The rescue option generates sharp debates as to its effectiveness and cost. Successful operations like those by the Israelis at Entebbe and the Germans at Mogadishu make dramatic stories. However, they do not blot out the costly failures of the Germans at the Munich Olypics in 1972, the Americans storming of the ship *Mayaguez* in 1975, which caused more deaths among rescuers and hostages than it saved, the American embarrassment in the Iranian desert in 1980, the Egyptians at Malta, and the Pakistanis at Karachi in 1986.

Questions about reprisals and preemptive strikes raise ambiguous issues of moral propriety and effectiveness, and they show that the United States depends on the political considerations of other governments. The United States has bombarded the bases of terrorists who acted against American personnel in both Lebanon and Libya. In neither case was it likely that the strikes would end terrorist attacks against Americans. At the most, such attacks may lessen the incidence of such attacks by persuading potential attackers or their supporters that they may pay an unduly high price for their activities. Again an Israeli example helps to illustrate the American problem.

Israeli raids on terrorist bases are said to be based on the assumption that they will strike their own terror into the hearts of the PLO and its associated organizations and encourage them to seek out softer targets.[48] Israel begins with the advantage of terrorist bases being within reach of the Israeli military without the assistance of foreign governments. Also, Israelis are—compared to Americans—relatively united in agreement about the need to strike hard on the sources of terror. Yet Israeli critics charge that their government's policy does not end terror.[49] Indeed, preemptive strikes and reprisals seem to assure a steady supply of terrorists, driven to action by the damage done to their homes and families. Israeli military activities in Lebananon from 1982 onward dealt a serious blow to the Palestine Liberation Organization. However, there has been a postwar wave of stabbings of Israelis by single attackers, seemingly without organizational affiliation. Reprisals and preemptive strikes may limit terrorist attacks that endanger large numbers of people. They cannot assure protection against enraged youths who use kitchen knives to attack individuals. The isolated individual acting alone against a single civilian target may be the ultimate terrorist, impervious to the known techniques of national security. American tourists who wander into crowded markets, as well as business executives, civilian government employees, and military officers on the way to work, are likewise exposed to a possibility of violence that cannot be eliminated entirely.

The U.S. military reprisal against Libya in the spring of 1986 offers its own insights into the international politics that are integrally associated with national security policy against terror. It was not easy for the United States to elicit international cooperation for the strike, despite considerable indications that the regime of Mu'ammar al-Qadhdhafi was involved in terrorist attacks on the terrain of several countries, with casualties to their own civilians. Other national governments feared reprisals from Libyan-aided terrorists, as well as the animosity of other Arab and Third World governments that might be led to identify themselves with a North African country attacked by a Western power. The British government of Mrs. Margaret Thatcher did consent to the use of its land and airspace for U.S. planes that participated in the attack. However, once the British role in the affairs was revealed, there began a domestic attack on Mrs. Thatcher—partly from members of her own Conservative Party—that may limit British cooperation in the future.

CONCLUSIONS

The international importance of the American economy, the many Americans who travel and live abroad, and the prominent international roles of the U.S. government expose American facilities and citizens to terrorist attacks abroad. Attacks occurring on foreign sites are in the jurisdiction of other countries' constitutions and laws, however, limiting the applicability of the U.S. Constitution to this issue. The political considerations of other governments are likely to determine the steps that may be taken to protect American citizens located in their jurisdictions.

Among the domestic elements that determine the policies of the U.S. government with respect to the protection of citizens abroad, the pervasive separation of powers and the plural nature of the American polity assure dispute between and within the various branches of the government. Criticism of the administration's policy or activities comes prominently from opposition members in Congress. Variations in stance have also been apparent in the comments of the president, vice president, and cabinet secretaries.

More than a score of federal agencies have roles in dealing with terrorism. Sorting out their responsibilities and establishing lines of cooperation with parallel activities of the private sector has required the appointment of cabinet-level committees. Although the State Department has been given prominence in coordinating operations, sharp criticism of the government's "no concessions, no negotiations" policy has come from ranking professionals within that department.

Civil liberties guaranteed by the Constitution limit the intelligence and security operations that the government can mount, especially within the United States. The assertiveness of the press in exercising its constitutional rights has constrained the executive branch in planning and carrying out missions that depend for their success on strict secrecy.

The United States has not been successful in promoting multinational enactments against terrorism. By one explanation, the weight of "Western" or "civilized" nations is too small in international forums.[50] By another explanation, the division of interests among all kinds of nations is too great for a politically loaded concept to acquire status in international law. Even countries strikingly similar in culture and law—like the United States and the United Kingdom—have had trouble convincing one another to work in tandem on issues pertaining to Irish and Iranian terrorists.

Observers who are troubled by the lack of finality in U.S. actions against terrorism may see some prospect for greater success in constitutional change or other domestic reforms. National identity cards, more effective border controls, and limited access to weapons may lessen the potential for terror against Americans at home. More integrated law enforcement and security forces within the United States may attain intelligence advantages against terrorists who attack Americans abroad. Yet such activities ought to be viewed in the light of several commentaries that caution against an overreaction in the face of terrorism.

According to some observers, excessive reactions against terrorists include intelligence and surveillance activities that violate the civil rights customarily associated with democratic regimes, taking too hard a line in refusing to negotiate with all terrorists, armed rescue attempts, preemptive strikes, and reprisals.

One example of overreaction in a Western democracy may be the record of detentions made under the United Kingdom's Prevention of Terrorism Act (Temporary Provisions) of 1974 and 1976. As of October 1977, only 247 of 5,875 persons detained had been charged with an offense, and only 129 of these were charged with an offense specifically falling under the act.[51]

The concern about an overreaction against terrorism includes an assertion that terrorism is a form of low-level warfare that does not threaten a society's destruction. Terrorism's recent popularity may reveal that its practictioners—and the governments that support them—have despaired of conventional assaults against their targets and strike out in anger. Terrorist groups often kill more of their own people in internecine struggles then they kill of their declared enemies. Roberta Goren's analysis of Soviet support for various terrorist movements takes account of the USSR's inability to topple its Western adversaries.[52] Rather than seriously seeking to undermine Western governments, the USSR may be providing modest aid to terrorists as a way of gaining political benefits in the Third World.

Perhaps no state has been more beset by terrorist threats than Israel. Moreover, the Palestinian terrorists are exceptional in the amount of resources that allied governments have put at their disposal. Yet the Israeli government gains domestic support in response to its firm policies toward terrorism.[53] A British observer writes that terrorism is a weapon of the weak: "It is extensively used in the initial stages, when the movement is at its weakest . . . and reversion to it probably indicates declining strength, and is likely to follow military defeats."[54]

In the light of skepticism as to the power of terrorists, a concerned citizen should ask if reform of the U.S. Constitution or political system is worth what might be a marginal contribution toward greater success in protecting Americans abroad. Terrorists cause individual tragedies and national embarrassment. They generate media attention and create pressure on politicians to do something. However, terrorists do not threaten the integrity of the United States. Moreover, the foreign setting of attacks against Americans puts the emphasis on international cooperation, as opposed to unilateral U.S. efforts. The Constitution as presently drafted and interpreted provides substantial authority for defense and making international agreements for the protection of citizens abroad. What is lacking is the capacity of American and foreign officials to agree about policy and to implement their agreements. In the thicket of international dispute that surrounds the issue of protecting citizens from terrorism, there are few clear victories.

NOTES

1. "Terror: Americans as Targets," *New York Times,* 26 November 1985, p. A1.
2. The 1978 revision of Edward S. Corwin's classic *The Constitution and What It Means Today* by Harold W. Chase and Craig R. Ducat (Princeton, N.J.: Princeton University Press) does not even comment on this provision.
3. Herman Pritchett, *Constitutional Law of the Federal System* (Englewood Cliffs, N.J.: Prentice-Hall, 1984), pp. 307f.
4. Martha Crenshaw, ed., *Terrorism, Legitimacy, and Power: The Consequences of Political Violence* (Middletown, Conn: Wesleyan University Press, 1983), pp. 1–37.
5. "International Terrorism: The Nature of the Threat," in Stephen Sloan and Richard Schultz, Jr., eds., *Responding to the Terrorist Threat: Security and Crisis Management* (New York: Pergamon Press, 1980), pp. 1–17.
6. William L. Waugh, Jr., "The Values in Violence: Organizational and Political Objectives of Terrorist Groups," *Conflict Quarterly* 3, no. 4 (Summer 1983): 5–19.

7. Grant Wardlaw, *Political Terrorism: Theory, Tactics, and Counter-Measures* (Cambridge: Cambridge University Press, 1982), p. 52.

8. Walter Laqueur, *Terrorism* (London: Weidenfeld & Nicolson, 1977), pp. 223–26.

9. Edward Mickolus, "International Terrorism" in Michael Stohl, ed., *The Politics of Terrorism* (New York: Marcel Dekker, 1983), pp. 221–53.

10. Paul Wilkinson, *Terrorism and the Liberal State* (London: Macmillan, 1977).

11. Robert H. Kupperman and Darrell M. Trent, *Terrorism: Threat, Reality, Response* (Stanford, Calif.: Hoover Institution Press, 1979).

12. John B. Wolf, *Fear of Fear: A Survey of Terrorist Operations and Controls in Open Societies* (New York: Plenum Press, 1981), p. 47.

13. Wayne A. Kerstetter, "Practical Problems of Law Enforcement," in Alona E. Evans and John F. Murphy, eds., *Legal Aspects of International Terrorism* (Lexington, Mass: Lexington Books, 1978), pp. 535–72.

14. George Shultz, "U.S. Government and Business: A Common Defense against Terrorism," *Department of State Bulletin*, March 1985, pp. 10–12.

15. Diane T. Berliner and L. Douglas Heck, "Thoughts on a Hijacking," in Martin F. Herz, ed., *Diplomats and Terrorists: What Works, and What Doesn't* (Washington, D.C.: Georgetown University Institute for the Study of Diplomacy, 1982), pp. 18–21.

16. Anthony C. E. Quainton, "The Starr Case: A Bureaucracy under Stress," in ibid., pp. 41–44.

17. Brian M. Jenkins, "Some Simple Principles Based on Experience," in ibid., pp. 48–54.

18. John Felton, "Reagan, Hill Move to Bolster Embassy Security," *Congressional Quarterly Weekly*, 29 September 1984, pp. 2401–3.

19. Pat Towell, "After Raid on Libya, New Questions on Hill," *Congressional Quarterly Weekly*, 19 April 1986, pp. 838–39.

20. "Shultz Asks Move against Terrorism," *New York Times*, 4 April 1984, p. A13; "US Plans Tough Policy on Terrorism," *New York Times*, 17 April 1984, p. A3; George Shultz, "Terrorism and the Modern World," *Department of State Bulletin*, December 1984.

21. Bernard Givertzman, "Shultz's Address Touches off Stir in Administration," *New York Times*, 27 October 1984, p. A1.

22. Ernest Evans, "American Policy Response to International Terrorism," in Yonah Alexander and Seymour Maxwell Finger, eds., *Terrorism: Interdisciplinary Perspectives* (New York: John Jay Press, 1977), pp. 106–17.

23. C. Herman Pritchett, *The American Constitution* (New York: McGraw-Hill, 1968), pp. 684–88.

24. By one count, business personnel were 54 percent of the kidnap victims taken after 1970. See Yonah Alexander and Robert A. Kilmarx, eds., *Political Terrorism and Business: The Threat and Response* (New York: Praeger, 1979), introduction.

25. See Shultz. "Terrorism and the Modern World" and "U.S. Government and Business: A Common Defense against Terrorism."

26. Laqueur, *Terrorism*, pp. 223–26.

27. Gary Sick, *All Fall Down: America's Tragic Encounter with Iran* (New York: Random House, 1985), p. 354.

28. Ibid.

29. Stuart Taylor, Jr., "Three Senators Foresee a Threat in Antiterrorism Bill," *New York Times*, 6 June 1984, p. 7.

30. Stuart Taylor, Jr., "Reagan Sends Congress Four Bills Aimed at International Terrorism," *New York Times*, 27 April 1984, p. 1.

31. "Resisting Terror—and Lawlessness," *New York Times*, 29 April 1984, IV, p. 20.

32. Kerstetter, "Practical Problems of Law Enforcement," claims that the White House

failed to take the required step of publishing certain memoranda in the *Federal Register*.
33. Walter Berns, "Constitutional Power and the Defense of Free Government," in Benjamin Netanyahu, ed., *Terrorism: How the West Can Win* (New York: Farrar, Straus & Giroux, 1986), pp. 149–55.
34. Ernest Evans, "American Policy Response to International Terrorism: Problems of Deterrence," in Alexander and Finger, eds., *Terrorism*, pp. 106–17.
35. Alona E. Evans, "The Realities of Extradition and Prosecution," in ibid., pp. 128–38.
36. On the issue of the Soviet support for terrorism, see Roberta Goren, *The Soviet Union and Terrorism* (London: George Allen & Unwin, 1984).
37. "A Blow against IRA Terrorism: Uncle Sam Gets Tough," *Newsweek*, 28 July 1986.
38. Paul Wilkinson, "Proposals for Government and International Responses to Terrorism," in Wilkinson, ed., *British Perspectives on Terrorism* (London: George Allen & Unwin, 1981), pp. 161–93.
39. Ernest Evans, "American Policy Response to International Terrorism: Problems of Deterrence," in Alexander and Finger, eds., *Terrorism*, pp. 106–17.
40. Alfred P. Rubin, "International Terrorism and International Law," in ibid., pp. 122–27.
41. Alona E. Evans, "The Realities of Extradition and Prosecution," in ibid., p. 130.
42. John E. Karkashian, "Too Many Things Not Working," in Herz, ed., *Diplomats and Terrorists*, pp. 6–9.
43. Wardlaw, *Political Terrorism*, esp. chap. 11.
44. Kerstetter, "Practical Problems of Law Enforcement," pp. 535–72.
45. Seymour M. Finger, "The United Nations Response to Terrorism," in Alexander and Kilmarx, eds., *Political Terrorism and Business*, pp. 267–80.
46. Alona E. Evans, "The Realities of Extradition and Prosecution," in Alexander and Finger, eds., *Terrorism*, pp. 128–38.
47. Ernest Evans, *Calling a Truce to Terror: The American Response to International Terrorism* (Westport, Conn: Greenwood Press, 1979), pp. 87–88.
48. J. Bowyer Bell, *Transnational Terror* (Washington, D.C.: American Enterprise Institute, 1975.)
49. For a critique of Israeli antiterrorist programs by a professional military analyst, see Hanon Alon, *Countering Palestinian Terrorism in Israel: Toward a Policy Analysis of Countermeasures* (Santa Monica, Calif.: RAND Corporation, 1980).
50. Laqueur, *Terrorism*, p. 224.
51. Wardlaw, *Political Terrorism*, chap. 7.
52. Goren, *The Soviet Union and Terrorism*.
53. Crenshaw, *Terrorism, Legitimacy, and Power*, introduction.
54. Brian Crozier, *A Theory of Conflict* (London: Hamish Hamilton, 1974), p. 129.

9

Conducting Diplomacy

ROBERT H. FERRELL

The conduct of diplomacy today, in the dangerous latter years of the twentieth century, constitutes the nation's most important challenge. Unless the arms race slows down; unless emplacement of nuclear weapons and carriers does not merely stop, but is reversed, moving toward their elimination; unless the spread of such weapons and carriers to other nations can be halted and reversed, the cost of the U.S. military establishment will continue to escalate, while national security plummets.

Having said this, one must remark on the intense awkwardness of attempting to deal with present-day diplomacy through an eighteenth-century Constitution. The idea of the Founding Fathers that there should be checks and balances, notably the division of government under the Constitution into executive and legislative branches, is perplexingly complicated. It has produced rivalries at a time when clarity, rather than confusion, is much needed in American diplomatic dealing.

This says nothing about the outside forces that necessarily impinge upon constitutional organization and requirements: interest groups, congressional constituencies, and the ever-present media—newspapers, radio, and television. They either seek to bend government (and in foreign relations that means diplomacy) to their will, ask consideration of parochial interests, or, in the case of the media, venture to define the purposes and discern the course of the government's diplomacy, and sometimes are not above attempting to change purposes and courses.

What can come of the conduct of diplomacy so cumbersomely organized under the Constitution, of diplomacy also likely to be assailed by outside forces? In 1987 the Soviet Union raised an attractive disarmament proposal that already had been heard in Europe several years earlier, namely, to eliminate all intermediate-range ballistic missiles. It was a technical proposition and required thought by all officials of the government, not to mention interest groups, congressional constituencies, and the media. But it would have to be decided by a Republican president and a Democratic Congress. Moreover, the executive and legislature were at loggerheads over the so-called Iran-Contra affair, a complex situation in which the president had secretly allowed the sale of arms to Iran in hope that the Iranians would influence Lebanese radicals to release American hostages, and in which a presidential assistant, apparently without the president's knowledge, and contrary to a congressional prohibition, then transferred the profit from the arms sale to the Nicaraguan rebels known as the Contras, so that the latter could purchase arms themselves. The Iran-Contra affair involved the constitutional prerogatives of the executive and the legislature. Interest groups, congressional constituencies, and the media at once entered the fray. In the resulting contretemps, the disarmament proposal could easily fail to receive the attention that it deserved.

DIPLOMACY AND THE CONSTITUTION

The Constitution refers to diplomacy in only six specific instances. How, then, has the nation's diplomacy—reporting of events abroad and representation of U.S. commercial and political interests, together with occasional distribution of foreign aid—been affected by the great document of 1787?[1]

Consider, first of all, the way in which the Founding Fathers subtly divided authority over diplomatic matters between the executive and the legislature. The Constitution provides that the president "shall nominate, and by and with the advice and consent of the Senate, shall appoint ambassadors."[2] There is no question but that the need to concert nominations with the Senate, to obtain the consent of the latter, has produced exceeding caution on the part of presidents, who prefer no open challenges to nominations. The result has usually been gentlemanly reception of nominations by the Senate, and yet there have been embarrassments cunningly arranged. In such cases the proposed envoys have often abandoned their hopes, discovering reasons why they should not undertake what they wished. Or the executive has found excuses to withdraw the nominations. Once in a while senators have asked unseemly questions, obtaining either no answers or poor answers, and nominations have then gone through, but they have been mortgaged, and the subsequent missions have gone poorly. A generation ago the Ohio clothing tycoon Maxwell H. Gluck, chosen by President Dwight D. Eisenhower to represent the United States in Sri Lanka, was asked by a perhaps bored, but also suspecting, senator to name the prime minister, Mr. Bandaranaike, of the country to which he was to be accredited. Gluck could not do so. There was a furor before the nominee, whose claim to the embassy was in some part his $21,500 campaign contribution to the Republican party treasury, did his homework and was appointed. Thereupon he exhibited his good fortune, inadvisedly perhaps, as he only reminded auditors and newspaper readers of his humiliation. "Gluck," he said waggishly to reporters: "Gluck. It rhymes with luck." But his mission was ill-starred; he remained in Colombo only a year, leaving few diplomatic results. The inquiring senator had asserted the authority of the Upper House; the executive and Gluck had been chastised; and American diplomacy had hardly been assisted.

Fortunately, the other constitutional references to diplomacy have not divided authority, although they have produced other troubles. In one passage the Constitution provides that the president "shall . . . receive ambassadors and other public ministers."[3] This might seem a matter of common sense, and ordinarily it would be, except that it can have a diplomatic meaning if the president decides—as happened in one notable instance—not to receive an accredited envoy. In 1919–20 President Woodrow Wilson was a very ill man, having suffered a severe stroke in October 1919 that required months of rest. Using his indisposition as a palpable excuse, he refused to receive the new British ambassador, Lord Grey, the former foreign secretary. The underlying reason was trivial in the extreme. A member of Grey's suite, a young military attaché, may have spoken disrespectfully of Mrs. Wilson, and the president refused to receive Grey until the ambassador dismissed the assistant, which Grey refused to do. It was possible also that the president believed Grey had been consorting with senators who opposed the Treaty of Versailles. The episode's real proportions are difficult to know. In any event Grey never saw the president and returned to England in bitterness, where he made a public pronouncement in favor of an amended Covenant of the League of Nations that infuriated the president and sadly harmed Anglo-American relations.[4]

A third reference to diplomacy in the Constitution is that the judicial branch of the government shall not merely deal in "all cases affecting ambassadors, other public ministers and consuls, and those in which a state shall be party"; the Supreme Court, the Constitution relates, "shall have original jurisdiction" in such cases.[5] This constitutional injunction has never been a serious issue. Nations are sensitive to legal awkwardness involving envoys and tend to withdraw ambassadors upon signs of trouble. Envoys who become inconvenient are always subject to recall for reasons of health, or other excuses easily manufactured. Moreover, it is possible for a host country to declare an ambassador persona non grata, which requires no explanation. As for involvement of states of the Union in disputes with foreign powers, the constitutional allocation of authority to the Supreme Court was a wise precaution, but in fact has resulted in little adjudication.

A fourth reference in the Constitution is that Congress shall have the power to declare war, and this specification rightly deserves discussion in other chapters of the present book. The fifth and sixth constitutional references, that the president shall have power to make treaties by and with the advice and consent of the Senate, and that treaties shall be the supreme law of the land, are likewise dealt with later (see chapter 10 below).[6]

To be sure, the Constitution has not been the only factor in determining American diplomacy. Diplomatic practice has introduced many novelties. In the eighteenth century the idea of wars fought by coalitions was fairly common, and yet once the coalitions formed, the war of the moment usually ran its course without much international cooperation. In the twentieth century, however, the United States has fought two world wars in coalition, and of course against coalitions of enemies. The need for a common strategy and for war against enemy coalitions has much changed American diplomacy. Closely allied with such coalition diplomacy in our present century has been the need, beginning with NATO in 1949, to negotiate within seemingly permanent peacetime alliances. And there has been the twentieth century's diplomacy of international organizations, notably the League of Nations after World War I and the United Nations after World War II.

But the principal reason that American diplomacy has been conducted the American way surely relates to its ordering under the Constitution, especially the division of authority between the executive and the legislature.

THE PRESIDENT, THE CONSTITUTIONAL SYSTEM, AND DIPLOMACY

The president of the United States, by virtue of his right under the Constitution to nominate ambassadors and to receive envoys, is of course the federal official who directs diplomacy. After confirmation, American envoys abroad usually receive an audience with the president, which includes instruction of some sort. When they present their credentials abroad, the latter are from the president to the chiefs of state of the nations to which they are accredited.

Because American diplomats represent the president—this was an imitation of European monarchical practice—there is a temptation for the president to become a diplomat, and such has often happened. Ministers and ambassadors (the United States began employing the latter rank on a reciprocal basis only in 1893) of foreign countries have sought to talk to the president, and presidents have encouraged the attention. Sometimes special representatives have appeared, as in the months before the American Civil War, when the Prince of Wales came to the United States. The first visit of a British prime minister, Ramsay MacDonald, occurred in 1929. MacDonald was followed two years later by a French premier, Pierre Laval.[7] In the summer of 1939, President Franklin D. Roosevelt received the king and queen of England, who came to the United States to demonstrate their country's plight just before the opening of World War II.

For many years American presidents carefully conducted their personal diplomacy at home; they did not journey to foreign nations, there to be received like visiting monarchs. The reason was that the Constitution, they believed, forbade their leaving the country. In this they were mistaken, for the practice of staying home originated out of inconvenience rather than constitutional prohibition. In the early days of the Republic, ocean voyages to Europe were lengthy, and presidents who wished to be diplomats could hardly have afforded the time, not to mention the peril, which often was considerable. By the mid nineteenth century and introduction of steamships, the practice that a president should remain in his own country had been established. By the early twentieth century, presidents took it as an article of faith that they must not leave the country. After the Spanish-American War, President William McKinley would have liked to have made a triumphal tour of Europe, but feared to raise the possibility, which would have concerned both his countrymen and the Senate. Theodore Roosevelt introduced a slight change in practice by visiting Panama during construction of the canal, but did not go out of the Canal Zone, which for all intents and purposes (a ninety-nine-year lease) was American territory. His successor, William H. Taft, gave up vacations in Canada for fear of criticism, although he did venture across the border into Mexico for a few moments to converse with the president of Mexico.

At last President Wilson broke this practice after World War I, when he went to the Paris Peace Conference and remained for six months, with the exception of a month during which he returned to the United States to sign legislation and meet with administration officials and congressional leaders. For a while thereafter matters reverted to tradition; Warren Harding journeyed only to Alaska, and Calvin Coolidge went to Cuba in 1928 for one day to make a speech to a Pan-American Conference. But then President Franklin Roosevelt met Prime Minister Winston Churchill at Placentia Bay off Newfoundland in 1941, and followed with wartime conferences at Casablanca, Teheran, and Yalta, diplomacy on a grand geographical scale. In the two generations since the end of World War II, presidential trips for diplomatic purposes have become commonplace, perhaps because of the ease of travel after introduction of jet passenger planes in the mid 1950s. The panoply accompanying foreign visits is instantly translated to American living rooms via the television screen, and an incidental result has perhaps been the creation of the so-called imperial presidency.

Presidential diplomacy, endorsed not by the Constitution but by the increasing ease of travel and probably the political advantages of pageantry when recorded by television, has been carried on not merely by presidents but by their alter egos—personal representatives of their own choice. The roster of special envoys begins with Gouverneur Morris, the stylist of the Constitution, whom President George Washington sent to England in 1790 at a time of confrontation between the British and Spanish governments over a Spanish settlement at Nootka Sound in Canada. Subsequent presidents have proved fond of personal envoys, such as the succession of representatives President Wilson sent to revolutionary Mexico. The same president's use of his friend and confidant Edward M. House as an envoy to European capitals before and during American participation in World War I is well known, and Franklin Roosevelt similarly employed special envoys before and during World War II.[8]

To assist their diplomacy, presidents have also surrounded themselves with White House staffers. In 1947 the National Security Act created the National Security Council, nominally to coordinate foreign affairs with military policy, but actually for what turned out to be the organization of a presidential staff largely to handle foreign affairs. President Eisenhower created the position of special assistant for national security affairs. President John F. Kennedy appointed to the post the dean of Harvard College, McGeorge Bundy, and thereafter, until the Reagan presidency, with the exception of Lieutenant General Brent Scowcroft, the national security advisers were academics—Walt W. Rostow, Henry A. Kissinger, Zbigniew Brzezinski. Reagan first appointed a quasi-academic from a "think tank," Richard Allen, and then mostly chose men of military background, the second of whom, Vice Admiral John Poindexter, resigned because of the linking of arms for Iran with money for the Contras. The office of national security advisor, legislatively an advisory office, had become a locus of both negotiation and operations.

THE SECRETARY OF STATE, THE DEPARTMENT, THE ENVOYS

The most important way of conducting diplomacy, however, has been negotiation not by the president, assisted by his staffers, but by resort to a secretary of state and the cabinet department known as the Department of State, which in turn has organized and supervised the work of envoys sent abroad.

The Constitution says nothing about a secretary or department, although it refers to "departments" of the government. Indeed, it says nothing about a cabinet. The Founding Fathers did not wish to produce a long, detailed document, preferring to pass details of administration to President Washington, who had presided over the constitutional convention.[9]

The secretaryship and the department thus came into being, not merely to manage diplomacy, but to handle many of the formalities of the new government, including the keeping of the great seal and affixing of it to state papers. Well into the nineteenth century, secretaries of state, and sometimes presidents, signed innumerable legal papers, such as land grants (any teacher of history in colleges and universities in the former Northwest Territory has had students bring in these papers, duly signed and sealed, now possessing considerable value because of their signatures). The early secretaries of state must have been busy men.

Gradually the diplomatic purpose of the secretaryship and department prevailed, and it was perhaps because of that change that the secretaryship was accorded formal primacy in the presidents' cabinets. The secretary sat at the cabinet table to the right of the president.

The secretaries of state have been appointees of varying personal qualities—they have not always been national leaders or individuals with special aptitudes for this important cabinet post. For a while there was a tendency to appoint men who could use the office to advance themselves to the presidency. The Virginia dynasty—Jefferson, Madison, Monroe— had all been secretaries of state. John Quincy Adams, Monroe's secretary, may have had in mind a subsequent Massachusetts dynasty, but after his "corrupt bargain" with Henry Clay, acquiring his electoral votes and then appointing him secretary of state in 1825, no further elevations from the State Department to the White House have proved possible. The office has sometimes attracted nonentities. Occasionally it has been a place for political rivals, as when President Wilson appointed William Jennings Bryan in 1913. President McKinley used the office for an even more deplorable purpose. Desiring that his friend and mentor Mark Hanna be elected senator from Ohio, he appointed Ohio Senator John Sherman secretary of state despite the fact that Sherman was senile (and had to be replaced after outbreak of the Spanish-American War).[10]

Gradually the secretaries accumulated staffs for their department, and together with the staffs supervised the envoys sent abroad. The diplomatic establishment grew slowly, and was quite small until the beginning of the present century. In the 1890s personnel in Washington numbered fewer than one hundred. Missions abroad were not merely small; there were so few nations that not many missions were necessary.

As was true of secretaries of state, so envoys varied markedly in their qualifications. At the beginning of American government, during the

Confederation era and the first presidencies under the Constitution, American diplomats were extraordinarily able. The first half century of government produced a diplomatic roster that probably excelled those of European countries. Then with President Andrew Jackson the quality went down rapidly. Jackson believed that any citizen could hold any office, and the less experienced the better. As for posts abroad, he hardly considered them necessary, and imagined them to be places for exhibition of American virtue rather than knowledge of foreign affairs.

Throughout much of the nineteenth century, the Jacksonian tradition of amateurism thrived, and added to it was the belief of Jackson's supporter William L. Marcy, who himself served as secretary of state during the 1850s, that "to the victors belong the spoils." President-elect Lincoln kept a little book in which, as he moved about the town of Springfield, prior to leaving for Washington, he wrote down the names of worthy politicians whom he might send abroad. In 1862 when Secretary of War Simon Cameron had thoroughly demonstrated incompetence in that important office, Lincoln wanted him far away and sent him as minister to Russia. Similarly, when World War I broke out in Europe in 1914, the Wilsonian diplomatic service was inhabited by a collection of political hacks and campaign contributors—this when the government of the United States needed all the information it could obtain about the diplomatic situation in Europe. None of the American ambassadors and ministers had the slightest idea that war was coming; they gave the Department of State no advice, and the department thus had no policy, not the slightest, for preventing, ameliorating, or otherwise responding to the holocaust of war. The minister to Belgium, Brand Whitlock, formerly mayor of Toledo, Ohio, was at his country place near Brussels writing a novel about rural life in Ohio, and when told that the Archduke Francis Ferdinand of Austria-Hungary had been assassinated at Sarajevo, he did not know where that locality was in the world, "if indeed it was in the world".[11]

After World War I it was almost dramatically necessary for the United States to bring some quality into appointments to embassies and legations, and the Rogers Act of 1924 incorporated all American envoys abroad into a new foreign service, replacing the old diplomatic and consular services. With subsequent congressional enactments, the foreign service has become a professional organization.

American diplomacy at the present time is still largely under the supervision of career ambassadors (the title of minister has continued, but only for secondary officers, in the large embassies), but there is a sizable group of ambassadors with political appointments—they number perhaps three-fifths of the names sent to the Senate for confirmation. Still, whether career or political, the envoys are surrounded with experts, known collectively as country teams. A present-day diplomatic team would be headed by the ambassador, seconded by political and economic counselors, and supported by military, commercial, agricultural, and public affairs attachés. Such a team is responsible for ceremonial representation, information about foreign objectives and programs, setting out of political positions, and informational—sometimes described as propaganda—initiatives. It makes recommendations to the department in Washington and persuades the host nation of the proper direction of relations in both broad policies and specific programs.

In addition to the work of the country teams, there are representatives of other cabinet departments and of independent agencies who must coordinate their activities with the local embassies. Many agencies in Washington, cabinet and other, have international programs that supplement the activities of the State Department. There are often accusations of undercutting, but coordination usually takes place. The ambassadors are the nation's representatives; if they wish to force recognition of that fact, the representatives of other agencies usually will come into line. When policy issues become large, and especially if they are controversial, troubles can multiply. But strong local leadership can put them down. Late in 1945 the U.S. Army's former chief of staff, General George C. Marshall, was named special ambassador to China. Marshall wrote his own instructions and President Harry S. Truman signed them. Included in his requirements was control over all programs in China. Marshall demanded, and received, sole authority to speak for the president and Secretary of State James F. Byrnes.[12]

As the years have passed, American diplomacy carried out by official representatives abroad has tended to become tightly supervised, until at the present time it is a rare envoy who attempts a demarche of any sort without clearing it with the Department of State. What a change from the time of President Thomas Jefferson, who once wrote his minister in Madrid that he had not heard from him for two years, and hoped he would hear from him before another two! Communication with envoys became easier after the laying of the Atlantic cable in the mid nineteenth century, and the telegraph meanwhile quickened communication overland. In the present century the wireless, and then the teletype, made control of diplomacy far easier. Apart from mechanical communication, control has tightened through appointment of ambassadors-at-large, either specialists who can handle technicalities or individuals who have the confidence of presidents or secretaries of state. During World War II the personnel of the Department of State in Washington came to number six thousand and it has continued at that figure. Supervision has expanded to include a deputy secretary of state, several under secretaries, and a dozen assistant secretaries, each with deputies. These individuals often go abroad to converse with ambassadors. At the last moment in an important negotiation, it is possible that the secretary himself will appear to take over diplomacy from the local envoy.

The creation of the office of secretary of state, of a Department of State, and of a foreign service, does not, to be sure, make certain that expert advice and knowledge from the field will save a president from error, for advice may come from some quarter other than the secretary and his assistants at home and in the field. President Reagan's initial diplomacy to limit ballistic missiles, conducted during a summit meeting at Reykjavik, Iceland, during the autumn of 1986, apparently occurred at the urging of an assistant secretary of defense, Richard Perle, rather than a member of the cabinet department established specially for the conduct of diplomacy. The president's advice on negotiating with Iran, to trade weapons for hostages in Lebanon, came not from the Department of State but from the National Security Council. All of which seems to imply that the formal allocation of duties to the admittedly primary cabinet department does not ensure that the conduct of diplomacy will occur within its bailiwick. Perhaps it was a failure of the document of 1787 that it did not itself define the responsibilities of the Department of State and prohibit the conduct of diplomacy by other representatives of the executive branch.

THE LEGISLATURE

Even though the Constitution stipulates that diplomacy is the prerogative of the executive, the need for Senate confirmation of secretaries of state and of envoys has ensured a sharing of diplomatic tasks with Congress. So has the House of Representatives' right to make or withhold appropriations, and its participation in joint resolutions. For presidents who lack supporters in the legislature, these arrangements can be deeply embarrassing. Heads of state abroad find them incomprehensible. Yet they are the ways that the Constitution has divided authority in the conduct of diplomacy.

The constitutional sharing of authority has been notably evident in the appointment of secretaries of state. Presidents make nominations that are assured of Senate support. There is even a tendency of presidents to choose senators as secretaries, as in the instance of Edmund Muskie in 1980 after Secretary of State Cyrus Vance resigned over the attempted rescue of embassy hostages in Teheran.

Similarly, the Senate has often demonstrated its constitutional authority by making trouble over appointment of ambassadors. Here one does not mean momentary bedevilment, such as the questioning of Gluck's qualifications to be ambassador to Sri Lanka, but the protracted hearings that sometimes accompany confirmation of envoys to crucial capitals. Hearings can serve as debates over the conduct of diplomacy—over policy, not the individuals seeking confirmation. Consider the case of Charles E. Bohlen, a career foreign service officer, who had been Roosevelt's interpreter at Yalta and similarly assisted President Truman at Potsdam. It was his misfortune to come up for confirmation as ambassador to Russia after the Republican party had triumphed in the presidential election of 1952, when some of its leaders desired to demonstrate a need for the United States to "stand up to" the Soviet Union. No matter that within the foreign service Bohlen was one of the acknowledged Russian experts, in a tiny group that included George F. Kennan (whom the USSR had just declared persona non grata). The senators desired to replace what they described as weak (Democratic) policy toward the USSR with strong (Republican) policy. A secondary purpose was to embarrass the party's new president, who seemed middle-of-the-road and was not their choice.[13] Bohlen had to face this opposition, and there was little that the new secretary of state, John Foster Dulles, and his chief, Eisenhower, could do, other than wait out the hearings. It almost goes without saying that Bohlen's difficult confirmation surely sent a message to the new post-Stalin leadership in the USSR that the American government was hardly united in the conduct of diplomacy.

The way in which the Senate has affected diplomacy is through confirmation, but the House of Representatives also has power over the conduct of diplomacy because of need for its assent to appropriations, together with the fact that major issues of diplomacy sometimes are taken through the formality of a joint resolution rather than consent of the Senate. After the Alaska Purchase, Secretary of State William H. Seward had to get the appropriation through the House, and rumor had it that the new territory's cost, the peculiar sum of $7,200,000, was arranged so as to give the Russian minister a purse of $200,000 with which to influence votes in the House. More than a century later, the House was up in arms over the Iran-Contra problem because the advance of money to the Contras defied its prohibition of support other than for humanitarian purposes. As for the use of joint resolutions in the conduct of diplomacy, two notable occasions were the annexations of Texas in 1845 and of Hawaii in 1898. In both instances presidents had attempted annexation by treaty, requiring a two-thirds vote of the Senate, and failed. Congressional resolutions on other subjects have given leverage in diplomacy, as in the extraordinary grants of power to the executive branch during the offshore islands controversy of 1955 (involving Quemoy and Matsu, island groups off the coast of mainland China belonging to Nationalist China); the Eisenhower Doctrine for the Middle East in 1957, offering support to any local country threatened by communism; the resolution preceding the Cuban missile crisis of 1962; and the Tonkin Gulf resolution of 1964 concerning American intervention in Vietnam. In these instances both houses of Congress granted the executive branch virtual blank checks in the conduct of diplomacy. Years later they took back these grants of power in what amounted to another display of control over the conduct of diplomacy.

As diplomacy has increased in importance during the years after World War II, both houses of Congress have increased the staffs of their diplomatic committees, the Senate Committee on Foreign Relations and the House Committee on Foreign Affairs. Congress needed staffing if only to match that of the White House; the executive branch's staff work, of course, has increased tremendously, both through enlargement of the presidential staff and through creation of the National Security Council. For members of the Senate and House, the need perhaps first came to mind over a matter distinct from the conduct of diplomacy: after World War II, Congress needed staff assistance to help with examination of the federal budget, drawn up in the executive branch. Because the latter possessed the Bureau of the Budget, presidents were in a far better position to advance budget initiatives than Congress was to examine them. From this need, but also because of the complexity of all parts of government in recent decades, has come the buildup of congressional staffs. Construction of the labyrinthine Rayburn Office Building for the House of Representatives was testimony to this fact, and Capitol Hill is now full of converted apartment houses containing congressional staffs. The result, incidentally, has been a curious shifting of roles within Senate and House committees, in which members of Congress are now virtually executives, raising questions with staff members, who then research them. Behind the sometimes spectacular scenes of congressional hearings on diplomatic matters is frequently a large amount of staff work.

Along with congressional staff work has come use of outside experts, including university specialists. Senate and House committees do not merely publish hearings that involve testimony of outside experts. They commission and publish virtual monographs on, among other subjects, diplomatic issues. Staff members of committees arrange these expert testimonies, or submission of expert papers. Hence, they are not merely in the business of researching inquiries from committee members and bolstering questioning or testimonies during committee sessions, but are involved in outside research and formal publication.

All the while, members of the Senate and House have not hesitated to conduct on-the-spot investigations, sometimes known as junkets. There has been freqtent criticism—accusations of tourism rather than inquiry. But there can be no question that congressional visits to areas of concern have often advanced understanding. Frequently members have discovered that the executive branch does not wish to investigate an issue, and conduct their own inquiries. A case in point was the trip of Congressman Frank McCloskey (D, Ind.) to Hanoi in 1986, in company of other representatives and staff members, to inquire into the allegation that the Vietnamese government was holding American prisoners from the Vietnam War, thirteen years after Secretary of State Henry A. Kissinger had negotiated what was presumed to be a return of all prisoners. McCloskey allied himself with a conservative colleague, and despite refusal of both the Department of State and of the House leadership to consider the problem, the two members conducted their own investigation. In a sense they were conducting their own diplomacy.

The visits of congressmen abroad, for whatever purpose, affirm the constitutional power of the legislative branch over the conduct of diplomacy. Sometimes, let it be added, they can have personal consequences for local envoys. Many years ago, in 1921, Minister Joseph C. Grew in Copenhagen inadvertently failed to pay attention to a visiting congressional group, giving the impression that he was snubbing them. For years thereafter this distinguished member of the foreign service, later minister to Switzerland, ambassador to Turkey and Japan, and twice under secretary of state, feared congressional retaliation. Each time his name went to the Senate for confirmation, he was unsure of the result.[14]

Envoys spend a large amount of their time assisting the visits of congressmen. One ambassador in a small European country in an off-election year, 1961, found himself entertaining two hundred members of the Senate and House.[15] One hesitates to think of the attentions necessary in such capitals as London, Paris, and Rome.

A last way in which the legislative branch, created by the Constitution for enactment of laws rather than the conduct of diplomacy, has influenced the executive in diplomatic matters has been presidential appointments of members of Congress, usually senators, to delegations to diplomatic conferences. The notable appointments have been to peace conferences—where the result will be treaties that require senatorial consent. President McKinley was the first chief executive to send senators to a peace conference—this in 1898 after the Spanish-American War. The Treaty of Paris of that year needed all the assistance the senators could give, for it provided for annexation of the Philippines, a subject on which public and senatorial opinion was deeply divided. Twenty years later President Wilson made the error of avoiding the Senate in his appointments to another Paris peace conference. Moreover, Wilson appointed a delegation that included only one member of the opposing political party—and the Republicans had won a bare majority in the Senate in the elections of November 1918 and could organize the committees, including the Foreign Relations Committee. How differently the Treaty of Versailles might have been received in the Senate if the president had appointed Henry Cabot Lodge, chairman of the Foreign Relations Committee, or, if not Lodge—with whom Wilson was on poor personal terms—then another Senate Republican! Or perhaps two or three senators. For a far less important treaty, the astute McKinley had appointed the chairman of the Committee on Foreign Relations, the leading minority member of the committee, and a third senator. For delegations to other, less important international conferences and for delegations to the United Nations, recent presidents have frequently chosen members of the Senate.

The Constitution carefully arranged for a division of power over the conduct of diplomacy, and on ordinary and even some extraordinary occasions, this seems to have been a good arrangement. And yet it does not always work. Sometimes Congress can outmaneuver the president. With good reason President Wilson disliked his Senate enemies, who eventually forced the rejection of his beloved Covenant of the League of Nations. On a clear night in early July 1919, he returned to Washington from the Paris Peace Conference and drove through the streets of a capital that was bright with lights of welcome. Federal buildings were floodlit, the scene exquisitely beautiful. The wife of the secretary of the navy, riding in the same limousine, expressed regret that everything was illuminated but the Capitol. "It never is," was the dour response.[16] But then the legislature can lose to the executive. When during the Reagan administration the prerogative of the executive came to an outright confrontation with that of the legislature, and Congress through joint hearings brought an apparently wayward president back to traditional ways, the lesson of the occasion was that Congress had lost control.

It is an awkward business to contemplate the excesses of the system—victories, so-called, for Congress or the executive. How to ensure that the conduct of diplomacy will be a joint matter, involving the two branches of government? What happens to issues when overlaid with institutional rivalries?

INTEREST GROUPS, CONGRESSIONAL CONSTITUENCIES, THE MEDIA

In writing of the cumbersome nature of a divided constitutional system, one must mention the role of outside forces, of which the first have been interest groups. From the beginning the document of 1787 contained clauses in support of what in the eighteenth century were known as the champions of privilege, principally of property, against the common people, usually the propertyless, and in the early 1790s, political parties also formed, in part to represent the owners of the bonded indebtedness created by the Hamiltonian fiscal measures. Foreign policy entered—what was considered the pro-French policy of the Jeffersonians against the pro-

British policy of Presidents Washington and John Adams. With appearance of national parties, it became possible for other interests to attach themselves to the parties. Interest groups, whether coalesced in national parties or working by themselves, were indeed a natural, to-be-expected part of politics. When the Constitution was drawn up, the Founding Fathers did not fully imagine what interest groups might do to the government they were creating. The notion that interest groups would appear had its classical statement in Madison's *Federalist,* no. 10, of course. But the pressures that interest groups might place upon government exceeded the founders' imaginations.

In the nineteenth and twentieth centuries, the procedures of interest groups varied, but beyond question affected both domestic and foreign policies, usually by attempting to influence Congress. Members of the Senate and House are more susceptible to persuasion than is the president, for their concerns are naturally local; the president of the United States necessarily has to represent all the people, and his wide outlook tends to belie or undercut the purposes of interest groups. The merchants of New England were singularly uninterested in the coming of the war of 1812, whereas the owners of western lands were up in arms over the depredations of Indians supported, they believed, by British frontier garrisons. Similarly, the southern slaveholders favored the annexation of Texas and war with Mexico, for they desired more virgin land for cotton culture. In the War of 1812, the Texas annexation, and the Mexican War, congressmen of both houses found themselves under intense pressure through petitions and visits by individuals and groups.

In the twentieth century the procedures of interest groups became more pressing because of better communication and the increasing ease of travel—petitions could circulate without difficulty and people could descend upon Washington in larger numbers. National organizations arose for this or that cause, and sometimes their procedure was to give the impression that they represented many other national organizations—they virtually tended to integrate themselves, so to speak. One of the most effective lobbyists in Washington during the present century was the late Carrie Chapman Catt, who took an interest in causes looking to world peace during the 1920s and 1930s and federated many national women's organizations into what she described as the National Committee for the Cause and Cure of War. She was active at a time when women were newly enfranchised, and when it seemed possible to organize them to vote separately from males, with a result that she often threatened to use the "woman's vote" against congressmen who did not do her bidding by championing international issues that her committee had endorsed. As the years passed, the initial crudities of nationally organized interest groups disappeared, their work becoming less assertive and more subtle in giving the impression of a vast support among the "grass roots," and they were thus even more impressive. Congressmen gradually discovered their techniques, however, and in recent years have often countered them with a vengeance by use of letter-writing machinery, including automatic pens. For personal visitations, there unfortunately has been little recourse except to interviews, and today's clever lobbyists understand this technique thoroughly.

Foreign governments also have sought to affect the conduct of diplomacy by influencing congressmen. In recent years the governments of Taiwan, the Dominican Republic, and Israel, to mention only three notable instances, have maintained lobbies in Washington, which watch for any legislation or diplomatic issues that would affect the lobbying governments. Sometimes congressmen have accepted campaign contributions or fees for speeches or expensive trips paid for by foreign governments. The division of power over diplomacy, arranged by the Constitution, has made these payments advantageous.

Little needs to be said about the pressures of congressional constituents, which are often parochial. If congressmen understand their districts, they can sometimes use countermeasures, or at least attempt to judge the consequences of not going along with inconvenient proposals. The force of constituents' ideas is nonetheless likely to be great, and any legislation that passes the Senate or House must reckon with the need to balance or otherwise express the views of local bodies of voters. In the conduct of diplomacy, this can mean that some representatives and senators, because of the favor bestowed upon them by their constituents, achieve reputations for their devotion to certain diplomatic issues.

Lastly one comes to another well-known outside influence on national issues, domestic and foreign, and that is the media—newspapers, radio, and television. Presidents and congressmen often find themselves attempting to judge the importance of advocates with access to the press or the airwaves.

Newspapers, to be sure, were the initial medium of public expression. Their importance in early America was profound, as they constituted the principal means of influencing voters in a country where distances made individual solicitation difficult. The speeches of the nineteenth century were widely reported, and foreign issues obtained attention by virtue of appearing in the printed speeches. Editorial pages sometimes formed opinion, although their importance is difficult to measure. The later twentieth century has probably seen a waning of the importance of editorials, and perhaps even of newspaper readership, certainly of evening newspapers.

Radio became important only in the early 1920s, and for thirty years, until the introduction of television in the early 1950s, competed for attention with the newspapers. Presidents and congressmen taking positions on diplomatic issues sought to obtain time to discuss or debate them.

Television followed, a difficult medium for political discussion. It stresses appearance, which often takes a toll of content. The costs of time, especially prime time, have skyrocketed. Extended time is almost prohibitively expensive, spot time is so short—counted in seconds—that it reduces messages to posters. As for coverage of issues as news, the medium again is likely to be superficial. It caters to viewers whose concentration is no longer than four minutes, and who because of remote-control gadgetry can switch channels. Public service programs, required of all stations, tend not to be on in prime time and often discuss matters of marginal importance.

What does it all add up to? Presidents and congressmen assuredly must pay attention to the outside forces—for the executive the interest groups and the media; for the legislature also the constituencies. And yet it is often anyone's guess as to what each outside force, however presented, really means.

CONCLUSION

The effect of the Constitution on the conduct of diplomacy is evident in almost all the ways in which the United States has acted for more than two centuries. While the Constitution does not set out much detail about the conduct of diplomacy, and is silent on many subjects, including the almost obvious need for a secretary of state and a Department of State, the organization of American government into executive and legislative (and judicial) branches has itself had a profound effect. Autocracies and parliamentary regimes produce lines of control that are fairly straightforward. In the American system, conflict is nearly inevitable. The very fact that the president serves for a four-year term and legislators hold office for different terms almost guarantees disagreement. Moreover, the two branches have surrounded themselves with traditions that make relations more formal, and hence more susceptible to clashes.

The division of government into executive and legislative branches was enough to ensure rivalry, but into this complexity the Founding Fathers inserted the seemingly innocuous proviso that the president shall nominate ambassadors by and with the advice and consent of the Senate. To be sure, they perhaps desired confusion; after their experience with royal governors, they distrusted all government. The power to confirm is nonetheless the power to conduct diplomacy. The Senate thereby obtained a clear constitutional right to assist the executive—and contend with the executive—on diplomatic issues. The responsibility of the House of Representatives for appropriations and for joint resolutions has had similar effects.

The pressure of interest groups and constituents, together with the role of a free press, and now radio and television, has added to the complexity. The result can be extreme awkwardness. If the executive branch is headed by a president knowledgeable in the arts of persuasion, he can almost dominate the media, because of the seeming daily need of the media to produce news.

The basic issue of the congressional hearings over the Iran-Contra affair held in the summer of 1987 was clear enough: it was an investigation into the acts of a president and his assistants who did not care to share the conduct of diplomacy with Congress. It was an investigation into the checks and balances of the Constitution—how in this instance they had failed to work. Both President Reagan and his assistants believed that the president alone made foreign policy. The assistants undertook to do what they thought he wanted. Admiral Poindexter testified that he himself had not told the president about the diversion of money to the Contras because he felt the president wanted it and could not have had it had he known about it.

Members of the president's cabinet went right along with the actions taken in the president's name. Secretary Shultz told Poindexter that while he did not agree with the Iran negotiations, the less he knew about them the better: "Look, you know my feeling on this. I don't think we ought to be doing it. Just don't bother me with details on stuff I don't need to know." Having made himself automatically ignorant about sale of arms to Iran, the secretary of state thereby opened himself to ignorance about the Contra diversion. During the hearings the secretary gave the impression that Poindexter had deceived him. Meanwhile, it came out that the White House had told the Defense Intelligence Agency, part of the Department of Defense, to withhold information on the Iran arms sales from Secretary of Defense Caspar Weinberger. During the hearings Weinberger, like Shultz, made much of his disagreement with the policy, but affirmed his loyalty to the president, under whose administration his own department had deceived him.

The underlying constitutional issue was soon lost from view because of the attention of interest groups and the media. For days in the summer of 1987, the Iran-Contra hearings dominated the electronic media. Poindexter's assistant, Lieutenant Colonel Oliver L. North, a photogenic marine who appeared in full uniform, including campaign ribbons, played to the feelings and ideas of conservative groups. North gave the impression that he was a patriot who had done what was necessary to deal with Iran to get back the hostages in Lebanon, help the Contras, defy Congress, and thereby accomplish the diplomacy of the president. The conservative groups and the media loved it. The president seemed to support North, as well as Poindexter; he assuredly did not disown them. He gave the impression that if a grand jury indicted them and a jury convicted them, he would pardon them—he did not say he would not pardon them.

How to explain to the man or woman in the street that these cabinet officers and the president's White House assistants (themselves commissioned officers of the armed forces) and perhaps the president himself were throwing the checks and balances of the Constitution into the dustbin of history? Not for many years had officials of the U.S. government so flouted the requirement that the executive and legislative branches must conduct diplomacy together.

The president won out in the Iran-Contra affair, at the expense of much bad feeling in Congress. Will the Senate now cooperate in limiting intermediate-range ballistic missiles in Europe? If so, will it consent to subsequent treaties to limit or abolish nuclear arms? One can confront the diplomatic challenge of the present time, the arms race, only with a feeling of foreboding, a sense that time may be running out. Perhaps an eighteenth-century Constitution is not efficient enough—is too full of checks and balances and too open to outside pressures—and will need to be replaced by something more workable. A scenario might then become possible in which the American people, reverent of their Constitution, would refuse to amend it, with the result that the government of the United States would become unable to conduct the diplomacy necessary to preserve it against its international enemies.

NOTES

1. Sir Ernest Satow, *Guide to Diplomatic Practice,* 5th ed. (New York: Longman, 1979), defines diplomacy as "the application of intelligence and tact to the conduct of official relations between the governments of independent states." The French ambassador to the United States in the early years of the present century, Jules Jusserand, once told an American audience that diplomacy was the art of bringing home the bacon without spilling the beans. See his *The School for Ambassadors and Other Essays* (New York: Putnam, 1925).
2. Article 2, sec. 2.
3. Article 2, sec. 3.
4. Robert H. Ferrell, *Woodrow Wilson and World War I* (New York: Harper & Row, 1985), pp. 171, 278–79.
5. Article 3, sec. 2.
6. For the fourth, fifth, and sixth references to conduct of diplomacy, see Article 1, sec. 8; Article 2, sec. 2; Article 7.
7. President Herbert Hoover vastly enjoyed the visit of MacDonald, and took him to his camp in Virginia for a rustic weekend, where the two men sat on a log and discussed their countries' problems. The Laval visit was less welcome. Hoover did not look forward to it and peevishly inquired of an assistant why "that frog" was coming to Washington. Secretary of State Henry L. Stimson could do nothing to temper the

presidential displeasure. "As I told him after we had been going for awhile, it seemed to me all he was thinking about was how he could best stop Laval from picking his pocket while he was here." Stimson diary, 30 September 1931, Yale University Library, New Haven.

8. The literature on presidential alter egos is extensive. For Morris, see Samuel Flagg Bemis, *Jay's Treaty,* rev. ed. (New Haven: Yale University Press, 1962). See also Alexander and Juliette George, *Woodrow Wilson and Colonel House* (New York: Day, 1956); Robert E. Sherwood, *Roosevelt and Hopkins,* rev. ed. (New York: Harper, 1950).

9. Catherine Drinker Bowen, *Miracle at Philadelphia* (Boston: Little, Brown, 1966), a careful, if popular, account, makes the point.

10. Sherman was so incapacitated that he failed to recognize friends when encountering them upon the street. His lament was: "They deprived me of the high office of senator by the temporary appointment of secretary of state."

11. Rachel West, *The Department of State on the Eve of the First World War* (Athens, Ga.: University of Georgia Press, 1978).

12. Harry S. Truman, *Memoirs: Years of Trial and Hope* (Garden City, N.Y.: Doubleday, 1956), pp. 66–92.

13. "In the contest of Bohlen's confirmation, eleven Republican senators voted against us. There were only two or three who surprised me by their actions; the others are the most stubborn and essentially small-minded examples of the extreme isolationist group in the party. I was surprised by the vote of Bricker and Goldwater. These two seemed to me a little bit more intelligent than the others, who sought to defend their position with the most specious kind of excuse and the most misleading kind of argument. . . . Of course, if this kind of thing were often repeated, it would give some weight to an argument that was presented to me only yesterday. It was that I should set quietly about the formation of a new party. The method would be to make a personal appeal to every member of the House and Senate; to every governor, and to every national committeeman whose general political philosophy and purpose seem to belong to that school known as 'the middle way.' It may come about that this will be forced upon us, but the difficulties are vast, and if we can possibly bring about a great solidarity among Republicans, if we can get them more deeply committed to teamwork and party responsibility, this will be much the better way," Eisenhower noted *(The Eisenhower Diaries,* ed. Robert H. Ferrell [New York: Norton, 1981], p. 234, entry for 1 April 1953).

14. Waldo H. Heinrichs, Jr., *American Ambassador: Joseph C. Grew and the Development of the United States Diplomatic Tradition* (Boston: Little, Brown, 1966), pp. 49–51. Possessed unfortunately of a lordly presence, attired in a claw-hammer coat and yellow waistcoat, Grew had gone to Nimb's Restaurant to attend a luncheon in honor of the American delegation returning from the Interparliamentary Congress at Stockholm. He arrived at the restaurant without meeting the senators and representatives, and without thought took the arm of the Danish foreign minister and stalked in to lunch, leaving the members of Congress, open-mouthed, to trail behind. Senator Joseph T. Robinson, the new Democratic minority leader, was furious. Grew's nomination as minister to Switzerland came up not long thereafter, and Senator Lodge was able to sneak it through on a day when his Democratic colleague was out playing golf.

15. Ellis Briggs, *Farewell to Foggy Bottom: The Recollections of a Career Diplomat* (New York: McKay, 1964).

16. Jonathan Daniels, *The End of Innocence* (Philadelphia: Lippincott, 1954), p. 291.

10

Negotiating International Agreements

NORMAN A. GRAEBNER

Treaties are the product of diplomacy, but not all diplomacy terminates in treaties. Nor is that its purpose. Still, the framework for the conduct of foreign relations embodied in the U.S. Constitution refers only to treaties, and for good reason. All diplomatic activity that concerned the American people directly before 1787 either pursued or resulted in treaties. The Treaty of Paris of 1763 eliminated the French from the North American continent; that of 1783 granted the United States its independence, with territories extending to the Mississippi River. Those who thereafter represented the young Republic in the courts of Europe—Benjamin Franklin, John Adams, John Jay, and Thomas Jefferson—sought commercial treaties with the major trading states of Europe and North Africa. For the Founding Fathers diplomacy was synonymous with treaty making.[1]

In establishing a procedure to govern treaty making, the Founding Fathers assigned the president the right to make treaties, but only with the Senate concurring by a two-thirds vote of those present. The Constitution declares, moreover, that the president, in the formulation of treaties, must seek the advice and consent of the Senate. These few phrases comprise the constitutional formula for the peaceful conduct of the country's foreign relations. The Founding Fathers granted the Senate a formidable veto power over treaties because they visualized the Senate as a body of informed, distinguished citizens whose advice no president should neglect. They doubted that the executive branch would necessarily be the repository of the country's best thought regarding its interests abroad. By distributing the power over treaties—and thereby all fundamental external policy—between the executive and legislative branches of government, the Founding Fathers sought to maximize the nation's wisdom and astuteness in the conduct of foreign relations.

In a sense the Constitution's provisions for treaty making are very limited, essentially advocating the sharing of knowledge and responsibility on matters of great importance to the country. Unfortunately, the balance of power between the executive and the Senate that the makers sought to establish has never been stable. Treaty making occurs in a political context, for the ultimate arbiter between the president and the Senate in a contest over treaties is the American people. Senate approval of any treaty recognizes not only the president's authority to negotiate treaties, but also the quality of the treaty itself and its general acceptability to the nation's citizens. Thus the Senate might reject a treaty for a variety of reasons—its antagonism toward the president or the secretary of state, its doubts regarding the necessity of the specific provisions of the treaty, or its conviction that the treaty would alienate important constituents. It is not strange that the division of powers over treaty making has encouraged a perennial struggle between the executive and Congress as each seeks to prevail through successful appeals to the American people. On issues of minor importance, where the political gains and losses may be minimal, the conflict over treaty approval may be subdued. On questions that touch the interests or emotions of large numbers of citizens, the struggle for control of treaty making may become intense, even divisive.

In time the country's external relations moved into areas in which the Constitution established no formal congressional restraints at all. As a result the general effort to control external policy differs little from the normal executive-congressional war waged over the determination of domestic policy. In practice, the president can dominate the Congress and the public most readily when the country is in a crisis mood—when external conditions appear to demand strong national leadership. What gives the president his ultimate advantage over his detractors, in Congress and out, is the broad assumption that the executive branch, because of its massive foreign affairs establishment, possesses knowledge superior to that available elsewhere in the country. In times of crisis, whether real or contrived, the chief executive has often behaved as if that assumption were correct and, through arguments and assertions that play on national insecurities, has gone to extreme lengths to override his congressional opposition. To control external policy the president must command the allegiance of the House of Representatives no less than the Senate; the House possesses the greatest of all governmental powers, control of the purse.

When they face apparently irresistible domestic opposition, presidents can bypass the Congress by negotiating "executive agreements" rather than formal treaties, although often such agreements are purely matters of convenience. The ultimate escape from congressional and public constraints is the clandestine operation, conducted within the executive branch itself. Such behavior simply underscores the limited control that the American constitutional system exerts over the conduct of external policy. Indeed, the Constitution permits the executive to do whatever the public will approve. When assured of public support in his clash with congressional and public critics, a president faces almost no limits in his control of external policy. In granting the executive that power, congressional and public majorities assume that the president is correct in his assessments of the external world. The Founding Fathers warned that such concentrations of power could lead to disaster. Indeed, in creating the Constitution, the Founding Fathers repeatedly demonstrated their fear of unbridled executive power in the area of external affairs.

This chapter focuses on the evaluation of treaty making in the United States. We shall first consider the position of the Founding Fathers on the roles of the executive and legislature in this realm and then review the institutional struggles over treaties during the last decade of the eighteenth century and throughout the nineteenth century. Thereafter, I analyze treaty making through the two world wars down to the present. In my conclusion, I argue that the current procedures for making agreements with foreign nations are very far from the founders' intentions.

THE INTENTIONS OF THE FOUNDERS

Any examination of the Articles of Confederation and the records of the constitutional convention makes clear the almost universal agreement among the Founding Fathers that the control of foreign affairs was a legislative, not an executive, function. With its decision of June 1776 to declare independence, the Continental Congress appointed a committee to prepare a plan of union. Article 18 of the committee report declared that "the United States assembled shall have the sole and exclusive right and power—of determining on peace and war . . . sending and receiving ambassadors under any character, enter[ing] into treaties, alliances, etc." The report of the Committee of the Whole, on 20 August, accepted the principle that Congress alone would have control of external affairs. Under the Articles of Confederation, ratified on 1 March 1781, Congress received the right to make treaties, but only with the assent of nine states. Treaties negotiated by Congress would take precedence over any imposts or duties levied by the states, but Congress could not prohibit imports or exports, and thus had no control over foreign commerce.[2] If Congress possessed the full power to make treaties, it lacked the power to enforce them.[3] British military pressures enabled Congress to uphold the wartime alliance treaty with France, but Congress could not enforce the Treaty of Peace with Great Britain. Several states passed laws that violated the treaty. Congress's failure to compel the states to abide by all the articles of the treaty gave England a welcome excuse to retain frontier posts inside the boundaries of the United States. In London, British officials assured

John Adams, the U.S. minister, that Britain would evacuate the posts only when the United States fulfilled all its obligations under the Treaty of Peace.[4] Encouraged by John Jay, then secretary for foreign affairs, state after state, beginning in March 1787, repealed laws that violated the Treaty of Peace, especially those that prevented the British from collecting prewar debts.[5]

Perceptions of national failure that led to the calling of the constitutional convention in 1787 strongly reflected the powerlessness of Congress in the areas of commerce and treaties. The absence of authority to regulate commerce, James Madison recalled, had enabled foreign countries, especially Great Britain, to adopt monopolizing policies injurious to American trade and destructive of American navigation. Equally troublesome had been the loss of prestige and effectiveness that resulted from the determination of states to violate not only the Treaty of Peace with Britain but, after 1783, the treaties with France and Holland as well. "Examine . . . your treaties with foreign powers; those solemn national compacts, whose stipulations each member of the Union was bound to comply with," Charles Pinckney of South Carolina implored the delegates on 28 May. "Is there a treaty which some of the States have not infringed?"[6] Madison wondered how long other countries would tolerate the treaty violations of the states and how long the weakness of the general government would permit the states to so endanger the peace of the United States.[7]

During the weeks before the Philadelphia convention opened, the Virginia delegates had perfected a plan of government, known as the Virginia Plan. On 29 May, Governor Edmund Randolph presented that plan to the convention. In his introductory statement he advocated the creation of a government with the power to defend the United States from invasion and control the nation's commerce. Among the defects of the Articles of Confederation that Randolph cited was the inability of Congress to punish infractions of treaties. The New Jersey Plan, presented to the convention on 15 June 1787, provided that treaties made by Congress should become "the supreme law of the respective States so far as these . . . treaties shall relate to the said States or their citizens."[8] In time the convention adopted this proposal without debate and embodied it in the Constitution.

That decision left unresolved the allocation of power in the making of treaties. The Articles of Confederation had carefully enumerated the powers to be exercised by Congress, but the Virginia Plan advocated only that the national legislature "ought to be empowered to enjoy the Legislative Rights vested in Congress by the Confederation."[9] The convention quickly agreed without debate that the national legislature would act in all cases where the states were incompetent, but Madison acknowledged his preference for an enumeration of the specific powers to be exercised by the national legislature, including the right to make treaties with foreign powers. The convention now faced the more exacting task of distributing powers among the three branches of government. Under the Articles of Confederation, all powers of government—legislative, executive, and judicial—were centered in Congress. The Virginia Plan proposed a government of three branches. It asked in its seventh provision for the creation of a national executive with the authority to execute the national laws and "to enjoy the Executive rights vested in Congress by the Confederation." When the convention turned to the seventh provision on 1 June, it readily accepted the notion of a national executive, but pointedly rejected the prescription that the United States, in the British tradition, consign all powers over foreign affairs, formerly embodied in Congress, to the national executive, unless the convention were prepared to limit those powers by a strict definition.[10]

Alexander Hamilton's plan of 18 June was the first presented to the constitutional convention that explicitly addressed the question of allocating power between the executive and legislative branches on the issue of negotiating treaties. For Hamilton, no less than other members of the convention, peace and war were not executive prerogatives. To the Senate he would give sole power "of declaring war, the power of advising and approving all Treaties, the power of approving or rejecting all appointments of officers except the heads or chiefs of the departments of Finance, War and foreign affairs." To the supreme executive Hamilton would extend the power to execute all laws passed by the legislature, "to have with the advice and approbation of the Senate the power of making all treaties; to have the sole appointment of the heads or chief officers of the departments of Finance, War and Foreign Affairs."[11] Hamilton offered no resolution for a vote. Throughout the following month, no delegate made any effort to alter this limited definition of executive power. By late July the convention had hammered out compromises on many critical issues; still, it had made no decisions relative to the conduct of foreign affairs.

On 23 July the convention assigned to a "committee of detail," consisting of five members, the task of "reporting a Constitution conformably to the proceedings" of the convention. The convention adjourned on 26 July to permit the committee to complete its assignment. On 6 August the committee of detail submitted its report to the convention. During the final six weeks of debate, the convention reconsidered and modified certain clauses in the report, but found the distribution of powers over external affairs generally satisfactory. For the committee of detail the treaty-making power was neither wholly legislative nor wholly executive. For that reason it refused to add the authority to make treaties to the list of powers granted to the legislative branch. It regarded such power, like the authority to make war, as essentially a legislative power, but one not to be given to Congress as a whole. The treaty-making power, believed the committee, belonged properly to the Senate because of its smaller size, its greater ability to maintain secrecy, and its presumed invulnerability to hysteria and the demands of special interests.

The article in the draft constitution detailing the powers of the Senate began: "The Senate of the United States shall have the power to make treaties, and to appoint Ambassadors, and Judges of the Supreme Court." The president did not even share these powers. The draft established a single executive, but the executive authority did not include the important powers to make war, make treaties, or appoint ambassadors; these powers the committee assigned specifically to legislative bodies. Clearly the committee of detail was no more convinced than the convention itself that national leaders would always display wisdom in the conduct of the country's external relations; it therefore sought to maximize the constraints on the exercise of the treaty making as well as the war-making powers.

Delegates soon questioned the decision of the committee of detail to grant the treaty-making power to the Senate by simple majority vote. The great compromise of 16 July that terminated the debate over representation had granted each state equal voting power in the Senate, while representation in the House of Representatives would be proportional to population. That compromise seemed to assign disproportionate authority over treaty making to the smaller states. James Wilson of Pennsylvania proposed that the House share the treaty-making power with the Senate. This disagreement over Senate control of treaty making raised the question of the two-thirds rule for the approval of treaties. The question did not pit the small states against the large, but the eastern commercial states against the southern states with their planting interests. To southern delegates it seemed clear that the protection of their regional interests required a two-thirds vote for the approval of treaties. The committee of detail, by advocating the approval of treaties by majority vote, had offered no special guarantees to the South on the matter of treaties, but it had proposed the requirement that navigation acts receive a two-thirds vote in each house. Ultimately, the convention sent these divisive issues to a special committee.

For some convention delegates a possible answer to the sectional conflict of interest lay in compelling the Senate to share the treaty-making power with the executive. During the debates of 23 August on treaty making, Randolph observed that no one liked the committee's decision to assign the power over treaties to a Senate majority. It was apparent to the convention that treaty making entailed some purely executive functions. Madison observed that the Senate represented the states alone, and that it was therefore proper that the president should be the agent in making treaties. In large measure Madison favored a return to the relationship between Congress and the secretary for foreign affairs under the Articles of Confederation.

Finally, on 31 August the convention referred the burgeoning sectional questions, including that of treaty making, to the so-called "grand" committee formed to deal with "such parts of the Constitution as have been postponed, and such parts of reports as have not been acted on."[12] The southern states, with some northern support, had sustained the principle that navigation acts should require a two-thirds vote in both houses. At the same time abolitionist delegates from the North insisted on the total abolition of the slave trade. As part of a sectional compromise that eliminated the two-thirds vote from navigation laws, the convention voted to permit the importation of slaves until 1808. When the convention dropped the recommendation of the committee of detail for a two-thirds vote on navigation acts on 29 August, thus breaking the South's veto power over U.S. commercial policy, southern delegates argued that they merited further compensation elsewhere. A new "committee on postponed parts" responded by adopting a two-thirds rule on treaty making. The committee's draft, presented on 4 September, read as follows:

> The President by and with the advice and consent of the Senate, shall have power to make Treaties; and he shall nominate and by and with the advice and consent of the Senate shall appoint ambassadors and other public Ministers, Judges of the Supreme Court, and all other Officers of the U[nited] S[tates], whose appointments are not otherwise herein provided for. But no Treaty shall be made without the consent of two thirds of the members present.[13]

Nowhere did the treaty clause give the president any exclusive right to propose a course of action in foreign affairs. Moreover, the convention called for the advice and consent of the Senate as an organized body, not for the advice of its individual members. The American tradition as it had developed under the Articles of Confederation had assumed that the legislature possessed the authority to determine the objectives in any treaty negotiation. Policy matters, at the beginning no less than at the end, were to reflect the collaboration of the legislature with the executive officers charged by Congress to conduct the actual negotiation. Madison, as a member of the committee on postponed parts, was probably responsible for the inclusion of the phrase "advice and consent." Hamilton had sent Madison a plan of government in which he dealt with the role of the president in such terms. Whether or not Hamilton's plan reached Madison before the deliberations of the committee on postponed parts, Madison had available Hamilton's remarks of 18 June, in which he declared that the executive shall "have with the advice and approbation of the Senate the power of making all treaties."[14]

Those who defended the Constitution in the ratifying conventions stressed the primacy of the executive in the actual negotiation of treaties. To perform effectively in the international arena, they argued, the United States, no less than the great powers of Europe, required a chief executive with the authority to conduct the nation's diplomacy. William R. Davie explained to the North Carolina convention that treaty making, as an executive function, "had not only been grounded on the necessity and reason arising from that degree of secrecy, design, and despatch, which is always necessary in negotiations between nations, but to prevent their being impeded, or carried into effect, by the violence, animosity, and heat of parties, which too often infect numerous bodies."[15] Successful negotiations, declared John Pringle of South Carolina, "must be conducted with despatch and secrecy not to be expected in larger assemblies."[16]

Still, even those who recognized the essential role of the executive in treaty making emphasized the importance of safeguards against excessive executive authority. Charles Pinckney assured the South Carolina convention that the president could not appoint to office or enter into any treaty without the concurrence of the Senate. So great was the fear of executive power, asserted William Davie, that the Philadelphia convention was compelled to grant approval authority over treaties to the Senate. Charles Cotesworth Pinckney of South Carolina found little comfort in even those restraints. The British king, concerned with his country's welfare and unable to leave it, would always negotiate wisely. But an elected president, he warned, was not worthy of such trust.[17] Hamilton clarified his continuing distrust of executive power in similar terms:

> However proper or safe it may be in governments where the executive magistrate is an hereditary monarch, to commit to him the entire power of making treaties, it would be utterly unsafe and improper to entrust that power to an elective magistrate of four years duration. . . . The history of human conduct does not warrant that exalted opinion of human virtue which would make it wise in a nation to commit interests of so delicate and momentous a kind as those which concern its intercourse with the rest of the world to the sole disposal of a magistrate, created and circumstanced, as would be a president of the United States.[18]

THE EVOLUTION OF PROCEDURE UNDER WASHINGTON

Nowhere did the Constitution define the process whereby the president would seek and obtain the advice and consent of the Senate in the matter of treaty making. Was the president to meet with the Senate to discuss the purposes of treaties to be negotiated, or would he submit treaties to the Senate for its approval after they had been negotiated by executive officials? The Constitution supplied no answer, leaving the question of procedure to future presidents and senators as they formulated treaties under the conditions of governing. The actual process of defining the Senate's role in treaty making began on 25 May 1789, when President George Washington sent the following message to the Senate:

> In pursuance of the order of the late congress, treaties between the United States and several nations of Indians have been negotiated and signed. These treaties, with sundry papers respecting them, I now lay before you for your consideration and advice, by the hands of General Knox, under whose official superintendence, the business was transacted; and who will be ready to communicate to you any information on such points as you may appear to require it.[19]

The Senate ordered all papers tabled for future consideration, thus exercising its concurrent power with the president to make treaties.

Two weeks later Washington submitted a French consular convention, signed on 14 November 1788, to the Senate. The Senate instructed Jay, as acting secretary of state, to prepare an accurate translation of the consular convention for all members of the Senate. Next the Senate asked Jay for all papers in his custody relating to the negotiations. On 22 July the Senate requested Jay to appear before it to explain the convention and express his opinion "how far he conceives the faith of the United States to be engaged . . . to ratify, in its present sense or form, the Convention now referred to the Senate."[20] The Senate was concerned, not with the merits of the convention, but with the moral obligation to approve. Jay feared that the convention would prove to be inconvenient but, in tracing the history of the negotiations, believed that the United States had no choice but to approve. The Senate, in giving its advice and consent, voted unanimously that the president ratify the convention. During its deliberations the Senate debated the method of giving its advice and consent and agreed finally on a voting procedure.[21]

In both the Indian treaties and the consular convention, the Senate approved documents already negotiated. Members of the Senate questioned this procedure and on 3 August 1789 adopted a motion that the Senate appoint a committee to "wait on the President of the United States, and confer with him on the mode of communication, proper to be pursued between him and the Senate, in the formation of treaties."[22] Five days later a Senate committee called on the president and assured him that the Senate desired nothing but an arrangement for making treaties agreeable to him. Washington observed that the committee seemed to favor some form of oral communication with the president. On 10 August the committee held another conversation with the president. Eventually Washington and the committee

Resolved, that when nominations shall be in writing by the President of the United States to the Senate, a future day shall be assigned, unless the Senate unanimously direct otherwise, for taking them into consideration. That when the President of the United States shall meet the Senate in the Senate chamber the President of the Senate shall have a chair on the floor, be considered as the head of the Senate, and his chair shall be assigned to the President of the United States.

That all questions shall be put by the President of the Senate, either in the presence or absence of the President of the United States; and the Senators shall signify their assent or dissent by answering, *viva voce,* ay, or no.[23]

Soon the president put this new procedure to the test. On the same day that the Senate passed the resolution on procedure, the president's secretary appeared in the Senate chamber and informed the clerk that the president would come to the chamber on the following day "to advise with them on the terms of a treaty to be negotiated with the Southern Indians." When the Senate convened, the doorkeeper announced the arrival of the president. The diarist, William Maclay recorded the event: "The President was introduced, and took our President's chair. He rose and told us bluntly that he had called on us for our advice and consent to some propositions respecting the treaty to be held with the Southern Indians. Said he had brought General Knox with him, who was well acquainted with the business."[24] After explaining the issues in conflict between the Indians and the United States, Washington asked the Senate for its advice. He met with dead silence. Finally Maclay requested that the president furnish additional information regarding the Indians, inasmuch as the Senate had no opportunity to inform itself on the subject before it. It was apparent to Maclay that there could be no free discussion "while the President of the United States sat there, with his Secretary of War to support his opinions, and overawe the timid and neutral part of the Senate. Mr. Morris . . . moved that the papers . . . should be referred to a committee of five." Washington, obviously displeased, declared: "This defeats every purpose of my coming here." He then went on to say, wrote Maclay, "that he had brought his Secretary of War with him to give every necessary information. That the Secretary knew all about the business, and yet he was delayed, and could not go on with the matter." Maclay recorded that Washington cooled by degrees and agreed to return to the Senate.

Years later William Crawford recalled Washington's reaction to this encounter with the Senate over the projected treaty. "They debated it and proposed alterations," said Crawford, "so that when Washington left the Senate Chamber he said he would be damned if he ever went there again. And ever since that time treaties have been negotiated by the Executive before submitting them to the consideration of the Senate."[25] Maclay judged Washington's behavior from the viewpoint of the Senate: "I cannot now be mistaken. The President wishes to tread on the necks of the Senate. . . . He wishes us to see with the eyes and hear with the ears of his Secretary only. The Secretary to advance the premises, the President to draw the conclusions, and to bear down our deliberations with his personal authority and presence. Form only will be left to us."[26]

On the following Monday, Washington again appeared in the Senate chamber. Now the president, General Knox, and members of the Senate discussed in turn the propositions put forward by the president. The Senate agreed with some, but rejected others. The experience illustrated again the reluctance of senators to argue treaty matters in the presence of the president. Washington continued to take the constitutional admonition that he seek the advice and consent of the Senate when negotiating treaties seriously, but never again did he appear in the Senate chamber to discuss a treaty. He submitted his treaty negotiated with the western Indians in a message carried to the Senate by his secretary.[27]

Jay's Treaty, signed with Great Britain in November 1794, established the Senate's role in treaty making in something approaching final form. John Jay's mission to London reflected the intense partisanship that had engulfed American policy toward Britain and France by the mid 1790s. James Madison, backed by Secretary of State Thomas Jefferson, had pressed Congress for tonnage dues to be imposed on all countries without commercial treaties with the United States. Through such retaliation Madison hoped to coerce Britain into negotiating a fair commercial treaty. The country's pro-British forces, led by Secretary of the Treasury Alexander Hamilton, argued that American financial and security interests demanded good relations with Britain above all else. Madison pushed his major proposal through the House of Representatives in February 1794.[28]

Hamilton and his Federalist allies, in firm control of the executive and the Senate, determined to bind U.S. policy to Britain through a treaty. Taking advice from the leading Federalists, Washington nominated John Jay, then chief justice of the United States, for the mission to London on 16 April 1794. Jay's instructions covered all disputes between the United States and Britain: evacuation of the frontier posts, settlement of the northeast boundary and claims arising from prerevolutionary debts, compensation for slaves removed by the British during the Revolutionary War and recent maritime losses, recognition of American rights of neutrality in wartime, and the question of trade with the British West Indies. Washington did not submit the administration's proposals to the Senate, knowing that they would meet resistance. On 17 April the Senate defeated a resolution demanding that the president "inform the Senate of the whole business with which the proposed Envoy is to be charged."[29] A bitterly divided Senate then confirmed Jay's appointment as special envoy to London, 18 to 8.

Jay discovered in London that he possessed little leverage. Lord Grenville, who conducted the negotiations with him, recognized the strength of Britain's diplomatic position and the extent of American dependence on the revenues from British trade. In the end Grenville made few concessions. In the final treaty the British refused to recognize America's neutral rights. Jay gave up for ten years any American right to impose tonnage dues or other discrimination against British shipping. In exchange he gained limited entry of U.S. vessels into the British West Indies. Jay expressed huge satisfaction with the treaty.[30]

Actually the treaty was so vulnerable to criticism that when Washington received it on 7 March 1795, he hesitated to submit it to the Senate. Finally he called a special session of the Senate for 8 June. Having kept the treaty secret, he submitted it to the Senate in confidence. Opponents failed to defeat the treaty by making it public, but even Washington's Federalist advisers suggested that the president expunge the twelfth article, which limited American trade with the British West Indies. On 17 June the Senate received a resolution favoring ratification but suspending a portion of Article 12 and asking the president to reopen negotiations with Britain on the question of the West Indian trade. The Senate rejected the motion. Then on 22 June Aaron Burr introduced a resolution to postpone further discussion of the treaty with the recommendation that the president "proceed without delay to further friendly negotiations with his Britannic Majesty, in order to effect alterations in the said treaty."[31] The Senate, regarding the proposal as totally impractical, voted it down, 20 to 10. The opposition then introduced a resolution that the Senate inform the president that it would not consent to the ratification of the treaty. Again the motion failed. The Federalists now called for a vote on the resolution of 17 June. The portion consenting to ratification passed 21 to 10. The Senate agreed unanimously to advise additional negotiations on the West Indian trade.[32]

Washington was puzzled. Did the request to renegotiate one article compel him to resubmit the entire treaty to the Senate? Or if the British agreed to the change in the treaty could he ratify it without reference to the Senate? Hamilton and other Federalists, for political as well as procedural reasons, agreed that the Constitution did not require the submission of new articles. One more adverse vote would defeat the treaty. Washington accepted that advice and refused to resubmit the treaty or even submit the additional article. That decision, and the Senate's acquiescence, established the pattern for all cases in which the Senate had given only conditional consent to the ratification of a treaty.[33]

Following the exchange of ratifications in London, Washington on 29 February 1796 proclaimed the treaty without further consultation with the Senate. On 1 March he placed the treaty before the Congress and asked for the legislation to implement it. Madison argued that, whereas the House had no treaty-making powers, any treaty that required congressional action came under the whole Congress. This gave the House the right to judge the expediency or inexpediency of any treaty; to that end it would request the diplomatic correspondence. The House passed Madison's resolution, but Washington stood firm and the House eventually capitulated. The final ratification of the Jay Treaty established a procedure for treaty making that changed little thereafter. The success of that procedure, with the president placing a negotiated treaty before the Senate for its approval, rested less on the Constitution than on the power of the president to command the necessary two-thirds majority in the Senate in defense of any treaty.

TREATY MAKING IN THE NINETEENTH CENTURY

Throughout the nineteenth century those diplomatic efforts that most notably measured the nation's progress as a member of the international community were embodied in treaties. The treaties that were especially advantageous to the United States—and they were numerous—benefited from the country's powerful geographic and demographic advantages. American power and energy, set against the actual goals the nation pursued, generally placed the United States in a commanding position diplomatically and militarily. By limiting its political objectives to the North American continent, where it possessed total strategic advantage, the United States benefited from the weakening effect of distance in its contests with Europe's two major powers, Britain and France. Still America's diplomatic advantages, great as they were, could underwrite a century of successful treaty making only because American diplomacy almost invariably pursued precise, tangible objectives that were subject to accommodation and international agreement.

In some measure each major U.S. treaty before 1900 was unique. At times the diplomacy that produced agreement followed precise instructions; on other occasions the diplomats simply responded to unforeseen opportunities without any instructions at all. What gave all the treaties a common denominator was the requirement that they convey sufficient gain to the country to render them acceptable to the Senate. Possessing trusted diplomats, successive administrations in the early nineteenth century permitted important negotiations to proceed without special instructions, on the assumption that those conducting the negotiations, using their own good judgment, would secure the country's interests.

Thomas Jefferson dispatched fellow Virginian James Monroe to Europe in 1803 to resolve the Mississippi question. He instructed Monroe to visit any capital and negotiate any agreement he could, quite convinced that Monroe would achieve nothing. Without specific instructions, Monroe found a French government already determined to sell not only New Orleans but all of Louisiana to the United States. Jefferson and the Senate accepted the arrangement. Similarly, President James Madison refused to encumber the American diplomats at Ghent—notably John Quincy Adams, Henry Clay, and Albert Gallatin—as they attempted to negotiate an end to the War of 1812. The Treaty of Ghent managed to save the American West despite the country's failure to protect it adequately against British arms during the war. British diplomats at Ghent, troubled by the continuing war in Europe, could not counter the spaciousness and remoteness of the contested territories in their exchanges with Adams and his associates.[34]

As president, James Monroe generally refrained from issuing instructions to John Quincy Adams, his secretary of state, and with good reason. Adams possessed a remarkable sense of the possible in his dealings with other countries. In his tedious negotiations of 1819 with Don Luis de Onis, the Spanish minister in Washington, over Florida and the southern boundary of the Louisiana Purchase, Adams's grasp of the possibilities of gaining a satisfactory agreement always exceeded that of the president and the cabinet. In holding out for the 42nd parallel as the northern boundary of California, rather than accepting the Spanish offer of 43° as the cabinet advised, Adams explained that "if Onis intends to conclude at all, we can obtain better."[35] Adams regarded the Transcontinental Treaty of 1819, which brought Florida into the United States, as his most important diplomatic achievement. Such treaties faced limited opposition in the Senate. Adams, facing stern opposition, was less successful in his effort to negotiate commercial treaties with Britain and France, always settling for the best that he could obtain.

Perhaps the classic episode in American treaty making in the nineteenth century occurred in Washington during 1842 when Secretary of State Daniel Webster and Britain's Lord Ashburton negotiated the famed Webster-Ashburton Treaty. Regarding the accumulated antagonisms between the United States and Britain as subject to accommodation, Webster retained his post as secretary of state, despite a serious cabinet shake-up, in anticipation of Ashburton's mission to the United States. Among the issues requiring some accommodation was the *Caroline* affair, resulting from the destruction of the vessel *Caroline* by Canadian forces on the American side of the Niagara River above Niagara Falls. The *Caroline* had been employed to run supplies to Canadians in revolt against British rule. Another conflict arose when the British in Nassau freed all slaves aboard an American brig, the *Creole,* brought into the Bahamas by its mutinous American slaves. But the central issue of 1842 was the need to reach a final definition of Maine's northern border with Canada. Webster, in a series of brilliant exchanges with Ashburton, conceded Britain's right to protect its interests against the *Caroline.*[36] The British stood firm on the *Creole* case as well, although Webster and Ashburton agreed to a statement on extradition. In marking the Maine boundary, Webster gave up land for which some Yankees had been willing to die, although actually the United States received a large portion of the disputed territory. Having negotiated away land claimed by Maine, Webster faced the need of pacifying his opponents in Maine and the U.S. Senate. By revealing an old map from the peace negotiations of 1782, which gave the British the territory that Ashburton now claimed, and by successfully prevailing on much of the press in Maine and elsewhere to laud the compromise, Webster managed to secure Senate approval, 39 to 9.[37]

Three major nineteenth-century treaties that conveyed territory to the United States reflected a measured use of force or, in the case of Oregon, a clear demographic advantage. As early as 1818 John Quincy Adams established the fundamental position that an Oregon boundary along the 49th parallel would give the United States access to the Strait of Juan de Fuca and Puget Sound, a magnificent and essential port for America's expanding trade in the Pacific. Thereafter, an Oregon settlement awaited the occasion when the London government would retreat from its preference for the Columbia River line to the U.S. position—a retreat it was prepared to make after 1844. Meanwhile, President James K. Polk had complicated the Oregon question by acceding to his party's demand for the whole of Oregon to the line of 54°40′, a popular stance that had no chance in diplomacy. Polk eventually eluded his over-demanding Democrats by forwarding a British treaty draft embodying a settlement at 49° to the Senate for its advice, knowing that far more than two-thirds of the Senate favored such a settlement. John C. Calhoun, South Carolina's noted conservative democrat, assumed the lead in preparing the Senate to accept the necessary compromise.[38] Calhoun's supporters, Whigs and democrats, disposed of the proponents of 54°40′ in the Senate.

Shortly after the outbreak of the Mexican War in May 1846, the Polk administration agreed that it would not make peace until Mexico agreed to cede California, with its two major ports of San Francisco and San Diego. In sixteen months of fighting, U.S. armies won all the battles and occupied Mexico City, only to face continued reluctance among Mexican leaders to negotiate a peace treaty on American terms. Finally, when Polk no longer anticipated a settlement, his recalled envoy, Nicholas P. Trist, negotiated the desired treaty. For Polk it was a stroke of good fortune, for Mexico might well have compelled the United States to take California, if it would, without benefit of a formal treaty.[39] The Senate approved the Treaty of Guadalupe Hidalgo of 1848 readily enough, the opposition divided between those who feared that the United States had acquired too much territory and those who complained that it had not acquired much more.

Again in 1898 and 1899 the United States acquired territory—Hawaii, the Philippine Islands, Guam, and Puerto Rico—as the result of a victorious war. As the actual fighting in the Spanish-American War ended in the summer of 1898, the McKinley administration, pressed by the country's expansionists, acquired Hawaii through a joint resolution of Congress and then moved to annex the Philippines. In his instructions to his peace commission in Paris, McKinley suggested that the United States acquire no less than the island of Luzon, knowing that the commission, facing the choice of taking all the Philippine Islands or none, would indeed prepare a treaty that would transfer the entire Philippine archipelago to the United States. Some American conservatives saw the acquisition of islands across the Pacific as a heavy burden and potential source of conflict with powers that had far greater interests in the western Pacific. Their arguments exceeded their power; the treaty passed the Senate, 57 to 27—one vote more than necessary. Henry Cabot Lodge, who led the treaty forces, reported to Theodore Roosevelt on 9 February 1899: "It was the closest, hardest fight I have ever known, and probably we shall never see another in our time when there was so much at stake."[40]

This successful experience in treaty making—from the purchase of Louisiana in 1803 to the acquisition of the Philippines in 1899—scarcely reflects the full record of U.S. treaty making in the nineteenth century. Actually the U.S. government negotiated some 300 treaties in the nineteenth century, most, obviously, of limited significance. If occasional treaties were not totally satisfactory, either in their language or in the quality of the agreements, the major criticism of the treaty-making process focused on the Senate. Some charged that the Senate required too much time to approve the treaties it received. Still, that complaint was not a measure of general procrastination but a judgment that the Senate had delayed a number of treaties for immoderately long periods of time, most notably twenty-one years in the case of the Isle of Pines Treaty. In practice the Senate was no slower in approving treaties than it was in passing other legislation. Over half the treaties were approved in less than one month. Often the delays resulted from less than satisfactory relations between the Senate and the executive.[41] Rarely, moreover, did a president have a two-thirds majority of his party in the Senate.

Some treaties the Senate rejected, others it amended, often incurring the criticism of executive officials and editors alike. The Senate tended to alter about one-fifth of the treaties it considered. In examining treaties closely, the Senate on occasion found them poorly executed or otherwise unsatisfactory. This led either to requests for renegotiation or to outright rejection. Many changes were insignificant; others strengthened the treaties by requiring the inclusion of related items or demanding that the administration better define and defend the interests of the United States.[42] In amending the Hay-Pauncefote Treaty of 1900 with Great Britain, for example, the Senate demanded the right of the United States to fortify any future American-built canal through Central America. The second Hay-Pauncefote Treaty of 1901 included the right to fortify. With good reason the Senate rejected treaties with Texas in 1844, with Mexico in 1860, with the Dominican Republic in 1870, and with Hawaii in 1897. The knowledge that any treaty would face close scrutiny in the Senate was sufficient to compel care in negotiation. Thus, on balance, the constitutional provision that treaties must have the endorsement of two-thirds of the Senate to become the law of the land advanced the country's interests. John W. Foster, secretary of state under President Benjamin Harrison, believed that the Senate had saved the country from serious errors.[43]

WORLD POWER AND THE RISE OF THE EXECUTIVE

Although the growing involvement of the United States in international life led to a higher incidence of treaty making after 1900 than before, treaties no longer measured the progress toward the resolution of conflicts between the United States and other states as they had in previous decades. In part the change reflected the increase in executive authority in the conduct of American foreign relations, a change that could only diminish the constitutional role of the Senate—indeed of the Congress—in external matters. With the augmented position of the United States in world affairs following the Spanish-American War and the acquisition of the Philippines, it appeared essential that the United States meet its new international responsibilities, an obligation that centered on the president and the Department of State.[44] Foreign nations had no choice but to present their demands to the executive branch in accordance with international law and the established treaties of the United States.

After 1900, students of American government emphasized the right of the president to make agreements with other states, often without the advice and consent of the Senate.[45] Important arrangements defining American relationships with other powers, such as the Root-Takahira Agreement of 1908 and the Lansing-Ishii Agreement of 1917 with Japan, consisted of executive agreements without Senate approval. President Theodore Roosevelt did not seek Senate advice when he sent Henry White to the Algeciras Conference of 1906. Writers and officials now emphasized the power of the president, as commander in chief, to place U.S.

armed forces wherever he deemed necessary to protect the nation's interests, all without reference to the Senate. Indeed, the Supreme Court
recognized that authority when it declared: "While no act of Congress
authorizes the executive department to permit the introduction of foreign
troops, the power to give such permission without legislative assent was
probablv assumed to exist from the authority of the president as Commander-in-Chief of the military and naval forces of the United States."[46]
In general, such freedom of executive action included the proviso that the
president would make no direct demands on the lives and resources of the
American people without Senate or congressional approval. Nor could
the president, on his own, accept changes in ratified treaties.[47]

From the outset, the demands that the country's twentieth-century
world role placed on decision making created an unprecedented conflict
between the burgeoning power and influence of the president and the
prerogatives of the Senate, established through a century of treaty making. For many American officials after 1900, the Senate had become an
impediment to the proper conduct of the country's external relations.
Secretary of State John Hay complained that the Senate eliminated the
normal give-and-take of diplomacy. He wrote to John Nicolay in 1900:
"No fair arrangement between us and another power will ever be accepted by the Senate. We must get everything and give nothing and even then
some malignant senator or newspaper will attack the deal—and say we
have surrendered everything—and that scares our cowardly friends out of
their wits."[48] In another letter Hay revealed even greater disgust: "A
treaty entering the Senate is like a bull going into the arena; no one can say
just how or when the final blow will fall—but one thing is certain, it will
never leave the arena alive."[49] For Hay the uncertainty about what the
Senate would do was sufficient to strangle any agreement that required
Senate approval.

Recognizing this growing conflict between the executive and the Senate, Woodrow Wilson, in the 1900 edition of his noted book *Congressional Government,* took up the cause of the executive:

> Much the most important change to be noticed is the result of the war with
> Spain upon the lodgment and exercise of power within our federal system; the
> greatly increased power and opportunity for constructive statesmanship given
> the President, by the plunge into international politics and into the administra-
> tion of distant dependencies, which has been that war's most striking and
> momentous consequence. When foreign affairs play a prominent part in the
> politics and policy of a nation, its Executive must of necessity be its guide; must
> utter every initial judgment, take every first step of action, supply the informa-
> tion upon which it is to act, suggest and in large measure control its conduct. It
> may be, too, that the new leadership of the Executive . . . may give the heads of

the executive departments a new influence upon the action of Congress. It may bring about, as a consequence, an integration which will substitute statesmanship for government by mass meeting.[50]

Clearly, for Wilson, the new conditions of international life demanded augmented direction of foreign policy by the executive, with the Senate merely checking and modifying executive decisions. As he wrote in 1908, "One of the greatest of the President's powers is his control, which is very absolute, of the foreign relations of the nation."[51] During World War I, Princeton University's noted constitutional scholar Edward S. Corwin emphasized executive primacy. The long American experience in treaty making convinced Corwin that the "contest for power and influence in determining the international destinies of the country remains decisively and conspicuously in favor of the President."[52] In analyzing such apparently profound changes in executive-congressional relations, the University of Chicago's distinguished student of international law Quincy Wright doubted that the new requirements for concentrated authority over the country's foreign relations would necessitate any change in the American constitutional system. They would, however, rely on the adaptation of the system to guarantee the primacy of the executive in all external matters. The Senate, with the House, might still approve the general ends of national decisions, but the president, observed Wright, must guide and control America's relations with an increasingly complex world.[53]

Despite such repeated claims for executive power over the external policies of the United States, the Senate demonstrated again that it still possessed the ultimate authority over treaty making by rejecting the Versailles Treaty in 1919 and 1920. President Wilson had committed his personal prestige and the full powers of his office by entering the congressional elections of 1918 and then joining the deliberations at Versailles. There he accepted decisions that he could not control, some subject to extensive vilification in the United States. To commit his country and the world to the maintenance of peace, largely through procedures that really committed no one, Wilson embodied the Covenant of the League of Nations in the Versailles Treaty. Despite the broad opposition in the United States to league membership, as well as to some treaty provisions, Wilson returned from Paris on 8 July 1919 determined to meet the Republicans, who now controlled the Senate, head on. Two days later a reporter asked the president whether the treaty with reservations prepared by Republican leaders would pass the Senate. Wilson replied firmly: "I do not think hypothetical questions are concerned. The Senate is going to ratify the treaty."

That day the president laid the treaty before the Senate, informing that body that he expected no less than prompt and unqualified approval. Throughout the long debate of 1919 over U.S. membership in the League of Nations, Wilson could not explain how this system of collective security would work. Henry Cabot Lodge, who led the Republican assault on the treaty, reminded the Senate that only if the league possessed the authority to issue decrees and enforce them could it be effective. "Are you ready," he asked, "to put your sailors at the disposition of other nations? If you are not, there will be no power of enforcing the decrees." Any reliable league, warned Lodge, would require such infringements on national sovereignty that no one, not even the president, would favor it.[54]

Lodge's observations required an answer; Wilson could not supply it. With public opinion slowly deserting the administration, Wilson took his case to the country with a speaking tour that carried him across the Midwest to the states along the Pacific. The effort failed. In November 1919 the Senate rejected the treaty with the reservations, 39 to 55, with isolationist Republicans joining the Democrats to create a large opposing majority. The Senate then voted down the unaltered treaty, 38 to 53, with the Republican majority voting as a solid bloc. The Senate took its final vote in March 1920, rejecting the amended treaty by a vote of 49 to 35, seven votes short of the necessary two-thirds. Twenty-three Democrats, refusing to desert the president, assured the failure of the treaty with reservations, the only form in which it could pass the Republican majority.

TREATY MAKING BETWEEN THE WARS

After Versailles, the United States could no longer resolve its major differences with other leading powers through the process of treaty making. In part this failure reflected the continuing changes in the relative authority of the executive and Congress in the conduct of the country's foreign relations. Minor agreements continued to appear before the Senate as treaties, although many, often important, arrangements with foreign governments assumed the form of executive agreements rather than treaties, thus requiring no formal Senate approval. But in greater measure the failure of treaty making after 1920, especially with the nation's antagonists, reflected an official devotion to the status quo. This eliminated any possibility that the United States would resolve its differences on issues of peace and war through diplomacy alone.

For Woodrow Wilson the answer to international aggression had been simple and reassuring. His notion that only peaceful change was morally and diplomatically acceptable denied the legitimacy, even the necessity, of dealing with aggressors. In a world allegedly governed by the principle that change, to be legitimate, must also be peaceful, no country had the right to bargain with aggressors over changes in established treaties, especially when such bargaining would merely stimulate the appetite for additional illegitimate gain. The pleasant assumption that the United States could avoid the necessity of confronting aggressors directly absolved Washington of the need to define the country's interests precisely in the face of aggression or to prepare a strategy for their defense.[55]

For Wilson's followers, who dominated America's intellectual outlook on world affairs after Versailles, the essential stabilizing role of the United States as the world's leading power would comprise a moral and diplomatic defense of the status quo, whatever the possibilities of success or the dangers to international peace and security in such an approach. Yet so acceptable was this purpose, so thoroughly did it satisfy the conservative interests and idealism of the American people, so completely did it promise peace without unwanted change, that only with difficulty would the country, despite its remarkable strength, accept the traditional obligations of a great power—which included dealing forthrightly with aggressors. The refusal to negotiate with expansionist states would not control their behavior. In the end the determination to avoid accommodation with aggressors would permit only the unfortunate choice between the acceptance of unwanted change, unmodified by mutual agreement, or war. Thus the mere desire to avoid direct negotiations with Japan, Germany, and Italy in the 1930s would not sustain the peaceful, unchanging international order that Americans favored. In a world of uncompromisable purposes, treaty making had no place.[56]

Nothing demonstrated the conflict between principle and reality, and with it the elimination of treaty making, more forcefully than U.S.–Japanese relations in the late 1930s. Diplomatic accommodation had no chance against Tokyo's determined search for lebensraum in East Asia and Washington's total rejection of such expansion in the name of principle. Indeed, the historic clash between Japanese interests and American principles in China virtually eliminated diplomacy as a means of avoiding war, whether the diplomacy itself centered in China, Japan, or the United States. This relegated the diplomatic corps to the role of functionaries, explaining national positions and carrying out instructions, but unable to influence the policies themselves. The diplomatic exchanges revealed not so much the failure of diplomacy and treaty making as the fact that negotiations had no chance of success at all.

Throughout the Far Eastern crisis, the U.S. ambassador to Tokyo, Joseph Grew, favored some binding agreement with Japan that recognized Japan's superior interests in China. His appeals made no impression on the Roosevelt administration, which became more and more uncompromising with the passage of time.[57] Stanley K. Hornbeck, the State Department's chief advisor on Far Eastern matters, argued, in his opposition to accommodation with Japan, that whereas the United States did not contemplate the use of force to defend the principles relating to peaceful change, it had "no right to take action in authorization of their impairment."[58] The United States, in its refusal to compromise Chinese interests, assumed that it could avoid war through some form of Japanese capitulation. Ultimately, no U.S. policy could bridge the gap. War came with the Japanese attack on Pearl Harbor. Unfortunately, not even war, the American people would discover, could guarantee the triumph of the principles of peaceful change and self-determination.

TREATY MAKING AFTER 1945

Perhaps the Senate (and the House) could not escape all responsibility for the failures in American foreign relations in the 1930s. Senators did not escape the pervading parochialism of the decade or appreciate the need to deal honestly and forthrightly with challenges from abroad. Still, if the Congress, no less than Americans generally, insisted on peace without accommodation or risk, it was in large measure because national leaders themselves claimed validity for such inexpensive and over-demanding formulas. Having reaffirmed its devotion to self-determination in the Atlantic Charter of August 1941, the country was not prepared to negotiate a general settlement after the Allied victory over Germany in May 1945. No national administration would have proposed, and no Senate would have approved, any fundamental postwar arrangement with Russia that embodied the political and territorial changes wrought by the Soviet occupation of East-Central Europe. During 1946 the victors managed to conclude treaties of peace for all of Germany's former satellites.[59] These treaties compromised a full spectrum of conflicting East-West issues; they did not recognize Soviet hegemony over most of the area involved. But Washington's refusal to negotiate with the Russians over the question of Soviet political and economic dominance in regions under Russian occupation did not eliminate the Iron Curtain or bring freedom to the peoples of Czechoslovakia, Poland, Rumania, Bulgaria, and other Soviet satellites. Abjuring the use of force, the United States would accept what it could not change even while it denied itself the possibilities of effecting some improvement through accommodation.

Although the United States and its wartime allies could never arrange a general postwar settlement reminiscent of Versailles, the burgeoning fears of Soviet power and influence eventually drove the United States and friendly states of Europe, the western Pacific, and East Asia into a series of security pacts. Two events of 1948 suggested that the Kremlin had not accepted the status quo along the Iron Curtain dividing Europe. In February a Soviet-backed communist coup toppled the neutral government of

Czechoslovakia. The ease whereby the USSR had drawn this important, democratic country behind the Iron Curtain terrified Europeans and Americans alike. In June the Soviet Union created another crisis by instituting a blockade of West Berlin in retaliation for Western policy aimed at the creation of a West German republic. Britain and the United States countered the blockade with a successful airlift. Clearly such threatening Soviet behavior required some unified response.

Following the fall of Czechoslovakia, representatives of five European countries—Britain, France, Belgium, the Netherlands, and Luxembourg—formed the Brussels Pact and turned to the United States for military support. Washington was prepared to accept the challenge. During subsequent months the United States, Britain, and ten other countries negotiated the North Atlantic Treaty Organization (NATO). They signed the completed treaty amid special ceremonies in Washington during April 1949. Dean Acheson, the new secretary of state, informed the Senate Foreign Relations Committee that the pact carried an obligation to act. The Senate debate over the treaty was vigorous, but brief. The Senate approved the North Atlantic pact on 21 July 1949 by a vote of 82 to 13. NATO quickly emerged as the centerpiece of America's burgeoning containment policy.[60] Soon American aid underwrote the new NATO military structure.

During the NATO debates, Acheson denied that the elements existed for a defense pact in the Far East. The Korean War, with its underlying assumption that Asian communism under Kremlin control now threatened other regions of the Orient, quickly eliminated such official caution. During 1951 the Truman administration, responding to the new fears, negotiated a series of permanent military alliances in the Far East. Japan emerged as the key to the new alliance structure. To encourage Japanese economic development, the Japanese treaty imposed no restrictions on Japanese commerce and industry. It stripped Japan of its island possessions, including Okinawa, but it acknowledged Japan's right to self-defense and established the foundations for future Japanese armament.[61] At the same time the United States retained the right to land and naval bases on Japanese territory. The Japanese treaty received international approval in special ceremonies in San Francisco during September 1951. Australia and New Zealand, remembering their narrow escape from Japanese invasion in 1942, demanded special security guarantees from the United States before they would sign the Japanese treaty. United States officials joined representatives of Australia and New Zealand in signing the ANZUS Pact at San Francisco in September 1951, hours before the Japanese treaty conference opened. Late in August the United States negotiated a similar bilateral defense treaty with the Philippines. The Senate approved these pacts overwhelmingly during the spring of 1952.[62]

To strengthen the defense of Southeast Asia, some American and Asian leaders favored a broader alliance system that would include Britain and France as well as other pro-Western states in the Southeast Asian region. The threatened fall of French Indochina in the spring of 1954 before the communist forces of Ho Chi Minh seemed to demand some application of the containment principle to Southeast Asia. Unable to gain vital British support for the defense of the French stronghold of Dien Bien Phu, Secretary Dulles extracted promises from several countries, including France and Britain, to join a Southeast Asian defense organization after the forthcoming Geneva Conference resolved the future of Indochina. Dulles announced to the press in early May 1954 that the proposed pact would check the "imperial colonialism of communism"[63] The Geneva Accords of the summer of 1954 recognized the independence of Laos, Cambodia, and Vietnam, with Vietnam divided at the 17th parallel between Ho's communist-led North and Ngo Dinh Diem's pro-Western South Vietnam. Prime Minister Nehru rejected Indian membership in any Asian pact; Indonesia, Ceylon, and Burma followed the Indian lead. The Japanese had no interest in any defense arrangement for Southeast Asia; even the British revealed little enthusiasm. The Geneva Accords eliminated the new states of Indochina from any defense arrangement. For reasons that scarcely coincided, Australia, New Zealand, the Philippines, Thailand, and Pakistan agreed to join the pact, although Pakistan announced that it would oppose any anti-Chinese or anticommunist arrangement.

Dulles departed for the organizational meeting of the new Southeast Asia Treaty Organization (SEATO) in Manila on 30 August 1954, declaring that he felt a sense of solidarity among the eight nations sending delegates. In Manila the Philippine leaders refused to join the new defense organization until Dulles assured them that the United States would defend the islands from attack. In his opening address Dulles informed the delegates that the United States wanted no NATO-style pact for Southeast Asia. He declared that the United States would furnish logistical and air support for the defense of Southeast Asia, but would not, because of its worldwide commitments, bring ground forces into another war on the Asian continent. Dulles added that for the United States, aggression was "communist" aggression. In a special protocol he included the three new states of Indochina in SEATO's defense area. The signatories of the pact agreed only to consult in case of aggression and made no provisions for an army under SEATO control. Committing the United States to very little in Southeast Asia, the SEATO treaty faced little opposition in the Senate.

America's defense efforts soon encompassed the Middle East as well as the Pacific rim of Eurasia. After 1952 NATO extended allied defenses as far east as Turkey; SEATO after 1954 brought the American defense perimeter as far west as Pakistan, leaving a gap across southwest Asia from Pakistan to Turkey. Its vast resources in oil, its location astride the major routes of communication from Europe to the Orient, and its proximity to Russia rendered the Middle East of major strategic importance. What concerned the Eisenhower administration was not that the region harbored powerful communist movements or had been one of traditional American involvement, but that the USSR be denied major influence in a portion of the globe deemed vital to the West. Dulles returned from the Middle East in 1953, convinced that the area lacked the elements necessary for an effective military alliance. Soon he discovered, however, that the three Northern Tier states—Turkey, Iran, and Pakistan—had some interest in a regional pact, hoping that such a pact would bring economic and military aid from the United States. At the same time the United States had an interest in sustaining the British and French positions in the Middle East against the force of Arab nationalism. By 1954 Iraq made clear its willingness to join a regional pact. Despite the vigorous opposition of both Arabs and Israelis to a Middle Eastern defense organization, the United States pushed the formation of the Baghdad Pact. Iraq and Turkey signed a treaty in February 1955; in subsequent months Britain, Pakistan, and Iran adhered to the pact. The United States agreed to cooperate with members of the pact, but only as an observer. The Baghdad Pact made no effort to designate an enemy.[64] Nor did it have a military structure.

More recent efforts at treaty making, especially after 1970, sought agreements with the Soviet Union on arms limitations. The mutual interest of the United States and the USSR in taming the arms race for reasons of economics and security led to the SALT I treaty of 1972 and the SALT II agreement of 1978. The first formula received ready Senate approval; eventually President Jimmy Carter withdrew the second from the Senate in the wake of the Soviet invasion of Afghanistan in late December 1979. President Reagan reopened the search for arms reduction agreements in 1982, only to have the Russians walk out of the Geneva talks over the disputed placing of medium-range missiles in western Europe in late 1983. When the talks reopened in Geneva in the spring of 1985, the impasse on arms limitations appeared as great as ever, despite the president's insistence that the U.S. military buildup after 1981 was forcing the USSR to seek relief from the arms competition by reaching an agreement with the United States. At times the dialogue between Soviet and American arms negotiators sounded more like two monologues.[65] Unfortunately, a comprehensive treaty on nuclear and conventional arms reduction, high on the agenda of world leaders, remained elusive, because nations fearful of one another could scarcely reach a settlement on means when they could not agree on ends. Treaties involving partial arms limitations always remained a possibility, both because of the high cost of defense and because of the redundancy in nuclear stockpiling. Indeed, amid the festivities of the Washington summit of December 1987, President Reagan and Soviet leader Gorbachev signed a limited nuclear arms agreement that eliminated all medium-range nuclear weapons from Europe—some three percent of the total nuclear arsenals. As in previous decades, the perennial East-West clash over principles and interests eliminated serious treaty negotiations on basic political and territorial questions.

CONCLUSIONS

In drafting the Constitution, the Founding Fathers sought to assign the control of American foreign relations to specific agencies of government to assure decisions that would best serve the interests of the Republic. If they recognized the need for executive leadership in the negotiating of treaties, especially after President Washington's unsatisfactory dealings with the Senate, they never compromised the Senate's role in passing judgment on those treaties. That judgment was to reflect the broad knowledge and accumulated wisdom of a body of experienced and distinguished public officials, and through them the combined wisdom of the nation. The Founding Fathers doubted that the executive would ever command a monopoly of the country's understanding of the world or the requirements for living successfully with it. Perhaps the Senate lost much of its reputation for special acumen when it rejected the Versailles Treaty. Those who condemned the Senate shared an illusion that the League of Nations offered the United States a unique opportunity to play a substantial role in world affairs and do so without any commitment to defend the specific territorial provisions of the Versailles Treaty. Still, as Henry Cabot Lodge had warned, without such commitments the league would amount to nothing. Other countries represented at Versailles were no more prepared than the United States to uphold the league's decisions with force. In the end it mattered little that the United States did not enter the league. The Senate's behavior, in short, did not seriously challenge the notion that the Constitution's provisions regarding the making of treaties had served the country well. Certainly those provisions were not responsible for administrative decisions that failed to meet the highest standards of wisdom and performance. The Constitution provides no limitations on executive policy making, not involving treaties, beyond the power of congressional and public opinion. The people alone, acting largely through their elected representatives, can defend themselves against the mistakes of those who govern.

Nothing in the Constitution compels the executive to limit the country's international agreements to formal treaties. Indeed, the perennial struggle for control of external policy scarcely touches the question of treaty making at all. Most agreements of the United States with other nations, especially amid the complexities and divisions of the postwar decades, have taken the form of executive agreements. The term *executive agreements* covers all international agreements other than formal treaties. Such agreements may result entirely from executive initiative; they may be authorized by congressional action or by treaty provisions. Some executive agreements embody arrangements of major importance, such as President Roosevelt's 1940 exchange of fifty overage destroyers for 99-year leases to British bases in the Western Hemisphere. Even the Yalta agreements of 1945 were executive agreements. The importance of the issue in no sense determines whether an agreement shall be viewed as a treaty and submitted to the Senate for approval. The courts, Congress, and the executive have never officially delineated what categories of agreements should take the form of treaties and which can properly be negotiated as executive agreements.[66]

Postwar presidents, no less than their predecessors, have agreed that the Senate should approve major international agreements under constitutional imperative. What determines whether a president fails to respect the unwritten boundary between what he may choose to do alone and what requires senatorial approval is largely his personal power and prestige. What curtails a president in his pursuit of international agreements on his own is the knowledge that if an agreement requires congressional implementation, it must be acceptable to Congress and the public. Congress's power of the purse can thwart any president. In postwar practice, especially in areas and at times when U.S. foreign policy has enjoyed a wide consensus, treaties can scarcely be distinguished from executive agreements by their superior importance.[67]

Throughout the era of Soviet-American conflict, the issue of executive-congressional relations has hinged less on agreement making than on the willingness of Congress, including the Senate, to underwrite the policies that successive administrations have regarded as essential to defend the security and welfare of the American people. What mattered in the evolution of Cold War policy after 1947 was not constitutional requirements relative to treaty making but the power and capacity of the executive to influence congressional and public opinion so as to assure appropriations that would underwrite purely executive decisions. Supported by perceived dangers of Soviet aggression, all presidents from Harry Truman to Ronald Reagan generally managed to control the congressional mood and the resultant appropriations. Senator Richard B. Russell of Georgia boasted that he could drive a $10 billion military appropriation bill through the Senate in thirty minutes. Claiming superior knowledge and employing the rhetoric of falling dominoes, the administrations of Lyndon Johnson and Richard Nixon managed, until 1973, to sustain Congress's financial support, if not public approval, for their war in Vietnam. As Senator J. William Fulbright once complained, the country's perennial war mood simply broke the power of the Senate to influence executive policy making.[68]

Covert operations, financed by general appropriations, foreign governments, or private contributions, have removed executive policies even further from Senate and congressional restraints. Yet it was precisely because such operations enabled executive officials to avoid public debate and other democratic inconveniences that they were so attractive. Officials determined to counter every Soviet presence in the Third World faced the simple choice of curbing their fears or skirting post-Vietnam majorities that often detected little danger in Soviet behavior. Covert operations permitted those in power to pursue objectives that they deemed essential, but that were of little concern to the vast preponderance of American citizens. Many key foreign policies in the 1980s—economic and military aid for the rebels of Angola and Afghanistan, Cambodians fighting the Vietnamese, the Contras of Nicaragua, and the ayatollas of Iran—followed clandestine channels, and thus required no attention to constitutional processes. So secret were some operations that not even responsible officials knew about them.[69] Unfortunately, covert operations never remain secret for long, and their exposure invariably exposes their short-term expediency. Such operations, as in Nicaragua, demonstrate a preference for military solutions to the exclusion of executive-congressional cooperation in search of more promising, democratically determined responses to such regional challenges.

It is not strange that the division within the country became more profound with the passage of time. As a consequence, the struggle for congressional and public support for Cold War policies, especially those operating in the Third World, became intense. The competition for control of the American mind became the central element in the country's political processes, more and more transcending the question of constitutional constraints. Indeed, the more pervasive the opposition to official preferences, the greater the claims to executive primacy in the management of external relations, and the greater the play on national fears. Presumptions of global Soviet expansion, proclaimed to sustain the public's anti-Soviet mood, left little room for accommodation with the country's antagonists. No formal treaty was placed before the Senate to terminate any of the issues raised by forty years of Cold War: the initial dispute over the Soviet satellites, the recognition of mainland China, the war in Vietnam, the Arab-Israeli conflict in the Middle East, the recovery of the hostages in Iran, the Soviet invasion of Afghanistan, or the struggle for power in Central America. Unrelieved by international agreements, the issues themselves persisted until overcome by boredom or exhaustion, usually finding solutions of their own. Whether, in the process, the decline of the Senate as a formative agency in the conduct of foreign relations resulted from executive primacy, and the fears that underwrote it, or from the intractability of the issues, the experience of recent decades is not what the Founding Fathers had in mind.

NOTES

1. For early American efforts at treaty making, see Norman A. Graebner, *Foundations of American Foreign Policy: A Realist Appraisal from Franklin to McKinley* (Wilmington, Del.: Scholarly Resources, 1985), pp. 1–76.
2. Royden J. Dangerfield, *In Defense of the Senate: A Study in Treaty Making* (Norman: University of Oklahoma Press, 1933) pp. 11–17. Article 6 of the Articles of Confederation granted Congress control of the country's foreign relations. Article 9 recognized Congress's sole right to determine issues of peace and war and to enter treaties "provided that no treaty of commerce shall be made whereby the legislative power of the respective states shall be restrained, from imposing such imposts and duties on foreigners, as their own people are subjected to, or from prohibiting the exportation and importation of any species of goods or commodities whatsoever."
3. American practice diverged totally from that of Britain, where all power over external relations centered in the king. For a thoughtful discussion of British practice, see Arthur Bestor, "Separation of Powers in the Domain of Foreign Affairs: The Original Intent of the Constitution Historically Examined," *Seton Hall Law Review* 5 (Spring 1974): 529–63.
4. For Adams's troubles in negotiating with the British government, see Graebner, "Adams in London," in *Foundation of American Foreign Policy*, pp. 25–46.
5. Dangerfield, *In Defense of the Senate*, p. 15; Graebner, *Foundations of American Foreign Policy*, p. 60.
6. *The Records of the Federal Convention of 1787*, ed., Max Farrand, 4 vols. (New Haven: Yale University Press, 1911), vol. 3, p. 113.
7. *Documentary History of the Constitution of the United States of America, 1786–1870*, 5 vols. (Washington, D.C.: Department of State, 1894), vol. 4, pp. 126–27.
8. Farrand, *Records of the Federal Convention*, vol. 1, p. 245.
9. Ibid., p. 21.
10. Ibid., pp. 64–67. Madison urged the convention "to fix the extent of the Executive authority; that as certain powers were in their nature Executive, and must be given to the department . . . , a definition of their extent would assist the judgment in determining how far they may be safely entrusted to a single officer." See ibid., pp. 66–67.
11. Ibid., p. 292. In the remainder of this section, the source is Farrand, *Records*, unless otherwise noted.
12. Ibid., p. 481.
13. Ibid., vol. 2, pp. 489–99.
14. For Hamilton's plan of government, see ibid., vol. 3, 624–25.
15. *The Debates of the Several State Conventions on the Adoption of the Federal Constitution*, ed. Jonathan Elliot, 5 vols. (Philadelphia: Lippincott, 1896), vol. 5, pp. 119–20.
16. Ibid., pp. 265–69.

17. Ibid., vol. 4, p. 264.
18. *The Federalist*, no. 75, in Alexander Hamilton, John Jay, and James Madison, *The Federalist*, ed. Edward Mead Earle (New York: Modern Library, 1937), pp. 486–87.
19. U.S. Senate, *Executive Journal* (Washington, D.C.: Duff Green, 1828), vol. 1, p. 3. For a superb discussion of Washington's efforts to conform to the "advice and consent" clause of the Constitution, see Dangerfield, *In Defense of the Senate*, pp. 31–49.
20. U.S. Senate, *Executive Journal*, vol. 1, p. 7.
21. Dangerfield, *In Defense of the Senate*, pp. 38–39.
22. U.S. Senate, *Executive Journal*, vol. 1, p. 12.
23. Dangerfield, *In Defense of the Senate*, pp. 41–42.
24. *Journal of William Maclay* (New York: Appleton, 1890), p. 122; Dangerfield, *In Defense of the Senate*, p. 44.
25. Ibid., pp. 45–46; *Memoirs of John Quincy Adams*, ed. Charles Francis Adams (Philadelphia: Lippincott, 1874–77), vol. 6, p. 427.
26. *Journal of William Maclay*, p. 132.
27. Dangerfield, *In Defense of the Senate*, pp. 47–48.
28. Graebner, *Foundations of American Foreign Policy*, pp. 91–92.
29. U.S. Senate, *Executive Journal*, vol. 1, p. 151.
30. Jay to Edmund Randolph, 19 November 1794, in *The Correspondence and Public Papers of John Jay*, Henry P. Johnston, 4 vols. (New York: Putnam, 1890), vol. 4, p. 138.
31. U.S. Senate, *Executive Journal*, vol. 1, pp. 183–84.
32. Dangerfield, *In Defense of the Senate*, p. 54.
33. Ibid., pp. 55–59.
34. For an excellent discussion of the Ghent negotiations, see George Dangerfield, *The Era of Good Feelings* (New York: Harcourt, Brace, 1952), pp. 64–91.
35. *Memoirs of John Quincy Adams*, vol. 4, pp. 244, 249–53.
36. For the Webster-Ashburton correspondence on the case of the *Caroline*, see *The Writings and Speeches of Daniel Webster* (Boston: Little, Brown, 1903), vol. 11, pp. 292–303.
37. Richard N. Current, "Webster's Propaganda and the Ashburton Treaty," *Mississippi Valley Historical Review* 34 (September 1947): 189–94.
38. Norman A. Graebner, *Empire on the Pacific: A Study in American Continental Expansion* (New York: Ronald Press, 1955), pp. 136–37.
39. I have developed this theme in "Lessons of the Mexican War," *Pacific Historical Review* 47 (August 1978): 325–42.
40. Lodge to Roosevelt, 9 February 1899, in *Selections from the Correspondence of Theodore Roosevelt and Henry Cabot Lodge, 1884–1918*, ed. Henry Cabot Lodge, 2 vols. (New York: Scribner, 1925), vol. 1, p. 391.
41. Dangerfield, *In Defense of the Senate*, pp. 90–111.
42. Ibid., pp. 150–70.
43. J. W. Foster, *The Practice of Diplomacy* (New York: Houghton, Mifflin, 1906), pp. 263ff.
44. Quincy Wright, *The Control of American Foreign Relations* (New York: Macmillan, 1922), p. 71.
45. Ibid., p. 233.
46. *Tucker v. Alexandroff*, quoted in ibid., p. 242.
47. Ibid., p. 245.
48. Foster Rhea Dulles, "John Hay," in Norman A. Graebner, ed., *An Uncertain Tradition: American Secretaries of State in the Twentieth Century* (New York: McGraw-Hill, 1961), pp. 26–27.

49. W. R. Thayer, *Life and Letters of John Hay,* 2 vols. (Boston: Houghton, Mifflin, 1914), vol. 2, p. 393.

50. Woodrow Wilson, *Congressional Government* (New York: Houghton, Mifflin, 1900), pp. xi–xiii.

51. Woodrow Wilson, *Constitutional Government in the United States* (New York: Columbia University Press, 1908), pp. 77–78.

52. Edward S. Corwin, *The President's Control of Foreign Relations* (Princeton, N.J.: Princeton University Press, 1917), p. 207.

53. Wright, *Control of American Foreign Relations,* pp. 368–73.

54. For Lodge's telling criticism of collective security, see his speech before the Senate, *Congressional Record,* 64th Cong., 2d sess., 1 February 1917, p. 2367; speech against the League of Nations, 12 August 1919, *Congressional Record,* 66th Cong., 1st sess., pp. 3779–84. Quotation taken from Lodge's speech of 21 December 1913, *Congressional Record,* 65th Cong., 3d sess., pp. 727–28.

55. For this analysis of Wilson's approach to world politics, see my introduction to *America as a World Power: A Realist Appraisal from Wilson to Reagan* (Wilmington, Del.: Scholarly Resources, 1984), pp. xxvi–xxvii.

56. Ibid., pp. xxvii–xxviii.

57. Paul W. Schroeder develops the view that Japan's demands decreased in 1941 whereas those of the United States expanded, thus eliminating any possibility of a diplomatic agreement. See Schroeder, *The Axis Alliance and Japanese-American Relations, 1941* (Ithaca, N.Y.: Cornell University Press, 1958).

58. Hornbeck quoted in Richard Dean Burns and Edward M. Bennett, eds., *Diplomats in Crisis: United States–Chinese–Japanese Relations, 1919–1941* (Santa Barbara, Calif.: Clio Books, 1974), p. xvii.

59. The negotiations in Paris and New York in the second half of 1946 were difficult and required occasional warnings from Secretary of State James F. Byrnes that the United States would make treaties unilaterally with Germany's wartime allies unless the USSR became more cooperative. See Graebner, *America as a World Power,* pp. 141–45.

60. For an insider's view of the creation of NATO, see Dean G. Acheson, *Present at the Creation: My Years in the State Department* (New York: Norton, 1969).

61. For the Japanese treaty, see Hollis W. Barber, *Foreign Policies of the United States* (New York: Dryden Press, 1953), pp. 383–86; Edwin O. Reischauer, *The United States and Japan* (Cambridge, Mass.: Harvard University Press, 1965), pp. 288, 363–78.

62. Barber, *Foreign Policies of the United States,* pp. 386–88; William Reitzel, Morton A. Kaplan, and Constance G. Coblenz, *United States Foreign Policy, 1945–1955.* (Washington, D.C.: Brookings Institution, 1956), pp. 311–12.

63. The following material on the SEATO treaty and the Geneva Accords was collected in articles in the *New York Times* and *The Times* (London) over the period of 8 May 1954 through 25 September 1954.

64. *America* 94 (29 October 1955): 120; *Newsweek,* 5 December 1955, p. 36; "Baghdad Bastion," *Time,* 5 December 1955, pp. 33–34; "Baghdad Pact Organization," Department of State *Bulletin* 33 (28 November 1955): 895; "U.S. Support for Baghdad Pact," ibid., 35 (10 December 1956): 918; "U.S. Welcomes Iran's Adherence to Northern Tier Pact," ibid., 33 (24 October 1955): 653.

65. Michael R. Gordon develops this theme in the *New York Times,* 2 March 1986, p. E3.

66. For a discussion of this issue, see Arthur E. Sutherland, Jr., "Restricting the Treaty Power," *Harvard Law Review* 65 (June 1952): 1305–38.

67. For a brief analysis of executive agreements, see William P. Gerberding, *United States Foreign Policy: Perspectives and Analysis* (New York: McGraw-Hill, 1966), pp. 33–34.

68. Fulbright quoted in the *New York Times,* 4 April 1971, p. A1.

69. Apparently both the State Department and the Department of Defense were bypassed in the White House's secret Iran operation that became public in November 1986. See Bernard Gwertzman and John H. Cushman, Jr., in *New York Times,* 14 December 1986, p. A1.

IV

ECONOMIC POLICY

11

Budgeting for National Defense

LEE DONNE OLVEY

The preamble of the Constitution lists providing for the common defense among the purposes for which our government was formed. Indeed, the ability of a government to sustain itself against enemies, foreign or domestic, is inherent in the notion of government. Although defense may not be the paramount concern, it is at least the equal of any other—a government that cannot sustain itself cannot hope to attain any of its values.

During the past two hundred years that vital function has been performed successfully. When external threats appeared, the nation rose to the challenge, created the necessary instruments of military power, and applied them with the desired effect. Perhaps criticisms of the manner and timeliness of the response are merited on some occasions, but in a global sense the success of the constitutional regime in providing for the common defense and securing the blessings of liberty cannot be denied.

Yet the nature of the defense challenge has changed so profoundly in the second half of the twentieth century that the demands it places on government bear little resemblance to the ideas that must have been uppermost in the minds of the Founding Fathers at the time the preamble was written. For the constitutional regime created at the end of the eighteenth century to be ideally suited to ensuring the nation's defense as we move toward the twenty first century would be remarkable indeed. Almost certainly meeting the defense challenge has changed more radically than any other function that government undertakes.

The nation has responded with a dramatic transformation in U.S. foreign policy goals and national security policies, accompanied by certainly significant, if not so dramatic, procedural changes for the implementation of those goals and policies. In broadest terms it can persuasively be argued that the response has been effective. Nevertheless, in most scholarly or political assessments of the health of the defense budgeting process, there is deep dissatisfaction. Although there is wide variation in the criticism, there are a number of common themes that call into serious question whether we are—indeed, whether we as body politic are even capable of—sustaining the defense effort in a sensible way. In contemplating reform, one is torn between zeal and despair.

The proposition to be examined in this chapter is whether the critics are right, and whether—to the extent they do seem right—the problems they identify are amenable to treatment without some fundamental revision in the constitutional provisions. To look ahead to the conclusion, I am going to argue that things are really not as bad as the critics maintain, that in fact a proper understanding of the nature of the defense budgeting process and of the role of criticism in that process can relieve much of the doubt about the current health of the process. On the other hand, a revolutionary change in the nature of the defense challenge has occurred, and despite significant adaptation to that change in recent decades, there are serious problems, which current trends seem certain to intensify. These problems create an imperative need for continuing adaptation of the ways the nation organizes itself to budget for defense.

THE CONSTITUTION AND NATIONAL DEFENSE

The object of defense is the preservation of peace under terms favorable to the sustainment of our national values. Defense epitomizes the functions of government—it is a public good whose benefits are shared impartially by all citizens, and it is a good that only government can provide. But whereas the benefits of defense are shared collectively, the costs must be borne privately, in the form of taxes on private consumption or reductions in other government services. It is also the case that the provision of defense confers benefits on particular locales in the form of employment and profit opportunities. When defense costs and the pressures on budgetary resources for other purposes are both high, the size and shape of defense budgets becomes an intense political issue.

The defense problem is, of course, in significant part an economic problem. Provision of the public good, defense, requires the use of scarce resources, thus denying their use for other purposes. This means that the conventional economic criteria of efficient resource allocation apply to the evaluation of the soundness of defense budgeting choices. To the extent that these economic criteria can successfully discriminate among policy choices, it is desirable that they be used. Indeed, to the extent that the public perceives these criteria to be operative, it becomes a political imperative that they be applied. Not all, but certainly a large part, of the criticism of the defense budgeting process is couched in terms that implicitly assume some framework of economic efficiency criteria.

Without denying the vital importance of the economic dimension of the defense budgeting problem, in the final analysis it is the political dimension that predominates. There are several compelling reasons why this is the case. Foremost among these is the crucial linkage between U.S. foreign policy, the military force structure required to support that policy, and the budgetary implications of that force structure. No serious attempt to define defense needs can be made without reference to U.S. foreign policy goals broadly defined. Second, even the economic dimension of the problem reduces to a political issue, because the complexity of the issues makes it virtually impossible to separate economic analysis from political competition. Finally, history will not judge us by whether we might have saved an additional percentage of the defense budget. The judgment will be of how well we as a nation were able to keep the peace in the nuclear age, preventing holocaust and sustaining the blessings of liberty to our posterity.

The constitutional provisions for performing the defense function employ the principle of the separation of "purse and sword" to guard against governmental abuse of power. Power is shared by the legislative and executive branches, giving both key roles that can serve to check or balance abuse of power by the other branch. The two branches share in decisions as to the size and structure of military forces, with Congress appropriating the financial resources and authorizing manning levels, subject to presidential approval. To Congress, in its express authority to declare war, is given the global authority to approve the use of military force. However, once war is declared, the conduct of a conflict is left to the president in his designated role as commander in chief.

Under the right circumstances, these lines of division of authority and responsibility make a great deal of sense. The gravity of a decision to go to war is such that authority to make it is appropriately reserved to Congress, as the direct representative of the people. A large, fragmented committee is not the right organization to wage war, however, and that role is appropriately entrusted to the president, who has the hierarchical organization and executive clout to get things done with dispatch and efficiency.

This division of roles implies clear-cut distinctions between states of peace and war and between raising and using military forces, and for most of our history these roles worked well. Separated by two oceans from the most likely adversaries, and with time available to mobilize forces in the event of a military crisis, the nation was not obliged to maintain a large standing force in peacetime. Political conflict over defense budgeting issues could be held to a minimum. If diplomacy failed, and the nation was compelled to mobilize and go to war, these extreme measures could be undertaken in good time, duly authorized by Congress acting to represent the popular will. With the nation thus appropriately behind the effort, the details of execution of the conflict could be left to the chief executive, the better suited to cope with the exigencies of war to the extent that he could act independently of congressional supervision. Whether things were ever quite as simple as this commonly held view is debatable; they certainly are not that simple today.

THE CHANGING CHALLENGE

The international security environment has changed fundamentally in the post–World War II era. The advance of nuclear weapons and the emergence of a hostile superpower with massive nuclear and conventional military forces have virtually eliminated the space and time buffers behind which the nation could take refuge in the past. We now live in a MAD world of Mutually Assured Destruction, paradoxically both the deterrent to and the likely consequence of nuclear war, a world in which the effective use of military power depends on forces in being, forces whose ultimate test of effectiveness is the successful avoidance of their use. Thus it is now the design and deployment of an unprecedentedly large peacetime force that plays the key role in providing for defense needs.

In this modern world, provision of an effective—that is to say, credible—deterrent requires not only a nuclear arsenal but also conventional forces capable of flexible response to aggression along the entire spectrum of possible military threats. These conventional forces comprise the bulk of the costs of defense, and their effectiveness as a deterrent has required that they in significant part be stationed overseas, in a strategy of forward deployment that raises the costs of maintaining them still further.

Furthermore, we have entered into a system of collective security arrangements in various parts of the world, most importantly in Western Europe, which means that the design and planned use of our military forces must be coordinated with those of our allies, with whom we seek to share the cost burdens of collective security on an equitable basis. We have made commitments to the security of Third World countries, given military and economic assistance in large amounts, and used U.S. military forces and lost U.S. lives in combat in far-off places without a formal declaration of war.

The impact of these fundamental changes in the security environment has been to place a new kind of burden on the body politic and the government in sustaining a coherent defense policy, and it has blurred the distinctions implicit in the constitutional provisions as to how defense policy will be conducted. In the two most recent major wars in which we have engaged, a state of war was never declared. In the Vietnam War, the reserve forces were never mobilized. The rationale for U.S. involvement was unclear to large numbers of people and the goals of that involvement were ambiguous. Neither the public nor the Congress were content for long to permit the executive to conduct the war free from criticism.

Providing a large standing force has increased the peacetime defense budget far beyond the level prior to World War II. Big defense means big business, and the local and regional impact of defense spending includes spillover benefits to the areas affected, providing employment and profit opportunities in every state in the Union to an extent that makes defense spending of vital importance to the political survival of members of Congress, whose tenure depends on local support. There are well-known stories of legislators intensely involved in seeking to curb overall defense spending or to reduce inefficiences, such as by closing bases deemed redundant, while at the same time fighting to preserve the level of defense activity in their own constituencies. For most congressmen, to ignore or resist such pressures would be tantamount to political suicide. The net effect of these changes in the security environment may be summarized by saying simply that the stakes of the defense budgetary process have increased enormously.

Management of this complex process in peacetime, subject to intense scrutiny from the press and constituents and the pressures of political competition, without the immunity afforded by the crisis atmosphere of wartime, poses an extraordinarily difficult challenge to democratic government. Market criteria of management effectiveness are absent completely, or at best seriously limited. On the output side, the ultimate test is success in deterring aggression and, if that should fail, victory in combat. But from the point of view of year-to-year management, all that is available to non-Pentagon observers is a narrow glimpse into this or that aspect of the health of the force, based on proximate measures of readiness or performance of particular systems or units, a game of statistical trends that are always vulnerable to manipulation to suit the taste of the evaluator.

On the input side of the equation, procurement costs, in most instances, are not subject to the test of market criteria. Defense procurement operates on the technological frontier. For most programs, off-the-shelf components are deemed unsuitable and specially tailored systems must be designed. The use of multiple sources is frequently economically prohibitive. The combination of technological uncertainty and absence of competitive supply conditions make the monitoring and evaluation of system costs enormously difficult.

The complexity and subjectivity of appraising resource use in defense make it especially fertile ground for political competition. Choices are inevitably politicized. The overall level of spending is an issue, the structures of the programs are issues, and these issues are the subject of public debate on which the political reputations of presidents, parties, administrations, and individual legislators rise and fall. Competition among the military services flourishes from time to time as well.

CRITICS AND REFORMERS

The process resulting from these changing conditions has been a continuing target for critics and reformers throughout the post–World War II era. The executive and legislative branches have criticized each other and themselves, and both have made substantial efforts at reform. The theme of the reformers has been to rationalize the budget process. Within the executive branch, this has involved a series of procedural and organizational changes, some enacted by legislation and some by executive order, to centralize the authority of the secretary of defense and to improve management resources and practices. The process has not been a continuous one. The National Security Act of 1947 created the post of secretary of defense and a small civilian staff to assist him, retaining the separate services and Congress's right to question each service separately about proposals for expenditure. Early experience with the problems of coordinating service budgets and planning led Secretary James Forrestal, who originally had been a strong defender of the "weak confederation" of the services and the weak defense secretary of the 1947 law, to reverse his position. By 1949 he testified before Congress: "I must admit to you quite frankly that my position on the question has changed. I am now convinced that there are adequate checks and balances inherent in our governmental structure to prevent misuse of the broad authority which I feel must be vested in the Secretary of Defense."[1] Subsequent legislation in 1949, 1953, and 1958 expanded the powers of the secretary and the chairman of the Joint Chiefs of Staff, but the predominant mode in the determination of service shares in the budget remained what Michael Hobkirk has termed "defense by bargaining."[2]

Then in 1961 Secretary Robert McNamara introduced the Planning, Programming, and Budgeting System (PPBS), which for many informed observers, certainly the majority of economists, represented a genuine milestone in the nation's efforts to cope with the new problem of massive, complex peacetime defense budgets. The basic concept of the approach, recognizing the inseparability of programming and budgeting, was to incorporate budgeting into the planning and programming process, organizing budget accounts to make trade-offs among outputs of various programs as explicit as feasible. This basic concept is incontrovertible. Legitimate differences can and did arise as to how the concept is properly implemented, especially with respect to the distribution of decision-making authority between the secretary and the services. Yet the principle of organizing choices to force explicit consideration of the costs as well as the benefits of alternatives at all levels of analysis is the very essence of rationality. At this juncture, it appears literally the only path to ensuring that the nation gets the most for its defense dollars.

Most would probably agree that the McNamara years had a lasting impact in terms of upgrading analytical capabilities and inducing a more systematic attention to the cost implications of governmental programs, not only within DoD and the military services but in other government departments as well. Yet at the time the services reacted with considerable hostility to the concepts. The most frequently voiced criticism of PPBS was the objection that it led to overcentralization of decision authority, transferring control from the hands of bona fide experts within the military services to the so-called "whiz kids" in the Office of Systems Analysis. Subsequent administrations, in their continuing campaign to curb costs and rationalize expenditures, have felt compelled to continue to distance themselves from the concept by coining new phrases such as "management by objective" (Nixon) and "zero base budgeting" (Carter). The Reagan administration has stressed the theme of "management reform" in its quest for efficiency.[3]

As imperfect as these reforms may have been in terms of rationalizing defense planning and budget choices within DoD, they unquestionably provided the executive branch with a new and, especially under Secretary McNamara, highly effective weapon in the ongoing debates with Congress over defense budget issues. Not surprisingly, Congress was not wildly enthusiastic about the PPBS innovations. The reformulation of arguments in quantitative terms tilted authority toward the executive side because the numbers were difficult to understand, verify, and manipulate. The congressional hearing process was put at a disadvantage by the sheer magnitude of the analyses DoD was able to produce. The main legislative response to the growing complexity of the budget problem and the attendant difficulties in Congress of setting priorities so as to match budget demands and resources was the 1974 Budget and Impoundment Control Act. The new congressional budget process, and expanded analytical staffs in the Congressional Budget Office and the General Accounting Office, have raised many expectations and continuing doubts about the overall role of Congress in fiscal policy. However, from the more limited perspective of Congress's ability to engage the executive branch in debate on defense budget matters, it clearly has been significant in recouping any loss of congressional influence in the preceding decade. Congress now has a much expanded in-house capability to do its own quantitative analyses and in-depth looks at particular issues. And the budget resolution process has certainly had the effect of focusing congressional attention much more sharply on the trade-offs between military spending and other priorities. The number of reports required of DoD by Congress, for example, has grown from 36 in 1970 to 200 in 1980 to 600 in 1986.[4] Congress has reasserted its authority in the defense budget process.

Despite these improvements in research and analysis capability in both branches of government, the quality of the resulting defense budgeting process has not been persuasive to the critics.[5] It is almost impossible to find a positive assessment of the process, and most assessments are highly critical. Criticisms involve the overall level of spending, the effectiveness of spending in terms of the mix of forces purchased, and the performance as well as the costs of individual systems. The main theme is that defense costs too much; many also question the effectiveness of the force. Within the past year yet another reorganization has been enacted to further centralize the control of resource management within DoD by strengthening the power of the chairman of the JCS, and other measures have been taken aimed at improving joint military analysis and planning.[6] Concurrently a presidential Blue Ribbon Commission on Defense Management (the Packard Commission) has recommended a number of management initiatives after taking a "broad and searching look at defense issues . . . to address the root causes of defense problems."[7] In addition to improved defense and budget planning within DoD, the commission calls for a significant streamlining of the congressional review process, with elimination of duplicative effort by numerous congressional committees and subcommittees. The commission also recommends biennial budgeting and authorization and appropriation of major programs not annually but only at key milestones of a system's life.

These most recent initiatives echo many of the themes of critics and reformers during the past forty years. They confirm continuing and serious dissatisfaction with the budgeting process, and they suggest moderate steps toward improvement.

ISSUES

In considering the radical transformation of the defense challenge in recent history and the swirl of controversy and criticism that have accompanied efforts to meet the challenge, two questions come to mind:

— Is the defense budgeting process working effectively, or is it seriously defective?
— Are the constitutional provisions for the process proving to be adaptable to the changing challenge, or is some modification indicated?

Does the Process Work?

Although the critics might not agree, most of the criticisms of the budget process can be articulated in terms of the economic model of rational allocation at the heart of the original program budgeting concept. In fact they rely on this model as a frame of reference for what would count as a "good" or "efficient" budget allocation. The rational allocation model addresses the determination of appropriate defense spending levels in terms of the trade-off with other resource uses, defining an efficient allocation as one in which the last dollar spent for defense provides a benefit just equal to the opportunity cost of that dollar in terms of forgone private consumption or other public services. The model further stipulates that resources should be applied in a "cost-effective" manner, so the level of defense preparedness achieved is obtained at the least possible cost or, to say the same thing in different words, so that the dollars spent achieve the maximum effect. These are correct criteria to use, and they make enormous good sense as an organizing approach for thinking rationally about defense budgeting issues. Indeed, there is really no other way to do it.

Nevertheless, there are some real problems involved in accepting analyses that assert that the levels of defense budgets are excessive or that the use of the funds is inefficient. The central problem is the absence of objective criteria for evaluating the worth of defense programs. This problem confuses analysis in several ways. With respect to the overall level of the budget, the difficulty begins with the so-called problem of incommensurables—the fact that the output of defense spending cannot be expressed in dollar terms. A standard cost-benefit analysis of a public spending program seeks to determine whether the expected benefits of the program exceed the costs, both measured in terms of dollars. When this is feasible, the decision criterion is straightforward and objective, provided of course that one accepts the many approximations normally required to translate all benefits and costs into dollar terms. In the case of defense, however, it simply is not feasible to convert the benefits into dollar terms. For many categories of defense spending, it is not feasible to quantify in any way the outputs of that spending. Even in the cases where some quantitative measure is feasible, dollar approximations of the value are not appropriate.

The most promising area for a quantitative assessment of "How much is enough?" is that of the strategic nuclear forces. For example, the impact of an additional strategic missile or bomber wing can be estimated in terms of the increment to the U.S. strategic forces that would be expected to survive an enemy first strike. That increment can in turn be translated into the additional damage that could be inflicted on the adversary in terms of expected target destruction. However, there is no practicable way of translating this increment of target destruction into a dollar value for the United States. Even the most enthusiastic proponents of quantitative analysis do not attempt to do that. So the question "How much is enough?" persists, even though a quantification of the outcome of various spending levels is possible, because that outcome cannot be measured in dollar terms.

The standard approach for resolving this dilemma is to appeal to the shape of the effectiveness curve—the "flat of the curve" argument.[8] The idea is that at some level of spending the marginal benefit of an additional increment begins to diminish. It might be argued, for example, that the effectiveness curve of strategic retaliatory forces begins to flatten out at some identifiable force level. In such a case, the analyst's policy prescription might well be to spend up to the breakpoint, but not beyond. A credible analysis that succeeds in identifying such a breakpoint can constitute a highly persuasive rationale for a specific spending level. Certainly strategic retaliatory forces constitute the most promising area for applying this technique. There is a relatively simple and quantifiable effectiveness criterion, namely, targets destroyed, and there is a finite set of targets.

Even in this best case for analysis, however, the complications are formidable. First, allowance must be made for a disarming first strike by the enemy, and this involves many assumptions and scenarios concerning enemy capabilities, deployments, and possible courses of action. Second, assumptions must be made about the reliability of U.S. systems, especially their ability to penetrate enemy defenses. Third, these analyses have to be projected quite far into the future, raising additional uncertainties about the survivability and effectiveness of the various elements of the forces, given the dangers of "technological breakout" in a variety of areas. Such uncertainties present needs for hedges in the form of redundancy in force levels and multiple systems, such as the "triad." Finally, the ultimate test of effectiveness of the force is its success as a deterrent. The task is not to produce a sufficiently capable force as to render unthinkable by our calculus a decision by the USSR to launch a nuclear attack. Rather, the task is to influence the Soviet leadership's own calculus of the likely outcome of an exchange so that the damage to them will be considered unacceptable *from their point of view.*

These considerations enormously complicate the task of sizing the strategic nuclear forces, certainly to an extent that permits very wide variations in the conclusions reached by responsible analysts and policy makers, be they military, independent civilian analysts, or elected representatives. The bottom line is that in the area of strategic nuclear forces, although the idea of a point where the effectiveness curve flattens makes excellent sense as a concept, as we begin to account for the risks as to miscalculation, technological change, and Soviet behavior, the hope dwindles of finding a sharp breakpoint that can command agreement in defining how much the nation needs. So if a critic asserts that we are spending too much in this area, what does this mean? Even if the assertion is based on a careful, analytical effort to determine how much the nation needs, the statement cannot possibly stand alone as a fact with which we are all compelled to agree. To make such an assertion is properly the beginning of the argument, not the end, and practitioners should be obliged to preface their evaluations with "In my judgment . . ." or "It is my view that. . . ."

If we move to other categories of the defense budget, such as the general purpose land or naval forces, problems of evaluating effectiveness become much more acute. The marginal contribution of one additional infantry division or an increase in the battle fleet cannot be measured in quantitative terms of targets destroyed. Rather, war scenarios must be developed and gamed so as to gauge the outcome of contests involving differing levels of friendly and opposing forces. However, the variety of scenarios, the limitations of simulation methods for predicting outcomes with confidence, and the complexity and ambiguity of the outcomes render such analyses highly subjective, dangerously sensitive to the assumptions and gaming design used. Nor is there a breakpoint in the effectiveness curve for general purpose forces. Additional carrier groups or combat divisions, at least within the range of force levels we would seriously contemplate, can always be argued to provide additional confidence in the ability to withstand attack and ultimately prevail in a future war.

What these observations mean is that there is no finite, achievable level of total defense spending that will satisfy all needs. Defense is after all an economic problem, and we cannot afford as much as we would like to have. Nor is there an available criterion for resolving this economic problem, a way of identifying the optimal allocation by balancing the value achieved by additional defense dollars against alternative uses of those resources. Failing such a criterion, the "correct" trade-off is ultimately nothing more or less than a matter of political choice. It is the political process that must do the job of making this choice. Expert analysis can help inform the choice and perhaps help prevent foolish behavior that in restropect no one would endorse. Indeed, the legislators and executive branch policy makers have to lean heavily on expert military advice. Yet the ultimate decision on how much to spend for defense cannot be simply "whatever the experts say we need." At any level of spending we are likely to achieve, we shall always "need" more.

The debate on where we draw the line on defense spending addresses an absolutely vital issue. It is appropriate that the debate be conducted with all the intensity and rigor that that only open political competition can provide. If we were to discover a lack of competition on this issue among the parties, between the Congress and the executive branch, or even among and within the military services themselves, it would not bode well for the health of the constitutional system. On the other hand, the fact that we have an ample supply of critics making the case that we are spending too much should not be a cause for pessimism or a conclusion that the defense budgetary system is bankrupt. Nor should we despair that last year's budget level is always the starting point for attempting to reconcile defense and non-defense goals. Given the complexity of attempting to make this choice collectively and intelligently, a first approximation is a valuable commodity, and that is the best approximation we have.

The second major line of criticism concerns the cost effectiveness of military spending. This criticism is in part directed toward the planning and programming of the force structure and in part toward the efficiency of the procurement process, or lack thereof. These kinds of concerns are popular with critics because in many cases data can be cited that appear to constitute proof of management failure. The most tangible forms of failure include cost overruns, excessive prices for ordinary items, failures of systems to meet design specifications, ineptitude of managers or outright contractor fraud. Enough examples of these kinds of problems have been publicized to make it clear that they do occur, indeed many may regard them as the rule rather than the exception. However, given the sheer magnitude of the defense procurement process and the technological and other uncertainties in the decision environment, such individual instances of mistakes and inefficiencies are always going to occur. How, then, do we know when we are making too many mistakes? Given the adversarial nature of the debate, a few horror stories can swamp the news and ignore hundreds of successful, well-managed projects. The real question is whether there is a practicable way of reorganizing management procedures to improve in those areas.

More subtle criticisms involve charges of inattention to costs, resulting in excesses in design specifications, often labeled "gold plating." According to this criticism, technological superiority is the characteristic pushed in the design and evolution of weapons, without regard to price or the quantity of systems that budget constraints will permit.[9] Another common assertion is that the wrong kinds or amounts of procurement items are selected because of "servicism," which involves a bias toward the more glamorous systems identified with the central mission of a service, to wit aircraft carriers and intercontinental, penetration bombers, and a bias against the "orphan" functions not central to the providing service's definition of its role, to wit, airlift and sealift for the army.[10]

What is to be made of these criticisms? Clearly, the real question is not how many individual mistakes can be identified, but whether there is a practicable better way of reorganizing management procedures to improve in these areas. Unless such remedies are available, we cannot properly say the existing system is flawed. And if remedies are proposed, there is the additional caveat that they not introduce other, worse problems.

Secretary McNamara chose civilian centralization of analysis and decision making in DoD to bridge service differences and require explicit consideration of costs. That centralization provoked a reaction, and calls were made for decentralization. The latest reorganization efforts, specifically the Goldwater-Nichols Reorganization Act, envision a movement back toward military centralization, presumably avoiding some of the pitfalls that beset the previous attempt.

In any event, the cost-effectiveness and management issues should be separate from the global issue of the overall size of the defense budget. We should continuously strive for more effective management, but even though the best attainable performance may appear to involve excessive waste, we must go ahead with the defense effort. If resources can be saved by greater management efficiency, then we can afford reductions in the defense budget without degrading capabilities. However, to cut the budget first, on the assumption that somehow a way will be found to take the cuts out of waste and avoid an adverse effect on the force, is neither realistic nor in the nation's interest. The American way of relentlessly seeking out and publicizing individual instances of mismanagement is the guarantee that the executive branch will be vigilant in its quest for efficiency. On the other hand, to the extent that publicity overstates the problem, assumes efficiencies that cannot be realized, and suggests public managers in general to be incompetent or worse, the public interest is not well served. Much of the criticism falls into this category.

The note on which I would end this brief consideration of the health of the defense management system is that things are not as bad as the critics would have us believe. The search for better ways of coping with these problems has been vigorous and has led to a series of organizational and procedural innovations in both the executive and legislative branches. The search and the reorganization goes on. There is good reason to believe that ongoing changes are appropriate ones, and there is also every reason to believe that they will not lay to rest the issues of the level of defense expenditures and the optimal mix of forces.

Are There Constitutional Implications?

The above assessment suggests that a radical transformation has occurred in the defense challenge and that, to date, by and large, the challenge has been met successfully. This new challenge places great demands on government, heightened demands for peacetime resources and demands that those resources be used wisely and efficiently. Despite continuing organizational and procedural innovations, there remains widespread dissatisfaction with the quality of the performance. The question arises of whether more radical changes are necessary.

The traditional metaphor for describing the constitutional provisions for defense is the separation of "purse and sword." For the problems of an earlier era, this metaphor was an appealing one. It assigned responsibilities appropriately—the legislature controlled the *size* of the force and the decision as to *whether* to use it, but to the president was left the executive function of controlling *how* the force was to be used.

The old metaphor does not fit the current defense problem. For the problem we now confront, budgeting and strategy have become inseparable. A good metaphor to describe the modern situation is one used by the advocates of systems analysis in the late 1950s, when a campaign was under way to persuade policy makers to think of defense as an economic problem: "Strategy and cost are as interdependent as the front and rear sights of a rifle. One cannot assign relative weights to the importance of the position of the front and rear sights."[11] The obvious moral is that a division of labor that has one member of the team controlling the rear sight and another controlling the front sight is not likely to score bull's-eyes. The more likely outcome is a struggle between the two team members for control of both sights. That of course is what happens, with Congress and the president competing for a larger share of power to determine both the budget and the strategy. Such competition can be invigorating or it can be debilitating. There is ample evidence that the governmental system produces both outcomes. The path to improvement, if there be one that can maintain fundamental constitutional values, would not be to shift the overall balance of power between these two branches of government, but to better define their roles to permit each to specialize more in those tasks to which it is inherently best suited. The constitutional question might be expressed by asking whether there is a feasible modern equivalent of the "purse and sword" distinction.

An initial complication in addressing this issue is that today's defense budgeting problems exist within a broader context of deep concerns as to the ability of the government to control spending in general. The real revolution in government spending has occurred in the non-defense sectors, with the total share of GNP allocated by government rising from under 10 percent in the 1920s to over 30 percent in the 1980s. The concern is in part over what is alleged to be excessive growth of government spending, and in part over the manner in which the spending is financed, namely, out of borrowing rather than current tax revenues. An unprecedented bout of inflation in the 1970s and unprecedented peacetime expansion of the national debt in the 1980s have raised these concerns to an all-time high. Congress has sought a legislative fix to this problem through the Gramm-Rudman bill. A constitutional fix in the form of an amendment requiring a balanced federal budget (or alternatively limiting spending or limiting taxation) has received wide support.[12]

The premise that the growth of government spending is excessive and out of control is a curious one, because to accept it is to question the viability of the constitutional system at a rather fundamental level. The issue has been phrased in a variety of ways, but the basic idea seems straightforward. In the process of making policy choices collectively in a democracy, particular interests drown out consideration of the general interest. There is an upward bias in government activity that benefits particular groups, the costs of which, however, are borne publicly by taxpayers and currency holders. Budgets and spending grow willy-nilly, without due regard to adverse consequences for the overall economic system, whose health and continued viability require stable prices, vigorous work incentives unhampered by excessive taxes and transfers, and investment incentives unstifled by excessive interest rates. Whether or not these concerns are well-founded, it is indisputable that a large majority of Americans, in and out of government, believe they are valid. The paradox lies in why people permit their government to spend in a fashion that appears to threaten their economic welfare. Are these perceived shortcomings correctable in the context of the constitutional system, or is this a fatal flaw in the viability of democratic government, or—on a less pessimistic note—are these criticisms exaggerated debating points in the continuing political struggle over national priorities?

However one feels about these broader issues of controlling spending, the certain implication for defense budgeting is increasing difficulty in maintaining public support for large peacetime defense budgets. The implication derives from the fact that some 90 percent of the discretionary resources of the U.S. government go to defense. Efforts to hold total spending down will inevitably focus on the defense budget. The corollary proposition is that the importance of wise use of limited defense resources, both in substance and in the perception of the various constituencies whose support is required, is steadily increasing and will continue to do so.[13]

One proposal for addressing the overspending symptom is to give the president authority to veto line items in the appropriations and authorization bills, a power states have accorded their executives and that presidents have yearned after for the past century.[14] A blanket item veto authority would have sweeping ramifications for the balance of presidential and congressional power in controlling budget matters, and it is not my purpose to address the merits of such a proposal here. In any event the prospects of Congress assenting to such a sweeping change are limited, to say the least. Yet a good case can be made that defense spending is quite different from spending in general, and recognition of this difference offers one route to improving at least the defense portion of the budgeting problem. There is an instructive contrast between the defense budget problem and most, certainly not all, of the non-defense programs. As noted at the outset, defense is very close to being a "pure" public good, in that the benefits are shared collectively in a totally undiscriminating way. For most other programs, that is not true. Benefits apply to particular groups, the members of which receive payments or goods and services of various kinds. Thus these programs have a distributional impact that must be assessed along with the benefits per se. Such assessments are inherently political, resolvable only by the political process and not amenable to rational analysis.

In the case of defense programs, there is also a distributional impact. The selection of defense contractors and the location of elements of the defense force have significant economic implications for specific regions and industries. On the personnel side, the design and management of compensation and retirement schemes for active and retired military and civilian employees have important implications for those groups, who constitute a formidable political force. Yet these distributional impacts are different; they are in essence a by-product of defense activity, not integral to the goal. A rational analysis of procurement issues can, and arguably should, be made completely independently of these side issues of distributional impact. The selection of defense contractors really should be blind to the political interests involved. An outmoded or unsuccessful weapons system should not be continued in order to provide employment opportunities in a given state or save a corporation from financial embarrassment. The laws make no allowance for equitable sharing of defense business opportunities. The specified criterion is least cost, and that is how choices should be made.

In practice that is not what happens. Both the initiation and the discontinuation of specific procurement programs can be heavily influenced by particular interests. Indeed, allegation of such influence comprises a major part of the criticisms of the defense budgeting process. In 1985 Assistant Defense Secretary Lawrence Korb assessed the congressional pork barrel costs as "at least $10 billion a year, things we don't want, things we don't need, but are in there to protect vested interest."[15]

That the defense committees are increasingly involved in detailed scrutiny of the budget is clear. The growth of staff resources has been accompanied by growth in the number of changes made by Congress to the president's budget submissions. Robert J. Art traces the growth of detailed congressional scrutiny of the defense budget, citing the advent of annual authorizations in the early 1960s and the expansion of staff capabilities in the 1970s as key factors. He also cites numerous studies that convincingly document in quantitative terms the growth in the number of line item amendments by the armed services and appropriations committees.[16]

This pattern is not surprising. To the extent Congress has the ability to influence such decisions, individual congressmen will of political necessity be compelled to use that influence. Nor is it likely that Congress as a whole will be able to effectively constrain the use of such influence. As one (retired) staff member observed, "there is a natural constituency for concentration on weapons systems in the here and now. It is difficult for members to focus on the big issues because of the lack of time, because of the need to get reelected, and because of the fact that constituency service, not policy oversight, is what is necessary today to stay in office."[17]

Of course the executive branch is vulnerable to these pressures as well. However, a compelling argument can be made that the executive branch, with its hierarchical structure, is inherently better suited to defend the public interest in this regard. Here is an area in which the notions of rational analysis and economic efficiency have a firm grounding. Just as the executive is better suited than the legislature to command the force in time of war, so is the executive better suited to manage the detailed design and deployment of the force in time of peace. Cost-effectiveness questions, involving matters such as the mix of forces and the cost and performance of individual weapons systems, are smaller issues, in the sense that rational choice in these cases can be confined to trade-offs within the defense budget. Although decision makers confront formidable problems in quantifying and comparing outcomes, the criteria for choice can at least be confined to military considerations. The choice criterion can be stated in terms of choosing among alternative force mixes so as to achieve some stated military objective at least cost or, equivalently, choosing mixes so as to attain maximum effectiveness in attaining the objective using a specified level of resources. Although difficult, these questions are an order of magnitude easier than the global question of how much for defense. Unlike that question, these issues can be made to yield to expert analysis, and it is appropriate that they be tackled in that way and not in the political arena. They represent precisely the kind of analytical challenge that systems analysis attempted to address in its heyday in the 1960s.

In essence the proposition is that a boundary zone needs to be recognized between the question of the overall size of the defense budget ("How much is enough?") and the allocation of the defense budget to achieve maximum effect (the "cost-effectiveness" kinds of questions.) This is not to say that the two questions are independent. Clearly, neither can be intelligently addressed without some prior knowledge or working assumption as to how the other is going to be answered. For that reason, decisions in one area are bound to have an impact on the other, and there is bound to be intense competition between Congress and the president in both areas. Nevertheless, these distinctions do offer a basis for a desirable shift in the division of labor between the branches, one with the potential for improving the overall outcome.

The argument is that the current budgetary process should be modified to reduce congressional power and propensity to intervene in the *structure*, as opposed to the *level*, of the defense budget. The key word is reduce, not eliminate. Congress cannot and should not be expected to abstain from evaluating defense budget structure issues. However, Congress should restrain itself, or be restrained, from using the power of the purse to micromanage the structure of the force. Such limitation by no means implies a surrender of congressional oversight. Indeed, relieving Congress of some of the burden of servicing *constituent needs* should enhance the time, resources, and incentives for Congress to evaluate executive budget proposals in terms of *defense needs*. And to the extent that occurred, executive incentives to cast budgetary proposals in terms of realistic, clearly articulated defense plans would also be enhanced.

Although the executive branch, by virtue of its hierarchical structure, is relatively better suited to impose rationality on trade-offs within the defense budget, a key question is whether it will, in fact, exercise that authority as effectively as practicable. Certainly the willingness of Congress to abstain from micromanagement is heavily dependent on its assessment of the performance of the executive branch in this regard, and certainly there are major problems in this area. Congressional scrutiny provides a vital stimulus to improvement, but it should be directed at improving and not supplanting the executive defense planning and budgeting process.

President Reagan, like many of his predecessors, has asked for blanket line item veto authority, but the slender prospects of Congress collaborating in such a significant devolution of power render that idea almost undeserving of serious discussion. The 1974 reform of the legislative portion of the budget process has moved in the opposite direction by divesting the president of most of his power to impound funds whose expenditure he does not deem to be in the national interest.[18] Insofar as non-defense programs are concerned, the current arrangement may well produce the appropriate sharing of power. However defense spending really is different. Clearly the executive is better suited for micromanagement of the defense budget. Congressional micromanagement in response to particular private interests is a luxury the nation can ill afford.

Future prospects are for increasing pressures on overall government spending that will most sharply affect discretionary funding concentrated in the defense budget. These pressures are exacerbated by public loss of confidence in the defense budget process. Hence the need for more effective division of labor between Congress and the president in the defense budget process has never been greater, and current trends imply that the need will continue to grow. Less drastic means to the same end may be more readily available, for example the approaches suggested by the Packard Commission. By reducing the frequency of the authorization and appropriation processes and reformulating the president's budget authority in terms of broad programs rather than line items, the same purposes could be served. As long as Congress retains the power to insert or extend specific programs, however, the incentives to exercise that power for the protection of constitutent interests are likely to be irresistible. The Packard Commission proposals do not appear to address that fundamental problem. By contrast, the line item veto would sharply attenuate the ability and hence, more important, the incentive for Congress to focus on the peripheral effects of defense spending at the expense of the central purpose. For these reasons, a line item veto limited to defense authorization and appropriation bills merits consideration.

FUTURE PROSPECTS

Whether the constitutional system endures for another two centuries will depend on continued success in providing for the common defense. Now, as always, we face uncertainty in divining what the dangers are and how best to meet them. We certainly cannot comprehend what form future challenges are likely to take. But we can reasonably expect that the response to the challenges is going to cost a lot of money. History will judge the response on the basis of the outcome, not on the basis of how well the budget processes worked.

The first question in assessing the prospects of success is whether as a body politic we have the capacity to sustain our defense effort over the long term. The question is one of political will, not economic capacity. Given popular support expressed through elected representatives, the nation has incomparable resources and ability to harness those resources to whatever task is deemed vital. Clearly the adversary in the current concerns has relative strengths and weaknesses just the opposite of ours. With the loss of the luxury of time for us to mobilize, and with the relentless Soviet accumulation of military power, the net advantage we enjoyed in the past has given way to parity. The relevant question now is whether we will be able to maintain parity. An assessment of the current situation suggests reasons for concern but also reasons for confidence.

Perhaps the most serious cause for concern is the current controversy over government deficits. If the government is unable to keep its house in order with respect to the overall budgetary process, the prospects for the defense budget, which comprises a major part of the total and an even larger part of the controllable portion, are certainly not helped. Without a better reconciliation of the tax and non-defense-spending issues, the potential for disabling reductions in the defense budget in the future is dangerously high.

A second cause for concern is the low esteem in which the budgeting and planning processes are currently held by the public, the media, and policy makers. I have offered a number of reasons to support the argument that the health of the process is better than the critics allow. Whatever the merit of those arguments, or lack thereof, the one fact on which virtually all agree is that defense budgeting and its corollary activities have an exceedingly bad name. If the American people are convinced that "fraud, waste and abuse" are as rampant as most critics allege, at some point they will withdraw their support for defense programs. Concern over deficits and low esteem for the defense planning and budgeting process make the defense program a likely target for future cuts, and the fact that discretionary funds are so highly concentrated in the defense portion of the budget make it virtually the only target. The challenges of allocating reductions rationally are even more formidable than those of allocating increases. Thus the need for adaptation and reform continues. A presidential line item veto for defense spending has been suggested as an important way to better structure the roles of Congress and the president in meeting these challenges, but clearly no panaceas are in sight.

The bright side of the picture is to be found in the continued demonstrated ability of the constitutional system to adapt, albeit at a moderate and sometimes halting pace that does not satisfy the critics. The successive reforms within DoD over the past thirty years and the reform of the congressional budget process have been evolutionary in nature, but the cumulative effect is a massive improvement in the resources our government needs to address these complex problems. This process of adaptation must continue.

NOTES

1. U.S. Congress, Senate, Committee on Armed Services, Hearings, *National Security Act Amendments*, 81st Cong., 1st sess. (Washington, D.C.: GPO, 1949), p. 9.
2. Michael Hobkirk, *The Politics of Defense Budgeting* (Washington, D.C.: National Defense University Press, 1983), p. 25.
3. Caspar W. Weinberger, *Annual Report to the Congress, Fiscal Year 1986* (Washington, D.C.: GPO, 1985), p. 81.
4. Cited in Michael Ganby, "An Exclusive AFJ Interview with Representative Les Aspin," *Armed Forces Journal International,* April 1986, p. 40.
5. See Robert J. Art, Vincent Davis, and Samuel P. Huntington, *Reorganizing America's Defense* (Washington, D.C.: Pergamon-Brassey's, 1985); Richard Halloran, *To Arm a Nation* (New York: Macmillan, 1986); and Richard A. Stubbing, *The Defense Game* (New York: Harper & Row, 1986).
6. Goldwater-Nichols Reorganization Act.

7. "A Quest for Excellence," Report of the President's Blue Ribbon Commission on Defense Management, 30 June 1986.

8. Alain C. Enthoven and K. Wayne Smith, *How Much Is Enough? Shaping the Defense Program, 1961–1969* (New York: Harper & Row, 1971), p. 208.

9. Jacques S. Gansler, *The Defense Industry* (Cambridge, Mass.: MIT Press, 1980), p. 32.

10. Samuel P. Huntington, "Organization and Strategy," in Art et al., *Reorganizing America's Defense,* p. 240.

11. Charles J. Hitch and Roland N. McKean, *The Economics of Defense in the Nuclear Age* (Santa Monica, Calif.: RAND Corporation, 1960), p. 3.

12. See Aaron Wildavsky, *How to Limit Government Spending* (Berkeley and Los Angeles: University of California Press, 1980), for a discussion of why constitutional provisions are needed.

13. James Schlesinger, "The Office of the Secretary of Defense," in Art et al., *Reorganizing America's Defense,* p. 270.

14. Robert A. Wallace, *Congressional Control of Government Spending* (Detroit: Wayne State University Press, 1960), p. 136.

15. Cited, with other examples in Stubbing, *Defense Game,* p. 100. See also Halloran, *To Arm a Nation,* p. 347.

16. Robert J. Art, "Congress and the Defense Budget," in Art et al., *Reorganizing America's Defense,* pp. 409–25.

17. Ibid., p. 413.

18. See Rudolph G. Penner, *The Congressional Budget Process after Five Years* (Washington, D.C.: American Enterprise Institute, 1981).

12

Engaging in International Trade

ROGER B. PORTER

In drafting the Constitution, the Founding Fathers could hardly have foreseen the shape of the U.S. and international economies two centuries hence. The magnitude, pace, and sophistication of international economic interaction today is daunting even to those whose lives have been spent wholly in the twentieth century.[1] Yet the constitutional framework governing our economic and trade policy-making arrangements has changed little in two hundred years.

The inspired men who gathered in Philadelphia reflected a widespread recognition of the need to strengthen the Articles of Confederation. Under these, the central government had no power to tax, no means to regulate commerce, and no way to pay its debts. It faced consistent humiliation in its relations with foreign governments. Although the framers acknowledged the necessity of a substantially strengthened central government, two other concerns decisively conditioned the constitutional provisions they finally adopted.

First, they were concerned about the potential for abuses associated with concentrated powers. The Revolutionary War had been fought in large part to free the colonies from a system in which governmental decisions were made without adequate representation by those affected by those decisions. Dividing and fragmenting authority would help protect against the danger of arbitrary and capricious acts.

Second, the framers' thinking was shaped by the concept of placing limits on what governments could do. Placing specific bounds on the scope of governmental powers was considered essential by many whose agreement to the new set of governmental institutions was needed. The Bill of Rights, consciously restricting the government from doing certain things, was an indispensable part of the package that produced a ratified constitution.

The purpose of this chapter is to examine how the constitutional framework adopted in 1787 affects the way in which trade policy is formulated and implemented today. Trade policy is especially interesting for such an examination because it brings together domestic, economic, national security, and foreign policy considerations. Before turning to this task, however, it is worth reviewing briefly the specific trade policy clauses in the Constitution.

TRADE CLAUSES IN THE CONSTITUTION

It is commonplace to observe that the process of shaping the Constitution involved a succession of compromises. The trade policy clauses were no exception. Several factors shaped the discussions concerning trade.

Among the most immediate problems requiring a solution was finances. Under the Articles of Confederation, the central government lacked sufficient revenues and desperately needed the means to finance the debts it had accumulated and to undertake its new responsibilities. Duties on trade were a major source of revenue in the eighteenth century and remained so during the nineteenth century.

Second, the duties and restraints on trade between states and on goods from abroad that passed from one state through another constituted a significant barrier to an integrated national economy. A third factor was the economic difficulties stemming from the lack of a strong central government to preserve and enhance the states' collective economic interests abroad. By the mid 1780s, a postwar economic depression was compounded by discrimination against U.S. shipping interests, especially by Great Britain. The Navigation Acts greatly limited the use of non-British vessels in trade with the United Kingdom.

Finally, and perhaps most important in shaping the specific trade clauses in the Constitution, sharp differences existed in the economic interests of many southern states that relied heavily on agricultural exports to Europe and those states, predominantly in the North, that desired protection against foreign competition for their manufactured goods. The former were reluctant to give the new Congress the power to regulate foreign trade; the latter, attracted by a mercantilist philosophy, looked to a stronger central government to prevent foreign domination of their struggling manufacturing industries.

The southern states, with good cause, also feared both the potential for interference with exports and the passage of restrictive navigation acts in retaliation against the British. The fear of interference with exports was not an idle one. In August 1780, the Congress had "recommended to the Legislatures of each of the United States to impose a tax upon all exports equivalent to 2½ percent . . . paid in specie or in kind." The purpose was "to provide for the discharge of . . . foreign debts as the United States have already contracted and to enable them to procure such further credit as the public exigencies may require."[2]

At one point in the debates at the constitutional convention, representatives from several southern states sought a requirement for a two-thirds vote of Congress on any act touching commerce. Ultimately, this stipulation was dropped in exchange for a specific prohibition of any federal taxation of exports. Thus, the shape of the final compromise included granting Congress the power to levy duties on imports and to regulate commerce with foreign nations and among the several states (Article 1, Section 8). At the same time, Congress was restrained from imposing a tax or duty "on articles exported from any state" (Article 1, Section 9). The power to affect trade directly was exclusively a federal one. "No state shall, without the consent of the Congress, lay any imposts or duties on imports or exports, except what may be absolutely necessary for executing its inspection laws" (Article 1, Section 10).

In seeking to understand the relationship between the Constitution and the way trade policy is made, this chapter first examines three distinguishing characteristics of the U.S. system of government—divided institutional arrangements, democratic participation, and deliberative processes. Second, it explores three persistent policy tensions between competing values that are permitted and encouraged by our fragmented constitutional structure. Third, it describes the institutional biases among the major trade policy actors and how they reflect these competing values, objectives, and tensions. Finally, it considers how these biases influence the ebb and flow of policy, and what challenges this presents for U.S. trade policy as we move into our third century under the Constitution.

DISTINGUISHING CHARACTERISTICS

The general provisions in the Constitution provide the framework for three pervasive characteristics that shape the way in which policies are formulated and implemented in the U.S. system of government.

Divided Institutions

The first and most frequently cited characteristic is a fragmented and divided set of institutional arrangements. One manifestation is a federal system in which extensive power and authority is exercised at the state and local levels and in which residual powers, those powers not expressly delegated to the federal government, are reserved for the states.

Although the Constitution reserves the imposition of duties on foreign commerce to the Congress, states play an important role in many policies and activities that bear on the flow of goods, services, and investment across national borders. Not only do states organize export promotion activities, but state tax policies, as in the case of unitary taxation, can significantly influence the location of investment and thus trade patterns.

Likewise, those seeking to expand U.S. coal exports have long advocated the construction of coal slurry pipelines to reduce transportation costs, but failure to secure federal eminent domain has stymied the construction of such pipelines. A third illustration of the importance of state action is the impact of the patchwork array of state product liability laws. Proponents of federal product liability legislation have thus far failed to overcome resistance, not only from trial lawyers, but from certain state governments uncomfortable with federal preemption on this critical economic policy issue.

At the national level, the diffusion and division of power *between* the three constitutional branches of our federal government is mirrored by a similar fragmentation *within* each branch. The Constitution specifies that the Congress has responsibility for regulating foreign commerce. Within the Congress, the Senate Finance Committee and House Ways and Means Committee have historically had jurisdiction over most trade issues. The proliferation of congressional staff and the heightened perceived salience of trade policy issues have now attracted the interest of numerous other committees. Shortly after its introduction at the outset of the 100th Congress, the Omnibus Trade Act of 1987 was sent to six separate House committees for work on its individual titles. A policy area once considered virtually the exclusive province of the Ways and Means Committee is now aggressively and successfully contested by others.

The executive branch is, if anything, even more fragmented on trade policy issues than is the Congress. Numerous departments and agencies take an active interest in trade policy matters. Still others have specific responsibilities for formulating or implementing trade policy.

The fragmented nature of the executive branch periodically leads to calls for greater rationality, functional consolidation, and streamlined decision making. The Nixon administration undertook one such effort in the early 1970s, culminating in its proposal for the creation of four "super" departments. One of these, the Department of Economic Affairs, would have brought trade policy under one roof along with other major economic functions. The enthusiasm for the scheme, which went counter to the prevailing ethos favoring fragmented and divided authority, was limited in both the executive and legislative branches. Eventually, the departmental reorganizational plans were quietly dropped in the early days of Nixon's second term.

The Carter administration's reorganization of trade policy sought to consolidate certain functions and clarify roles and responsibilities. Administration of the antidumping and countervailing duty statutes was shifted from the Department of the Treasury to the Department of Commerce, and the international trade elements of Commerce were strengthened. In general, the Office of the U.S. Trade Representative in the Executive Office of the President was given responsibility for coordinating the formulation of trade policy, with the Department of Commerce having the lead in administering and implementing most of the trade statutes. The independence and role of the U.S. International Trade Commission, created in the Trade Act of 1974 to replace the Tariff Commission, were preserved. Time has shown that the line between policy formulation and policy implementation is imprecise and, for many of those involved, frustrating.

More recently, stimulated by the alluring image of Japan's Ministry of International Trade and Industry (MITI), proposals for creation of a new Department of International Trade and Industry (DITI) have emanated from both the executive branch and the Congress. Yet these proposals have run aground, despite much fanfare and sustained efforts by their proponents, on the shoals of resistance by critics throughout the government who make two central arguments.

First, they claim that such a department would soon become the home of protectionist policies and a breeding ground for industrial policy proposals to fine-tune the economy or support particular sectors and industries. The Department of Commerce, whose officials would form the core of the new department, has long been viewed as the representative of business within the executive branch. The contributions and roles played by those representing the Department of Commerce have, of course, varied greatly from administration to administration. There is no guarantee that a powerful Department of Trade and Industry would push an administration's policies in a more protectionist direction. But the fear of such an outcome is felt by many throughout the executive branch.

A second widespread concern about the DITI proposal is that a powerful new department, seemingly with sole responsibility for trade policy, would not fully reflect the interests of other executive departments and agencies, or would fail to include them fully in its decision-making process. The argument here is that trade policy issues are invariably interagency in nature, and that one could not direct them from a single department unless it were to encompass virtually the entire executive branch. This is because trade issues invariably touch on a wide array of domestic, economic, national security, and foreign policy interests. Creating a Department of International Trade and Industry would do nothing to alter this fact.

The Constitution originally envisioned that the Congress would have the primary responsibility for determining trade policy and the level of protection afforded America's industries against foreign competition.

The increased magnitude and complexity of the international economy inevitably meant that the Congress would delegate large chunks of authority on trade policy matters to the executive branch. The capacity to undertake detailed bilateral and multilateral negotiations is clearly greater for an executive agency than for a legislative body.

Moreover, the leadership assumed by the United States in international economic affairs during the twentieth century, and particularly following the conclusion of World War II, contributed to a major expansion of responsibilities for the executive branch, greater delegations of authority from the Congress, and a proliferation of new agencies to carry out an ambitious set of activities.

This proliferation of executive agencies contributed to the need for and creation of elaborate interagency mechanisms to coordinate policy. Much of the interagency machinery dealing with trade policy has been congressionally mandated.[3] The congressional role in executive branch trade policy-making arrangements is further underscored by the designation, at congressional initiative, of the U.S. trade representative as an Executive Level I official. Interestingly, the U.S. trade representative is the only official other than the secretaries of the thirteen executive departments who is accorded Executive Level I status. As such, he is the highest ranking official in the Executive Office of the President, except for the president and the vice president. This designation was made in part to signal the intensity of congressional interest in trade policy matters and in part to impress upon the U.S. trade representative the importance of keeping his congressional fences mended.

Within the executive branch, each administration has augmented the congressionally mandated interagency machinery with additional entities to coordinate policy. Some of these committees and councils have dealt with economic policy writ large; others have focused on particular problems or specific issues.[4] The persistent creation of new entities reflects the challenge of coordinating policy in an environment in which issues are complex and interrelated and authority is divided.

The level of congressional delegation of authority to the executive branch has ebbed and flowed over the past four decades. The Congress has consistently used the threat (and sometimes the reality) of removing or circumventing the executive's discretion to play a major role in influencing the course of U.S. trade policy. Vietnam and Watergate provided fertile ground for those within the Congress who argued that steps should be taken to redress the imbalance and restrain the excesses of executive power. Use of the so-called "legislative veto" expanded. In foreign policy, the War Powers Act of 1973, and in economic policy, the Budget and Impoundment Control Act of 1974, sought to augment the role of the Congress in shaping policy and bounding executive discretion.[5]

Whatever the precise distribution between the branches of the federal government and between the national, state, and local governments at any point in time, the fundamental characteristic of divided institutional arrangements and of separate institutions sharing power remains a consistent feature of the U.S. political system.

Democratic Participation

A second distinguishing feature of our political system, a broad base of participation in our policy-making processes, has reached new heights in recent years. Throughout our history, the federal government has never relied on a cadre of career officials, a permanent government, to the same extent as most other developed industrial democracies, such as those in Canada, Western Europe, and Japan.

Rather, the U.S. system has given greater scope to political appointees with relatively short tenure in office and often with little, if any, prior government experience. This churning of officials at the top has provided opportunities for a large number of individuals to be involved in shaping decisions from inside the government. It has also tended to produce what one perceptive observer has called "a government of strangers,"[6] with less institutional memory than many of the governments it deals with in international arenas.

Consistent with the desire not to aggregate too much power in any single set of hands, the U.S. system also provides numerous avenues for parties outside the government to play a major role in influencing what is on the policy agenda and in shaping the decisions that are taken. The breadth of participation by those formally outside the government is enhanced by two important features of the U.S. system.

First, it is a highly transparent system in which those outside the government are able to learn much about what is going on inside the government. The press, including a highly specialized trade press, has shown great ingenuity and persistence in piecing together accounts of the deliberations within the government while they are occurring. Legislation under the generic headings of government in the sunshine and freedom of information has also contributed to a general ethos in which there is a widespread presumption that those outside the government have a right to know what is going on inside the government. This is, of course, nothing approaching a blanket right. Moreover, the accounts that do appear in the press are often partial or incorrect. Nonetheless, the relative openness of the process permits and encourages participation from those outside the government.

The hunger for information on the government's internal deliberations often produces efforts by officials to limit the number of people involved in the most sensitive issues, where premature disclosure could seriously undermine the effectiveness of an initiative. These efforts, not surprisingly, are frequently unsuccessful. For the overwhelming majority of issues, it is possible for those outside the government to learn enough about the decision-making process to develop strategies for seeking to influence the outcome.

Second, the U.S. system provides numerous opportunities for parties outside the government to initiate actions that force issues onto the public agenda. The experience with investigations undertaken in accordance with the escape clause provisions of U.S. trade law over the past four decades illuminates the major role played by organizations outside the government.

The escape clause provisions permit the possibility of granting relief to firms or industries that are suffering serious injury, or face the threat of serious injury, from imports. The process of obtaining relief under the escape clause provision is begun with the filing of a petition with the U.S. International Trade Commission (USITC), formerly the U.S. Tariff Commission. The commission then undertakes an investigation and makes a determination as to whether it has found evidence of serious injury. Investigations may be initiated upon the request of the president or the U.S. trade representative, upon resolution of either the House Ways and Means Committee or the Senate Finance Committee, or by the USITC itself. A petition may also be filed "by an entity, including a trade association, firm, certified or recognized union, or group of workers, which is representative of an industry."[7]

Between 1949 and 1985, 217 escape clause investigations were conducted. Of these, three (1.4 percent) were requested by the president or the U.S. trade representative, six (2.8 percent) were undertaken subsequent to a congressional resolution, ten (4.6 percent) were set in motion by the commission itself, and 198 (91.2 percent) were initiated by a petition from a nongovernmental organization. Given the time limits for an investigation and for a subsequent presidential determination, industry groups have frequently filed petitions for relief with an eye toward the heightened political sensitivities during election campaigns. Industry groups and associations play a similar role in the initiation of antidumping and countervailing duty suits.

Much of the day-to-day work in shaping trade policy in the United States is spent responding to initiatives by affected groups outside the government. The wide latitude and scope for action accorded those outside the government reflects the attraction of democratic participation that is especially characteristic of twentieth-century America.

Deliberative Processes

Bayless Manning has suggested that "hyperlexis is America's national disease—the pathological condition caused by an overactive law-making gland."[3] At all levels of government, an explosion of statutes, regulations, and ordinances of all kinds has occurred, leading to the assertion that "we are drowning in law."[9] In addition to the proliferation of statutes, an attachment to the phenomenon of checks and balances and to the concept of due process contributes to a system characterized by much deliberation and extensive opportunities to revise, reargue, reassess, and reappeal.

Once again, the sequence of events associated with the escape clause provisions in U.S. trade law illustrates the point. After a petition or request has been filed with the U.S. International Trade Commission, an independent regulatory agency outside both the executive and legislative branches, the commission undertakes an investigation involving extensive fact finding through the efforts of its own staff and through public hearings and submissions from the petitioners and other affected interests. The sheer volume of material amassed in an escape clause investigation is staggering. Every opportunity is afforded those seeking import relief, and those opposing it to offer evidence and make their case.

The USITC then votes as to whether the evidence presented merits a finding that serious injury has occurred. If the vote is affirmative, the commission discusses and recommends a remedy. The finding and remedy are then transmitted to the president, who has sixty days to make his determination. He is advised through another formal process, in which interested parties have an opportunity once again to present their arguments to executive branch officials. It is common for escape clause provisions to be reviewed by at least two subcabinet interagency committees—the Trade Policy Staff Committee and the Trade Policy Review Group—as well as by the cabinet-level Trade Policy Committee or a comparable cabinet-level council. If the president's determination differs from the USITC's recommended remedy, the Trade Act of 1974 made provision for a legislative veto of the president's action by resolution of a majority of the members present. The resolution must pass both houses of the Congress within ninety days of the president's report.[10] Moreover, the law specifically permits an industry to file for a new investigation within one year if desired. Industries, either arguing that their situation has deteriorated or sensing that they may receive a more receptive hearing from a new administration, frequently avail themselves of this option.

An attachment to due process and thorough deliberation is also found in the administration of other trade relief provisions. The extensive documentation required and the time and expense involved in pursuing relief under the antidumping and countervailing duty statutes is one of the most frequently heard complaints by U.S. firms regarding their ability to secure timely relief.

The result of these characteristics—divided institutional arrangements, democratic participation, and deliberative processes—is a government in which the checking and balancing of power works with remarkable regularity. This is particularly true with respect to economic policy, both foreign and domestic. In military and diplomatic affairs, the constitutional responsibilities of the president have given him somewhat greater scope for independent action. With respect to trade policy, no entity or individual is in a position to articulate policy unequivocally for the United States.

PERSISTENT TENSIONS

The shaping of U.S. trade policy involves not only a large number of actors but a host of considerations that policy makers must weigh. Many of these considerations are recurrent ones and involve three persistent tensions between competing values and objectives.

Macroeconomic and Microeconomic Management

Since the mid 1930s and the disillusionment with the global economic repercussions of the dramatically increased tariffs instituted earlier in that decade, the United States has played a major role in a series of multilateral trade negotiations designed to reduce tariffs and other barriers to trade. U.S. leadership in pressing for a liberal world trading system during the past half century is based in large part on widely held convictions about the macroeconomic benefits of free trade. The economic arguments involving specialization, more efficient use of resources, and economies of scale are well known. Indeed, large numbers of economists have long been at the forefront in opposing "protectionist" trade legislation. In 1930, 1,028 U.S. economists, including many of the profession's most prominent members, petitioned President Herbert Hoover to veto the Smoot-Hawley Tariff Act of 1930, largely on grounds of the damage it would do to the domestic economy.[11]

Within every administration, Republican or Democratic, there is rarely a shortage of voices prepared to articulate the economic benefits associated with free trade and the dangers associated with protectionist policies.[12]

There are, however, inevitably voices that argue strongly for policies that take as their touchstone the concept of "fair trade." A conventional form of this argument is that U.S. firms should be permitted to compete with their counterparts abroad on a level playing field. This involves taking steps to deal with "unfair practices" engaged in by foreign companies or governments such as dumping goods or subsidizing exports, since such practices advantage such firms vis-à-vis their U.S. competitors. Those who articulate this set of arguments view themselves as fair traders rather than as protectionists. They see trade as a reciprocal rather than unilateral exercise. They also are more inclined to focus on the impact of trade on particular sectors of the economy rather than on purely macroeconomic measures of performance and economic vitality.

A third group often engaged in the debate over the economic effects of trade measures are those who see a major role for government in shaping specific economic outcomes. The reasons for their interest vary widely. Some desire to protect industries they consider essential to an industrial economy. Others want to assist, through trade and other measures, those industries that show extraordinary promise or future potential. Trade policy is merely one of many tools that can be used to help guide an economy into areas of ultimate comparative advantage or long-term good. Most frequently, this is a form of the infant industry concept. Trade intervention is viewed as temporary, not permanent, and is used to assist an industry through a difficult period or to secure a long-term advantage. This line of argument is premised on the belief that governments can and do make wise judgments about microeconomic interventions and that these produce greater good for a specific sector than they do harm for the economy as a whole.

There are, of course, varying shades and degrees of these major lines of argument. What is consistent is the persistent debate between those who hold quite different views regarding the appropriate role of trade policy in macroeconomic and microeconomic management.

National Security and Economic Policy Considerations

A second set of tensions most frequently engages those from the foreign policy or national security community on the one hand and those from the economic policy community on the other. Here the arguments are on different terrain.

Those from the foreign policy community frequently claim that noneconomic considerations should play a decisive role. With respect to import relief cases, the bread and butter of trade policy, those in the foreign policy community generally argue against granting import relief, especially for products coming from allies in a difficult economic situation. In the mid 1970s, Italy and Spain were both major exporters of shoes to the United States. Critical elections in both countries coincided with deliberations on the footwear escape clause petition. Not surprisingly, foreign policy officials argued vigorously that providing import relief for the U.S. domestic footwear industry would severely damage the electoral prospects of candidates in Italy and Spain who supported strong ties with the United States. Frequently, these arguments are based on an assessment of particular bilateral relationships or on the need for cooperation from certain countries in achieving some foreign policy or diplomatic objective.

A variant of this tension is the argument over whether the United States should take certain actions to protect an industry on the ground of its importance for national security purposes. This is an oft-used argument, but the instances in which it has proved decisive are rare. In part this is because of the difficulty of determining when one has crossed the threshhold between what is needed for national security and what is not.

National security provisions have long been a prominent feature of U.S. trade laws. In the Trade Agreements Extension Act of 1954, provision was made that no trade agreement reduction in duty should be made if it "would threaten domestic production needed for projected national defense requirements."[13] In the Trade Agreements Extension Act of 1955, the act was amended to provide procedures for investigation and action by the president if he agreed with the finding of the director of the Office of Defense Mobilization that any article was being imported in such quantities as to threaten to impair the national security.[14]

During the 1955–62 period, the director of the Office of Emergency Planning and his predecessors considered twenty-three petitions under the so-called national security amendment. Nine of the petitions were denied; five were suspended; four were withdrawn by the applicant; four were pending; and in only one case, dealing with petroleum, did the investigation produce a finding of threatened impairment.[15] The national security provisions were also strengthened and additional criteria added in the Trade Agreements Extension Act of 1958.[16] These provisions were retained in their strengthened form in section 232 of the Trade Expansion Act of 1962.[17]

What is striking about the use of this section is the infrequency with which it has been invoked. Despite the rather broad language in section 232 concerning the criteria that the president is to take into consideration, the section has been used neither often nor successfully.

In discussions of specific trade policy issues, one finds that economic policy free traders and those in the foreign policy community share many of the same objectives, although often for different reasons. Interestingly, one much less frequently finds alliances between those who want to provide import relief for economic or for national security reasons respectively.

Trade as a Foreign Policy Tool

A third persistent tension involves whether and when to use trade as a foreign policy tool. These discussions are much more likely to involve export policy. Richard N. Cooper has suggested that "interference with imports results largely from domestic policy or political pressures within the United States, whereas interference with exports results largely for reasons of foreign policy."[18] In his farewell address, George Washington offered advice to the new nation on this subject:

> The great rule of conduct for us in regard to foreign nations is, in extending our commercial relations to have with them as little political connection as possible. . . . Harmony, liberal intercourse with all nations are recommended by policy, humanity, and interest. But even our commercial policy should hold an equal and impartial hand, neither seeking nor granting exclusive favors or preferences . . . establishing with powers so disposed, in order to give trade a stable course.[19]

The possible foreign policy uses of trade policy are many and varied. An embargo or less severe form of trade sanction can serve powerful symbolic purposes. Export controls on particular products can seek to limit the military or economic capacity of a potential adversary. Alternatively, extending Most Favored Nation treatment can positively assist a specific bilateral relationship. The Generalized System of Preferences and portions of the Caribbean Basin Initiative involve providing special trade benefits to certain countries in an effort to assist their economic development and strengthen their ties with the United States.

Not least, leverage, defined as influencing or modifying the behavior of another party by withholding or threatening to withhold some good or service or by threatening to take some action, is a frequently discussed concept. The interest in leverage is understandable in an age dominated by diplomacy rather than the simple use of military power. Enthusiasm about leverage is also fueled by the concept of international interdependence. The argument runs that in an interdependent world, foreign policy makers have both the opportunity and the challenge to "manage" interdependence. In doing so, leverage is considered an important tool.[20]

The debate on the efficacy of trade as a foreign policy tool, and to what extent its use is justified, occurs both within the executive branch and increasingly as a source of congressional initiatives. Congressional action relating to the export of nuclear materials, human rights stipulations relating to the sale of certain equipment and materials, exports to countries supporting international terrorism, the granting of Most Favored Nation status, immigration policy, and, most recently, sanctions against

South Africa passed over a presidential veto are illustrative of the more assertive foreign policy role many members of Congress seek to play.

Different Criteria and Divergent Mandates

Our trade laws explicitly acknowledge a clash of competing objectives by giving certain institutions or officials one set of criteria to use in carrying out their responsibilities and giving another set of officials a different set of criteria to apply in carrying out their responsibilities. The escape clause provisions found in section 201 of the Trade Act of 1974 illustrate this phenomenon.

In making its finding and determinations, the U.S. International Trade Commission is directed to take the following economic factors into account: significant idling of productive facilities in the industry; the inability of a number of firms to operate at a reasonable level of profit; significant unemployment or underemployment within the industry; a decline in sales; a higher and growing inventory; a downward trend in production, profits, wages, or employment in the domestic industry concerned; an increase in imports (either actual or relative to domestic production); and a decline in the proportion of the domestic market supplied by domestic producers. All of these measures focus on the effect of imports on a particular industry. The purpose is to determine whether injury, or the threat of serious injury, has occurred.[21]

The president, in making his determination as to whether providing import relief is in the national economic interest of the United States, is directed to take into account a quite different set of criteria. He is to consider the extent to which workers and firms are likely to receive adjustment assistance; the probable effectiveness of import relief as a means to promote adjustment; the efforts being made or to be implemented by the industry concerned to adjust to import competition; the effect of import relief on consumers (including the price and availability of the imported article); the effect of import relief on the international economic interests of the United States; the impact on U.S. industries and firms of import restrictions that may result from international obligations with respect to compensation; the geographic concentration of imported products marketed in the United States; the extent to which the U.S. market is the focal point for exports by reason of constraints on exports into third country markets; and the economic and social costs that would be incurred by taxpayers, communities, and workers, if import relief were or were not provided.[22] These criteria focus on a much broader array of considerations. Rather than concentrating on the effects on a single industry, the president is directed to weigh the implications for the economy as a whole, as well as for our foreign policy. It is an institutional recognition of the competing objectives at stake in making trade policy decisions.

The shaping of U.S. trade policy involves not only a host of participants but a wide range of considerations. The leadership role assumed by the United States, especially in the post–World War II period, has made the challenge of shaping trade policy more rather than less difficult. It is the United States that has taken the lead in pressing for multilateral negotiations to reduce trade barriers. It is also the United States that has aggressively pursued export controls as a tool of foreign and defense policy, often at the expense of harmony within the Western alliance. The size of the U.S. trade deficit for much of the 1980s has prompted a challenge to the traditional arguments for free trade and strengthened the hand of those who urge policies based on "fair trade" or who advocate greater government intervention to assist particular industries. These developments have brought to the fore virtually all of the persistent tensions that have characterized the shaping of U.S. trade policy in the post–World War II period.

INSTITUTIONAL BIASES

The wide range of considerations involved in formulating trade policy are represented institutionally throughout the federal government. Simple caricatures of individual departments or agencies are often misleading and fail to capture important nuances. Nevertheless, institutional biases that extend across administrations, irrespective of party affiliations, are important in understanding the positions taken by various officials and in calibrating what kinds of arguments are likely to be made by whom.

Within the executive branch, the Department of State has taken the lead on trade policy issues for most of the past two centuries. The creation of the Office of the U.S. Trade Representative in the Executive Office of the President shifted the focus of trade policy coordination out of the State Department. State remains a central actor, however, and tends to emphasize two types of considerations in interagency discussions. The first is the role of the United States as leader of the Western alliance and proponent of the free flow of goods and services. As such, the State Department is invariably hostile to protectionism. Henry Kissinger, among others, has articulated this theme:

> The vulnerability of American policy to protectionist pressures . . . remains a serious weakness of the American system. . . . Protectionism is above all an untenable posture for a nation that seeks to be the leader of the alliance of industrial democracies. . . . This has thrown us into conflict when the necessity of statesmanship is to reemphasize in the economic field the fundamental community of interest that would surely operate in the face of obvious external threats to our security.[23]

State is thus often found siding with those economic departments and agencies most attracted to free trade.

Secondly, State is particularly sensitive to the impact particular trade actions will have on individual exporting countries and on our bilateral relationships with those countries. The emphasis is generally on the ways in which a trade action will affect the tone of our relationship with another government and on the array of other issues that are currently under discussion with them. In general, the National Security Council staff, when it is actively involved in interagency trade policy discussions, usually tends to emphasize the same types of concerns.

The core of market-oriented, free trade support within most administrations is usually found in the so-called Troika agencies—Treasury, the Office of Management and Budget, and the Council of Economic Advisers. Representatives from Treasury, OMB, and CEA are generally wary of most restraints on trade and export subsidy schemes. In voting on particular issues, more frequently than not they find themselves in agreement. Yet each brings a slightly different emphasis to the discussion. CEA invariably carefully analyzes the macroeconomic effects of particular trade actions on prices for consumers, aggregate employment effects, and real growth. The Office of Management and Budget is understandably sensitive to the budget implications of particular proposals, whether directly, as in the case of export promotion or subsidy programs, or indirectly through inflation. The Department of the Treasury emphasizes how particular actions may affect the balance of payments and current account positions of trading partners, particularly those who have heavy indebtedness to U.S. financial institutions. Treasury is also sensitive to the ease or difficulty of administering proposals that would rely on the U.S. Customs Service to bear the burden of implementing them.

The Department of Commerce is widely viewed as the representative, protector, and defender of the interests of U.S. business. Commerce has the largest staff analyzing the health of individual industries and the implications for them of specific trade actions. Not surprisingly, Commerce officials often urge consideration of the effects of various actions on particular sectors or industries. Generally, they articulate microeconomic considerations more frequently than their counterparts in Treasury, OMB, and CEA.

Likewise, the Department of Labor closely examines the impacts on specific industries or sectors, particularly how various alternatives will influence jobs for American workers. Labor also presses consideration of the difficulties associated with adjustment for workers and the need for governmental assistance in facilitating such adjustments.

The Department of Agriculture, especially since the export-led boom of the 1970s, has assumed a larger role in trade policy matters. Agriculture is anxious for initiatives that hold out the prospect of opening U.S. markets abroad, fearful of actions that could lead to retaliation by other countries against U.S. agricultural products, nervous about any actions that may call into question the reliability of the United States as a supplier, and sensitive that agricultural trade policy interests not receive short shrift in complicated multilateral negotiations involving trade-offs across sectors of the economy.

The Office of the U.S. Trade Representative has the formal responsibility for overseeing the formulation and coordination of U.S. trade policy. Although modest in size, with a total staff of approximately 130, USTR has assumed a variety of roles. In practice, USTR is a formulator (and sometimes major advocate), a coordinator (often cast in the role of honest broker), an articulator of administration trade policy, and a negotiator with responsibility for undertaking the negotiations required to implement many trade policy decisions. The conflicts among these multiple roles are frequent and require a careful balancing act for those at USTR who find themselves in the forefront of an administrator's relationships on trade policy with both the Congress and foreign governments. As one senior USTR official described it: "We are at once on the top of the mountain and down in the trenches."

Finally, the White House staff is often a major executive branch player on trade policy issues, particularly those issues with high visibility and great political salience. The White House is, in reality, a collection of staff offices dealing with congressional affairs, domestic policy, national security, political affairs, and so on. The interest, capacity, and time availability of individual staffers varies enormously, and the role played by the White House is thus quite different from administration to administration. As a general rule, however, those in the White House view themselves as responsible for protecting the president's policy and political interests. In this sense, they are usually much more heavily involved in the most controversial trade policy issues and are often in the role of developing and shaping a compromise position or legislative strategy.

A distinguishing and oft-noted feature of the U.S. Congress is that members are elected from individual states or districts and view themselves as representing their particular geographic locales. This is different than in many other industrial democracies, where party affiliations are a much more powerful electoral factor. As a result, members of Congress tend to reflect the set of interests in their districts. They are much more apt to become heavily involved in a trade policy issue when it directly affects a group of their constituents. Much congressional interest in trade policy issues thus revolves around the implications for particular industries. Similarly, a major concern for many in the Congress is the set of procedures to provide opportunities for individual industries to protect their interests in international trade.

Congressional Views of the Executive Branch

These institutional biases in the executive and legislative branches have contributed to the views that members of each branch tend to hold of the other. It is commonplace for those in the Congress to view administration trade policy as lacking sufficient coherence. Representatives and senators hear various shades and nuances from different executive branch officials with whom they talk and who testify before them. They are aware of the differences that exist within the executive branch and often seek to exploit those differences.

A second widely held view by many in the Congress is that the executive branch is too heavily biased toward free trade solutions. This contributes to concern over the amount of discretion Congress should grant the executive in trade matters. In the floor debates on the Trade Act of 1974, those who opposed the legislation invariably argued that the principal defects of the legislation were that it gave the president too much power, that it reversed the trend of attempts to reassert congressional authority in trade policy, and that it provided no true or certain relief for sectors injured by trade.

Finally, many in the Congress view the executive branch as biased against taking tough actions in dealing with foreign governments. They sense that diplomatic objectives often overwhelm a willingness to aggressively pursue trade policy objectives and to take actions unpopular with foreign governments. As Senator Edmund Muskie observed in the debate on the Trade Act of 1974: "We have been promised this kind of relief in international negotiations for all of the 16 years I have been in the Senate. We have always found the State Department and those in charge of our negotiations with other nations . . . less than the ardent advocates that we would like to have to persuade other countries that we mean business."[24] This sentiment was echoed by Senator Abraham Ribicoff: "I think it ought to be pointed out that the committee is deeply concerned with the lack of sympathy that has always been shown by the State Department, the executive branch, or the President."[25]

Indeed, the State Department has typically received among the most scathing reviews by those in the Congress. In debating the Fishery Conservation Act of 1976, Rhode Island Senator John Pastore passionately declared:

We want them to come in. We want to give them a fair share. But we want our fisheries to come under some management, some kind of orderly control. That is the reason we brought out this bill—not to hurt anybody, but, for once in our lifetime, to help Americans.

What is so bad about that? We bleed for the Russians, we bleed for the Chinese, we bleed for the Japanese. We bleed for everyone under the sun. Down there in the State Department, they have an Asian desk, they have an African desk, they have a European desk, but they do not have an American desk.

Is it not about time we had an American desk? This is what this is all about. All I am saying is, give us a chance. Do not give us the hokus-pokus of this strategy, this treaty, that treaty. We have been trying that for years. And every time we try, we end up behind the eight ball.[26]

Executive Branch Views of the Congress

Congressional views of the executive branch are mirrored by a similar collection of views that executive branch officials hold of the Congress. Many in the executive branch view the Congress as driven by concern more for microeconomic or geographically concentrated effects than for more general economic effects. Executive branch officials generally consider this congressional perspective understandable and appropriate, but one that often results in a greater attraction for protectionist policies. In the debates leading to passage of the Trade Act of 1974, one of the leading trade policy figures in the Senate, Abraham Ribicoff, in urging support for the legislation, assured his colleagues: "This bill has been written in such a way as to reflect the deep concerns on both sides of the aisle of protecting American industry and American labor. There is more protection in this bill than were [sic] ever in any trade bill to come before the Congress of the United States."[27]

One manifestation of this congressional perspective is found in one senator's account of the evolution of his thinking on trade policy issues.

> I came here as a strong believer in free trade and that we ought to be able to compete. I am confident that we can compete. But when we begin to see these pressures growing and then begin to look and see whether or not we are in fact getting the same kind of treatment in other countries as far as selling our products, then you have to, I think, take another look at the situation.
>
> I have come to the conclusion that we really do need to get the attention of the rest of the world and of our trading partners. . . . I believe that in every trade agreement that we have made . . . we lost those negotiations not because we are not good negotiators; we lost them because we went there with a bottom line that was against our interests to start with, and we came out with our people put at a disadvantage. . . . We are not above passing legislation that may very well put some very strong restrictions on the manner in which our market is going to be available to them.[28]

A second executive branch perception of the Congress is that members in the House and the Senate are generally less fiscally concerned over the cost of export subsidy or export promotion programs. Beset by pressures to "do something," legislating measures designed to stimulate exports is an attractive response. This view of the Congress is particularly prevalent in those elements of the executive branch, such as Treasury, OMB, and CEA, that concentrate much of their efforts on macroeconomic and budgetary matters.

A third perception is that many members of Congress are in reality less protectionist than their rhetoric would suggest. Members of Congress face a steady barrage of complaints by constituents for which a trade remedy is one possible response. As such, members of Congress inevitably find themselves seeking ways of demonstrating concern and showing sympathy for those facing severe competition from abroad. This sensitivity to the genuine adjustment problems facing many American workers is one of the elements contributing to much of the trade policy commentary by members of Congress. Most members also support establishing procedures that will ensure an adequate hearing for the particular problems facing individual firms or industries. Yet, as the structure of provisions in section 201 suggests, many members of Congress are quite willing to allow the president to "take the heat" for the difficult trade-offs associated with many trade policy decisions.

THE EBB AND FLOW OF POLICY

These institutional biases in the executive branch and the Congress and the mutual set of perceptions that each branch has of the other influence the ebb and flow of power and influence in the shaping of U.S. trade policy. The complex, detailed nature of much trade policy decision making, coupled with the large negotiating component involved in implementing trade policy, has led inevitably to major delegations of authority by the Congress to the executive branch.

As long as the executive branch uses that delegated authority in ways that a majority in the Congress views as consistent with its intentions, these grants of authority remain relatively unimpaired and occasionally are enlarged. When an administration's trade policies diverge too sharply from the majority sentiment in the Congress, there is inevitably much talk about directly legislating specific trade policies, such as quotas on particular goods or commodities, or devices such as domestic content legislation. There is also movement toward generally eliminating the discretion of the executive in deciding individual cases and petitions or toward imposing time limits for the accomplishment of certain actions.

As outside pressures on the Congress rise, such as the persistent large annual trade deficits during the mid 1980s, congressional pressure to more actively shape trade policy decisions increases. Throughout this most recent period, the executive branch has maintained a reasonably firm commitment to a liberal world trading system and to the goal of free trade in its statements, but has shown considerable flexibility and accommodation in its actions on specific issues.

Few would doubt the commitment of the Reagan administration to its free trade, market-oriented economic policies. Yet, in a host of instances its desire to retain control of trade policy has contributed to its willingness to take specific actions providing for import relief. The oft-renewed voluntary restraint agreement with Japan on automobiles, the negotiated steel agreement with the European Community, the increased tariffs on specialty steel and on motorcycles, the orderly marketing agreements on machine tools and carbon steel, the strengthened enforcement of quotas on textiles and apparel, the September 1985 round of administration-initiated section 301 cases, and the agreement, albeit with limited enthusiasm, to support an agricultural export enhancement program amply illustrate the point.

Congressional pressure has also contributed to a greater willingness to attempt to find common ground.[29] What specific proposals will survive in trade legislation in the 100th Congress is unknown as the new Congress begins its work. What is more clear is that the result will reflect much give-and-take between the executive and legislative branches.

CONCLUSION

The Constitution has succeeded magnificently for two centuries in providing a flexible framework for the shaping of trade policy. The division and fragmentation of power, the opportunity for widespread participation, and the deliberate procedures that govern most policy actions have contributed to two major strengths of U.S. trade policy development.

First, it is a system that for the most part fully exposes the broad array of considerations policy makers should take into account. It generates much information and analysis and engages officials with multiple perspectives in the task of assessing the consequences associated with various alternatives. As such, it provides for a full debate, with extensive representation by affected parties. There is little that is arbitrary or capricious. In this sense, the Founding Fathers would be pleased.

Second, it is a system that provides ample scope for policy entrepreneurs. And this latitude for entrepreneurship has produced a large number of initiatives that have kept the United States in the vanguard of trade policy making in international forums. The division of powers and multiple hurdles that policies must clear have not generally produced stalemates or gridlock. U.S. leadership in the sense of providing initiative for the direction of trade policy has been remarkable over the past half century.

What the constitutionally mandated system of divided and shared powers has not produced are consistently coherent policies. The constant turnover in officialdom and the multitude of checks and balances have produced what often appears to be a patchwork of policies. Initiatives are begun, only to be reversed when competing pressures build up elsewhere in the system. In an environment in which no one individual or entity is responsible for policy, continuity and coherence are often sacrificed. This is a source of considerable frustration to those involved in shaping policy in both the executive and legislative branches. And it is not a limitation easily remedied, given the attraction for divided and limited powers. Producing coherent and sustained policies while retaining the initiative, representativeness, and sensitivity to political realities that the U.S. system now provides remains the great challenge for U.S. policymakers as America begins her third century under the Constitution.

NOTES

1. Richard N. Cooper, "The United States as an Open Economy," Harvard Institute of Economic Research, Discussion Paper no. 1193 (November 1985), describes many of the most striking features of how closely the United States is now integrated in the world economy.
2. Three years later the focus had shifted to subsidizing exports as part of an overall trading package. An amendment in the Revenue Report recommended import duties on a long list of products (wine, liquors, rum, tea, sugar, spices, cocoa, coffee, salt, molasses), "provided that there be allowed a bounty of ⅛ of a dollar for every Quintel of dried fish exported from the U.S., and a like sum for every Barrel of pickled fish, beef, or pork to be paid to the exporter thereof at the port from which they shall be exported." Within a month, a new resolution eliminated the recommended bounty on exports. *Journals of the Continental Congress, 1774–1798*, compiled by Kenneth Harris and Steven Tilly (Washington, D.C.: National Archives and Records, General Services Administration, 1976), vol. 25 (1783), pp. 926–27, and vol. 26 (1783), pp. 170–72.
3. For example, see the Trade Expansion Act of 1962 (P.L. 87-794), chap. 5, sec. 242.
4. Roger B. Porter, "Organizing International Economic Policy Making," in William P. Avery and David P. Rapkin, *America in a Changing World Political Economy* (New York: Longman, 1982).
5. In *Immigration and Naturalization Service v. Chadha*, 46 U.S. 919, the Supreme Court ruled that forms of the legislative veto that do not involve passage by both houses of the Congress *and* concurrence by the president are unconstitutional. Useful discussions of the legislative veto are found in Arthur Maass, *Congress and the Common Good* (New York: Basic Books, 1983), chap. 11; Joseph Cooper and Patricia Hurley, "The Legislative Veto: A Policy Analysis," *Congress and the Presidency* 10 (Summer 1983); William West and Joseph Cooper, "Congressional Adaptation in Modern America: The Legisla-

tive Veto and Administrative Rulemaking," *Political Science Quarterly* 97 (Spring 1983); Robert S. Gilmour, "The Congressional Veto: Shifting the Balance of Administrative Control," *Journal of Policy Analysis and Management* 2 (Fall 1982); and Robert S. Gilmour and Barbara H. Craig, "After the Congressional Veto: Assessing the Alternatives," *Journal of Policy Analysis and Management* 3 (Spring 1984).

6. Hugh Heclo, *A Government of Strangers* (Washington, D.C.: Brookings Institution, 1976).

7. Trade Act of 1974 (P.L. 93-618), sec. 201(a)(1).

8. Bayless Manning, "Hyperlexis: Our National Disease," *Northwestern University Law Review* 71 (1977).

9. Ibid., p. 767.

10. Trade Act of 1974 (P.L. 93-618), sec. 203(c)(1).

11. Sidney Ratner, *The Tariff in American History* (New York: Van Nostrand, 1972), p. 144.

12. The annual economic report of the president and the annual report of the Council of Economic Advisers typically include statements and arguments in support of free trade. See, for example, *Economic Report of the President, January 1978* (Washington, D.C.: GPO, 1978), pp. 133–37; *Economic Report of the President, January 1979*, pp. 157–62; *Economic Report of the President, January 1980*, pp. 180–83; *Economic Report of the President, January 1981*, pp. 182, 207–13; *Economic Report of the President, January 1982*, pp. 167–68, 176–84; *Economic Report of the President, January 1983*, pp. 51, 59–61; *Economic Report of the President, January 1984*, pp. 57–60, 86; *Economic Report of the President, January 1985*, pp. 111–27; *Economic Report of the President, January 1986*, pp. 105–11, 122–28; *Economic Report of the President, January 1987*, pp. 125–45.

13. *Trade Agreements Extension Act of 1954* (P.L. 83-464), sec. 2.

14. *Trade Agreements Extension Act of 1955* (P.L. 84-86), sec. 7.

15. U.S. Congress, House, Committee on Ways and Means, Hearings, *Trade Expansion Act of 1962*, part 2 (Washington, D.C.: GPO, 1962), p. 766.

16. *Trade Agreements Extension Act of 1958* (P.L. 85-686), sec. 8.

17. *Trade Expansion Act of 1962* (P.L. 87-794), sec. 232.

18. Richard N. Cooper, "Trade Policy as Foreign Policy," Harvard Institute of Economic Research, Discussion Paper no. 1160 (June 1985), pp. 18–19.

19. Henry Steele Commager, ed., *Documents of American History*, 9th ed. (Englewood Cliffs, N.J.: Prentice-Hall, 1983), p. 174.

20. There is an extensive literature on the uses of economic tools for foreign policy purposes. One of the best discussions is Cooper, "Trade Policy as Foreign Policy" (cited no. 18 above). Others include Gary Clyde Hufbauer and Jeffrey J. Schott, *Economic Sanctions in Support of Foreign Policy Goals* (Washington, D.C.: Institute for International Economics, 1983); Klaus Knorr, "International Economic Leverage and Its Uses," in Klaus Knorr and Frank N. Trager, eds., *Economic Issues and National Security* (Lawrence, Kans.: Regents Press, 1977); and Homer E. Moyer, Jr., and Linda A. Mabry, "Export Controls as Instruments of Foreign Policy: The History, Legal Issues and Policy Lessons of Three Recent Cases," *Law and Policy in International Business* 15 (1983).

21. *Trade Act of 1974* (P.L. 93-618), sec. 201(b)(2) and (b)(3).

22. *Trade Act of 1974* (P.L. 93-618), sec. 202(c).

23. Henry A. Kissiger, *The White House Years* (Boston: Little, Brown, 1979), p. 340.

24. *Congressional Record*, 93d Cong., 2d sess., 13 December 1974, p. 39815.

25. Ibid., p. 39816.

26. *A Legislative History of the Fishery Conservation Act of 1976* (Washington, D.C.: GPO, 1976), p. 238.

27. *Congressional Record,* 93d Cong., 2d sess., 13 December 1974, p. 39817.
28. Walter D. Huddleston, "Domestic Content Legislation," in *Congress and U.S. Trade Policy* (Dallas: LTV Forum, 1983), pp. 121–22.
29. Clayton Yeutter, the U.S. trade representative, reportedly observed in February 1987: "Last year there was such a thrust toward protectionism that we saw no real possibility of sensible, responsible trade legislation emerging. It would have been Christmas-treed with protectionism and a veto would have been inevitable. We came to a different conclusion this year. Chances of responsible legislation are substantially higher" (*New York Times,* 14 February 1987, p. 8).

13

Managing International Monetary Policy

NORMAN C. THOMAS

On the weekend of 21–22 February 1987, the finance ministers of the United States, the United Kingdom, West Germany, France, Japan, and Canada (Italy had been invited but refused to attend) met in Paris in an attempt to halt the downward slide of the U.S. dollar, which had begun two years earlier. The United States and its five allies announced that they would "cooperate closely" to stabilize the dollar. They expressed fear that a further fall of the dollar against other major currencies, such as the yen and the mark, would damage the world economy. However, other than an implicit notice that the six countries intended to have their central banks intervene in international currency markets if the dollar resumed its decline, there were no proposed changes in the international monetary system that has existed since 1973.[1] The two-year fall in the value of the dollar was by no means over, and it could not apparently be arrested by the United States acting alone or in concert with its major allies.

International monetary policy is one of the two major components of foreign economic policy, the other being international trade policy. International monetary policy encompasses the effects of capital flows in and out of the United States on the exchange value of the dollar. The principal capital flows result from foreign direct investment by U.S. multinational corporations (MNCs), loans by U.S. banks and the U.S. government, direct investment in the U.S. economy by foreign MNCs, and investment by foreign governments, firms, and individuals in U.S. government securities. The growing dependence of the U.S. economy on financial and commercial dealings with other countries has accentuated the importance of international monetary policy:

> International capital movements have become a significant determinant of the overall availability of funds for borrowing domestically; external fluctuations of the dollar have come to have marked effects on [U.S.] internal unemploy-

ment and inflation rates. The authorities in Washington have no choice but to count economic interests among the goals of [U.S.] international diplomacy.[2]

International monetary policy is important to national security for two principal reasons. First, the exchange value of the dollar reflects the economic condition of the United States. A healthy dollar denotes a vigorous U.S. economy in which the rest of the world has a high degree of confidence, whereas a weak dollar indicates weakness in the economy and a lack of foreign confidence in it. The caveat must be added, however, that it is possible for the dollar to become too strong, and at times a degree of weakness is advantageous. The second way in which the exchange value of the dollar affects national security is that it determines the cost to the United States of deploying its forces overseas, providing military aid to its allies and economic assistance to developing countries, and pursuing other objectives. With a strong dollar, either security can be strengthened with little or no additional cost or the desired security programs can be obtained at less expense to the taxpayers. Conversely, a weak dollar either increases the cost or reduces the degree of national security.

The international monetary policy of the United States since World War II has been different from that of its major allies, because of the dollar's role as the world's primary reserve currency. The status of the dollar as a reserve currency gave the United States advantages over other countries, but eventually it imposed responsibilities as well. The willingness of other countries to use dollars as the principal means of exchange in international financial transactions created a greater demand for dollars than would otherwise exist. To some extent this freed the United States from the international balance-of-payments constraints that affect other countries. Their willingness to accept and use dollars in effect financed American deficits, thus enabling the United States to pursue domestic economic policy goals with limited regard to the effects of those actions on exchange rates and to pursue national security objectives with less regard for their cost than might otherwise have been the case. The disadvantage that accompanied the reserve currency role of the dollar was that eventually the willingness of other countries to accept dollars reached its limit. Then the United States confronted the difficult choice of whether to modify its domestic economic policies and national security goals to reflect balance-of-payments constraints or to risk damaging the international monetary system. The Paris meeting of February 1987 resulted from the reluctance of the United States to choose either option.

DOMESTIC POLITICS AND INTERNATIONAL MONETARY POLICY

Scholars have employed three distinct theoretical approaches to explain international monetary policy. The first approach is of most interest to us here. Based in political science, it views foreign economic policy as the product of behavioral and institutional factors in domestic politics. The second approach, drawn from the study of international relations, concentrates on the acquisition and use of power by nation-states in pursuit of security. The third approach, which reflects the influence of economics, regards international market conditions and the behavior of markets as the principal determinants of policy.

The three approaches are not mutually exclusive and often overlap. As Peter Katzenstein observes, "strategies of foreign economic policy of advanced industrial states grow out of the integration of international and domestic forces."[3] This analysis considers international monetary policy as the product of the interaction between domestic political factors, the activities of the United States in pursuit of its security interests, and international market conditions. The first factor is of primary concern, but the emphasis placed on it does not imply that the other two factors are unimportant.

This chapter examines the impact of five principal elements of the U.S. domestic political system on the content of U.S. international monetary policy. These elements include the constitutional allocation of power among the three branches of government; the diffusion of authority within the executive and legislative branches; partisan and electoral politics; social, economic, and political pluralism in American society and the pattern of interest group politics that it produces; and ideas. They do not necessarily work independently and may at times reinforce or conflict with one another. The overall effect of domestic political factors on international monetary policy is to limit the authority of U.S. central decision makers and the range of options open to them. The fragmentation of power within government and in society makes the formulation and implementation of coherent and cohesive international monetary policy that is consistent with national security objectives and with domestic economic and social policies quite difficult.

The Constitutional Allocation of Power

The Constitution, as Richard Neustadt has observed, establishes "a government of separated institutions sharing powers."[4] Both the executive and legislative branches perform important functions in the realm of foreign policy. However, because the Constitution lacks specificity as to those functions, there is inherent institutional jealousy between the president and Congress regarding them. Both carefully guard their prerogatives against the intrusions of the other and seek to expand their authority at its expense. Yet neither can operate independently of the other, and both must ultimately secure, at a minimum, the acquiescence of the other branch, if not its cooperation.

The Constitution does not give the president any specific powers over foreign economic policy. Such powers as he possesses have either been derived from the general grant of executive power, the power to make treaties, and the duty to "take care that the laws be faithfully executed," or delegated to him by Congress. (Statutory delegations have been substantial, as Congress has recognized that it is the president who must negotiate with foreign governments, monitor the ongoing condition of international markets, and adjust policy to changes in them.)

The Constitution grants Congress specific powers to lay and collect taxes, duties, and excises, to regulate foreign commerce, to coin money and regulate its value, and to borrow money on the credit of the United States. It also requires that treaties be approved by a two-thirds vote of the Senate. The effect of these affirmative grants of power is, in the words of Edward S. Corwin, "an invitation to struggle for the privilege of directing American foreign policy."[5] Corwin adds, however, that history's verdict is "that the power to determine the substantive content of American foreign policy is a *divided* power, with the lion's share falling usually, though by no means always, to the President."[6]

Congress has mostly been content to leave international monetary policy to the president and the executive branch. It has not accorded exchange rates and capital flows the same degree of attention that it has paid to trade. Such matters are in the technical realm of finance and do not directly appear to affect individual or group interests. Congressional interest in international monetary policy rises only when the exchange value of the dollar is so high or so low that it manifestly affects domestic economic conditions. For example, the very strong dollar of 1981–85 appeared to be an important cause of the falling competitiveness of U.S. exports, while the weak dollar of 1986–87 sparked fears of inflation. In both of those recent situations, however, congressional concern over exchange rates was secondary to trade issues and to the effect of domestic macroeconomic policies on the economy.

Executive Branch Fragmentation

Although the executive branch has assumed responsibility for international monetary policy, that authority is fragmented, and coordination can be a major problem. The missions of various agencies differ and sometimes overlap or conflict with one another. Major policies almost always affect the responsibilities of several agencies. The result is a pattern of politics within the federal bureaucracy in which agencies are the major actors. Agencies compete with one another for funds, jurisdiction, and status. Their policy recommendations often reflect agency interests and concerns, one of the most important of which is the survival and growth of the agency and its mission. Policies tend to be the outcome of bargaining among agencies more than command decisions of the president.

In spite of the fact that the presidency is the focus of policy leadership, the limitations on presidential power are great, and the expectations that the public has of presidential performance are unrealistic. Neither the presidency nor the leadership of individual presidents are sufficient to overcome the fragmentation and dispersion of power and authority that are the central feature of the American political system. The capacity of the president to provide policy leadership through persuasion, bargaining, and compromise is less than his position at the apex of a vast bureaucracy might suggest.[7] The fragmentation of authority within the executive branch enables agency heads to force the president to bargain with them. While policy is not solely the product of bureaucratic politics, the concerns of the major agencies almost always enter into it.

With respect to international monetary policy, the State Department, the Treasury Department, and the Federal Reserve System (the Fed) are the major agencies involved. State is responsible for the overall conduct of foreign economic policy and the secretary of state is the president's principal foreign policy adviser. The department also handles most economic reporting from abroad. However, State's primary expertise is political rather than economic or technical. Foreign economic policy matters are necessarily integrated in the State Department with its security, diplomatic, and political considerations.

Since World War II the Treasury Department has gained ascendancy over foreign economic policy. Its rise to dominance in this area is the product of several factors.[8] First, the relative decline since World War II of U.S. economic strength, as measured by the deterioration of the U.S. balance of payments. Second, the growing interdependence of the U.S. and other economies, which has increased the impact of external events and conditions on domestic economic management. Third, the broad range of economic policy goals that have accompanied the international leadership role of the United States. In addition, presidents beginning with Richard Nixon have tended to regard the secretary of the treasury as having primary responsibility for the government's overall economic policy. As a consequence, Treasury has acquired the largest body of economic expertise within the government, with the possible exception of the CIA. A fifth factor contributing to Treasury's ascendancy over foreign economic policy has been the rising concern over the external deficit. This has subjected every dollar the government spends abroad to its scrutiny.

Finally, Congress has contributed to Treasury's leadership of foreign economic policy by making the secretary responsible for U.S. participation in the International Monetary Fund and the World Bank. Treasury's influence predominates over balance-of-payments policy, international capital flows, exchange rates, the price of gold, and international monetary reform.

The Federal Reserve System is independent of direct congressional and presidential control. Its primary concerns are with the domestic economy: the supply of money and credit, the banking system, and the operation of capital markets. But the increase in economic interdependence between the United States and the rest of the world has expanded the Fed's involvement with international monetary policy. Its intervention in currency markets is the principal means that the United States has to influence exchange rates. This is done through the sale and purchase of dollars and other currencies by the Federal Reserve Bank of New York. The Fed's interest in international monetary policy has grown sharply with the advent of the debt crisis of less developed countries (LDCs) such as Brazil, Argentina, Mexico, and Nigeria. (Major U.S. banks made massive loans to LDCs in the 1970s at relatively low rates of interest; when interest rates rose worldwide in the 1980s, many LDCs had difficulty carrying their debts.) The Fed's principal concern over international monetary policy is with its impact on the banking system and the supply of money and credit.

In addition to the Fed and the Departments of State and Treasury, the Departments of Commerce and Agriculture are interested in the effect of international monetary policy on American business and agriculture. They do not, however, have a major role to play in shaping and implementing monetary policy.

The president's role in international monetary policy is to provide overall direction and coordination. Several staff units are available to assist him with this task, including the Council of Economic Advisors, the Office of Management and Budget, the National Security Council, and the Office of the Special Trade Representative. He also must coordinate the recommendations he receives from the operating agencies with advice that he gets from his staff units. He must consider the institutional positions and responsibilities of the Treasury, the State Department, the Federal Reserve, and other agencies. Often he will be under conflicting pressures from within the executive branch. He must recognize that the Treasury focuses on inflation, economic growth, and the health of the domestic economy, while the Fed is preoccupied with money, credit, and the banking system. Meanwhile, the State Department is attentive to national security considerations, relations with our allies, requests for foreign aid, and our overseas commitments. The Departments of Commerce, Agriculture, and Labor are concerned primarily with stimulating exports of American products and increasing the employment of labor and capital in the domestic economy.

Internal conflict over policy does occur, and the president is responsible for managing it. He can do so by delegating authority to a subordinate, such as the secretary of the treasury or the secretary of state, or by arranging a compromise. In the Reagan administration, the secretaries of the treasury, Donald Reagan (1981–85) and James Baker III (1985–88), took the lead in formulating international monetary policy. Baker worked closely with the chairmen of the Fed, Paul Volcker (1985–87) and Alan Greenspan (1987–88), as the Fed coordinated its interventions in currency markets with the Treasury's exchange rate objectives.

The fragmentation of executive branch authority over international monetary policy may or may not result in conflict between the Treasury, the Fed, State, and other agencies, but the potential for damage from bureaucratic politics is always present. Avoidance of such conflict depends on the president's operating style, which includes his effectiveness as a coordinator and the use that he makes of his staff, the personalities of his principal subordinates in the area, and international and domestic economic conditions. There is little that the president can do by way of changing the process for making policy, as it is largely determined by statute.

Congressional Fragmentation

Congress, with its bicameral structure and extensive committee system, parallels the bureaucracy with its fragmentation of authority. Yet Congress is deeply involved with foreign economic policy. It offers proposals of its own, it revises and criticizes administration proposals that require legislative authorization, and it must appropriate funds to implement authorized programs. The labyrinthine legislative process in Congress consists of a sequence of mandatory approvals, each of which provides opponents of policy change with the opportunity to defeat or modify it. Consequently, the president must take congressional opinion seriously into account in making foreign economic policy decisions. Failure to do so can result in reversals that deeply embarrass the administration or even undermine the basis of its policies. But Congress does not provide coherent alternatives to administration policy. It lacks the means of coordinating its policy proposals.

At the heart of the congressional policy process are the committees. Jurisdiction over international monetary policy is divided among four congressional committees. The House and Senate Banking Committees have jurisdiction over exchange-rate and gold policy. House Banking also is responsible for international financial and monetary institutions, which in the Senate are within the purview of the Foreign Relations Committee. The Joint Economic Committee exercises oversight over the international monetary and finance sectors, but it does not have the authority to act on legislation. Professional staffs of the committees, the Congressional Research Service, and the Congressional Budget Office provide the technical expertise that Congress requires to deal with international monetary policy.

The potential negative consequences of congressional fragmentation for international monetary policy are substantial. Congressional committees in domestic policy areas and in the area of defense procurement establish strong ties with interest groups and administrative agencies. The resulting triangular policy subgovernments tend to be autonomous centers of power that are largely impervious to external influence. Members of Congress often strengthen their constituency support bases through subgovernment relationships.[9] Since World War II, however, Congress has not concerned itself extensively with international monetary policy. The technical complexity and strategic nature of the policy limit the opportunity that it affords members to claim credit for legislation or perform services demonstrably beneficial to their constituencies. As is the case with foreign economic policy generally,[10] subgovernmental alliances seldom develop, and Congress and the executive approach international monetary issues with broad unity of purpose and distinctive preferences and predispositions. Most of the time, there has been sufficient reciprocal trust and responsiveness to produce coherent and cohesive policies. However, should international monetary policy manifest a distinct impact on inflation and unemployment in the domestic economy, it is unlikely that congressional deference to executive judgment with respect to the matter would continue.

Party and Electoral Politics

Theoretically, party and electoral politics can influence foreign economic policy through a direct causal chain from public opinion, to elections, to the decisions of Congress and the president. In practice, the electorate's control over most public policy is indirect. It is exercised by placing limits on the range of feasible policy alternatives and voting out of office parties and officials who cannot solve major problems.[11] Parties and elections have little direct potential impact on international monetary policy, which is far removed from, and not clearly understood by, most voters.

It is possible that a change in party control of the national administration could produce significant shifts in policies in which the public has little interest and that are not salient issues, especially if the two parties have different positions with respect to government intervention in the economy.[12] The Democrats, as the party traditionally more favorably disposed toward interventionist policies, might be mote inclined to try to manage exchange rates than the Republicans, who have historically relied more on market forces. Alternatively, the Republicans, as the party usually identified with financial responsibility, might be more willing to devalue the dollar than the Democrats, who tend to be regarded as big spenders. (Interestingly, the two devaluations since World War II occured in 1971 and 1973, during the Republican administration of Richard Nixon.)

International monetary policy has never been the central issue in a modern American election campaign, and it is most unlikely that it ever will be. If it is involved in electoral politics at all, it will probably be as an adjunct to the much more salient issue of trade.

Interest Group Politics

One of the most important consequences of the pattern of party and electoral politics in the United States is the development of an environment in which vigorous interest groups flourish and play a major role in shaping public policy. Also, the involvement of interest groups in, and their influence over, domestic economic policy affects foreign economic policy indirectly through the impact of budget deficits, interest rates, and the competitiveness of American products in world markets.

The pluralistic pattern of private power in American society limits the capacity of U.S. central decision makers to mobilize domestic political resources in support of their foreign economic policies. The need of the government to generate and maintain group support is a permanent constraint on its discretion. Resistance from powerful groups can stop or modify major policy initiatives. In addition, powerful interest groups have extensive access to decision makers and enjoy great success in shaping public policy in accordance with their interests. Pluralistic policy politics results in "the infusion of private interests into the definition of public preference and the exercise of public choice."[13] Pluralism also has a strong tendency to preserve the status quo in public policy.

Interest groups, at least in theory, may have substantial potential involvement in exchange rate policy.[14] On the one hand, exporters, firms competing with imported goods, and farmers could be expected to support a devaluation of the dollar. On the other hand, manufacturers using many imported components, importers, consumers, and tourists would tend to favor strengthening the dollar's exchange value. The absence of examples of group behavior according to this theory suggests either that group interests are multiple or uncertain or that most groups do not regard exchange rates as relevant to their immediate concerns.

Banks are one major economic interest that has played a central role in international monetary policy involving capital transfers, especially since the mid 1970s. Enormous amounts of dollars held in Europe, Japan, and by oil-producing countries, plus worldwide inflation, provided U.S. and other Western banks with surplus funds to lend. They found eager borrowers in the less developed countries. Many of their loans were imprudent, however, and when interest rates rose in the 1980s, a debt crisis developed. The banks worked with the U.S. and other Western governments and the International Monetary Fund to avoid defaults and damage to the international monetary system. The result has been a close overlapping relationship between U.S. international banks and the government. As Benjamin Cohen puts it, "high finance . . . now impinge[s] on high politics. Strategic interactions between governments . . . increasingly are linked with the public sector and private financial institutions both here and abroad."[15]

Such interactions involve attempts by banks to influence foreign policy in accordance with their interests and governmental efforts to use the banks to achieve foreign policy objectives. The U.S. government has not attempted systematically to coordinate the activities of U.S. international banks in support of its security and foreign economic policy objectives. But it has on occasion, as in February 1987, pressured banks to make loans on easy terms to countries facing default. However, there is no policy—explicit or implicit—with respect to the role of U.S. banks in the international monetary system. Moreover, it is likely that any attempt to utilize them to achieve foreign policy objectives would meet strong opposition. An instrumental attitude toward private business on the part of the government is alien to American politics. Private corporations exist to make money, not to promote the achievement of governmental policy goals, however laudable they may be.

Ideas

Ideas not only constrain the policy choices of U.S. central decision makers, they also play a vital role in mobilizing support for those policies in the public, among interest groups, and in Congress.[16] The ideas that affect foreign economic policy fall into three categories: general beliefs, theories, and ideology.[17] General beliefs and values shape the predispositions that officials have toward information and policy options based on it. For example, an official trained in economics would be likely to consider the cost effectiveness of a policy option, while one with a background in international relations might stress its implications for national security.

Theories, or schools of thought, provide conceptual frameworks within which officials can explain or predict phenomena in the political and economic worlds. They evaluate and advocate policy options on theoretical grounds. Keynesianism and monetarism have been two of the most influential economic theories employed by American foreign policy makers since 1945.

Ideologies are closed belief systems that purport to explain all social, economic, and political phenomena. Marxism is the best-known ideology affecting international relations in the modern world. However, it has not influenced the economic foreign policy choices of American officials.

If there is a dominant American ideology, it is a vision of a liberal world order in which peace and prosperity flow from "a free and open international economic system."[18] In the post–World War II era, the United States established, and has sought to maintain, international regimes for money and trade that manifest that liberal ideology. John Ruggie characterizes the normative framework of the two regimes as "embedded liberalism," the essence of which is to establish a pattern of multilateral international economic transactions that is "consistent with the requirements of domestic stability."[19]

As the predominant economic power of the United States relative to such countries as West Germany and Japan has declined, and as the American economy has become more dependent on imports and exports, the liberal ideology with its faith in markets has come under attack. Industries facing competition from imports and those experiencing difficulty competing in export markets have demanded that the government protect them. However, in spite of increased protectionist sentiment, a politically viable alternative to liberalism has not yet emerged.[20]

The relative decline in American economic power and the rise of global economic interdependence has increased the importance of domestic political factors shaping foreign economic policy. The number of domestic interests affected by international economic conditions has increased substantially.[21] International monetary and trade policy can no longer be determined primarily by security considerations. Concerns arising in the domestic political economy and domestic political forces and structures have become important determinants of foreign economic policy. The United States has a strong society but a weak state.[22] The central decision makers in the American state have difficulty mobilizing political resources in support of their policies, power is dispersed and fragmented, the state cannot easily transform society, and its foreign policies can be strongly influenced by interest groups. The multiple opportunities for organized interests to influence policy, the sensitivity of U.S. central decision makers in Congress and the executive branch to group and electoral politics, and the fragmentation of authority between the legislative and executive branches of government and within each branch ensure that international monetary policy will reflect domestic as well as international political pressures and considerations.

U.S. INTERNATIONAL MONETARY POLICY, 1944–87

The United States took the lead in establishing a liberal international monetary regime after World War II. The regime emerged from a conference of forty-four nations held at Bretton Woods, New Hampshire, in 1944. The design of the Bretton Woods system reflected the dominant position of the United States, which at the time possessed two-thirds of the world's monetary gold supply. Three features characterized the system.[23] First, exchange rates were pegged at par values and permitted to fluctuate within 1 percent margins. Second, there was free convertibility among the currencies of industrial countries. Third, the American dollar was the primary currency. The primacy of the dollar rested on the commitment of the U.S. government to convert foreign-held dollars into gold at a fixed price ($35 per ounce).

In the immediate postwar years, from the mid 1940s until the late 1950s, the Bretton Woods system worked to the advantage of the United States and its European allies. The United States financed the recovery of war-torn European economies through foreign aid and loans. As European economies recovered, their reserves were increased through the U.S. balance-of-payments deficit. European acceptance of surplus dollars freed U.S. central decision makers to attend to domestic economic issues and to finance their global security commitments without regard to the impact of their policies on the international political economy. During this period, domestic political factors had little effect on U.S. international monetary policy, as it was not an issue that led to conflict between economic interests or within the government.

Eventually, however, the willingness of participants in the Bretton Woods system to finance U.S. balance-of-payments deficits declined. The sizeable and growing body of foreign dollar holders began to doubt the ability of the United States to keep its commitment to convert dollars into gold, since by 1960 its foreign exchange liabilities exceeded its reserve assets. In addition, the relative economic power of the United States declined as a result of the increased strength of the Western European and Japanese economies and the reduced competitiveness of U.S. exports due to lagging productivity and obsolescent industries. However, there was no strong domestic political pressure that challenged the consensus supporting the Bretton Woods system. No grass-roots congressional movement or demands from the financial community, export industries, or organized labor emerged to insist that the United States balance its international payments by restricting imports or limiting the outflow of capital for foreign direct investment, or that it modify its domestic economic policies to support the dollar.

Not surprisingly, the United States adopted a strategy of "benign neglect" that disclaimed any responsibility for the problem. It refused to devalue the dollar and pressured its European allies and Japan to revalue their currencies. U.S. central decision makers found it politically less painful to rely on other countries to finance U.S. deficits than to make adjustments in fiscal and monetary policies to correct them. This led to a decline of confidence in the dollar in international currency markets. The absence of economic, partisan, and electoral pressures and the persistence of the consensus supporting the Bretton Woods system precluded action to support the dollar.

In 1971 the U.S. balance-of-payments deficit soared as speculative pressure on the dollar mounted. Confronted with an apparent choice between domestic prosperity and "the well-being of external accounts and confidence in the dollar," President Richard Nixon opted for the former.[24] In August 1971 he announced a new economic policy designed to curb inflation, promote recovery, and transfer the burden of the balance-of-payments deficit to other countries. The domestic goals were to be accomplished through a 90-day wage-price freeze and a 10 percent investment tax credit. Formal termination of the convertibility of dollars into gold and a 10 percent import surcharge were intended to restore an acceptable balance in America's international accounts. In December 1971 the United States, its Western European allies, and Japan reached an agreement for a modest devaluation of the dollar and revaluation of their currencies.

The Nixon administration's 1971 decisions to abandon dollar convertibility to gold, impose an import surcharge, and devalue the dollar reflect the collapse of the consensus supporting the Bretton Woods system. President Nixon and his key advisors, Secretary of the Treasury John Connally and Secretary of Commerce Peter Peterson, accorded a higher priority to continued autonomy in domestic economic policy than to maintenance of the Bretton Woods system. These central decision makers believed that U.S. international economic problems were due to foreign countries that would not change their behavior unless coerced.[25] Also, Nixon appeared to be in a politically weak position as he prepared for his 1972 reelection campaign. His decisions, which would reduce unemployment and control inflation at least temporarily, seem to have been designed, at least in part, to ensure his political survival. Thus, changes in ideas and electoral politics contributed to the first major postwar shift in international monetary policy. Congressional-presidential conflict, bureaucratic politics, congressional fragmentation, and interest group lobbying do not appear to have played major roles.

Continued stimulation of the domestic economy in 1972, an election year, resulted in further speculation against the dollar and renewed payments difficulties. In January 1973 the United States announced an additional 10 percent devaluation. Two months later, after the failure of American and European efforts to stabilize world currency markets, the United States took the lead in replacing the Bretton Woods system of fixed exchange rates with a system of managed floating exchange rates. Under the new system, all major currencies float, i.e., their values are determined by market forces. Governments can intervene to increase or decrease the value of their currencies through purchases and sales by their central banks. However, they are limited in their ability and willingness to do so by the large number of speculators in international currency markets. The new system, which was expected to be temporary, but continues to the present, relies primarily on markets to set exchange rates, while recognizing that governments may intervene to support their currencies.

The United States changed the international monetary system that it had created in 1944 when it could no longer ignore the effects of its domestic economic policies and its national security expenditures on the system, and the system would no longer continue to finance U.S. payments deficits. The belief among central decision makers that floating exchange rates would more effectively insulate domestic economic policy from international currency speculation than would fixed exchange rates, the decision makers' preference for market rather than government determination of exchange rates, a decline in the relative economic power of the United States, and the growing impact of international currency markets on the U.S. economy were the primary factors that led to the change. There is no evidence that bureaucratic politics, congressional influence, or partisan, electoral, or interest group pressures had any appreciable effect on the decision. The ideas and beliefs of the decision makers were of critical importance.

The flexible exchange rate system came into being just before a fourfold increase in the price of oil set off worldwide inflation. Also, the U.S. economy was feeling the impact of its growing dependence on imports of raw materials and its need for export markets. The oil price shock of 1973–74 created payments deficits in oil-importing countries and a surplus of dollars in the hands of oil producers. The new exchange rate system was able to accommodate the payments imbalances.[26] The United States supported flexible exchange rates on the grounds that stability could not be maintained under conditions of large-scale international capital transfers, inflation, and extensive speculation.

The dollar strengthened in the mid 1970s and then fell sharply as the U.S. government adopted stimulative fiscal and monetary policies to move the economy out of a recession in 1975–76 as a presidential election approached. Domestic economic policy changes, made to strengthen President Ford's reelection prospects, had adversely affected the exchange value of the dollar. Clearly, international monetary policy was less important than electoral politics.

The economic recovery that the stimulation induced moved faster in the United States than in other major countries. However, the United States ran a large trade deficit, especially with West Germany and Japan, which had adopted policies to restrain economic expansion. When efforts to induce those countries to stimulate their economies proved unsuccessful, Treasury Secretary Michael Blumenthal launched a campaign to "talk down" the value of the dollar against the mark and the yen as a means of correcting trade imbalances. His efforts were so successful that the dollar fell through most of 1978. The falling dollar and a consequent rising trade deficit exacerbated inflation in the U.S. economy, where macroeconomic policies were directed mainly at unemployment.

The U.S. government intervened massively in November 1978 to support the dollar. It borrowed $28 billion in foreign currencies, accelerated the sale of gold, and increased interest rates.[27] These actions halted the erosion in the value of the dollar. However, a second round of oil price increases in June 1979 and continuing inflation in the United States brought renewed activity by speculators who sold dollars and bought gold.

In October 1979 the Federal Reserve Board, responding to rising domestic inflation and pressure from West Germany, Japan, Saudi Arabia, and other major holders of dollars, announced a major change in U.S. monetary policy. The Fed stated that henceforth it would target monetary policy on the money supply rather than on interest rates, which would be free to fluctuate more widely in the money market.[28]

The tight monetary policy imposed in October 1979 achieved its immediate objectives. The inflation rate fell sharply as growth in the money supply declined. Interest rates in the domestic money market rose rapidly, reaching 17 percent by mid 1981, and the dollar's value began to climb in late 1980. The price paid to curb inflation and strengthen the dollar was painful: two severe recessions, from January to July 1980 and from July 1981 to November 1982. Also, many Western European and Third World countries vigorously protested the effects of U.S. tight money on their economies. Higher interest rates in the United States had pushed up interest rates around the world. European countries had to tighten their economies more than they felt desirable, and countries with large foreign debts experienced a doubling of their interest charges.

The change in U.S. monetary policy occured because the Carter administration feared the domestic political consequences of continued inflation. It was willing to risk a recession in 1980, another presidential election year, in order to curb double-digit inflation. Although the change in domestic monetary policy had positive consequences for international monetary policy, its primary causes lay in domestic political considerations. The probable effect of the shift on U.S. international monetary policy was not a major factor in the decision.

The Reagan administration, with its strong pro-market ideology, adopted a policy of non-intervention in foreign exchange markets.[29] Its position was that inflation would be controlled and competitiveness restored to U.S. industries through appropriate domestic economic policies. Then the market value of the dollar would stabilize and the trade deficit would move into surplus.

The fiscal policy of the Reagan administration sharply affected its international economic policies. The Reagan fiscal policy involved massive stimulation of the economy through sweeping individual and corporate tax cuts that took effect in 1982 and substantial increases in defense spending starting in 1981. The original plan anticipated cuts in non-defense spending to match the costs of the military buildup and stimulation of the economy from the tax cut to produce enough revenue to enable the budget to be balanced. President Reagan never conceded that his fiscal policies rested on unrealistic assumptions about his ability to persuade Congress to cut non-defense programs to the bone and the rate at which the economy would grow in response to the tax cut.[30]

Although the United States experienced a vigorous period of economic growth starting in late 1982, annual federal budget deficits exceeded $100 billion beginning in fiscal 1982 and, in 1985 and 1986, were above $200 billion. The deficits initially strengthened the dollar by maintaining pressure on interest rates. High interest rates attracted foreign capital, with the result that foreign investors were financing both the federal budget deficit and the deficit in the U.S. balance-of-payments. This proved to be of considerable short-run political advantage to the Reagan administration. The president won a landslide reelection victory in 1984, with minimal change in Republican strength in Congress, and he sustained a high level of popular support until late 1986. However, the strong dollar contributed to a substantial U.S. trade imbalance by making American products less competitive than foreign goods.

Nevertheless, the United States enjoyed a period of sustained real economic growth with little inflation. The strong dollar proved a boon to both the United States and most other countries. The inflow of foreign capital and cheap imports were essential contributors to American prosperity. The resurgent U.S. economy was the "locomotive that pulled the world economy out of the recession."[31] Even a modest reduction in interest rates in 1982 and 1983 did not weaken the dollar or stem the flow of capital into the United States, as confidence in the vitality of the U.S. economy remained strong.

Eventually, however, the persistence of massive budget deficits, high interest rates, and a strong dollar led to the rise of protectionist demands, as U.S. industries, even the most efficient and highly productive, encountered increasing difficulty meeting foreign competition. The U.S. government responded with complaints that the dollar was overvalued and urgings that West Germany and Japan revalue their currencies and stimulate their economies.

The dollar reached its peak against major foreign currencies in February 1985 and then began a rapid decline in which it lost 47 percent of its value over a three-year period. Speculators who had ridden the dollar upward for four years became uneasy over growth prospects for the U.S. economy and the inability of the government to reduce the budget deficit. In addition, the Fed and other major central banks undertook an intervention between January and March 1985 in which $10 billion were sold against the yen, the mark, and other major currencies.[32] In December 1985 Treasury Secretary James Baker III announced a shift to an exchange rate policy of active intervention to bring down the value of the dollar. Also, the Federal Reserve relaxed monetary policy through much of 1985 and 1986. This was done primarily to maintain economic growth, but the drop in interest rates also contributed to the decline of the dollar.

The principal reason for the Reagan administration's 1985 reversal of its exchange rate policy was to combat the rapid growth of protectionism among business and labor interests and in Congress. By causing the dollar to fall against other currencies, U.S. industries could become more competitive. Increased sales of U.S. goods and services in domestic and international markets would result from cheaper dollars, and calls for protection would abate. In the view of the Reagan administration, currency interventions were far less damaging to its liberal economic policies than protectionist trade legislation. Also, there were congressional initiatives to enact legislation that would return the United States to the gold standard, thus ending floating exchange rates. Although unsuccessful, these efforts signaled a strong congressional desire for a more active effort by the government to manage the exchange value of the dollar.

The shift in the Reagan administration's exchange rate policy also coincided with the appointment of James Baker III as secretary of the treasury. Baker was much less committed to a laissez-faire, free market ideology than his predecessor, Donald Regan. Baker was also much more sensitive to domestic politics than Regan and was quite willing to use exchange rate policy as a means to the achievement of political objectives. In his view, a fall in the value of the dollar, even if accomplished through government intervention in foreign exchange markets, was a wholly appropriate way to increase employment in the domestic economy and to respond to demands from businesses and labor organizations under pressure from foreign competition. Secretary Baker dominated U.S. foreign economic policy during the first two and a half years of President Reagan's second term, just as Secretary Regan had dominated it during the first term. The approach of each secretary served the domestic political interests of President Reagan at the time.

The interventionist foreign exchange policy adopted in 1985 succeeded in bringing down the value of the dollar to the point in late 1987 when the Fed began to support it. However, that policy has failed as of this writing (January 1988) to correct the U.S. trade imbalance, and it has not resulted in a stable dollar. In part, the limited success of interventionism is due to the presence in the international monetary system of "autonomous speculative fluctuations in exchange rates, which have real disturbing consequences."[33] Currency speculators consistently overshoot, so that fluctuations in exchange rates are excessive relative to economic conditions. More important, the United States has not reduced its budget deficit enough to diminish its need for foreign capital. As long as it has to borrow from foreigners to finance its public sector operations, including national security activities, and some of its private investment, it will continue to have a payments problem.

The persistence of large budget deficits in the 1980s is due to domestic political factors. A president with strong ideological convictions is locked in protracted stalemate with a Congress responsive to organized interests (both labor and business), constituency pressures, and its own electoral concerns. The impact of the deficit on U.S. international monetary policy is not an important consideration to either of these institutional participants in the struggle over how best to reduce the deficit. When the Reagan administration has moved to adjust the value of the dollar, it has done so as a means to other ends—the defusing of protectionist sentiments.

The probable effects of the dollar's current decline and how far it will fall cannot be determined. Like currency speculators, we do not know the fiscal and monetary policy intentions of U.S. central decision makers or their plans regarding interventions in currency markets. Nor are we able to predict economic performance accurately. What does seem apparent is that the United States will continue to need large infusions of foreign capital until domestic savings are able to finance the federal budget deficit and private investments. That will not happen until the impasse over the federal budget deficit is resolved, either by increases in taxes, cuts in spending, or some combination of the two. However, as long as foreigners remain willing to finance U.S. budgetary and payments deficits, U.S. central decision makers have little incentive to end the budgetary stalemate and are unlikely to make much effort to adjust domestic and economic policies to changing international market conditions. If and when those adjustments occur, it will happen as a result of domestic political pressures and the adoption of new ideas by central decision makers.

CONCLUSIONS

As of early 1988 the United States remains committed to the liberal international economic order that it has dominated since 1944. It has not adapted its international monetary and trade policies to the changes that have occurred in the international political economy since 1970—the relative decline of U.S. economic power, increased international economic interdependence, and the growing power of U.S. international banks. Nor has the United States adjusted its domestic economic policies to maintain confidence in the dollar or to manage international capital flows.

The United States presents a classic case of what Daniel Bell describes as the "double bind" of advanced industrial democracies.[34] It must simultaneously meet domestic political expectations of sustained economic growth at a high rate of employment and a low rate of inflation, while responding to external demands for a stable dollar and favorable trade and payments balances. Failure to meet the internal demands may result in loss of power at the polls, while inability to satisfy the external ones may undermine domestic economic policies. Unfortunately, policies adopted to meet both sets of demands often tend to be incompatible.

Any attempt to explain U.S. international monetary policy must necessarily be eclectic. Domestic political considerations have prevailed over national security needs and international market forces. Ideas have been the most important of the five political factors shaping international monetary policy since World War II, followed by considerations of partisan and electoral politics. Since 1980 interest group politics and congressional pressures have begun to play a more important role, as U.S. industries have had increasing difficulty meeting foreign competition in domestic and export markets.

Until now the United States has been strong enough to pursue its post–World War II goal of autonomy in its economic policies in spite of increasing interdependence with other economies. However, it is in a period of transformation in its foreign economic policy as it seeks ways that are compatible with domestic political pressures and national security interests to reduce massive balance of payments and trade deficits. It faces a major challenge because security goals and international market conditions increasingly conflict with domestic political forces. Fortunately, it has so far not had to contend with the divisive impact of internal bureaucratic conflict or jurisdictional squabbles between congressional committees over foreign economic policy.

The declining competitiveness of the U.S. economy may lead to an increase in the impact of political parties on foreign economic policy, especially if the Democrats embrace protectionism. Interest groups, principally labor and industries weakened by foreign competition, are already exerting enormous pressure for protectionist legislation. Longstanding ideological support of liberal international economic regimes for money and trade is under strong attack within the United States.

What can an administration seeking to make international monetary policy more supportive of security needs and adaptive to international market conditions do? The fragmentation of power within American society and the diffusion of authority within the U.S. government are fixed constraints. New processes for making and implementing foreign economic policy are not in prospect and, even if they were to emerge, are unlikely to affect the basic alignment of domestic political forces and the interests they pursue. Electoral politics, as reflected in the political business cycle whereby administrations in power stimulate the economy as presidential elections approach,[35] and the sensitivity of members of Congress to local consistituency pressures[36] are unlikely to change either. Another major problem confronting U.S. central decision makers is the bureaucratic and legislative inertia that is a salient feature of the American political system.

A change in the liberal ideology that dominates the formation of U.S. foreign economic policies will be required if central decision makers are to overcome the fragmentation of political power, the diffusion of governmental authority, and the inertial strength of existing policies. Such a change can only take place when domestic political forces demand that central decision makers adapt U.S. international monetary and trade policies to the transformation that is in process in the international political economy. (Such an adaptation must also be compatible with national security needs). The decision makers will do so when it is manifest that it is no longer in their immediate political interest to maintain existing foreign economic policies. The February 1987 Paris meeting may have been one of the first instances of such a response.

The unanswerable question is the speed with which central decision makers will accept new ideas that will facilitate adaptive policies. Resistance to new ideas will lead to policies that are reactive and defensive. Active search for new ideas will increase prospects for creative and proactive policies. No one can predict what kind of central decision makers the United States will have in the critical period of transformation. Nor is it

possible to prescribe how to obtain a set of decision makers that are
receptive to new ideas and attentive to the long- as well as the short-term
effects of the policies they pursue.

NOTES

1. Peter T. Kilbourn, "U.S. and 5 Allies Promise to Seek Dollar Stability," *New York Times,* 23 February 1987, p. 1.
2. Benjamin J. Cohen, *In Whose Interest? International Banking and American Foreign Policy* (New Haven: Yale University Press, 1986), p. 7.
3. Peter J. Katzenstein, "Introduction: Domestic and International Forces and Strategies of Foreign Economic Policy," *International Organization* 31, no. 4 (1977): 591.
4. Richard E. Neustadt, *Presidential Power* (New York: Wiley, 1960), p. 33.
5. Edward S. Corwin, *The President: Office and Powers, 1787–1984,* 5th rev. ed. (New York: New York University Press, 1984), p. 201.
6. Ibid.
7. John S. Odell, *U.S. International Monetary Policy: Markets, Power, and Ideas as Sources of Change* (Princeton, N.J.: Princeton University Press, 1982), p. 51.
8. Stephen D. Cohen, *The Making of United States International Economic Policy* (New York: Praeger, 1977), pp. 46–49.
9. Randall B. Ripley and Grace A. Franklin, *Congress, the Bureaucracy, and Public Policy,* 3rd ed. (Homewood, Ill.: Dorsey Press, 1984).
10. Robert A. Pastor, *Congress and the Politics of U.S. Foreign Economic Policy* (Berkeley and Los Angeles: University of California Press, 1980), p. 345.
11. Odell, *U.S. International Monetary Policy,* p. 40.
12. Ibid, p. 42.
13. Katzenstein, "Domestic and International Forces," p. 602.
14. Odell, *U.S. International Monetary Policy,* p. 43.
15. Cohen, *In Whose Interest?* p. 58.
16. Stephen D. Krasner, "US Commercial and Monetary Policy: Unravelling the Paradox of External Strength and Internal Weakness," *International Organization* 31, no. 4 (1977): 645.
17. Odell, *U.S. International Monetary Policy,* pp. 63–66.
18. Krasner, "U.S. Commercial and Monetary Policy," p. 637. Also see Judith Goldstein, "The Political Economy of Trade: Institutions of Protectionism," *American Political Science Review* 80, no. 1 (1986): 161–84. Goldstein argues that there is a strong liberal bias in U.S. trade policy that has thus far prevented the adoption of protectionist measures.
19. John Gerard Ruggie, "International Regimes, Transactions, and Change: Embedded Liberalism in the Postwar Economic Order," *International Organization* 36, no. 2 (1983): 399.
20. However, see the alternatives examined in Robert Gilpin, *U.S. Power and the Multinational Corporation: The Political Economy of Foreign Direct Investment* (New York: Basic Books, 1975), chap. 8.
21. Katzenstein, "Domestic and International Forces," p. 595.
22. Stephen D. Krasner, *Defending the National Interest: Raw Materials Investments and U.S. Foreign Policy* (Princeton, N.J.: Princeton University Press, 1978), p. 61.
23. Thomas L. Ilgen, *Autonomy and Interdependence: U.S.–Western European Monetary and Trade Relations, 1958–1984* (Totowa, N.J.: Rowman & Allanheld, 1985), pp. 10–11.

24. Ibid, p. 81. Also see Joanne Gowa, *Closing the Gold Window* (Ithaca, N.Y.: Cornell University Press, 1983), p. 69.
25. Odell, *U.S. International Monetary Policy,* p. 201.
26. Ilgen, *Autonomy and Interdependence,* pp. 117–19.
27. Odell, *U.S. International Monetary Policy,* p. 334.
28. Ibid, pp. 337–38.
29. Ilgen, *Autonomy and Interdependence,* p. 133.
30. David A. Stockman, *The Triumph of Politics: Why the Reagan Revolution Failed* (New York: Harper & Row, 1986).
31. Gottfried Haberler, "The International Monetary System," *AEI Economist,* July 1986, p. 4.
32. Ibid, p. 5.
33. Herbert Stein, "Thoughts on Exchange Rates and All That," *AEI Economist,* November 1986, p. 3.
34. Daniel Bell, "The Future World Disorder," *Foreign Policy* 27 (Summer 1977): 16.
35. Edward R. Tufte, *Political Control of the Economy* (Princeton, N.J.: Princeton University Press, 1978).
36. David R. Mayhew, *Congress: The Electoral Connection* (New Haven: Yale University Press, 1974); and Gary C. Jacobson, *The Politics of Congressional Elections,* 2d. ed. (Boston: Little, Brown, 1987).

Conclusion: The Constitutional System and National Security

GEORGE C. EDWARDS III and WALLACE EARL WALKER

We have examined the impact of the Constitution on national security policy in considerable detail. As we would expect, the authors of the preceding chapters have found that the political system in which national security functions are carried out influences those essential activities in fundamental ways. In this chapter, rather than summarize the details of the contributions of each author in his specific functional area, we review the broad findings about the impact of the Constitution on national security functions to highlight our overall theme. With this as our foundation, we then reach some generalizations about the relationship between the political system and policy.

STATECRAFT

Nations that desire success in the international realm are concerned with statecraft. Establishing national objectives, ranking priorities among them, and determining the most appropriate means to those ends enhances the prospects of a nation attaining goals in the international realm. Making national strategy requires consensus among those both in and outside government on the means and ends of policy and good foreign intelligence upon which to base decisions.

Mobilizing Political Support

The Constitution's dispersion of powers among different branches of government makes the president dependent upon at least tacit congressional support for nearly every significant aspect of national security policy. Whether it is foreign aid, weapons systems, or international trade that is at issue, the White House needs the support of Congress to act. Moreover, despite conventional wisdom to the contrary, Congress has typically not been deferential to the chief executive on most of these matters. This complicates the president's efforts to develop and implement coherent national security policy and forces him to attempt to mobilize the public to win the support of the legislature.

Although the constitutional system forces the president to seek public support, he is often frustrated in his efforts. Bert Rockman shows that there is a lack of political foundation for a coherent and complex national security policy strategy in mass public opinion and little support for policies entailing broad sacrifices, especially the protracted engagement of military force. The public is largely inattentive to, and indifferent and uninformed about, national security matters. It is difficult to make sophisticated strategy simple enough to resonate with the general public. Policies of restraint, prudence, and caution can easily become political liabilities for the White House. When national security matters become more salient to the public, they become more political, and when this occurs, the public is typically less likely to be open to presidential leadership.

Elite opinion is more structured than mass opinion, and in theory elites are more easily mobilized than the mass public. Yet there has rarely been a broad consensus on national security policy among elites in the public or in Congress, and the elements of society most easily mobilized may be the most strongly opposed to presidential policy, as in the case of the Vietnam War. Moreover, interest groups are active on many national security policy issues, and they often represent interests that are parochial from the president's viewpoint. Because these concerns may be quite salient to individual members of Congress, organized interests can exploit the fragmentation of the policy-making system to further confound efforts to develop coherent policy, or they become additional targets of presidential mobilization. Either way, groups play an increasingly important role in national security policy.

Thus, the structure of American government determines that the president must seek to mobilize broad public support early in the policy process. This adds legitimacy to decisions that are made, but it inevitably constrains the president and makes coherent policy more difficult to attain. Some chief executives may respond to this environment by taking risks, hoping that others will follow, or they may engage in subterfuge to bypass the distinctively decentralized American political process.

Making National Strategy

Developing a clear and consistent national strategy of the ends and means of national security policy is analytically demanding under the best of conditions. Stansfield Turner and George Thibault demonstrate that in the United States this task is made more difficult by the number and diversity of participants in setting national strategy and the necessity for them to work together.

Although Congress has broad powers in the national security policy realm, it is not in a strong position to make national strategy. As an institution it has a difficult time reaching a policy consensus, and it is not structured to take a comprehensive view of national needs. Instead, it tends to make policy piecemeal, which may lead to inconsistencies. Domestic considerations may narrow its perspective, and it often responds in a reactive mode, criticizing presidential action post hoc. This may contribute to perceptions among other countries of an absence of strategy.

The president is in the best position to set priorities and take broad, long-range views of national security needs. He is constrained, however, by Congress, public and organized group opinion, and even his own executive branch. It is difficult to obtain help in his responsibility for thinking about national strategy, because aides and officials have operational or constituency interests as well as concerns for strategy. The decentralization of the system pulls them in many directions at once.

The collaborative effort at making national strategy, based upon the Constitution's checks and balances, tempers extreme views and rash actions, and this is a strength in the nuclear age. At the same time, the multitude of players may produce inconsistency in U.S. strategy, confusion as to its content, and the waste of scarce resources. There has been a stable national strategy regarding American goals (but not means), and the system guarantees accountability, even if its complexity may obscure the roles of others than the president. Moreover, although it is difficult to make rapid changes in policy in the absence of crisis conditions, the United States has been able to accommodate changing conditions with flexibility in its national strategy, and the president has been able to respond rapidly in crises.

Producing Foreign Intelligence

Accurate and timely information about other nations is essential for national security policy. Intelligence gathering requires secrecy and central management. Yet, as Harry Howe Ransom illustrates, American government and political culture are hostile to secrecy and do not permit the monopoly of power, even in intelligence activities. This confronts the United States with a secrecy-accountability dilemma that it has never resolved. Moreover, the pluralism of the American political process has impeded the rationalization of intelligence organization.

The world's freest press, protective of its First Amendment rights, is seen by many as a natural enemy of intelligence agencies. To much of the modern press, disclosure of information on the workings of government is always in the public interest. At the same time, intelligence officials argue that publicity inhibits foreign sources of information and allied intelligence services from cooperating with the United States because of their fear of disclosure, and American agents may lose their cover, and thus their usefulness, because of revelations of their identities or activities in the press. Yet the press may also play a crucial role in keeping intelligence agencies accountable and making it more difficult to conceal incompetence, errors, and abuses of power under the cloak of national security.

Although the courts have typically deferred to the president on foreign intelligence issues, Congress has at times been more aggressive in constraining the executive's intelligence activities, including covert operations. In the process it has revealed much about American intelligence activities, and the incorporation of intelligence policy into the more normal checks and balances of government encouraged the politicization of intelligence. Yet congressional oversight does not seem to have had much impact on most important issues in the collection of intelligence or the protection of American security interests.

Indeed, the quality of the intelligence product may be higher as a result of the participation of Congress in intelligence. If they can overcome the instinct to play it safe with conservative and ambiguous conclusions, analysts may gain freedom to analyze events more objectively when they have a wider clientele for their studies and consumers to whom they may have to justify their analyses. There is also less chance that intelligence will be misused when there are more players in the intelligence game. Moreover, the checks and balances in the American system may stimulate the intelligence system to perform with greater efficiency and creativity, and congressional participation in the intelligence process may foster a deeper appreciation of the difficulties facing intelligence agencies.

Congress has been especially active in attempting to restrain covert action, and a president can now not expect to sustain such policies without the support of the legislature. Covert action can no longer be used as a means of evading constitutional requirements for consensual policy making and accountability. If presidents try to do so, they are likely to face widespread condemnation. This restricts the executive's use of one possible resource in national security policy, but it also lends legitimacy to covert operations that receive congressional approval.

Despite the accountability-secrecy dilemma inherent in being a democratic nation with broad national security interests, the United States possesses the world's widest range of information, gathered by methods and techniques of the greatest variety and scope. Most intelligence failures are not attributable to the system's demands for consensus, no matter how much they might confound the production of intelligence.

NATIONAL DEFENSE

It may be surprising that the impact of the Constitution on national security policy is perhaps most clear in the area of defense policy. We typically view defense policy as distinctive, as an area in which there is less fragmentation, less of a role for the states (and thus less impact for federalism), and more legitimate restrictions of fundamental freedoms than in other areas of policy. It is easy to infer from these premises that the Constitution is less relevant when it comes to matters of defense. Yet the authors of the four papers in this section make clear that the impact of the U.S. system on defense policy is direct and substantial.

Raising the Armed Forces

Raising the armed forces is fundamental to a nation's defense. Determining who and how many will serve in the armed forces are difficult questions that every political system must address. The resolution of these potentially divisive questions varies widely, however, reflecting both the political culture and the structure of policy making in a country, as Hobart Pillsbury shows.

Consistent with the strong emphasis on personal freedom in American culture and in the Constitution itself, the United States has normally relied upon the market to supply its military manpower needs. Volunteerism rather than conscription has typified the American experience. Yet volunteers have not always provided the armed forces with either the quantity or quality of soldiers, seamen, or airmen that U.S. security has required. Moreover, the greatest need for recruits occurs when volunteers are least likely to come forward—when hostilities are imminent or have already begun. At such times conscription is necessary, and conflict between individual rights and national security is most evident. In addition, concern for equity in sacrifice moves questions of the social and economic characteristics of draftees to the forefront of the debate over defense policy.

We would not expect such vital questions to be taken lightly by the elected representatives of the American people, and they are not. The Constitution assigns responsibility for raising the armed forces directly to Congress, but historically it has delegated much of its discretion to the president in his role as chief executive and commander in chief. During times when the manpower issue is most salient, however, Congress takes an active role in the design and implementation of raising the armed forces. The courts have essentially accommodated the other branches and endorsed the compromises they have hammered out. The states also have an important role in manpower policies because of the militia, the National Guard, which is under their control in peacetime. Because of the decentralization of the American political system, the differing perspectives of the participants in the policy-making process are accorded not only a fair hearing but also substantial influence over the ultimate policy. Thus the separation of powers and federalism further complicate the raising of the armed forces.

The outcome of this system has been an inconsistent policy, in which liberty has sometimes been constrained in the interests of the common defense, while at other times the United States may have jeopardized its security in the interests of personal freedom. There is no simple solution for this trade-off, and as long as Americans value both their liberty and their security, the system will reflect these divergent viewpoints.

Organizing the Armed Forces

The armed forces must be organized after they are raised. Once again, both the president and Congress have important constitutional roles in carrying out this function. So, through their maintenance of the National Guard, do the states. The dedication of Americans to civilian control of the military, their preoccupation with matters of domestic policy, and their fear of centralized power, all prominent components of the American political culture, reinforce the extraordinary decentralization of American government in defense policy.

As a result of the fragmentation of defense policy making, the U.S. armed forces are not centralized, and there is no general staff. The uniformed services are not in a position to take a broad national perspective on defense policy. As Dan Kaufman demonstrates, the individual armed services, and thus service interests, dominate decision making about the forces, the weapons, and the capabilities that are available to carry out national military strategy.

In addition, strategic planning, a potentially centralizing force linking means with national objectives, is neglected by the armed services. To the extent that the services do develop strategic plans, their parochialism often precludes them from operating under realistic fiscal constraints. This inability to conduct effective strategic planning has forced civilian agencies to assume the function. Although not inherently undesirable, the process of strategic planning does not fully incorporate the expertise and experience of the nation's military leadership and those who must implement defense policy.

The services are also not strong in setting cross-service priorities and analyzing the trade-offs necessary for a coherent defense policy. Individual service programs predominate over strategic thinking. The responsibilities and inevitable interest of Congress in resource allocation and the annual budget cycle create both further diversions from strategic planning and the possibility of end runs around civilian leadership by the Department of Defense.

The lack of centralization and the dominance of the services has a pronounced influence on force structuring. Each service's structure reflects its view of its organizational essence. This has led to imbalances in military capabilities. These are especially evident in capabilities required for effective joint military operations. Of equal concern, the services have not been quick to adjust their traditional missions in developing capabilities to meet the changing needs of warfare. Finally, decentralization of the military services has produced an unintegrated force structure and inadequate command arrangements for the direction of deployed forces.

Equipping the Armed Forces

Equipping the armed forces has always been crucial to American defense policy, since outproducing the enemy has been the country's greatest strength in wartime. Procurement has taken on added importance as weapons and command, control, and communications systems have become ever more sophisticated and central to the nation's defense. Moreover, concomitant with technical sophistication, there have been enormous expenditures for equipment, placing extraordinary demands on scarce budgetary resources.

Harvey Sapolsky shows that the decentralized nature of the U.S. political system, with its many participants in decision making on procurement, coupled with the high stakes involved in individual decisions, makes equipping the armed forces highly politicized. Opposition, bargaining, delay, and stalemate characterize procurement policy making. This increases the already heavy burdens of long-range strategic planning for defense, adding uncertainty and inefficiency to an inherently difficult task, in which policy makers attempt both to press the limits of technological knowledge and to anticipate future needs.

The fragmentation of the system not only complicates procurement decisions, but also decreases accountability for them, which is already nebulous due to the technical nature of such decisions and the long lead time that is often necessary to develop modern equipment. Equally important, fragmentation often produces indecision or contradictory strategic objectives. Since these serve as the basis for procurement policy, equipping the armed forces is likely to suffer as a result.

Conversely, a more centralized system would have drawbacks of its own. If power to make procurement decisions was located even more squarely in the Pentagon, there would be less competition between the services over weapons systems and thus probably less stimulation for innovative thinking on these critical matters. In addition, if there were considerably more secrecy surrounding equipping the armed forces, there would be less criticism of military decisions and less accountability on issues of undoubted importance to the public. Procurement may be highly technical, but its implications are profound.

Waging War

The ultimate defense policy is waging war, which includes both the process of deciding to go to war and the conduct of war once hostilities have begun. Although it might seem that because of the extraordinary nature of war, constitutional structure would play a minor role at such times, this is not the case. The Constitution allocates, albeit without clarity, war-waging power to both the presidency and Congress, reinforcing the system's broad decentralization. As Asa Clark and Richard Pious demonstrate, these institutions represent the competing values of effectiveness and legitimacy, and their reconciliation poses a major dilemma for constitutional democracy.

Our fragmented policy processes generate open debate about waging war and increase the potential of accountability, but they may also produce policy paralysis, tethering of security policy to parochial constituency interests, and an inability to engage in secret diplomacy or covert operations. Flexibility in the rapid shift of commitments and resources is an advantage in waging war, and it is increased if there are fewer decision makers and less accountability for their decisions. Conversely, the support of the public is essential to sustain even a partial mobilization for war.

A more unified system would increase the prospects of coherent, consistent, flexible, comprehensive, and well-executed waging of war, but may induce groupthink, insulation from competing viewpoints, and a strain toward consensus on a comprehensive but inadequate "world view." The costs of such a system may include the loss of legitimacy as well as the development of poor policy.

Because the United States is in a state of "semi-war" in the post–World War II era, it must face a new variety of complex and intractable small wars: surrogate wars, terrorism, civil wars, and various types of low-intensity conflict. Matters internal to other societies are critical to understanding these wars and complicate analysis of them. Moreover, it is difficult to generalize from one to another.

In a crisis the American political system typically functions in a unified manner, because there is no time for many players to become involved, the threat of nuclear war is relatively easy to understand, and defense against nuclear attack is a public good, with the costs and benefits equally distributed. When consensus exists, the fragmentation of the system is not an obstacle to effective waging of war.

When it comes to semi-war, we lack consensus. Such wars are difficult to understand, the costs are not borne equally, and there is normally ample time for participation by all interested parties. Fragmented policy making is compatible with waging small wars, however, because it provides time for reflection and debate. Unified policy making on grand strategy for small wars may stifle debate and produce inappropriate polices. Thus, the open process that can so frustrate policy makers in the U.S. can be a considerable advantage.

FOREIGN RELATIONS

Modern nations cannot act in a vacuum. Their interdependence demands that they carry on relations with one another, even with nations viewed as potential adversaries. Sometimes foreign relations take the form of direct negotiations about matters of mutual benefit, while at other times they consist of reporting on foreign events or representing U.S. interests to other governments. They may also involve the distribution of foreign aid. At the extreme, foreign relations encompass efforts to protect the well-being of American citizens in other countries.

Protecting Citizens Abroad

Protecting citizens abroad is one of the national security functions most likely to arouse intense interest and feelings of responsibility among both officials and the public. The large population of the United States, its wealth, its role as leader of the West, and the millions of Americans who travel or live overseas expose the country to abuses of its citizens by people or organizations in other nations. Ira Sharkansky shows that although this issue arises in foreign settings in which the Constitution does not apply, and although the founders did not directly address protecting citizens abroad, their handiwork has a significant impact on how the U.S. government responds to the problem.

The decentralization of American government produces a plurality of participants in the formulation and implementation of policy regarding protecting citizens abroad, including the many police forces and security bodies established by the various states. Responsibility for dealing with the problem is not clear, and responses are difficult to coordinate. Competing perspectives further complicate efforts to develop coherent policy.

Extensive civil liberties, including free expression, assembly, and petition, privacy, due process of law, and the right to bear arms, increase the burdens of preventing or terminating harm to American citizens abroad. They limit the means officials can use to gather intelligence and apprehend suspected terrorists, especially within the United States. They also make it easier for them to obtain firearms. The press gives hostage takers copious publicity, perhaps encouraging other terrorists. Moreover, the preoccupation with hostages can place extraordinary pressure on officials to respond prematurely, while at the same time increasing the difficulty of taking secret action to rescue them.

Conducting Diplomacy

There are many facets to international diplomacy, including representing U.S. interests in international forums and in bilateral relations with other countries, reporting on events abroad, and distributing foreign aid. Although responsibility for American diplomatic policy is centered in the executive branch, as Robert Ferrell illustrates, the Constitution ensures that there are a multitude of players and a wide range of perspectives influencing the conduct of diplomacy.

The most profound impact of the Constitution on the conduct of diplomacy results from the role of Congress. The Senate has the responsibility for confirming the nominations of diplomatic personnel and ratifying treaties. Both houses appropriate funds for foreign aid and the implementation of U.S. commitments to other nations. The president can take little for granted, and often finds that Congress not only fails to defer to the White House, but exercises very independent judgment. Without question, the role of the legislature complicates diplomatic activity, making it more difficult to make commitments and maintain continuity in policies toward other nations.

The openness of the American political system also provides the opportunity for many of the same forces that affect domestic policy to influence diplomacy. Groups representing economic or ethnic interests actively participate in the policy process and attempt to pressure both the executive and the legislature to support their positions. Even foreign nations hire lobbyists and public relations firms to represent their interests. The media actively report diplomatic activity, further limiting the executive's ability to shift its positions and express and commit itself in secrecy. It is safe to say that the fragmentation of the process of conducting diplomacy has evolved beyond anything imagined by the Founding Fathers and made it difficult for the country to send clear, consistent signals to other nations.

It is also worth noting that the Constitution is generally silent about the actual conduct of diplomacy. Although this accords the president some flexibility, it has also provided for substantial variance in the qualities of secretaries of state and diplomatic personnel, and it has allowed a wide range of agencies and officials to conduct diplomacy, further decentralizing the process.

Negotiating International Agreements

Negotiating international agreements was the form of foreign relations with which the founders were most familiar, and the one that they expected to be at the core of relations between nations in the future. As Norman Graebner demonstrates, they also intended Congress, particularly the Senate, to be an equal partner with the president in the control of foreign affairs.

Things have obviously changed over the ensuing two hundred years. The president's role in conducting international relations has grown substantially, and treaties are far from the typical form in which U.S. international agreements occur. As the world outside the borders of the country has grown more complex, and as the role of the United States in international relations has increased in dramatic fashion, the Constitution has accommodated America's need to respond to its changing environment.

At the same time, the dispersion of power in the constitutional system has had consequences for making international agreements. The Senate's role in treaty ratification makes it more difficult for the president to negotiate treaties. Knowing that partisan, ideological, and constituency interests will influence the Senate's decisions on treaties reduces the president's flexibility in negotiations and ability to make firm commitments to the representatives of other nations. This is frustrating to the chief executive, but it adds legitimacy to the agreements that are ratified and serves as a check on poor policy proposals, which are just as likely to occur in foreign as in domestic affairs. In addition, however, the deliberateness of the process may induce presidents to attempt to bypass Congress through executive agreements or secret negotiations.

ECONOMIC POLICY

The relationship between national security and economic affairs is a salient one to virtually every country. Because the influence of the economy is pervasive, affecting the lives of individual citizens and the collective capabilities of a nation, countries always place economic policy high on the agenda. Without an effective economic policy, resources are wasted, opportunities for growth are lost, and potentially productive ties with other nations are not established.

Budgeting for National Defense

Budgeting is the crucial government activity for allocating scarce resources and setting priorities. Moreover, budgeting and national security strategy are inseparable because of the great cost of defense policy, especially in an era of large standing military forces in what is ostensibly peacetime. Perhaps no aspect of national security policy is subject to more criticism than the defense budget. Lee Donne Olvey asks whether there is something about the American political system that makes defense budgeting inherently unsatisfactory.

Several features of defense policy make budgeting particularly difficult. The fundamental question of "how much is enough?" requires a measure of output. We do not have units of defense to measure output, however. Defense is primarily a public good in which all citizens benefit equally, so there is no market price with which to assign values to defense policy. There is also no objective criterion for evaluating the benefits of defense programs (except to defense suppliers and employees). Much of the benefit of defense is deterrence, but measuring deterrent effects is difficult, because it is not possible to know reliably either the perceptions of potential adversaries or the impact of those perceptions on their behavior. As a result, analysts are not able to determine with confidence the marginal contributions to defense of additional expenditures.

Questions of cost-effectiveness are more narrow than the trade-offs between policies or between public and private consumption, but they also pose substantial budgeting challenges. Since much of the defense budget is allocated to components on the frontiers of technology and since economic considerations make competitive suppliers prohibitive, it is difficult to take advantage of the normal market forces of competition.

The high stakes of national defense for both the country and some discrete beneficiaries of defense expenditures such as contractors, the high cost of defense programs, the direct linkage between foreign policy and the military structure to support it, and the complexity and indeterminate nature of budgeting issues ensure that budgeting decisions will be dominated by political rather than technical dimensions. The prominent roles of both Congress and the president in budgeting, the responsiveness of the former to constituent interests, the intense scrutiny of defense expenditures from a free press, and the competition for resources among and within executive agencies in the fragmented U.S. constitutional system contribute to the predominance of political, rather than economic, considerations in defense budgeting decisions. This undoubtedly results in some waste of resources and some failure to spend on critical defense needs, but it is not clear that it is the system rather than the inherent nature of defense budgeting that is the principal cause of unhappiness with budgeting for national defense.

Engaging in International Trade

Nations are rarely self-sufficient and must engage in foreign trade to acquire the resources they need to obtain the raw materials and finished products that either do not exist or cannot be produced efficiently at home. Whether a nation's economy is rudimentary or complex, increasing foreign trade is likely to be a primary objective of public policy. Despite its large size and resource base, the United States has been active in foreign trade from its earliest years.

The Constitution encourages international trade and a free market with its ban on export taxes and its centralization of the power to regulate international commerce and lay import duties in Congress. At the same time the document establishes a divided government, both between and within branches, the potential for broad participation in a transparent and highly permeable policy-making process, and extensive opportunities to revise, reassess, and repeal decisions.

As a result of the openness and the fragmentation of the system, Roger Porter points out, there are a series of persistent tensions in American international trade policy making. One is the basic conflict between free trade and the protection of domestic industries. A second is the strain between the goals of economic policy (selling as much as possible) and national security (withholding resources from potential adversaries). Finally, there is the possibility of employing trade as an instrument of foreign policy, using the threat of limiting U.S. exports or foreign imports as leverage to influence the behavior of other countries. These tensions are not resolved but are expressed through different institutions and officials with disparate criteria for evaluating options in international trade policy.

The clash of competing objectives and the institutional biases that reflect them have several important consequences for international trade policy. On the one hand they generate a great deal of information and analysis and multiple perspectives in a full policy debate. They also provide ample opportunities for policy entrepreneurs, supporting innovative thinking about trade policy. On the other hand, the system precludes a consistent, coherent trade policy. Instead, it is one characterized by ebbs and flows, with differing emphases at different times.

Managing International Monetary Policy

The second major component of foreign economic policy is international monetary policy, which encompasses the effects of capital flows on the exchange value of the dollar resulting from investments by U.S. corporations abroad, foreign loans by U.S. banks and the federal government, investments by foreign corporations in the American economy, and foreign investments in U.S. government securities. As the U.S. economy becomes more dependent on financial and commercial dealings with other nations, the value of the dollar has greater implications for national security policy because it affects the cost of deploying forces abroad, aid to other countries, and other objectives, and it influences the confidence of other nations in the leadership of the United States.

Throughout most of American history, international monetary policy has been of little interest to most elements in American society, and Congress has been deferential to the president in this area, except when policy visibly affects domestic economic conditions. American ideas of a liberal world order with a free and open international economic system have been more important influences on policy than structural aspects of the political order.

However, the relative decline in American economic power and the rise of global economic interdependence has increased the importance of domestic political factors in shaping foreign economic policy. More domestic interests are affected by international monetary policy. The multiple opportunities for organized interests to influence policy, the sensitivity of U.S. decision makers to group and electoral politics, and the fragmentation of political authority assures that international monetary policy will reflect domestic as well as international pressures and considerations.

Norman Thomas shows that the fragmentation of policy-making responsibility across several components of the executive branch, the Federal Reserve Board, and Congress poses problems of coordination and the necessity of reaching decisions through bargaining among competing agencies rather than by unitary analysis. In this environment, the system's overall effect is to decrease the authority of central decision makers and the range of options open to them, making it more difficult to formulate and implement a coherent international monetary policy consistent with national security objectives and domestic economic and social policies.

IMPLICATIONS OF CONSTITUTIONAL GOVERNMENT

A number of generalizations emerge from the foregoing discussion. We first consider the impact of various American political institutions on the U.S. performance of national security functions and then offer some broader generalizations about the impact of the entire constitutional system on the conduct of national security policy making.

Institutions and Policy Making

One of the central questions in our study has been the impact of various elements of the political system on national security policy making. Table C.1 lists the political institutions that play an important role in current national security policy making by functional area. Table C.2 denotes the relative contemporary influence of four of these by functional area.

We find that the president, Congress, national security agencies such as the Department of Defense and the Central Intelligence Agency, and

TABLE C.1. Important Systemic Components by Function in National Security Policy Making

	President	Congress	Bureaucracy	Courts	Interest Groups	Press	Public Opinion	State and Local Governments
Statecraft								
Mobilizing political support	x	x			x	x	x	
Making national strategy	x	x	x		x			
Producing foreign intelligence	x	x	x			x		
National Defense								
Raising the armed forces	x	x	x		x	x	x	x
Organizing the armed forces	x	x	x					x
Equiping the armed forces	x	x	x		x			x
Waging war	x	x	x			x	x	
Foreign Relations								
Protecting citizens abroad	x	x	x			x	x	x
Conducting diplomacy	x	x	x		x	x		
Negotiating international agreements	x	x				x	x	
Economic Policy								
Budgeting for national defense	x	x	x		x	x	x	x
Engaging in international trade	x	x	x		x			x
Managing international monetary policy	x	x	x		x			x

TABLE C.2. Relative Influence of Components by Function in National Security Policy Making

	President		Congress		Bureaucracy		Interest Groups	
	More	Less	More	Less	More	Less	More	Less
Statecraft								
Mobilizing political support	x		x			x	x	
Making national strategy	x		x			x		x
Producing foreign intelligence	x		x		x			x
National Defense								
Raising the armed forces	x		x			x		x
Organizing the armed forces		x		x	x			x
Equiping the armed forces		x	x		x		x	
Waging war	x		x			x		x
Foreign Relations								
Protecting citizens abroad	x			x	x			x
Conducting diplomacy	x		x		x		x	
Negotiating international agreements	x			x		x		x
Economic Policy								
Budgeting for national defense	x		x		x		x	
Engaging in international trade		x	x		x		x	
Managing international monetary policy	x		x		x			x

interest groups are the most influential systemic components in the making of national security policy. Not surprisingly, these reflect both the decentralization and the openness of our constitutional system. Although public opinion, the press, and state and local governments are certainly significant players in some functional areas, they are typically of secondary importance.

In U.S. national security affairs, the president is the epicenter of initiative. Although the Congress does initiate policy proposals, it must gather at least tacit presidential approval for policy acceptance and implementation. In times of crisis the president has enormous flexibility; few constraints are imposed on him in such circumstances, although almost invariably he is subject to post-crisis legislative sniping for not "consulting" with Congress, especially if his initiatives are judged to be a failure. His ability to lead and organize in routine national security affairs is highly constrained. He has room for maneuver early in his term, and then only if his public popularity is high. Specifically, in mobilizing political support for security policy, designing national strategy, budgeting for defense, and organizing the defense establishment, the president is constrained by other actors and by legal restrictions. The exceptions to this rule appear to be in the protection of citizens abroad and the negotiation of international agreements, and even in those realms the number of congressional restrictions are growing (see Table C.2).

Because of these constraints, presidents have routinely sought techniques to circumvent the restrictions imposed by the resurgent, post–Vietnam War Congress or, in Norman Graebner's more succinct words, to avoid "public debate and other democratic inconveniences." Among the newer techniques are "black programs" in the area of weapons procurement and use of the National Security Council staff to coordinate covert action, as in the Iran-Contra arms sales. More established techniques such as crisis making through "going public," sustaining the myth of bipartisan consensus, and using secret envoys and executive agreements have been resurrected and used. Such techniques are risky, temporary palliatives for the issue at hand. Without public support and congressional backing, no initiative will be enduring and policy will certainly fail in the longer term. As Bert Rockman so nicely observes, "the ultimate logic of the American constitutional system [is] do not proceed without agreement unless an immediate crisis impinges."

Thus the post–Vietnam War Congress is now a key partner in national security affairs. For instance, in manning the armed forces, there is a clear trend toward detailed and growing involvement by the Congress. The legislature is also an active participant in constructing the national strategy and ever more disposed to provide specific instructions, such as the Boland amendment that limited covert action in Nicaragua. Only in the area of international monetary policy does Congress eschew routine involvement, and only because individual and group interests do not discern the relationship of this technical realm to their immediate concerns.

Unlike the Congress, the courts have remained quiescent in the recent past. This quiescence held true in manpower policy and in intelligence collection even in the face of widespread social and political resistance to the draft during the Vietnam War and the intense use of secrecy to safeguard intelligence operations (see Table C.1). Thus in national security affairs, the courts continue to cede responsibility to the president and to Congress.

In virtually every realm, the disaggregated constitutional system has spawned fragmented public organizations. The function of trade, diplomacy, and fighting terrorism are fractionalized, with responsibilities spread among numerous agencies. The organizations of the Defense Department and the CIA resemble collections of fiefdoms more than integrated agencies possessing clearly delineated lines of authority. These decentralized structures are mostly a result of the inability of our presidents and our legislature to agree on organizing criteria.

Furthermore, in some cases the variety of agencies involved in national security affairs and in other cases the disaggregated nature of government departments have institutionalized tensions and disparate approaches to policy making. In the conduct of foreign trade, the divergent biases among such departments as State, Treasury, Commerce, and Labor and such offices as those of the president's Council of Economic Advisers and the U.S. trade representative, as well as the legislative branch, have produced a patchwork of policies. In the Defense Department, service dominance is so pervasive that the secretary of defense has been unable adequately to centralize decision making; inadequate centralization has meant that strategic planning, military advice, resource allocation, force structuring, and joint operations are insufficient to meet the needs of a great power.

In the post-Vietnam era, special interest groups and business corporations have taken a much more active role in national security affairs. They are not only prominent players before the Congress, but are also much more aggressive in arguing their cases to presidential staffers, as in the recent Wedtech scandal in defense procurement involving Reagan White House aides, and national security agencies. For instance, ethnic groups with loyalties to nations abroad and defense contractors dependent on government procurement of weapons systems at home play a large role in the public debate and in congressional deliberations on national security policy. Business groups are also the principal proposers of escape clause provisions to the U.S. government's International Trade Commission for relief against foreign nations restricting the free flow of commodities.

The role of state and local governments in national security affairs may be growing, but as yet has not become substantial. These governments do have a salient role in defense manpower and in countering terrorism. The reserve combat power of the United States is primarily in the National Guard, which is simultaneously commanded by state governors and yet supplied and advised by federal officers in peacetime. This fractured structure has created considerable tension between state and national governments during peacetime training and mobilization for war. Local governments are also involved in national security. Their police forces provide an important deterrent to U.S.-based terrorism. Although there has been a low incidence of terrorist attacks in the United States, attacks may increase if foreign-based groups continue their focus on American targets and learn to exploit the political fragmentation that characterizes law enforcement in the United States.

In spite of the adversarial nature of government-press relations, the news media do not appear to have a particularly salient role in national security affairs. Their role is more that of conveyors of political information and recorders of events. That is, the press is used by political elites to carry their messages to other elites and to mass publics and as a source of information about world and national developments. Only in the areas of gathering intelligence and covert operations is it an inhibitor in policy making or implementation. These conclusions will almost certainly be disputed by participants in the political process, who are convinced that the press has enormous influence in security affairs and that editors have an inherent negative bias. What such participants overlook, of course, is that the sources of most information that journalists like to call "news" are political elites intent on manipulation of the political process for their own purposes. What editors then choose to publish is a reflection of their own recognition of the continued need for access to elite sources and their inbred professional predisposition to regard "news" as something "new."

The Constitution and National Security Affairs

The previous discussion reveals that the influence of the Constitution for national security policy is significant and varied. The most uniformly positive consequences are for the political system as a whole. The United States has the oldest and longest surviving democratic Constitution in the world. This alone provides eloquent testimony to the legitimacy accorded government decisions by the American people. It is difficult to abuse power when it is widely dispersed and other power holders have strong incentives to hold authorities accountable for their actions.

Although at first glance the stability of the system might seem relatively insignificant to those focusing on the narrower picture of specific national security functions, it is the foundation upon which national security policy is built. In the absence of a durable political system, it is difficult, if not impossible, to develop and implement effective national security programs, requiring as they often do substantial human and material sacrifice and widespread cooperation of diverse elements of society.

In addition, a system that is biased toward the status quo because of its requirement for consensus and provision of multiple veto points is one that tempers extreme policies and the rash actions of individual public officials. At the same time the Constitution has been able to accommodate long-term policy change. The fragmentation of power ensures that there is always someone with both the stature and resources to advocate departures from prevailing national security policies effectively. The openness of the system to a wide variety of viewpoints and the necessity for building broad coalitions discourages rigidity and insulation and places a premium on being responsive to changing conditions and demands.

The open and fragmented political system of the United States also has an advantage for decision making on discrete policies. Free debate enhances the prospects of locating weaknesses in policy proposals and removing crucial decisions from the sole purview of possibly parochial "experts," who might overlook important societal values in their drive to accomplish their missions.

Finally, the system works in crisis situations requiring very rapid response. The characteristics discussed in this section combine with environmental imperatives to provide the confidence necessary to delegate short-term concentrations of power to the chief executive.

Conversely, the need to reach consensus, the number and diversity of the players, and the abundant opportunities for participation do not yield an efficient process for making national security policy. Under normal conditions the system is indecisive; it may take months or even years to reach a decision, reducing the speed and flexibility of responses to particular circumstances in the short run. Moreover, the absence of centralized power may cause policy to suffer from incoherence and inconsistency as a result of the ebbs and flows of influence of various officials and institutions and the necessity of meeting their competing demands.

The piecemeal manner of making decisions under such conditions is not conducive to comprehensive policy planning. It is difficult to organize information in a centralized fashion so that all decision makers may benefit from it and approach issues from a broad and informed perspective. In addition, the system incorporates a basic element of uncertainty in policy making that makes long-range planning very difficult. This is not only deleterious to the development of national strategy, but it also makes it more difficult to make international commitments and maintain policy continuity. Perceptions among allies of U.S. dependability and adversaries of U.S. resolve may suffer as a result of the uncertainty generated by such a complex policy process.

The central role of domestic considerations in national security affairs complicates policy making and inevitably wastes scarce resources as potential coalition partners are bought off with a wide variety of programs and side payments that a more centralized policy-making process would reject. Moreover, public pressures for action on some matters, usually articulated in Congress or the press, can force the executive's hand when it may want to downplay a matter or act with more restraint.

Constraints on action inevitably frustrate the executive branch and may encourage efforts to bypass the system through subterfuge. Such actions carry with them the potential for serious political damage to a president and his policies. Limitations on secrecy in an open political system may inhibit the planning or execution of even legitimate policies.

Considerations for Constitutional Reform

The conventional wisdom among many scholars, practitioners, and commentators holds that the U.S. constitutional system so constrains the executive that the nation is now unable to respond to international threats and challenges. As a result, Americans may be in danger of losing their cherished freedoms to adversaries who are both implacable and possess highly centralized political systems that generate coherent policy. Thus, they argue, the system is inadequate to the needs of a great power.

It is significant that the contributors to this volume did not share a consensus on the conventional wisdom. Instead, they have provided a remarkable variety of opinion on the impact of the Constitution on the making and implementation of national security policy. Some find the system enormously constraining, especially in the areas of organizing the armed forces, purchasing weapon systems, and making national strategy.

In other areas, however, the U.S. constitutional system is not the principal cause of incoherence or inflexibility in national security policy making. Or, if it is a primary confounding influence, it shares that distinction with other factors. For instance, in the protection of citizens abroad and in the making of treaties, other factors are primarily responsible for the difficulties policy makers encounter. That is, relations with states where American citizens are held hostage and moral imperatives impeding the negotiation of treaties are the salient constraints on policy making. In the intelligence community organizational arrangements that have fused intelligence collection and covert operations into one organization, the Central Intelligence Agency, have created most of the difficulties. In budgeting for national defense, it is the nature of policy analysis, not the constitutional system, that provides the greatest barriers to rational decisions.

In other instances the authors find that the constitutional system dominates the making of national security policy and that this dominance produces very satisfactory, if not salubrious, policy. In mobilizing public and congressional support for national action in a crisis, the U.S. system is more responsive to executive initiative than parliamentary systems and provides considerable legitimacy to such action. In the realm of international trade, the constitutional system provides a broad array of information and analysis, thereby constraining arbitrary and capricious policies. Furthermore, the latitude of the system has encouraged policy entrepreneurs, whose initiatives have produced imaginative policies that are frequently copied by other nations.

In the realm of national defense, the Constitution may well be more specific as to responsibilities than in any policy area. Power appears to be clearly divided among political institutions, with the president designated as commander in chief and the Congress given the power to declare war. And yet, as in this example, such specificity is far from precise. The commander-in-chief clause fails to adequately detail what authority is thereby given to the president and the war-declaring clause, drafted as it was in the eighteenth century, fails to meet the ambiguities of the twentieth century. In fact, such specific allocations of power seem to have considerably less significance in the conduct of security affairs than the larger institutional arrangements of separate legislative and executive branches and the variety of informal rules, such as customs, cultural predispositions, and precedents, that condition institutional and organizational behavior. In some cases these informal rules have been codified in law, but in no case have they been incorporated into the Constitution by amendment. Thus the Constitution alone does not dominate the way we conduct security affairs.

It must be conceded that the national security functions discussed in this volume are very tough nuts to crack. The making of national strategy is a task at which very few governments succeed. Collecting foreign intelligence is another demanding challenge, particularly for a democratically constituted regime, and yet we are reported to be more effective at this than our principal adversaries. No less difficult are such choices as which weapons to procure and how to budget and provide manpower for defense.

Not only are these problems very difficult, they are appreciably more difficult now than at any time in our history, and they seem to be getting more difficult with each decade. As Asa Clark and Richard Pious observe, "never in its history has America been confronted by a tougher world." For example, the variety of wars with which the U.S. must contend, stretching as they do from space-based strategic defenses to protecting foreign-owned ships flying the American flag in the Persian Gulf to openly supplying anti-Marxist guerrillas in Central America, are peculiar to the post–Vietnam War era. The U.S. political system has been overwhelmed by these demands. One need only look at the unending defense budgeting process, with its heavy use of continuing resolutions and supplementary appropriations, for confirmation.

Furthermore, many of our nonconstitutional devices for forging or sustaining consensus seemingly evaporated in the 1970s. These devices served, in Harvey Sapolsky's words, as "compensatory mechanisms that permitted the effective functioning of government." Before the Vietnam War, there was some semblance of discipline in congressional parties; now subcommittee government is the norm, with some members of Congress actually conducting their own brand of diplomacy overseas. Interest groups are now more vibrant and intrusive. Finally, public trust in government leaders and our pre-Vietnam consensus on containing communism have been shattered. The absence of these compensating mechanisms has, depending on one's point of view, either significantly complicated policy making or created an impasse that threatens our very existence. These changes have had more of an impact on the way the United States conducts national security affairs than constraints imposed by the Constitution.

As a result of frustrations with the policy-making process, many observers yearn for change in the U.S. constitutional regime to produce more coherent, flexible, and responsive national security policy. Yet as this analysis suggests, the U.S. Constitution is only one of many influences on policy making, and it has both positive and negative consequences. The Constitution creates the broad outlines of the political system through the separation of powers and through a federal structure sharing responsibilities for governance. Although these broad arrangements set the context for national security affairs, they alone cannot be blamed for failures in the making of policy, and, as detailed above, they provide many advantages to policy makers.

The only constitutional changes that are likely to have a profound impact on policy making are dramatic ones that shift the balance of power among political institutions and levels of government or that limit free expression. It is highly unlikely that Americans will be willing to forgo the advantages of the Constitution by consenting to major changes in the political system that might yield some benefits but also a host of unintended and unforeseen consequences. This is yet another reason why it is essential that we understand the broad range of implications of our system in the vital area of national security policy.

Contributors

Asa A. Clark IV is professor of international relations and national security studies at the U.S. Military Academy. His recent publications, as contributing editor, include *The Defense Reform Debate* and *Conventional Deterrence in NATO*.

George C. Edwards III is visiting professor of social sciences at the U.S. Military Academy and professor of political science at Texas A & M University. He is the author or editor of a dozen books and numerous articles on the presidency and the public policy making, including *At the Margins, The Public Presidency, Implementing Public Policy, Presidential Leadership, Presidential Influence in Congress,* and *The Policy Predicament.* He has also served as president of the Presidency Research Section of the American Political Science Association.

Robert H. Ferrell is Distinguished Professor of History at Indiana University and the author or editor of nearly three dozen books on modern American history and diplomacy. These include *Peace in Their Time, American Diplomacy in the Great Depression, The American Secretaries of State and Their Diplomacy, Foundations of American Diplomacy, America as a World Power, America in a Divided World, The Eisenhower Diaries, Woodrow Wilson and World War I,* and *Harry S Truman and the Modern American Presidency.* He has also served as president of the Society for Historians of American Foreign Relations.

Norman A. Graebner is professor emeritus at the University of Virginia where he was Randolph P. Compton Professor of History and Public Affairs and before that the Edward Stettenius, Jr., Chair of Modern American History. He is the author or editor of nineteen books on American history and diplomacy, including *The Age of Global Power, Cold War Diplomacy, The New Isolationism, Empire on the Pacific, Traditions and*

Values: American Diplomacy (two volumes), and *The Cold War*. He has also served as president of the Society for Historians of American Foreign Relations.

Daniel J. Kaufman is associate professor and director of national security studies at the U.S. Military Academy. He has served on the staff of the National Security Council and has published a number of articles in the field of national security affairs. His latest book, as co-author, is *U.S. National Security: A Framework for Analysis*.

William W. Kaufmann is professor emeritus in the Department of Political Science at the Massachusetts Institute of Technology and currently a lecturer at the Kennedy School of Government at Harvard University. A long-time consultant on defense issues throughout the executive branch, his many publications include *The McNamara Strategy* and *The 1986 Defense Budget*.

Lee Donne Olvey is an army colonel and head of the Department of Social Sciences at the U.S. Military Academy. An economist and a Rhodes scholar, his publications include *The Dynamics of International Politics, The Economics of National Security*, and *Industrial Capacity and Defense Planning*.

Hobart B. Pillsbury, Jr. is associate professor of social sciences at the U.S. Military Academy. He has authored a number of articles on military compensation, military unionization, and the public policy process.

Richard M. Pious is professor of political science at Barnard College of Columbia University. He is the author of *The American Presidency* and *The President, Congress and the Constitution*. He has also written numerous articles on executive branch politics.

Roger B. Porter is professor of government at the Kennedy School of Government at Harvard University. A Rhodes scholar and a White House fellow, he has extensive White House experience, serving as executive secretary of the President's Economic Policy Board in the Ford administration and as director of the Office of Policy Development in the Reagan administration. He is the author of *Presidential Decision Making* and *The U.S.–U.S.S.R. Grain Agreement*.

Harry Howe Ransom is professor of political science at Vanderbilt University. He is the author of *The Intelligence Establishment, Can America Survive Cold War?* and numerous articles and essays on the intelligence function in national security.

Bert A. Rockman is professor of political science at the University of Pittsburgh. He is the author of *The Leadership Question* and numerous articles, co-author of *Bureaucrats and Politicians in Western Democracies*, and co-editor of *Elite and Communist Politics*. He has also served as president of the Presidency Research Section of the American Political Science Association.

Harvey M. Sapolsky is professor of public policy and organization at the Massachusetts Institute of Technology. He has written widely on defense policy issues. Among his many publications are *The Polaris System Development*, *Science and the Navy*, and *Consuming Fears*.

Ira Sharkansky is professor of political science and public administration at Hebrew University in Jerusalem. He is the author or editor of two dozen books on American politics and public policy and comparative politics, including *What Makes Israel Tick? Wither the State? The Routines of Politics, Spending in the American States, The United States: The Study of a Developing Country*, and *The Maligned States*.

George Edward Thibault is chairman of the Department of Military Strategy at the National War College. He has served in a wide range of positions in the Department of Defense and the Central Intelligence Agency and has authored numerous articles on national security issues. He is the author of *The Art and Practice of Military Strategy*.

Norman C. Thomas is Charles Phelps Taft Professor of political science at the University of Cincinnati. He is the author of *Education in National Politics, Rule 9, The Politics of the Presidency*, and numerous articles, and has edited several volumes. He has also served as president of the Presidency Research Section of the American Political Science Association.

Stansfield Turner is head of Stansfield Turner Perspectives. A Rhodes scholar, he attained the rank of admiral and served as Commander of the Second Fleet and NATO Striking Fleet Atlantic and Commander in Chief of NATO's Southern Flank. In 1977 he was named Director of Central Intelligence and served in that position throughout the Carter administration. He is the author of *Secrecy and Democracy*.

Wallace Earl Walker is professor of public policy and director of public policy studies at the U.S. Military Academy. A White House fellow, he is the author of *Changing Organizational Culture* and numerous articles on defense policy making and the role of professionals in government.

Index

Acheson, Dean, 224
Adams, John Quincy, 188, 204–5, 215, 216
Aerospace Corporation, 125
Agriculture Department, 273, 287, 288
Allen, Richard, 187
Almond, Gabriel, 19, 21
Ambassadors, 188–89, 190, 191, 194
American Civil Liberties Union, 171
Anderson, Jack, 168
ANZUS Pact (Australia, New Zealand, United States; 1951), 244. *See also* Security pacts
Armed forces: centralization of, 96, 99, 105–7, 124; conventional, 241; decentralization of branches, 98–99, 103, 105, 107–8, 114–17, 124; deployment of, 6, 47; deficiencies of, 99, 114–15, effectiveness of, 84, 114–17, 118, 247, 255; enlistment and retention, 5, 79, 84, 85, 309; force structure, 111, 114, 116–18, 248; imbalance of capabilities, 114–15; Joint Chiefs of Staff, 96, 99, 100, 101, 105–7, 109–12, 118; joint military operations, 114–15, 116, 117; lack of general staff, 98, 99, 107; nuclear, 240, 245–46; pay, 79, 84; presidential supervision of, 98, 99; reorganization of, 99, 100–101, 103, 118, 244, 250; resource allocation within, 112–13; service dominance, 104–5, 107–8, 109, 112–14, 118; service missions, 101–3, 114–16, 117, 248; strategic

planning by, 108–9, 112–13, 310; structuring of, 114–15, 117, 119; unified and specified commands in, 103, 104, 117–18, 119n.15; unionization of, 84. *See also* Key West Agreement; National Security Act; National security policy; Weapons systems
Art, Robert J., 252
Articles of Confederation: Congress and, 206, 208; economic policy in, 259; military manpower, 75; need to strengthen, 258; revenue and taxation, 259–60; treaty making powers, 204, 205, 208
Atlantic Charter (1941), 223
Attorney General, 56
Australia, 224, 225

Baghdad Pact (1955), 226
Baker, James, III, 228, 298–99
Banks, 290–91
Barrett, Archie, 108
Beirut Resolution (1983), 152
Bell, Daniel, 300
Berns, Walter, 171
Blumenthal, Michael, 296
Board of Foreign Intelligence Advisors, 56
Bohlen, Charles, 192, 201n.13
Boland Amendment, 321
Bretton Woods Agreement (1944), 293–94
Bryan, William Jennings, 188

Brzezinski, Zbigniew, 187
Budget, defense, 7–8, 97, 113, 241, 315–16; determining spending levels in, 245–46
Budget and Impoundment Control Act (1974), 243
Bundy, McGeorge, 187
Bush, George, 169
Byrnes, James F., 190

Cabinet system, 29, 31
Calhoun, John C., 216
Cameron, Simon, 189
Caribbean Basin Initiative, 59–60, 270
Carter, Jimmy: Carter Doctrine, 40–41; consensus in administration, 25; Iran hostage crisis, 170–71; and news media, 59–60; SALT II Treaty, 47, 226; trade policy, 261–62
Carter, Beverly, 169
Casey, William, 59–60, 64
Catt, Carrie Chapman, 196
Census, 326
Central Intelligence Agency: congressional investigations of, 55; crisis in, 55; establishment of, 51–52, 53–54; Hughes-Ryan Amendment, 55; Iran-Contra scandal, 66; and national defense, 93; Office of General Counsel, 56; role in Communist containment, 54; Soviet Union and, 60–61; spying on citizens, 55
Chadha case, 152
China, Nationalist, 192
Churchill, Winston, 186
Citizens, protection of abroad, 6, 313–14; and civil liberties, 169; and Congress, 162–63; and Constitution, 162; constraints against action, 171–72; federalism and, 167; "no concessions, no negotiations" policy, 168–69; and president, 162; responsibility for, 167–68, 177–78
Clay, Henry, 188, 215
Cohen, Benjamin, 291
Commerce Department, 262, 273, 287, 288
Congress: and ambassadors, 183, 192; budgets, 40, 42, 95, 113, 239, 250, 252–55; committees of, 56, 288–89; and conscientious objectors, 85;

constituents, 197; and creation of national security establishment, 2–3; draft, 82, 86; foreign policy, 230–31; fragmentation of, 29–30, 288–89; intelligence functions of, 51, 54–56, 58, 61, 63–64; lobbies, 27, 28; military manpower, 84, 85; monetary policy, 285; national security, 2, 17–18, 28; outside experts and, 193; president and, 24–25, 34, 263; priority setting, 39; powers of, 42; regulation of armed forces and, 94–95, 96; role in military reform, 94–96; role in waging war, 137–38, 149–52; separation of powers and, 2; staffs, 193; strategy, 39, 40, 42–43; trade and, 274–75, 278; treaty making and, 202–3, 204, 217–18; use of veto, 152, 263
Congress of Industrial Organizations, 77
Congressional Budget Office, 243
Connally, John, 294
Conscription. See Draft
Constitution, 3, 4, 156–57; accountability and ambiguity in, 30; armed forces, 73–74, 75–76, 95; comparison with parliamentary system, 29; doctrine of subordination, 153; federalism and, 3; flaws in, 155–56; foreign affairs, 204; intelligence gathering, 51, 53; national security and, 30–31, 33, 309, 323, 325; reform of, 324–25, 327; separation of powers, 2, 3, 27–28, 57, 321; strategy and, 39–40; trade policy and, 262–63; treaty making and, 151, 202–3, 227; waging war, 136–37, 149–50, 151, 155–56
Constitutional Convention, 204–9
Contractors, defense, 125–26, 251. See also Weapons systems
Coolidge, Calvin, 186
Cooper, Richard N., 270
Corwin, Edward S., 285
Council of Economic Advisors, 273, 277
Council on Foreign Relations, 24
Country teams, 190
Covert action, 62–63, 65, 69, 308. See also Intelligence
Crawford, William, 211
Crenshaw, Martha, 163

Croly, Herbert, 13, 14
Cuban Missile Crisis, 137, 139, 192–93
Currency: exchange rates, 293–95; speculation, 295, 299
Czechoslovakia, 67, 223–24

Daoud, Abu, 173
Davie, William R., 209
Defense budget, 97, 113, 237–38, 247–49; Congress and, 95, 239, 250, 252–54; cost effectiveness of, 244–46, 248–49, 253; local impact of, 241, 252; market criteria, 241; president and, 239–40, 251, 253; program evaluation, 245; public support for, 97, 251, 254; reforms in, 242–44
Defense Department, 94, 98, 124, 129
Defense Intelligence Agency, 199
Defense Secretary, 104–6, 107, 109–11, 112
Department of International Trade and Industry (DITI), 262
Destler, I. M., 37
Deterrence, 141–42, 146, 240
Diplomacy, 6, 187, 190, 314; coalition, 185; Congress and, 191, 192–94, 194–95, 198–99; Constitution and, 182–83, 195; definition of, 183, 200n.1; eighteenth century (U.S.), 214–15; foreign service and, 189; interest groups and, 196–97; joint resolutions and, 192–93; and mass media, 197–98, 199; nineteenth century (U.S.), 214; presidential, 186–87
Dollar, 283, 293–94, 295, 298–99
Draft, 73, 80–83, 85, 89, 309; Civil War, 76–77; in peacetime, 77–78, 79, 80–81; in Vietnam War, 79; in World War I, 81; in World War II, 78, 81
Dulles, John Foster, 33, 192, 225

Economic policy, 7, 292–93, 300–301; and domestic politics, 292–93, 294, 296–97
Edwards, George, 24–25
Eisenhower, Dwight David, 33, 103–4, 153, 187, 201n.13; and ambassadors, 183–84, 192; Bohlen confirmation, 201n.13; consensus and, 25–26
Eisenhower Doctrine (1957), 157

Elites, 23, 24
Energy Department, 93
Espionage Act of 1917, 59
European Economic Community, 278
Executive agreements, 228
Extradition, 172, 173

Federal Aviation Administration, 167
Federal Reserve Board, 296, 298–99
Federal Reserve System, 286, 287
Fishery Conservation Act (1976), 275
Foreign Intelligence Surveillance Act, 56
Foreign policy, 6, 37, 65, 313; and Cold War, 228–29; policy of nonnegotiation with aggressors, 222; public response to, 21, 22
Forrestal, James, 242
Foster, John W., 218
Franklin, Grace, 15, 16
Freedom of Information Act, 57
Fulbright, J. William, 28, 229

Gallatin, Albert, 215
Galvin, John, 142, 145–46
General Accounting Office, 243
Gluck, Maxwell H., 183–84, 191
Gold standard, 293, 298
Goldwater-Nichols Reorganization Act, 249
Gorbachev, Mikhail, 227
Goren, Roberta, 179
Gramm-Rudman bill, 250
Greenspan, Alan, 288
Grenada, 47, 116, 117
Grew, Joseph, 194, 201n.14, 222–23

Haas, Richard, 43
Halperin, Morton, 114
Hamilton, Alexander, 136, 206, 208, 209, 212
Hanna, Mark, 188
Harding, Warren, 186
Hawaii, 192, 217
Hay, John, 219
Hay-Pauncefote Treaties, 218
Hijacking, airplane, 167, 172, 173. See also Terrorism
Hobkirk, Michael, 242
Holsti, Ole R., 23–24
Hoover, Herbert, 54, 200n.7
Hornbeck, Stanley K., 222–23

Hostages, 42–43, 168–69, 170–72, 174–76. *See also* Kidnapping; Terrorism
House, Edward M., 187
Hughes-Ryan Amendment, 55, 57
Huntington, Samuel, 24, 28, 113
Hyman, Sydney, 136
"Hyphen vote," 26–27

Ideology, 292, 301
Impoundment of funds, 254
Inflation, 294, 295–96, 297
Intelligence, 4–5, 50–52, 60–61, 68–69; accountability in, 52, 68, 307, 308; analysis and interpretation, 61–62, 68–69; collecting, 61, 307–8; Congress and, 54, 60–66, 68; Constitution and, 52; covert action in, 62–63, 308; evaluation of, 61–62, 69; failures, 61, 66–67; mass media and, 58, 60, 68, 307–8; National Security Council, 51–52; oversight of, 54–55, 308; politicization of, 66–68, 69; president and, 54, 63–66; secrecy in, 52, 61, 307, 308; "secrecy-accountability dilemma," 50, 57; separation of powers, 62, 68; successes of, 67, 68; terrorism and, 171
Intelligence Oversight Act (1967), 56, 57
Intelligence Oversight Board, 56
Interest groups, 26–27, 170, 290–91, 298, 300; Congress and, 196, 197
International Monetary Fund, 291
International political system, 139, 141
International Trade Commission, 262, 265, 266; escape clause, 271, 322
Iran-Contra arms sales, 64–65, 183, 187, 191–92, 199–200, 233n.69, 321
Irish Republican Army, 170, 172
Israel, 26, 175, 179

Jackson, Andrew, 189
Japan, 222–24, 296, 298
Jay, John, 52–53, 205, 210, 212–14
Jay Treaty (1794), 214
Jefferson, Thomas, 188, 190, 215
Joint Chiefs of Staff (JCS), 99, 107–9; reform of, 96, 97; strategic planning, 109–10; weaknesses of system, 106–7, 109–12. *See also* Armed Forces: Joint Chiefs of Staff

Jones, General David, 111, 116–17, 122

Katzenstein, Peter, 284
Kennan, George R., 157, 192
Kennedy, John Fitzgerald, 25–26, 78, 137, 187
Kennedy, Robert, 137
Key West Agreement (1948), 102, 114–16
Kidnapping, 168, 170, 172–73, 174–75. *See also* Hostages; Terrorism
Kissinger, Henry, 37, 187, 194, 272
Knox, General Henry, 211, 212
Korb, Lawrence, 109, 252
Korean War, 26, 148, 224
Kristol, Irving, 147

Labor Department, 273, 287, 288
Laqueur, Walter, 164, 170
Lasswell, Harold, 163
Laval, Pierre, 186, 200n.7
League of Nations, 185, 220–21, 227
Lebanon, 47, 168, 176
Libya, 47, 168, 176, 177
Lincoln, Abraham, 171, 189
Lincoln Laboratory, 125
Lobbies. *See* Interest groups
Lodge, Henry Cabot, 20n.13, 195, 217; and League of Nations, 221, 227
Louisiana Purchase, 215

MacDonald, Ramsey, 186, 200n.7
Maclay, William, 211–12
McCloskey, Frank, 194
McKinley, William, 186, 188, 194–95, 217
McNamara, Robert, 97, 242–43, 249
Madison, James, 188, 196, 212; treaties and, 205, 206, 207–8, 215
Mahan, Alfred Thayer, 48
Management by objective, 243
Manning, Bayless, 266
Marcy, William L., 189
Marshall, George C., 103, 190
Mass media: censorship and, 58–59; diplomacy and, 197–98; government operations, 264–65; intelligence functions, 58, 60; national security, 60, 322–23; news leaks and, 63; terrorism, 170

Military industrial complex, 130. *See also* Weapons systems
Military manpower policy: colonial period, 74–75; Congress and, 84–85; Constitution and, 75–76; draft, 82–83, 309; executive-legislative relations, 86, 89; federalism and, 310; inconsistencies in, 310; judiciary and, 86; reserve forces, 87–89; role of women, 82; separation of powers in, 310; volunteer forces, 309
MITRE Corporation, 125
Monetary policy, 8, 300, 317–18; budget deficit and, 299; changes in system, 301–2; Congress and, 288–89, 321; definition of, 282; dollar and, 283; effect of domestic politics on, 289–90, 300–301; executive-legislative relations, 288; history of, 293–94; ideology and, 291–92, 300; president and, 285–86, 287; national security, 283; separation of powers and, 301; theoretical approaches to, 284
Monroe, James, 188, 215
Morris, Gouveneur, 187
Morrison, Samuel L., 59
Mueller, John, 19, 20
Muskie, Edmund, 191, 275
Mutually Assured Destruction (MAD), 240
MX missile, 115

National Committee for the Cause and Cure of War, 196
National Defense Act (1920), 77
National Guard, 74, 87, 309, 310, 322; in Berlin crisis, 87–88; in Central America, 88–89; congressional influence on, 90; and McNamara, 97; mission of, 88–89; nationalization of, 88; as state militia, 87, 88–89, 96–97
National Security Act (1947), 53–54, 100, 103, 124, 322; amendments to, 100–101, 104; creation of, 124, 242
National Security Advisor, 93
National Security Council: conduct of diplomacy, 187, 193; Congress and, 305; and covert action, 45, 65, 229, 321; intelligence and, 51–52; international influences on, 141; and national defense, 93; president and,

45; role in strategy development, 45–46; trade policy and, 273
National security policy: budgeting and, 7, 238–39, 247–48; categories of, 15–18; coherence of, 18; and Cold War, 2, 23, 33, 229–30; Congress and, 321; consensus for, 33, 144, 147, 326; in crisis, 16, 320; decentralization of, 98, 105; decision making in, 15–17; domestic politics in, 238, 324; executive-legislative relations and, 305–6; fragmentation of process, 117, 143–45, 148, 310, 322; functions of, 4–5, 238, 318–19; inefficiency of system, 324–25; interest groups and, 306, 322; mass media and, 60; president and, 14, 320; public perceptions of, 4, 18–19, 306; role of institutions in, 31–32; unified, 143–44, 145
NATO (North Atlantic Treaty Organization; 1950), 185, 224, 225–26. *See also* Security pacts
Neustadt, Richard, 40, 93, 284
New Jersey Plan, 205
"New nationalism," 13–14
New Zealand, 224, 225
Nicaragua, 64–65, 229
Niskanen, William, 106
Nixon, Richard, 25, 46, 168, 260; economic policy, 290, 294; military manpower policies, 40–41, 79; Nixon Doctrine, 40–41
North, Oliver L., 199–200

O'Brien, Conor Cruise, 163
Office of Defense Mobilization, 269
Office of Emergency Planning, 269
Office of Management and Budget, 273, 287
Oil prices, 93, 273, 277, 295, 296
Omnibus Trade Act (1987), 261
"One Army" concept, 88
Overseas Security Advisory Council, 167

Packard Commission, 244, 255
Palestine Liberation Organization, 176
Parliamentary system, 28–30, 129
Pastore, John, 275
Perle, Richard, 191
Peterson, Peter, 294

Philippines, 217, 224–25
Pinckney, Charles, 29, 205
Planning, Programming, and Budgeting
System (PPBS), 242–43
Poindexter, Admiral John, 187, 199
Polk, James K., 216, 217
President: advisors and, 44, 45–46;
ambassadorial appointments, 183, 184;
armed forces organization, 94;
authority of, 218–19; budgets and,
39–40, 43–44, 228, 239–40, 253; and
cabinet, 45; constraints on, 27, 28,
43–44; covert action and, 63–64, 65–
66, 229; crisis authority, 46–47, 203;
decision making, 16–17, 18, 39;
diplomacy and, 87, 185–87, 192–93;
domestic policy and, 46; foreign policy
of, 17, 46–47, 218, 220, 228, 229;
foreign travel, 186–87; intelligence
and, 51; monetary policy and, 284,
285; National Security Council, 45;
national security policy, 16–18, 22,
26, 28, 32–34; popularity of, 32;
relations with Congress, 31, 219, 228,
276–77, 305–6; risk-taking, 33–34;
role in policy development and
implementation, 93–94, 307; role in
strategy development, 38, 40, 43–45;
trade policy, 274; treaty making, 202–
3, 209; "two presidencies" thesis, 24;
use of veto, 25, 254; vision of, 44–45;
war making powers, 47, 136–37, 149,
150–52
Procurement, military, 5–6, 311–12. See
also Weapons Systems
Public opinion: electoral consequences of,
20; foreign policy and, 18–19, 22–23;
war waging and, 19–21

Qadhdhafi, Mu'ammar al-, 177

RAND Corporation, 125
Randolph, Edmund, 205
Reagan, Ronald, 34, 45, 169, 191, 195;
arms reduction agreements, 226–27;
free trade policies of, 278;
international monetary policies of,
297; Iran-Contra arms sales, 65–66,
199, 200; response to terrorism, 152,
169
Regan, Donald, 288, 298–99

Reserve forces. See National Guard
Reykjavik Summit (1986), 191
Ribicoff, Abraham, 275–76
Ries, John, 105
Ripley Randall, 15, 17
Rogers Act (1924), 189
Roosevelt, Franklin D., 123, 186, 187,
222
Roosevelt, Theodore, 186, 217
Rosenau, James N., 23, 24
Rostow, Walt W., 187
Ruggie, John, 292
Russell, Richard, 55

SALT treaties, 61–62, 226–27
Saxe, Maurice de, 140
Schlesinger, James, 110–11
Schultz, George, 167, 169, 199
Schultz, Richard, Jr., 163
Scowcroft, Brent, 187
SEATO (South East Asia Treaty
Organization; 1954–77), 225–26. See
also Security pacts
Security pacts, 223–27
Selective service. See Draft
Selective Service Act (1948), 83
Seward, William H., 192
Sherman, John, 188
Sloan, Stephen, 163
Smart, Ian, 144
Smoot-Hawley Tariff Act (1930), 267
South Africa, 38
Spanish-American War, 103
Starr, Richard, 168
State Department, 187; Constitution and,
187–88; and foreign economic and
trade policy, 272–73, 286–87;
formation and growth of, 188;
organization of, 190–91; role of
Secretary of State, 188, 191
Statecraft, 4, 305–8
Stimson, Henry L., 200n.7
Strategy: collaboration and consensus in,
37, 42, 305; criteria for and definition
of, 37, 39, 305; effect on domestic
politics, 46; evaluation of, 48–49;
formulation of, 4, 38–39, 40, 307;
inconsistencies and weaknesses in, 41,
49, 307; intelligence, 4; pressure
groups, 43; resource allocation in, 39;
role of Constitution in, 41; role of

president in, 43–45; use of weapons, 130

Strategic Defense Initiative, 40–41, 46

Supreme Court: and ambassadors and envoys, 184–85; draft law and, 85–86; intelligence policy, 58; and presidential power, 219; waging war and, 151–52

Taft, Robert, 77–78

Taft, William H., 186

Temple, Herbert R., 89

Terrorism, 146, 161; and American political system, 166; characteristics of terrorists, 165–66; defense against, 166; definitions of, 163, 172–73; incidence of, 164, 175; international agreements on, 174, 178, 179; Israeli experience, 175; lack of consensus on, 179; legislation against, 172–73; mass media and, 170–71, 175; overreaction to, 178–79; president and, 168, 169, 170–71; Privacy Act and, 171; reprisals for, 176; rescue operations, 176; role of local governments in, 322; State Department and, 169; U.S. citizens and, 161–62; U.S. policy on, 174–76; within U.S., 165. *See also* Hijacking; Kidnapping

Texas annexation, 192

Thatcher, Margaret, 177

Thomas, Norman, 77

Tocqueville, Alexis de, 69, 157

Trade Act (1974), 262, 266, 275–76; escape clause provisions of, 265–66; 271; Extension acts (1954, 1955, 1958, 1962), 269

Trade policy, 8, 262, 272, 277–79, 316–17, 322; agenda setting in, 265; Caribbean Basin Initiative, 270; Congress and, 261; executive-legislative relations and, 263–64; fair trade, 267–68, 272; in foreign policy, 270; free trade, 267, 278; Generalized System of Preferences in, 270; impact of federalism on, 260–61; interagency coordination of, 263; leverage in, 270; national security provisions of, 269; president and, 261–62, 271; protectionism in, 267, 268–69, 270; trade relief provisions and, 265–67

Trade Representative, U.S., 262–63, 272, 274

Treasury Department, 262, 273, 277, 286–88

Treaty making, 7, 315; arms limitation treaties, 226–27; pre-1900, 214–15, 216–17, 221–22; post-1900, 218, 221–22; post-1945, 218, 223

Treaty of Guadalupe Hildago (1848), 216–17

Treaty of Paris (1898), 194, 195

Trist, Nicholas, P., 216–17

Truman, Harry, 25, 33, 83, 190; intelligence policy of, 54, 63

Union of Soviet Socialist Republics (USSR), 48, 223–24, 226–27

United Kingdom, 59, 178

United Nations, 185, 195; and terrorism, 171, 173–74

United States: budget of, 250–51, 255–56; characteristics of, 164–65, 264, 266; relations with USSR, 48, 223; as a world power, 222

Universal military training, 81–82

Vance, Cyrus, 191

Vandenberg, Arthur, 14

Versailles Treaty (1919), 220–22, 227

Vietnam War, 47, 148, 194, 240–41; appropriations for, 229; Geneva Conference and, 225; lack of national consensus for, 19–21, 23, 26; service autonomy in, 116–17, Tonkin Gulf Resolution, 193

Vinson, Carl, 55

Virginia Plan, 205–6

Volcker, Paul, 288

Volunteer forces, 77–80, 82, 84, 89

War: conventional, 142; high intensity, 146–47; low intensity, 142–43, 147–48, 156; nuclear, 142, 146, 240. *See also* War waging

War Powers Resolution (1974), 2, 47, 84, 137; failures of, 151–52, 168, 263

War waging, 6, 137, 145, 148–49, 153, 222; Congress and, 148, 154–55, 239; courts and, 152; definition of, 138, 312; nuclear deterrence and, 141–42, 146; in parliamentary model, 153,

War waging (*cont.*)
154–55; policy process in, 143, 146, 312; in presidential supremacy model, 153–54; role of presidency in, 146–47, 149, 239
Washington, George, 98, 187–88, 270; and treaties, 212–14
Waugh, William L., 163
Weapons systems, 5–6, 114, 115–16, 132; arsenals, 122–23; benefits of research, 131; constraints on development, 115–16; contractors, 125, 126; costs of, 130–31; design and production of, 122–23, 125; and political system, 127, 128, 130, 132; procurement of, 122, 123–24, 126, 128, 131, 248; and social issues, 126–27; and technology, 123, 124–25, 127–28
Webster, Daniel, 76, 215–16
Wedtech scandal, 322

Weinberger, Caspar, 199
West Germany, 296, 298
Wheeler, Burton, 77
Whigs, 154
Whitlock, Brand, 189
Wieseltier, Leon, 141
Wildavsky, Aaron, 24
Wilson, James, 207
Wilson, Woodrow, 184, 186, 188, 219–20; and League of Nations, 195; and Treaty of Versailles, 194–95, 220–22
Women's Armed Services Integration Act (1948), 82
World War I, 77, 189
World War II, 23, 123, 124, 143–44

Yeutter, Clayton, 281n.29
Yugoslavia, 173–74

Zero base budgeting, 243